# Praise for *Work in the Digital Age*

'*Work in the Digital Age* is a superb collection of articles that together provide a wide-ranging, comprehensive analysis of the challenges and opportunities for labour in a period of rapid technological change. This volume is essential reading for academics and policymakers alike'.

—**Kathleen Thelen**, MIT

'Everybody is in favour of technological innovation and modernisation, yet not enough research and discussion is devoted to the actual consequences for society. *Work in the Digital Age* brings together leading European academics and thinkers to help us find our course, as the future hurtles toward us at breakneck speed'.

—**László Andor**, European Commissioner for Employment, Social Affairs and Inclusion (2010–2014)

'*Work in the Digital Age* should be required reading for the many groups around the world that are being formed to plan for the future of work in the age of digitisation. These European experts explore the broad terrain of private actions, public policies, and social dialogue needed to ensure that technological innovations can be shaped to benefit society while providing adequate compensation and adjustment opportunities for those who might otherwise bear the costs. As such, they lead the way for the rest of us'.

—**Thomas A. Kochan**, MIT Sloan School of Management

'*Work in the Digital Age* is a valuable contribution to understanding how technology is disrupting the way we work and threatening the safety net that has long undergirded successful economies. We need a clear vision for the path forward, and this book helps provide that'.

—**Steven Hill**, Berlin Social Science Center

'This edited volume provides a very valuable overview over the general discussion about the potential impact of new technologies on the future of work. The book is unique in the way in which it brings together a series of case studies showing how the topic is discussed in different countries. It is essential reading for everybody interested in this crucial public policy debate'.

—**Henning Mayer**, Social Europe

'The transformation of employment in the digital era raises fears of insecurity, technologically induced unemployment and more stress at work. The political and academic discourse of digital technology and its impact on work is often alarmist and resorts to drastic policy recommendations. The collection of essays in *Work in the Digital Age* is a highly welcomed contribution that offers a rich understanding of the complex interaction between the role of new technologies in the world of work and the welfare state. There will be no simple solutions to maintain good work and a good society in the digital age. Policymakers have to shape it themselves and need high quality intellectual input of this sort'.

—**Anke Hassel**, Hertie School of Governance
and Institute of Economic and Social Research (WSI)

'*Work in the Digital Age* is a cutting-edge collection of articles on the future of work, offering a comprehensive treatment of current debates regarding the effects of new technology on employment, labour relations and inequality. As the authors make clear, the implications for public policy are profound. This book is an essential guide to the challenges of equity and policy that are emerging as digital technologies reshape the workplace'.

—**Michael J. Handel**, Northeastern University

'The editors of *Work in the Digital Age* have done the rest of us a great service in bringing together this remarkable group of contributors. Carefully balancing broad themes and detailed country studies, the collection is a must-read for scholars and students from multiple disciplines interested in how current technological change is affecting work and employment'.

—**Christian Lyhne Ibsen**, Michigan State University

'*Work in the Digital Age* is the major contemporary challenge. This book not only provides access to the outstanding trends, developments and challenges in the world of work and how to deal with them, it also provides country-specific access to the topic of digitalisation through country case studies'.

—**Wolfgang Schroeder**, University of Kassel

'How does the process of digitalisation transform the nature of work? Do the new technologies lead to labour disruption including rising wealth inequality or increasing regional disparities? Do they offer the potential for new and exciting business opportunities and economic growth? What are the major challenges for policymakers? This excellent volume offers a range of compelling answers to these pertinent questions by some of the world's leading labour market experts'.

—**Jette Steen Knudsen**, Fletcher School of Law and Diplomacy, Tufts University

'We are living in a time of major change in the labour market. Automation is altering both the amount and the nature of work as well as the skills, protections, and opportunities of people in all corners of society. Coming alongside unprecedented advances in human health and the ageing of populations, these changes throw up many challenges for policymakers. The proposals outlined in this impressive collection are an important contribution to the conversation about how to enable all citizens to have the opportunities they need to succeed in the new world of work'.

—**Seamus Nevin**, Institute of Directors, London

'The thematic arc of *Work in the Digital Age* makes clear that many futures of work are possible – and these futures are the consequences of choices that will be made by governments, businesses, technologists, educators, unions and activists working at the grassroots. Prior periods of technological innovations ushered in great social changes as people explored the uses and functions of new tools and systems. What is singularly remarkable about the digital age is that innovations are driving unpredictable, black swan events that are occurring at increasing frequency, in many forms, on multiple fronts and at a global scale. The challenge for policy makers is to see past each new technological event and, instead, establish and articulate and enduring set of principles that will guide the uses of unimagined technologies to the benefit of people and societies. *Work in the Digital Age* provides a great foundation that will help policy makers meet this challenge'.

—**Peter A. Creticos**, Institute for Work & the Economy

'This is a refreshingly broad and original exploration of the current upheaval in work and employment. The power of the contributions by remarkable team is greatly enhanced by their brevity. It will be important in shaping the gathering international debate on policy choices'.

—**William Brown**, Cambridge University

'Going beyond the buzzwords Work in the Digital Age provides a comprehensive analysis of how emerging technologies reshape the workplace and the labour market. Particularly the comparative perspective is highly valuable for academics and policymakers. This book is a major reference point in ongoing discussions on the future of work'.

—**Professor Dr. Werner Eichhorst**, IZA – Institute of Labor Economics

# WORK IN THE DIGITAL AGE

# About Policy Network

Policy Network is the international ideas exchange for progressives. More than just a thinktank, its network spans national borders across Europe and the wider world with the aim of promoting the best progressive thinking on the major social and economic challenges of the 21st century.

What makes Policy Network unique is our ability to connect policymakers and policy implementers. We combine rigorous analysis of the biggest questions facing modern societies with creative thinking on how to turn those fresh solutions into dynamic political narratives that can deliver electoral success for progressive parties.

- A platform for research and ideas
- Promoting expert ideas and political analysis on the key economic, social and political challenges of our age.
- Disseminating research excellence and relevant knowledge to a wider public audience through interactive policy networks, including interdisciplinary and scholarly collaboration.
- Engaging and informing the public debate about the future of European and global progressive politics.
- Building international policy communities comprising individuals and affiliate institutions.
- Providing meeting platforms where the politically active, and potential leaders of the future, can engage with each other across national borders, with the best thinkers who are sympathetic to their broad aims.
- Engaging in external collaboration with partners including higher education institutions, the private sector, thinktanks, charities, community organisations, and trade unions.
- Delivering an innovative events programme combining in-house seminars with large-scale public conferences designed to influence and contribute to key public debates.

www.policynetwork.org
@policynetwork

# About Das Progressive Zentrum

Das Progressive Zentrum is an independent thinktank, founded in 2007 as a non-profit initiative. In other countries, thinktanks have long established a dynamic market for ideas and have become key players in public debates. Like all industrialised countries, Germany will need to find answers to the challenges triggered by the rapid socio-economic, cultural, technological and ecological transformations of the 21st century. Thus it can only benefit from a lively conglomerate of innovative institutions catering to the need for modernisation. Das Progressive Zentrum aims to:

- Pursue a political agenda that promotes progressive politics and reform in Germany.
- Shape a new understanding of progress a new progressive narrative for a modern dynamic society, a just economy and a modern state of the 21st century.
- Analyse future problems and develop progressive, scientifically based solutions.

- Link discussions in Germany to international debates through bringing together key actors from academia, the media, business and politics.
- Provide a platform for an international exchange of ideas, in particular for the next generation of progressive thinkers, researchers and policymakers.

## About Foundation for European Progressive Studies (FEPS)

The Foundation for European Progressive Studies is the only progressive thinktank at European level. FEPS establishes an intellectual crossroad between social democracy and the European project, putting fresh thinking at the core of its action. As a platform for ideas and dialogue, FEPS works in close collaboration with social democratic organisations, and in particular national foundations and thinktanks across Europe, to tackle the challenges that Europe faces today. Close to the Party of European Socialists (PES), the S&D Group in the European Parliament, the PES Group in the Committee of the Regions, Young European Socialists and PES women, but nevertheless independent.

FEPS embodies a new way of thinking on the social democratic, socialist and labour scene in Europe.

Our main purpose is to nourish a fresh progressive debate through research including the Next Left and Millennial Dialogue programmes. With research activity available in a range of formats, including online, we are able to engage with the largest possible audience, notably through the FEPS Progressive Post magazine and our digital platform, the European Progressive Observatory.

**Disclaimer**

European Parliament

FOUNDATION FOR EUROPEAN
PROGRESSIVE STUDIES
FONDATION EUROPÉENNE
D'ÉTUDES PROGRESSISTES

This volume is developed in partnership with the Foundation for European Progressive Studies (FEPS) and published with the financial support of the European Parliament. The study does not represent the European Parliament's view.

**Editors**

Max Neufeind is a researcher and policy adviser on the future of work.

Jacqueline O'Reilly is professor of comparative human resources at the University of Sussex Business School.

Florian Ranft is head of policy and international at Policy Network, senior research analyst at the Centre for Progressive Policy and policy fellow at Das Progressive Zentrum.

# WORK IN THE DIGITAL AGE

## Challenges of the Fourth Industrial Revolution

**Edited by
Max Neufeind, Jacqueline O'Reilly
and Florian Ranft**

Published by Rowman & Littlefield International Ltd
Unit A, Whitacre Mews, 26-34 Stannary Street, London SE11 4AB
www.rowmaninternational.com

Rowman & Littlefield International Ltd. is an affiliate of Rowman & Littlefield
4501 Forbes Boulevard, Suite 200, Lanham, Maryland 20706, USA
With additional offices in Boulder, New York, Toronto (Canada), and Plymouth (UK)
www.rowman.com

The views and opinions expressed in this book are those of the authors and do not
necessarily reflect the official policy or position of any of the institutions they are
affiliated with.

**British Library Cataloguing in Publication Data**
A catalogue record for this book is available from the British Library

ISBN: PB 978-1-78660-906-9
eBook    978-1-78660-907-6

**Library of Congress Cataloging-in-Publication Data**
Library of Congress Control Number: 2018941712

∞™ The paper used in this publication meets the minimum requirements of
American National Standard for Information Sciences—Permanence of Paper for
Printed Library Materials, ANSI/NISO Z39.48-1992.

Printed in the United States of America

# CONTENTS

# PREFACE

The first industrial revolution at the end of the 17th century was possibly the first time in human history that sustained economic growth and technological progress collided with falling living standards and employment conditions, resulting in the great social upheavals described in Karl Polanyi's *The Great Transformation*. By now, it is undeniably clear that technological development and economic growth do not necessarily go hand in hand with social progress. Therefore, it should be the goal of our politics to ensure industrial and societal transformations provide opportunities for social mobility and citizens' personal and professional development – rather than being cause for concern and insecurity.

We must not be misled by recent electoral defeats: the current frustration of social democracy across Europe is not due to our fundamental values becoming less relevant. If anything, our mission towards freedom, fairness and equality of opportunity is more important than ever in the digital age, and these values should be the cornerstone of our renewal. Crucially, we must focus on how to better communicate these values through a convincing narrative, with a political agenda and concrete policy measures that address the difficult challenges faced by modern society.

But how can we design a narrative that combines our enthusiasm for innovation and technological change with a commitment to individual security and fairness across society? How do we put into practice our mission for socio-economic development and social justice in the context of disruptive changes brought about by the fourth industrial revolution?

A strong progressive narrative will not be sufficient to face the challenges of the digital transformation. Our movement needs to be able to translate our vision into concrete solutions, firstly through adapting and modernising existing policies, particularly in the areas of labour market regulation, social protection and welfare. On top of this we must think ahead to develop brand new policy instruments to address those problems that may have not yet fully materialised. Only by looking forward will we be able to fully address citizens' concerns and ensure their wellbeing is secure, enabling them to view our transformed society as a land of opportunity.

To achieve this, public participation will be particularly valuable, expanding our understanding by allowing us to keep a close eye on different country case studies and evaluate a range of concrete measures. As president of the Foundation for European Progressive Studies, I am glad that our organisation and the editors of this book have been able to compile such a wide range of expertise into one accessible volume and provide a valuable resource for policymakers across Europe. The purpose of our collaboration is to avoid a fragmentation of expertise and enthusiasm within our movement among those keen to develop a progressive approach to social democracy fit for the modern world of work.

If we have learnt one thing from the advent of the digital age, it is that collaborative models can be enormously valuable. It is therefore with a collaborative spirit and an open-minded approach that we should develop a new plan to ensure the digital transformation has more winners and fewer losers. In terms of immediate actions, in the short term we must move quickly and with conviction to implement the recently adopted European Pillar of Social Rights, which provides a new opportunity for political reform on social protection, work-life balance and improved security for atypical workers, such as those who peddle their labour on digital platforms. It is this new generation of workers that our movement must adapt to advocate for to ensure social democracy and its values can have maximum impact in the midst of a fourth industrial revolution.

Maria João Rodrigues

President of FEPS – European Foundation of Progressive Studies

# ACKNOWLEDGEMENTS

This book is the result of a long and adventurous intellectual journey the editors have taken to understand the seismic impact of new technologies on work and welfare in modern economies. This volume originates in the close and longstanding relationship between Policy Network, Das Progressive Zentrum and the Foundation for European Progressive Studies (FEPS) and our commitment to advance progressive thinking and inform public policy reform debates on the key social and economic challenges of our time. As international thinktanks based in London, Berlin and Brussels, we have drawn on our respective networks to engage progressive thinkers and academics and provide the reader with state-of-the-art public policy research on the main challenges of the fourth industrial revolution.

We would like to thank the Policy Network team, in particular Charlie Cadywould, Barry Colfer, Alex Porter and Samuel Siguere, who have done a tremendous job in assisting research, editing chapters and co-ordinating over 50 contributors of this impressive volume. In addition to the book's contributors, we would like to thank Steven Hill, Patrick Diamond, Josh Simons and Michael Schönstein for their thoughtful comments on earlier drafts. Matthew Laza and Katherine Roberts warrant special thanks for making sure the book was on track organisationally and intellectually. We would also like to convey our thanks to Dominic Schwickert, director of Das Progresive Zentrum, Dhara Snowden and the team at our publisher, Rowman & Littlefield, and Vincent Aussilloux and Cécile Jolly from France Stratégie.

Finally, we would like to thank Maria João Rodrigues, Ernst Stetter, David Rinaldi and Lisa Kastner of FEPS for the rewarding partnership.

# INTRODUCTION

## Identifying the challenges for work in the digital age

Jacqueline O'Reilly, Florian Ranft and Max Neufeind

The enormous growth in the rate of IT computing power, storage capacity, connectedness and software applications is transforming employment, disrupting businesses and challenging labour regulations. Businesses and governments grapple to contain the quasi-anarchic deployment of apps, data analytics and new forms of business and employment. Employees scramble to be, or to stay, connected. A proliferation of digital platforms is creating new kinds of good and poor quality jobs and businesses opportunities. Positive and pessimistic scenarios abound of an increasingly fragmented, digitalised and flexible transformation of work across the globe, a transformation that is hoped will boost economic growth, raise productivity levels and create an inclusive new vision of social integration for all in the digital age.

The fourth industrial revolution, according to (Schwab 2016; 2018), is characterised by a blurring of the distinctions between physical, digital and biological spheres, as major technological advancements are having a profound impact on economies, businesses and the personal lives of people throughout the world. Some of the technological forces in this transition include the development

of big data, algorithmic management, 3D printing, quantum computing, smart robots, artificial intelligence (AI), the internet of
things, nanotechnology, biotechnology and alternative forms of
energy technology. These debates have recently received considerable media and government attention, for example in the German
Industry 4.0 debate (see Rahner and Schönstein this volume), and
in the 2017 independent, UK-government-commissioned Taylor
review of modern working practices report (Taylor, 2017).

However, some authors are critical of the 'revolutionary' claims
of this transition (Atkinson this volume), others point out that this
multi-layered transformation is a longer term process that was first
identified back in the 1990s (Castells 1996; see also Soete this
volume). Nevertheless, the poignancy of changing forms of work
through the process of digitalisation makes it an apposite time to
examine the consequences of these emerging trends.

With this aim in mind, drawing on a wide range of international expertise, contributors to this volume examine a range of
existing empirical examples to assess the policy challenges that
arise from the transformation of work in the digital age. They
discuss the effects of labour disruption including the rising levels
of wealth inequality, low social mobility and increasing regional
disparities within and between countries. They consider how to
unlock the vast economic potential of new technologies and the
implications for policy innovations at firm, governmental and
societal levels.

Contributions to this book are structured around two main sections. In Part I contributors examine particular dimensions raised by
debates around the fourth industrial revolution, and consider how
it is affecting the changing face of work, labour relations and the
welfare state. In Part II contributors focus on country case studies
that range between high, medium and low digital density economies.
Authors here outline the context of digital transformation and recent
policy reforms in specific countries and regions that are related to
the issues raised in Part I. We conclude by bringing together this
analyis, discussing the policy challenges that have been identified by

the authors in this volume, and presenting tentative policy solutions and considerations.

## DEBATING THE FOURTH INDUSTRIAL REVOLUTION

The volume opens with Luc Soete situating current concerns with the emergence of the fourth industrial revolution in a broader historical perspective. He argues, first, that levels of fear and anxiety concerning the consequences of automation for employment today are comparable to those of the 1970s and 1980s, or even of the 1930s and 1940s, an opinion that is echoed by Colin Crouch. However, Soete points out that this anxiety was higher in earlier periods and today appears to be more of a concern in the US than in Europe. Cécile Jolly also argues that in some countries people are unaware or underestimate the potential consequences of the digital era, while in other countries media reporting suggests that people are anxious about digitalisation and the internet in general. Negative opinions about digital communication via the internet have also been associated with more populist and protectionist attitudes, as evidenced in the result of the Brexit referendum (O'Reilly 2016).

Despite identifying similar levels of anxiety to earlier periods of significant industrial change, there are also some important differences that distinguish the current period, which Soete suggests is becoming increasingly recognised as the emergence of a new form of digital 'winner-take-all' monopoly capitalism, from pervious eras. First, the digital transformation is characterised by what Haskel and Westlake (2017) have called "capitalism without capital": the growth of investment in the intangible economy of knowledge-based assets. Compared with traditional tangible assets, intangibles are more likely to be scalable, have sunk costs, and create spillovers and synergies with other intangibles. The capacity for disproportional 'rent taking' from intangibles is significant. Whereas capital investment requirements imposed limits to growth in previous periods, today the 'winner-takes-all' dynamic lasts much longer. Second, a major difference with previous periods of economic development is that entry barriers to the digital economy have been significantly reduced and the process of creative destruction through the constant updating and development of technology is now possible as a result of the internet and 'app economy'.

Soete reasons that private investment in information and communications technology (ICT) in Europe has been lagging, compared with the US. Zysman and Kenney argue that in the US a growing ecosystem of different types of venture capital and private equity investors, ranging from expert 'angels' to crowd funding vehicles, are chasing 'unicorn' investment opportunities.[1] Such investors are not overly concerned about immediately generating profits, but rather are more interested in market domination strategies. In these circumstances labour is a cost to be minimised, rather than an asset contributing to the long-term value of the firm. As a result Zysman and Kenney suggest that the disruptive effects of these venture capital and private equity investment ecosystems are likely to have dire consequences for the increased commodification of labour in platform companies.

Yet, the increased commodification of labour will affect particular groups of workers differently. In their examination of the digital gender gap Debra Howcroft and Jill Rubery illustrate how persisting gender inequalities are perpetuated through the process of digitalisation, and how emerging forms of employment reinforce women's role in social reproduction in new ways. They argue that we need to think about the consequences of these transformations in relation to structural changes in the growth and decline of particular sectors, changes to the nature and quality of work affected by patterns of displacement and recruitment, change to the employment relationship, and change to access to work over the period of childbirth and childrearing. Their policy recommendations focus on issues related to working-time flexibility, revisiting the societal value of care and 'caring jobs', and the regulation of new forms of employment.

Digitalisation will change jobs, but this does not mean that robots will replace them; new jobs and tasks will also emerge.

Daniel Arnold, Melanie Arntz, Terry Gregory, Susanne Steffes and Ulrich Zierahn argue that the potential for job automation has been greatly exaggerated. 'Non-automatable niches' within the bundle of tasks constituting a job make many jobs less vulnerable than suggested by Frey and Osborne (2017). According to Arnold et al. these threats also vary significantly by country, and in workplaces where qualifications and communications are higher, the threat is lower. There are a number of barriers to the more extensive implementation of Industry 4.0. These barriers include the need to provide data protection and cyber security, to improve employee training, to acquire high levels of investment, and to create ecosystems that generate new forms of dependency on external contractors. The authors suggest that there is less need to be anxious about automation per se. Instead it is the policies around automation that ought to be cause for concern. Three key policy areas are identified that will be essential: upgrading workers' qualifications and skills, deciding how displaced workers should be supported, and determining how the distribution of the economic benefits of digitalisation are translated into taxes and wages that are beneficial to local economies and workers.

Paul Hofheinz reinforces the argument that the revolution will be political and social rather than industrial or technologically in nature. He contends that the four most fundamental shifts have become the dematerialised state of "capitalism without capital" (Haskel and Westlake 2017), the dramatic improvement in life expectancy, increased access to education, and data as the equivalent today of what raw materials were in previous periods of industrialisation. The key issues for Hofheinz are not how much industry is adapting, because it will do so anyway. Rather, what is of more concern should be the social disruption and discontent that this transformation will likely cause. While Hofheinz considers the introduction of a basic income as a "primitive solution" to a complex problem, that "would lead to poor social results", he argues that it reflects a move in the right direction. Data sharing has become the contemporary currency in the workplace, but the 'sharing economy' that extends to the inclusion of information about us also needs a sharing of the rents that are generated by it.

Other authors like Robert Atkinson challenge the whole concept of the fourth industrial revolution as both inaccurate and exaggerated. According to Atkinson, we are already approaching the sixth industrial revolution.[2] He expects that technological innovation associated with ICT and AI will be modest, but progressive, as improvements to technology will develop relatively slowly. There will be productivity gains, but these will depend on the right policy combination, which should not involve taxing robots or introducing a basic income. He argues that the question and concern with job quality is misplaced. Job creation, he argues, will be based on consumption patterns, and some of these trends will create good quality jobs, for example in education, and also poorer quality jobs in personal services, or what Morel (2015) calls "servant" jobs.

For Atkinson the key issue is related to raising productivity and how this would reduce the costs of goods and services. Reduced costs could generate further consumption and job growth in better-paid jobs. He argues that there is no reason to believe that this would lead to a disproportionate growth of self-employment or "crowdwork". Atkinson also argues that growing inequality has been largely attributable to changing pay rates within occupations as some workers make winner-take-all incomes at the expense of others in their occupation, with workplaces becoming dualised between insiders and outsiders. But, he argues, this is not about a general polarisation of the labour market and a hollowing out of the middle-level occupations; contrary to the arguments of Bruno Palier. Atkinson is also quite sanguine about the need to develop future skills as a large proportion of Europeans already say that they are overqualified for their current jobs:

> Automating low wage jobs will mean not only the creation of fewer low-wage jobs and more middle- and higher-wage jobs, but also this will usually lead to higher output per worker in the remaining workforce, meaning that their wages can be more easily increased.

For him a progressive agenda will require governments to help workers make the transition to new employment, but basic income is not the way to protect workers from temporary periods of job loss. Inspired by Nordic flexicurity models and systems of lifelong-learning in France, he suggests that models of higher education must be overhauled and disrupted. For him these are the ingredients necessary to bring about a progressive vision of future growth.

As these contributions illustrate, the concept of the fourth industrial revolution is contested, and assessments of its expected implications are diverse and complex. Inevitably there will be some very significant changes in the way that work is organised in the future, but the speed and extent of these changes are disputed. To get a sense of what some of these changes will look like, in the following section authors identify some of the key transformative technologies and the implications of digital platforms for new forms of employment. One theme running throughout these contributions is that the consequences for jobs that are displaced, or created, by the process of implementing digital technologies will require new forms of governance and consultation between employers, social partners and governments.

## THE CHANGING FACE OF WORK IN THE DIGITAL AGE

Looking at the labour displacement and productivity effects of AI on employment, Georgios Petropoulos argues that middle-level jobs that require routine manual and cognitive skilled are the ones that are most at risk. In the long run, initial labour displacement effects of jobs with routinised manual or cognitive skills, as in previous industrial revolutions, will be compensated for by the growth in non-routine jobs at the high and low end of the economy. However, the speed of change today is significantly faster than it was in the past. Petropoulos focuses on the growth of machine learning and improved machine performance and explains how these advancements are produced through the development of so-called 'deep neural networks' that are inspired by the architecture of the human brain. Although these are still very far from achieving the level of complexity associated with the human brain, on very specific tasks machines have outperformed humans. The author draws attention to the nexus between what is possible, and which firms will be willing to invest to implement these technologies. The introduction of multifunctional robots has been most extensive in the EU, followed by the US and China. The sectors that have adopted these with the greatest enthusiasm include car production, and plastic and chemical production, where job displacement effects will be felt the most. Policymakers will need to develop a framework of rules for the operation of machines and AI systems. This should involve collective consultation with affected parties and experts, and a comprehensive debate on the regulation of the liability, safety, security and privacy of these technologies, alongside the updating of relevant skills and training programmes working with these new technologies.

Manufacturing has always been at the forefront of game-changing technological innovation. Enrique Fernández-Macías, drawing on a Eurofound (forthcoming) study, examines the impact that advanced industrial robotics, additive manufacturing, the industrial internet of things, electric vehicles and industrial biotech may have on the future of work. He identifies four trends: the increasing centrality of digital information, mass customisation, the increased importance of the service relationship ('servitisation'), and increased resource efficiency. Like Petropoulos he agrees that the effect of new technologies is likely to have a profound impact on employment, by displacing jobs, but it will also lead to an upgrading of occupations, the development of more hybrid skill sets, a decrease in repetitive routine work and a reduction in hazardous industrial tasks. Despite these advantages, firms interviewed in the Eurofound study also expressed concern for how this would affect the degree of privacy and control for workers who will feel permanently monitored through an intensification of work and a declining sense of autonomy. Fernández-Macías argues that greater social dialogue around policy is required, similar to that which exists in Germany around Industry 4.0 and Work 4.0 (see Rahner and Schönstein this volume).

Examining the idea of an 'inclusive robot agenda', Monique Kremer and Robert Went are more sceptical of the exaggerated claims regarding the roll out of the fourth industrial revolution. Between the hyperbolic commentary they make a distinction between long standing traditions of research in AI, where technology is intended to replace people, and intelligence augmentation (IA), where computers are used to enhance human learning and innovation. Questioning the idea of technological determinism, they argue that the process of implementing technology through regulation and reforms to skills and education will shape its outcomes.

While tempering the most radical claims regarding the future of work, the problem for Kremer and Went is one of work and money, and how it is distributed, a theme that runs through many of the contributions in this volume. They situate this problem in relation to a long running debate that makes a distinction between skill-biased technological change that is beneficial to the well educated and higher skilled, in contrast to capital-biased technological change, where those who own the robots benefit more. An 'inclusive robot agenda' covers a number of dimensions. This includes co-production, educational expertise, the distribution of productivity gains through co-ownership and the possibility of a universal 'robot dividend' to be paid into a social wealth fund. There are a variety of opinions on policies such as a robot or 'bit' tax (see Soete this volume). While some like Crouch are more positive of such proposals, Atkinson dismisses them as 'progress-killing ideas'. These contributions clearly illustrate how new ideas are being proposed to identify a portfolio of innovative policies to ensure the pursuit of an inclusive agenda that prevents the exclusion of an increasingly fragmented workforce; but there is also considerable disagreement on how such an agenda should be implemented and what it should include.

Turning to examine workforce perspectives of the changing face of employment in the digital age and the consequences of new forms of work for social protection, Huws et al., Schor, and Berg and De Stefano draw on some recent international studies of clickworkers and crowdworkers. Precise measurement of this sector is difficult and contested, as are the range of policy challenges that it presents.

Berg and De Stefano draw on an International Labour Organization (ILO) survey of clickworkers in 2015 that suggests over 40% of respondents said this platform work was their principal source of income, and the average time spent on platforms was 30 hours per week (Berg 2016). But for most crowdworkers this is as an additional income stream to a more regular job (Huws et al. 2017). Schor argues that platform work effectively 'free rides' on conventional employment, which raises questions about how sustainable it will be. In the US there is a discussion about whether or not platform work may have peaked (Farrell and Grieg 2017) because income rates for clickworkers have been falling, there is a very high turnover rate, and the relative proportion of those want to do this type of work is declining due to changing demographic trends.

While appreciating the flexibility that this form of work can offer different communities, crowdworkers also complained about difficulties in communication, the way that work was allocated and paid, the impossibility of challenging negative ratings from customers, and the sometimes arbitrary deactivation of their accounts. Sources of stress came from long or unpredictable working hours, the reluctance of workers to refuse work in case they would be excluded from future offers, as well as risks of sexual harassment and sometimes being asked to conduct illegal tasks (see Huws et al. this volume).

Schor highlights the negative environmental consequences of using these platforms, and evidence of racial discrimination. Ge et al. (2016) and Edelman, Luca and Svirsky (2017) found that non-white participants using platforms were more likely to experience discrimination when acquiring services, and this cohort also received lower ratings and lower prices for the services they offered in the US.

As Berg and De Stefano argue, the digital revolution is rebranding casual work. A key message coming out of these contributions relates to the gap in existing labour regulations and social provisions. A number of legal judgments in the UK and at the European Court of Justice illustrate the questionable status of these workers being self-employed and autonomous. According to Berg and De Stefano regulatory reforms would involve platforms guaranteeing a minimum number of hours of paid work, as is the case for zero hour contract workers in the Netherlands, as well as the introduction of a ban on exclusivity clauses for this type of work, as is seen in the regulation of zero hour work in the UK. The authors also suggest that technology could be improved to reduce the time spent searching for work and to facilitate the accrual of social security contributions. They cite examples where collective bargaining for ride-hailing platforms in Seattle has been introduced, as initiatives that mark a step forward to help protect platform workers to organise and achieve collective rights.

The growth of crowdwork raises some significant issues concerning existing regulation of welfare systems and labour markets. This requires guidelines on the definition of self-employment relating to tax, national insurance contributions and social protection entitlement, where the onus of proof rests with the employer rather than the worker (Prassl 2015). Further clarification of workers' rights to minimum wages, holiday entitlements and other benefits is needed. While some authors have suggested that a basic income policy could address these problems, Huws et al. point out that this raises a number of additional problems with regard to who should be entitled to these benefits, how immigration from outside Europe affects this policy, and whether it would encourage employers to withdraw their contributions to social welfare. According to Schor three areas for future policy makers to focus on are the need to reduce worker's dependency on this form of crowdwork through social measures, monitoring carbon impacts, and tackling racial discrimination.

## LABOUR RELATIONS AND THE WELFARE STATE

This volume also considers the potential actors who might bring about some of the changes that are required for improvements to labour relations and welfare reform. Colin Crouch expects that the threat to jobs is as likely to affect better-qualified workers as those in middle- or lower-skilled jobs. He argues that the growth of 'non-employees', those not covered by legal and social protections, can affect a very diverse array of people. While these working arrangements can be attractive at particular times during the life course for some, it prevents others from establishing the stability that is required in adult life (O'Reilly et al. 2017; 2018). Current labour law disputes over which economic sectors these firms operate in is a clear illustration of how these platforms are reshaping the employment relationship. For example definitions of employers and workers, contractors and dependent contractors are being contested in the courts and in some countries subject to new statutory definitions (Jolly this volume). Recent judicial decisions in the UK have found Uber to be an employer and not a transport company (Berg and De Stefano this volume). Crouch argues, like Zysman and Kenney, that 'non-employees', such as those who drive for Uber, are less likely to be seen as an asset to be invested in. The autonomy of 'non-employees' at work is more likely to be reduced through digital technology, increased surveillance and new digital systems of managerial control. These changes all contribute to a redefinition of the employment relationship (Howcroft and Rubery this volume).

The global implications of these disruptive processes for different groups of workers are illustrated in the contribution from Virginia Doellgast. Drawing on extensive international research of call centre workers (Batt, Holman and Holtgrewe 2009), telecom firms (Doellgast et al. 2016) and unions (Doellgast, Lillie and Pulignano 2018), Doellgast points to how the changing balance of work in the networked economy is taking shape through global and regional outsourcing. This undermines workers power and increases inequality and precariousness. Returning a larger share of power and voice to workers has to be part of a larger project designed to address inequality and to extend democracy. She proposes the closing of existing legal loopholes and the extension of collective agreements across companies to their subcontractors and staffing agencies. These suggestions illustrate the need for new and internationalised governance systems.

Examining the transformation of social dialogue Cécile Jolly also argues that we need new institutions of collective bargaining, as existing institutions are not well adapted to address the changing nature of work. A continuous dialogue is required over a number of crosscutting issues related to jobs, skills, working life and personal data protection. Currently social dialogue is organised around rigid timeframes, and largely focused on issues of working time and wages. Nevertheless, Jolly points to some innovative company level initiatives in France, Germany and Spain where employers have sought to establish clearer boundaries around email communications outside business hours. Furthermore, new forms of regulating tele-workers have been found in a number of European collective agreements. There has also been an emergence of new forms of unionism to represent these new workers and freelancers in Canada, the UK and the US (Vandaele 2018). Reforms to labour law have been introduced in Italy and Spain to recognise the category of 'the economically dependent self-employed' and 'para-subordinated workers'; French reforms have also resulted in conflict between different national actors. However, despite these initiatives, much remains to be done to attempt to grapple with the integration of casualised labour resulting from the growth of platform organisations.

The issue of labour market deregulation is particularly pertinent in recent discussions around the UK's departure from the EU. Kate Bell examines whether Brexit will lead to a race to the bottom for workers' rights and productivity. In February 2018 the UK minister responsible for UK's withdrawal from the EU, David Davis, dismissed the idea that Brexit would result in a dystopian 'Mad Max' style exit (Brown 2018). However, Bell illustrates, on a number of dimensions, that the UK's poor performance – low productivity, low wages, precarious employment, limited employee voice and inadequate skills training – does not provide a fertile bedrock for transition to the digital age. She argues that, given these shortcomings, trade unions today have as much relevance as they did at the beginning of the industrial revolution.

The need to develop new adaptive skills to capitalise on technological change is examined by Thomas Aubrey in his investigation of the long-term deficiency in technical skills provision in the UK and its effects on productivity. Employers in the UK frequently complain that it is very difficult to fill jobs that require core technical skills, and Brexit is expected to exacerbate this problem. Students are often unaware of the skills that they will need to find work as they receive poor careers advice. Given the pace of technological change and its implementation, it is an urgent requirement for policymakers to establish a programme of adaptive skills development, to be delivered through local collaborations at a regional level, in order to build up a strong skills ecosystem that is essential to ensure that communities across the UK are not left behind.

Taking up this issue of those who are most vulnerable to the consequences of the digital transformation, Bruno Palier examines the politics of social risks and the existing gaps in social protection. He suggests that digital workers in lower status jobs face higher risks of not being covered by social and employment protection. This exacerbates trends towards labour market dualisation and a hollowing out of middle-skilled jobs, although not all contributors to this volume agree with this. For Palier the challenge is to build a new social contract between the winners in the knowledge economy (the productive and 'creative' types) along with the emergent class of 'servant' gig workers (Morel 2015). Palier identifies five groups of precarious workers who are most at risk: women, the young and ethnic minorities in precarious non-standard employment, unskilled workers on short-term contracts, independent workers or microentrepreneurs, and platform workers. Renewed forms of social protection will need to be adapted to the different types of welfare state regimes that currently exist in Europe. Palier identifies three types of welfare state regime: a liberal solution based on a universal, unconditional, basic income; a Bismarckian model that improves conditions for independent workers; and a flexicurity model that develops and finances social rights for all. While none of these regimes will definitively solve all of the risks these workers may face, Palier's piece asserts that Europe's welfare systems need urgent reforms.

In the final contribution in this section on the changing face of digital work and the new conceptualisation of the future of work in 2030, Salima Benhamou outlines four possible scenarios. She distinguishes between the development of learning organisations, new virtual learning organisations, the super-interim model and a new age of Taylorism. Learning organisations capture those organisations that seek to encourage high quality jobs where employees with different skill sets are integrated in the delivery of the services and caring sectors. New virtual learning organisations refers to collaborative platforms for high quality production where virtual teams manage complex processes. In contrast, the super-interim model is about improving working conditions for low skilled workers by integrating them into highly skilled networks where they can access a variety of different sources of employment from different employers. Finally, the new age of Taylorism includes homeworkers performing individual tasks remotely. These four scenarios provide a heuristic device to think about the future of work and how different models can coexist, but will also be affected by differences in the skills and qualifications of the local labour market.

A major thread running through all these contributions points to the need for new forms of collective dialogue to anticipate the major risks and opportunities and to identify which policy bundles are required in different national contexts. The implementation of these changes is evident from some of the examples of company level initiatives cited by Jolly. In some cases there has been evidence of these being expanded to the sectoral level, and that national governments are beginning to initiate new forms of regulation to cover these newly emerging labour markets and forms of social protection. However, these initiatives are in their infancy. To capture how these developments are evolving in more detail, Part II of this volume provides a selection of country case studies from the EU and across the world, including Canada, India and the US, to understand the historical context in which digitalisation is happening in these different societies, to identify how political agendas are evolving, and to assess the impact of locally developed solutions to address change.

## COMPARING THE DIGITAL TRANSFORMATION OF WORK ACROSS COUNTRIES

While global in nature, it is clear that the impact of the fourth industrial revolution has been embedded to different degrees in different national contexts, and has moved at different speeds in advanced industrial economies. An incredible volume of international research is being produced from a wide range of organisations, which attempts to measure and estimate the likely consequences of the fourth industrial revolution in general, for particular sectors and between countries. This includes the business intelligence community (the World Economic Forum) and management consultants (PricewaterhouseCoopers, McKinsey, Accenture, and collaboration with academics such as Oxford Economics); thinktanks (Pew); and international organisations, such as the Organisation for Economic Co-operation and Development, Eurofound and the ILO (2016). These are to a large degree in their infancy in developing comparative methodologies and reliable, comparable cross-national data. This volume seeks to contribute to this body of research, and to address its shortcomings by going beyond a mere quantitative or single case study analysis.

One measure to differentiate between countries has been to draw on data that measures ICT usage in the population at large measured through household access to the internet and internet speeds (Eurostat 2017a). A second approach compares the density and nature of digital technologies used in enterprises (Eurostat 2017b), while a third approach has been to aggregate these individual dimensions to generate the Digital Economy and Society Index (DESI), which ranks and compares advances in the digital sector in the EU (European Commission 2017); see Figure Int 1.

Using the DESI index we differentiate between three types of countries in the EU: high, medium and low digital density countries. Four countries stand out from the rest as digital forerunners:

Denmark, Finland, Sweden and the Netherlands. Middle digital density countries are those ranking above the EU average, and all those below are considered to be low digital density countries. Some of the countries found in these categories and rankings might at first be a little surprising. For example, Estonia performs particularly well because it is seen as the egovernment champion in the EU; Spain is not far behind it on this dimension and performs better than Germany. The countries in the low digital density group are quite varied, ranging from France at the top to Romania at the bottom; this category could be further differentiated, but for our purposes here this rather rudimentary demarcation allows us to talk at a broader level about overall similarities and differences in the evolution of digitalisation in Europe. Although these figures change annually as countries improve, to varying degrees on the different dimensions,

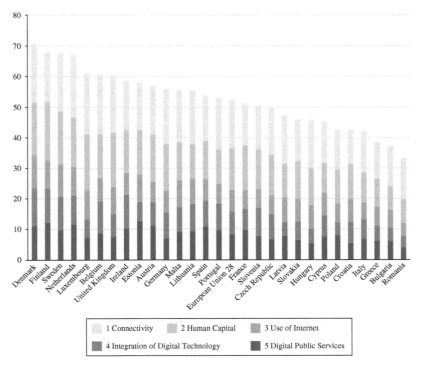

**Figure Int.1   Digital ranking of EU countries in the Digital Economy and Society Index, 2017.** *Source*: European Commission (2017).

the overall rankings between the forerunners and those lagging behind have not changed very significantly in recent years.

The DESI ranking is based on five key dimensions: connectivity, human capital and digital skills, citizens' use of the internet, business integration and digital public services.[3] Connectivity measures the speed and quality of the broadband infrastructure, as fast broadband speeds can be seen as essential for competitiveness. Human capital measures both basic and advanced digital skills ranging from simple internet use to the proportion of ICT specialists and science, technology, engineering and mathematics graduates in the labour force, drawing on various Eurostat surveys. Citizens' use of the internet includes consumption of online content, communications, online shopping and banking. The integration of digital technology by businesses measures the use of electronic planning and management software, social media, cloud services and ecommerce for sales. And egovernment measures the proportion of public services accessible through the internet.

While the index provides a basic benchmark to compare the extent of digitalisation between European countries, we go further by providing empirical evidence and country specific expertise from across the EU28, and beyond the boundaries of Europe, to understand how policy debates in this field are being developed within different national contexts. Contributors to this volume provide in-depth country case studies, which are used to draw more general conclusions on the causes and policy options needed to address the challenges of the digital age and the changing nature of work in different societies.

Contributions from high digital density countries (DESI score greater than 60) include Denmark (Anna Ilsøe), Finland (Jenni Karjalainen), Sweden (Fredrik Söderqvist) and the Netherlands (Maarten Keune and Fabian Dekker). Contributions from middle density countries (DESI score lower than 60 and greater than EU average) include Belgium (Patrizia Zanoni), the UK (Olivia Bailey and Andrew Harrop), Ireland (Seán Ó Riain and Amy E. Healy), Austria (Jörg Flecker), Germany (Sven Rahner and Michael Schönstein), Spain (Rafael Grande) and Portugal (Joana

A. Vicente). Contributions from countries that are below the EU average DESI score (= 51) include France (Enzo Weber), eastern Europe (Jan Drahokoupil), Slovenia (Aleksandra Kanjuo Mrčela), Latvia (Dmitrijs Kravcenko), Poland (Maria Skóra), Italy (Carlotta de Franceschi) and Greece (Sotiria Theodoropoulou). Finally, by including perspectives from Canada (Juan Gomez and Rafael Gomez), the US (Arne L. Kalleberg) and India (Marc Saxer) we provide a global perspective on these developments, while recognising that despite having an already large volume of contributors, an issue for future research and debate would be to include more extensive coverage of Asia and developments in Africa and Latin America. This book should be seen as a catalyst to developing these future comparisons and debates.

## CHALLENGES OF WORK IN THE DIGITAL AGE

In this high-risk, high-opportunity era (Ranft 2016) a mixture of new technologies and less regulated labour markets have led to contractual employment agreements becoming more flexible and hybrid, especially for young people in Europe (O'Reilly et al. 2018). The standardised employment relationship is in decline and distributional conflicts between labour market 'outsiders' and 'insiders' are on the rise. Middle-income jobs that drove social mobility in the US and Europe during the second part of the 20th century are at risk of erosion, with digitalisation of work systems replacing jobs across the spectrum from low to medium-skilled managerial positions (Eurofound 2017; Goos, Manning and Salomons 2014). Job creation is also polarised between those at the lower and upper end of the income scale and between advanced and less advanced societies and regions (OECD 2017, 85–88).

As a consequence, in most countries welfare systems are facing escalating pressures in their capacity to tackle the new social risks of the 21st century and in relation to demographic and fiscal sustainability. Pay gaps are very likely to widen and women and minorities are likely to be hit the hardest in the initial phases as low-wage jobs – where these cohorts are concentrated – have a higher risk of automation (Lawrence, Roberts and King 2017; Nelson 2018). Supporting those who fall through the social safety net as a result of emerging forms of employment is one of the most significant challenges facing advanced societies on the threshold of the fourth industrial revolution.

The main objective of the contributions to this volume is to discuss a wide range of the challenges that have been identified, and to outline how these are being addressed in particular countries or regions. The guiding questions shaping these discussions revolve around: What will the decent jobs of tomorrow look like? Where will they come from? What forms will they take? And, how can policymakers capture and combine the innovative dynamism of these changes with enhanced social justice?

Finding answers to these questions is crucial as the negative consequences of the digital revolution might provide a feeding ground for the spread of emerging populist politics that are widely recognised to be opposed to the consequences of globalisation and the internet. Our contribution here is intended to inform a progressive agenda on how we can develop shared narratives and solutions across a range of advanced industrialised countries. It touches on the core mission of how progressive movements and trade unions can contribute to the ongoing policy debate about the future of work in modern economies, and the opportunities, threats and potential solutions we need to identify to address some of the most intriguing and gripping economic and social challenges of our time. We conclude by outlining the key challenges and political realities identified by these contributions, and how they can inform a progressive framework for policy reform to address the consequences of digitalisation at work.

## NOTES

1. Unicorn investments are software start ups that reach US$1bn valuations. The term derived from Aileen Lee, founder of CowboyVC, a venture

capital fund from Palo Alto. She estimated that of the software start ups founded in the 2000s only 0.07% every reached US$1bn valuations. Their rarity made them comparable to mythical unicorns. This has become a widely accepted term in financial circles with Fortune magazine listing the top 100 unicorns.

    2. The first industrial revolution of steam power was in the late 1700s and early 1800s. The second, based on iron, in the 1840s and 1850s was followed by the third at the turn of the millennium with steel and electricity. The fourth revolution in the 1950s and 1960s was based on electromechanical and chemical technologies, and the present fifth revolution is based on ICT. The sixth wave, grounded in AI, robotics and perhaps nanotechnology and biotechnology, will not emerge until after a relatively long period of stagnation.

    3. The main dimensions of DESI indicators are weighted in equal terms.

## REFERENCES

Batt, R., D. Holman and U. Holtgrewe (2009), 'The Globalization of Service Work: Comparative Institutional Perspectives on Call Centers, Introduction to a Special Issue of ILRR', *ILRReview*, 62(4): 453–488.

Berg, J. (2016), 'Income Security in the On-Demand Economy: Findings and Policy Lessons from a Survey of Crowdworkers', *Comparative Labour Law & Policy Journal*, 37(3): 543–76.

Brown, J. M. (2018), 'Davis Dismisses Fears of a 'Mad Max-style' Post-Brexit Dystopia', *Financial Times*, 20 February, https://www.ft.com/content/bd5f1078-162d-11e8-9376-4a6390addb44.

Castells, M. (1996), *The Rise of the Network Society*, Oxford: Blackwells.

Doellgast, V., K. Sarmiento-Mirwaldt and C. Benassi (2016), 'Contesting Firm Boundaries: Institutions, Cost Structures, and the Politics of Externalization', *ILRReview*, 69(3): 551–78.

Doellgast, V., N. Lillie and V. Pulignano (eds) (2018), *Reconstructing Solidarity: Labour Unions, Precarious Work, and the Politics of Institutional Change in Europe*, Oxford: Oxford University Press.

Edelman, B., M. Luca and D. Svirsky (2017), 'Racial Discrimination in the Sharing Economy: Evidence from a Field Experiment', *American Economic Journal: Applied Economics*, 9(2): 1–22.

Eurofound (2017), *Occupational Change and Wage Inequality: European Jobs Monitor 2017*, Luxembourg: Publications Office of the European Union.

Eurofound (forthcoming), *Game Changing Technologies in European Manufacturing: Exploring the Impact on Production Process and Work*, Dublin: Eurofound, https://www.eurofound.europa.eu/publications/report/2018/game-changing-technologies-in-european-manufacturing.

European Commission (2017), *The Digital Economy and Society Index (DESI)*, https://ec.europa.eu/digital-single-market/en/desi.

Eurostat (2017a), *Digital Economy and Society Statistics: Households and Individuals*, http://ec.europa.eu/eurostat/statistics-explained/index. php/Digital_economy_and_society_statistics_-_households_and_individuals.

Eurostat (2017b), *Digital Economy and Society Statistics: Enterprises*, http://ec.europa.eu/eurostat/statistics-explained/index.php/Digital_economy_and_society_statistics_-_enterprises.

Farrell, D. and F. Grieg (2017), *The Online Platform Economy: Has Growth Peaked?*, New York City: JP Morgan Chase Institute, https://www.jpmorganchase.com/corporate/institute/document/jpmc-institute-online-platform-econ-brief.pdf.

Frey, C. B. and M. A. Osborne (2017), 'The Future of Employment: How Susceptible are Jobs to Computerization?', *Technological Forecasting and Social Change*, 114(C): 254–280.

Ge, Y., C. R. Knittel, D. MacKenzie and S. Zoepf (2016), *Racial and Gender Discrimination in Transportation Network Companies*, NBER Working Paper 22776.

Goos, M., A. Manning and A. Salomons (2014), 'Explaining Job Polarization: Routine-Biased Technological Change and Offshoring', *American Economic Review*, 104(8): 2509–526.

Haskel, J. and S. Westlake (2017), *Capitalism Without Capital: the Rise of the Intangible Economy*, Princeton: Princeton University Press.

Huws, U., N. H. Spencer, D. S. Syrdal and K. Holts (2017), *Work in the European Gig Economy: Research results from the UK, Sweden, Germany, Austria, the Netherlands, Switzerland and Italy*, Brussels and Hatfield: European Foundation for Progressive Studies, UNI Europa and University of Hertfordshire, http://www.feps-europe.eu/assets/9d13a6d2-5973-4131-b9c8-3ca5100f92d4/work-in-the-european-gig-full-report-pppdf.pdf.

ILO (2016), *Non-standard Employment Around the world: Understanding Challenges, Shaping Prospects*, Geneva: International Labour Office, http://www.ilo.org/wcmsp5/groups/public/---dgreports/---dcomm/---publ/documents/publication/wcms_534326.pdf.

Lawrence, M., C. Roberts and L. King (2017), 'Managing Automation: Employment, Inequality and Ethics in the Digital Age', *IPPR*

*Commission on Economic Justice*, London: Institute for Public Policy Research, https://www.ippr.org/files/2018-01/cej-managing-automation-december2017.pdf.

Morel, N. (2015), 'Servants for the Knowledge-based Economy? The Political Economy of Domestic Services in Europe', *Social Politics* 22(2): 170–92.

Nelson, E. (2018), 'Job Automation Will Hurt Women First but Will Ultimately Hurt Men More', *Quartz*, 6 February, https://qz.com/1198953/after-three-waves-of-automation-men-will-face-greater-job-losses-than-women-a-pwc-study-shows/?mc_cid=a47e86c151&mc_eid=7a8caf6ba0.

O'Reilly, J. (2016), 'Brexit: Understanding the Socio-Economic Origins and Consequences', *Socio-Economic Review*, 14(4): 807–54.

O'Reilly, J., C. Moyart, T. Nazio and M. Smith (eds) (2017), *Youth Employment: STYLE Handbook*, Brighton: CROME, http://www.style-handbook.eu.

O'Reilly, J., J. Leschke, R. Ortlieb, M. Seeleib-Kaiser and P. Villa (eds) (2018), *Youth Labour in Transition: Inequalities, Mobility and Policies in Europe*, New York: Oxford University Press.

OECD (2017), *OECD Employment Outlook*, Paris: OECD Publishing.

Prassl, J. (2015), *The Concept of the Employer*, Oxford: Oxford University Press.

Ranft, F. (ed.) (2016), *Aiming High: Progressive Politics in a High-Risk, High-Opportunity Era*, London and New York: Rowman & Littlefield.

Schwab, K. (2016), *The Fourth Industrial Revolution*, Geneva: World Economic Forum.

Schwab, K. (2018), *Shaping the Fourth Industrial Revolution*, Geneva: World Economic Forum.

Taylor, M. (2017), *Good work: the Taylor Review of Modern Working Practices*, London: Department for Business, Energy & Industrial Strategy.

Vandaele, K. (2018), 'How Can Trade Unions in Europe Connect with Young Workers?', in J. O'Reilly, J. Leschke, R. Ortlieb, M. Seeleib-Kaiser and P. Villa (eds), *Youth Labor in Transition*, New York: Oxford University Press.

# Part I

# Debating the fourth industrial revolution

# A

# The destructive creation of employment in the digital age

# DESTRUCTIVE CREATION

## Explaining the productivity paradox in the digital age

## Luc Soete

The technology in itself is neither good nor bad. It is the use which human beings make of any technology which determines both the nature and extent of the benefits.

—Christopher Freeman

**D**ebate regarding the impact of new technologies on jobs and the organisation of work has raged for decades, if not centuries. While notable, this is hardly surprising. After all, we talk today about the fourth industrial revolution, following on from the first, second and third industrial revolutions. To gain insights into what the potential impact of the current phase of disruption might be, taking a look at previous industrial revolutions is both logical and revealing.

In this short contribution, I will attempt to provide some analytical insights into the possible consequences of the fourth industrial revolution for work and incomes. In doing so, it follows the more detailed analysis of Daniel Arnold and colleagues on the digitalisation and automation of manufacturing processes (Arnold et al. 2016; see also Arnold et al. this volume). My analysis will primarily be based on comparing current developments with the immediately foregoing, third industrial revolution, the one most closely linked to the emergence and rapid diffusion of microelectronics and the computer in the last quarter of the 20th century. I limit myself to such a comparison for two reasons.

First, most of the technologies associated with the fourth industrial revolution can undoubtedly be described as 'new' and 'disruptive' in their current and future applications, but are in essence based on improvements and developments to technologies which are characteristic of the third industrial revolution, including microelectronics and in particular the continuous exponential improvements in the performance of integrated circuits following Moore's law.[1] As Klaus Schwab of the World Economic Forum put it, this built on the foundations prepared by the third industrial revolution. The improvements of these technological advancements, and improvements to processing speeds, continuously opened new areas for further research in robotics, and many other technologies associated with the fourth industrial revolution: 3D printing, quantum computing, artificial intelligence (AI) (Petropoulos this volume), the 'internet of things' (Fernández-Macías this volume), nanotechnology, biotechnology, materials science, energy storage, and in many other fields. Unsurprisingly, since the 1990s, microelectronics has been identified by economists as the most characteristic example of a so-called general purpose technology – one that affects all sectors of the economy (Bresnahan and Trajtenberg 1992).

Second, having written articles and books in the 1980s and 1990s on the impact of microelectronics and computerised technologies more broadly on employment and the organisation of work,[2] I feel that I am well placed to highlight in these pages some of the similarities and differences that exist between these two phases of industrial transformation as they have confronted our economies over the last 40 years. In particular, when debating the possible consequences of revolutionary transformations one can enter quite quickly into debates in which speculation and visions based more on science fiction of future societies can become dominant, which ultimately offers little help to policymakers. This contribution seeks to address this shortcoming in the literature.

## SIMILARITIES WITH THE PAST: THE FEAR OF JOB LOSSES AND A PRODUCTIVITY PARADOX

The first similarity when comparing the third with the fourth industrial revolution is the fear of significant job losses. The similarity between Clive Jenkins' 1979 book *The Collapse of Work* and the multitude of current analyses on the likely job losses associated with AI and robotics is striking and characteristic of the intrinsic fear of the way that new technologies can replace labour and automate routine jobs (Jenkins 1979). Arntz et al. (2016) refer to a widespread "automation angst". In the 1970s and 1980s, following the widespread adoption of microelectronics, similar references were made to the literature of the 1930s and 1940s about the fear of 'permanent' technological unemployment, that would be brought about by automation.[3] Whereas such fears were particularly articulated in Europe in the 1980s,[4] far fewer concerns were raised about these issues in the US, where the debate shifted quickly to a more positive vision of the potential employment 'displacement' aspects of new technologies and the potential 'skill-bias' dimension associated with it – the fact that new technologies favoured skilled over unskilled labour, which increased the productivity of skilled labour, and hence the demand for skilled labour.[5] Thus, the temporary friction that new technologies could introduce would be solved by education and training.

Paradoxically, the debate today regarding the fourth industrial revolution appears much more a feature of the US American rather than the European academic and public discourse, with important contributions from the likes of Erik Brynjolfsson and Andrew McAfee – curiously called *The Second Machine Age* – focusing on past trends towards jobless growth following economic recovery in the 1990s, and the role played by new digital technologies in replacing routine jobs (Brynjolfsson and McAfee 2014). The focus of the debate on employment displacement today has also shifted from the consideration of unskilled to routine jobs. The possibility that technology could be causing jobless US recoveries was first suggested by Jaimovich and Siu (2012), who argued that middle-skilled jobs involving routine tasks are susceptible to replacement by new technologies, and were likely to become permanently destroyed during recessions, which would result in slower job growth during any recovery. The focus here was again on new computer-based technologies, but the impact of employment displacement on routine white-collar work would be far greater than in the past. As Jerry Kaplan (2015), author of *Humans Need Not Apply*, puts it: "automation is now blind to the colour of your collar". Brian Arthur (2011) describes this as the arrival of an underground, totally automated, digital 'second economy' that involves little to no physical employment in the 'first economy', while the title of Martin Ford's (2015) book is *The Rise of the Robots*.

The dominance of the debate on the implications of new technologies linked to the fourth industrial revolution on jobs can be explained by the fact that no evidence for such trends can be found outside the US, where modern technologies appear unlikely to be causing jobless recoveries (Graetz and Michaels 2015). This is in all likelihood also a reflection of US global dominance in the new digital technology industries, as illustrated by the impact of the public statements on these topics by some of the leading American high-tech chief executive officers such as Elon Musk and Bill Gates (Delaney 2017; Kharpal 2017). In the 1980s it was similarly IBM who asked Chris Freeman and me to write a report on the impact on employment of computers (Freeman and Soete 1985). The report had no impact in North America, however. In Europe, by contrast, with unemployment remaining stubbornly high and barely recovering from the 1982 recession, the report led to a European Commission-backed expert study on the information society (European Commission 1996) and the inclusion in the Jobs Study launched in the mid-1990s by then secretary general of the OECD, Jean-Claude Paye, of a specific chapter on the potential impact of technology on employment and skills (OECD 1994). Today despite high levels of youth unemployment in many European countries there is, paradoxically apart from Germany, little interest and attention being paid to the emergence of new technologies that affect future jobs and the organisation of work.

A second, more striking similarity between the third and fourth industrial revolutions is the puzzling evidence of trends in productivity growth following the emergence of the aforementioned radical new technologies that are identified with the fourth industrial revolution, the 'core' variable in any econometric analysis on the impact of research and innovation on growth and welfare. Generally speaking, productivity refers to a measure of how much output (or income) is generated for a fixed amount of input, typically an average hour of work. Productivity growth is essential for understanding any discussion on the impact of new technologies on employment. Over the long run, the only way a society can generate higher standards of living is if the average level of productivity grows.

Rather surprisingly, and in contradiction to the revolutionary evidence on the emergence of new technologies, productivity did not increase following the third industrial revolution. In the 1980s, this became known as the 'Solow paradox', following a remark by Robert Solow (1987):

> what everyone feels to have been a technological revolution, a drastic change in our productive lives, has been accompanied everywhere, including Japan, by a slowing-down of productivity growth, not by a step up. You can see the computer age everywhere but in the productivity statistics.

Even more surprisingly, the current evidence regarding the fourth industrial revolution appears to be accompanied by a similar lack of evidence of productivity growth. As Millar and Sunderland (2016) point out:

in a period where not only many new technologies are being introduced, more firms and countries are integrated into global value chains, [and] workers are more highly educated than ever, it remains surprising that productivity growth is not rising. For sure the financial crisis may be part of the explanation, but OECD data show that productivity growth has been slowing since the early 2000s in Canada, the United Kingdom and the United States (Millar and Sunderland 2016).

The link between productivity growth and technological change is not that straightforward, however. In earlier analyses I compared the evolution of technological change and its impact on productivity growth to the movement of a snake, where the head (technological progress) moves ahead while the tail remains more or less in the same place.[6] In this analogy, productivity growth, as expressed by the average progress of the snake, is relatively limited, versus the tail moving to join the head, which remains more or less in the same place with little or no technological progress, while average productivity increases rapidly. It is as if the gap in productivity growth between global firms and the more domestically oriented firms has grown during the fourth industrial revolution, with the body of the snake expanding. As the current OECD secretary general, Angel Gurria (2016), put it: "The knowledge and technology diffusion 'machine' is broken."

A lot has been learned over recent decades from research that analyses previous productivity 'paradoxes'. There is broad agreement that much more attention needs to be paid to the time lags involved in the diffusion of new, 'radical' technologies. Those new technologies might for example involve a first phase of declining capital productivity as Paul David and Gavin Wright (1999) argued on the basis of historical comparisons, or might require essential organisational changes to fully exploit the often, in the first instance at least, unnoticed efficiency gains associated with new technologies, as Chris Freeman and Luc Soete (1987) and Paul David (1990) argued with respect to the second industrial revolution and the introduction of electricity. Here the authors point to the importance of the discovery of unit electric drive replacing line shaft (Devine Jr. 1983). Such changes also required the development of new skills and on-the-job learning before new technologies would result in overall efficiency gains, dubbed "the race between technology and schooling" by Jan Tinbergen (1975).

To conclude this first section; given the current low global productivity growth trends, concerns about the negative impact of the fourth industrial revolution on employment and job displacement appear not entirely convincing. There seems to be a tendency to overestimate both the speed and the impact of the new technologies associated with the fourth industrial revolution (Atkinson this volume), including AI, robotics, 3D printing, automotive driving, quantum computing and nanotechnology. For example, just look at the complexity involved in using robots simply to lift patients in a hospital, which requires numerous physical security interaction problems, or using AI to assess written exams. Historically, the evidence of skills disappearing as a consequence of the introduction of new technologies has not ushered in mass unemployment. Rather, digital technologies appear to have dramatically increased the distribution of the gains associated with the emergence of new technologies, as if monopoly capitalism has re-emerged now in digital form. Let me turn to these concerns in the next section.


## DIFFERENCES WITH THE PAST: FROM GENERAL PURPOSE TO GLOBAL PLATFORM TECHNOLOGIES

In so far as the core of the fourth industrial innovation is primarily associated with the application of digital technologies across the board – not just in production processes but also in the delivery of goods and services – it has become associated with a more systemic 'digital transformation' process across society and across the world – what many economists today describe as 'digitalisation'. Contrary to the previous third industrial revolution, digital innovation in this transformation process is based much more on a number of well-known principles of information economics, which are discussed below.

Traditionally, industrial innovation involves major structural transformations in the economy as incumbents, and sometimes whole sectors, are challenged by new unexpected innovators which force them to adjust or disappear. The previous industrial revolutions are dramatic historical illustrations of such structural transformations, in which Joseph Schumpeter's process of 'creative destruction' became dominant. Such structural change came to be seen as essential to lead society to a higher level of economic development and welfare, as many incumbents are destroyed to the benefit of newcomers. In this process newcomers can benefit from extraordinary innovations in market 'rents'. Introducing an innovation endows the innovator with an advantageous but temporary exclusivity over their rivals. This is sometimes formalised through intellectual property rights (IPR) protection. Sometimes it is based on secrecy, which allows the innovating firm to set prices well above marginal costs gaining extraordinary rents. Those gains should be considered temporary, however. While the innovating firm would often have incurred substantial costs in the R&D phase of any new innovation, and must absorb the risks of launching the new product or process, competitors are often quick to acquire and exploit the knowledge behind the innovation, which economists explain by the non-rivalrous nature of knowledge. As a result, Schumpeterian competition involves the continuous emergence of new innovating firms which undermine the initial extraordinary innovation rents yielded by innovative firms. History is full of examples of innovating 'boom and bust' firms, which illustrates the process of creative destruction, as described by Schumpeter.

Guellec and Paunov (2017) highlight how the process of digitalisation is being magnified in two ways. First, thanks to the much wider use of information, software and data in the current 'digital transformation' process, the marginal cost of production of goods and services is coming close to nil with the intangible component of capital including IPR, branding and reputation now representing most, if not all, of the value of digital products. As a result, one is now witnessing the emergence of what Jonathan Haskel and Stian Westlake (2017) have called 'capitalism without capital' – a new form of intangible capitalism. In previous industrial revolutions, physical tangible capital led to significant scale and increasing returns, linked to continuous improvements associated with incremental product and process innovations and 'learning by doing'.[7] However, gains were always ultimately limited, as variable costs never reached zero, but required additional materials, labour, energy and other inputs. Notably, this is not the case with digital transformations. Here so-called 'winner-take-all' dynamics become dominant as market concentrations allow the winners to extract profits globally, and for a much longer period of time. Going back to our previous analogy, the long tail of the snake has grown significantly while at the same time its head has grown exponentially.

The process of digitalisation raises dramatic, near endless, opportunities for 'creative destruction' by potentially reducing significantly barriers to entry (Kenney and Zysman this volume). As Guellec and Paunov (2017) point out,

> the capital requirement for programming software, the core of digital innovation, is much lower than for other types of innovative activities, such as those requiring special facilities to develop innovations (eg laboratories and experimental settings in pharmaceuticals).

The intangible nature of knowledge, and the opportunities for rapid scaling-up, facilitate creative destruction. This is exemplified by the 'app economy' (Guellec and Paunov 2017) – the full range of economic activities, from selling applications and advertising revenues as well as hardware devices, on which apps are designed to run for mobile applications. Digitalisation can potentially lead to significant reductions in the costs of incremental innovations and product design, and the versioning of products and services for different consumer and users groups. Furthermore, digitalisation allows for global markets to be reached practically instantaneously, which opens up many new opportunities for product and service delivery, including product upgrades, which obviate the need to purchase a new product. For example, the word processing programme used to type this chapter is based on a 10-year-old software programme, which is updated nearly every month.

In short, while digitalisation has increased the fluidity of markets and the ease of entry, it has also dramatically increased society's dependency on global digital platforms. These digital platforms enable direct digital interaction between producers and consumers, but they also facilitate interactions of almost any kind involving two parties – so-called 'two-sided markets', with one selling, and the other buying services in areas as diverse as jobs, finance, travel, advertising, medicine, entertainment and leisure.[8] The increase in global market access, fluidity – the speed with which prices will clear markets – and the achievement of scale without mass resulting from digitalisation, has undoubtedly contributed to much more competition. At the same time, though, the fact that digital platforms are crucially dependent on network externalities on both sides of the market leads naturally to monopolistic structures with various 'locking in' strategies. Compared with the general purpose technologies of the third industrial revolution (Bresnahan and Trajtenberg 1992), the general purpose platforms of the fourth industrial revolution appear intrinsically more monopolistic, which reflects the emergence of a new form of digital monopoly capitalism, in which winner-take-all features are becoming world leading.

## CONCLUSIONS

Back in the mid-1990s, while I was chairing a high-level expert group for the European Commission on the information society, the prevailing view was that

> a large proportion of public opinion was sceptical about the new opportunities offered by the information society and even fearful

about the job losses, employment displacement and work insecurity associated with a future Information Society (European Commission 1997).

Let me quote from the group's report in some detail:

The lack of public support is also a reflection of the 'technology dominated' nature of the European Information Society policy debate. The latter offers little freedom of manoeuvre for policy action. Such an 'international competitiveness/technological determinism' argument runs as follows. We are forced through international competition to adopt new information technologies as rapidly as possible. It is an illusion to think we would be able to govern the speed of such change. Consequently, the only relevant policy issue is one of liberalising and deregulating. Any delay would be extremely costly. At the social level, while there could be 'local' employment destruction, the cost of such destruction is minimal when compared to the aggregate employment 'price' rigid societies might have to pay in terms of loss of competitiveness when failing to adopt the new information and communication technologies quickly enough. In other words, these employment losses have to be accepted as a minimal cost, outweighed by the positive global welfare impact of the Information Society and the employment growth in new areas (European Commission 1997).

Viewed in retrospect, the 'ideological' line of the high-level expert group report that the information society is malleable and that there could be different models of information societies, just as one had different models of industrialised societies, seems somewhat naive. However, this view was based on a strong conviction that the so-called European model of social welfare, with its strong ethos of solidarity, would ultimately also come to characterise any European version of the information society. To achieve this, so it was argued, would imply substantial changes in the traditional structures of the welfare state, and in particular a shift towards an active rather than passive concept of solidarity. Despite this logic, little happened in this respect, and while the welfare state has remained, it has become based even more on a passive concept of solidarity.

Thirty years on, at the advent of the fourth industrial revolution, concerns about massive employment losses have again led to widespread moves away from long-term jobs towards self-employment, linked more closely to new digital technologies, robotics, AI, the internet of things, the cloud, 3D printing, blockchain, virtual and augmented reality and big data analytics. Cecilia Reyes, chief risk officer of Zurich Insurance Group, was quoted in a recent article in Computer Weekly:

> Unless there is a concerted effort from governments and the private sector, this [digital technology] will put pressure on economies and may lead to social unrest. . . . Without proper governance and reskilling of workers, technology will eliminate jobs faster than it creates them. . . . Governments can no longer provide historic levels of social protection, and an anti-establishment narrative has gained traction, with new political leaders blaming globalisation for society's challenges. Governments, academics and businesses should be planning for huge social disruption because there are many real-life examples across the world of AI replacing people in the workplace (Flinders 2017).

It is important to realise though that the social disruptions that some, including Reyes, predict are yet to manifest. Following the historical evidence on the productivity slowdown, it is clear that most of the impact on productivity of the new digital technologies has either not yet occurred, or remains more or less invisible. At the same time private investment in new technologies in Europe has been lagging behind other parts of the world. One notable line of argument is that the slowdown of private capital investment is directly linked to the macro-economic policies pursued in most European countries following the financial crisis of low-wage competition. This in itself provided little incentive for most firms to invest in productivity enhancing capital. From this perspective, the lack of productivity growth calls for the diffusion and more rapid implementation of more robots and AI, despite the growing shortage of labour following the retirement of baby-boomers in many

European countries. In short, employment displacement following automation is in the present context of increasing labour shortage not really an issue.[9]

What has arguably become the central concern in the current industrial revolution debate is the increasingly skewed distribution of the innovation rents associated with digital innovations and the digitalisation transformation. The record on addressing the distribution of innovation rents since the third industrial revolution has been disappointing to say the least. The current stage of development is typified by rising inequality, and a trend towards a race to the bottom in existing European social welfare systems (Bell this volume). As Guellec and Paunov (2017) neatly illustrate in their OECD paper, the 'rents' from digital innovation affect income distribution and benefits directly, particularly in the top income groups through shareholders and investors, top executives and key employees of the 'winning firms' who often own capital and hold managerial and leading positions in firms:

> In line with a Schumpeterian vision, innovation gives rise to rents from market power and scale economies. This is magnified with digital innovation, in which the intangible component (the source of rents) is much larger than in traditional manufacturing innovation. Highly concentrated market structures ('winner-take-all') allow rent extraction. In addition, digital innovation tends to increase risks because even only marginally superior products can take over the entire market, hence rendering market shares unstable. Instability commands risk premia, hence higher expected revenues, for investors. Market rents accrue mainly to investors and top managers and less to the average workers, hence increasing income inequality.

By contrast, average workers have been confronted with more competition in the labour market, are increasingly employed in temporary work arrangements, and are becoming subject to national low-wage competition policy pressures. Adding it all up explains why the share of capital (as opposed to labour) in national income has increased, particularly in innovation-intensive economic activities.

It is therefore essential to reframe the technology employment debate by focusing on the need for alternative income
systems that are disconnected from employment, such as the
notional 'basic income' (Palier this volume). Following Jahoda,
Lazarsfeld and Zeisel's (1932) study of unemployment in
Marienthal, Austria, in the 1930s, employment could still be considered to represent one of the most important factors for social
integration and personal recognition today. At the same time,
and given the tremendously increased opportunities for social
contact outside the sphere of employment following the development of social media over the last 20 years, it is also reasonable
to assume that an unconditional 'basic income' could well lead to
a substantial voluntary shift in labour market participation, based
on free choice and ultimately to the benefit of the individual,
even to the health and happiness of the individual, as well as to
the overall benefit of society.

Once 'basic income' is viewed as the monetised 'digital manna
from heaven', resulting from technological change, the concept
seems like a simple and attractive way to redistribute the gains from
technical change to all throughout society. At the same time, the
erosion of social welfare systems and more general state revenues
following the digitalisation of society should also become a central
issue of policy debate in experimenting with new tax revenues. More
than 30 years ago, as part of our deliberation process on the information society, I proposed that states should levy an internet tax, or
so-called 'bit tax'.[10]

It is clear that the global digitalisation transformation of society
has many more implications than those dealing with employment
and the organisation of work, as has been discussed here. Probably
the most immediate question is the extent to which the extreme
concentration of wealth and economic power associated with
digital innovation will ultimately lead to a similar extreme concentration of political power, which might ultimately undermine
democracy.

# NOTES

1. In 1965, Gordon Moore, co-founder of Fairchild and Intel, predicted that the number of transistors on an integrated circuit would double every two years, at least until 1975. What became known as Moore's law proved valid at least until 2015. This continuous logarithmic improvement in microchip performance has been one of the major enabling factors behind the processes of digitalisation and the emergence of smartphone technology, 3D printing, robotics and AI.

2. This is something we referred to as The Biggest Technological Juggernaut that ever rolled, which is the title of chapter 3 in *Work for All or Mass Unemployment* (Freeman and Soete 1996).

3. For further insight into this, see for example Neisser (1942).

4. For further insight into this, see for example *Unemployment and Technical Innovation* (Freeman and Soete 1982) and more recently *The Economics of the Digital Society* (Soete and ter Weel 2005).

5. Typically, the use of computers requires certain human skills in order to be fully operational and to make use all available new opportunities the machines offer.

6. For further insight into this, see for example 'Technology Diffusion and the Rate of Technical Change' (Soete and Turner 1984).

7. These have been studied in more detail in industrial economics. The process of industrial innovation was first and foremost characterised by incremental process innovation improving nearly continuously such scale advantages and the accompanying increasing returns leading to various forms of monopoly capitalism as described by Paul Baran and Paul Sweezy. The process of creative destruction linked to new, radical innovations now and then undermined such trends towards monopoly capitalism (Baran and Zweezy 1996).

8. For further insight into this, see for example 'Two-sided Markets: a Progress Report' (Rochet and Tirole 2006).

9. For an argument along similar lines on the US economy, see the *Washington Post* interview with Josh Bivens (Bivens 2017).

10. Arthur Cordell first developed the proposal for a 'bit tax', which would be applied to all interactive digital services. It was based on a simple count of bits flowing over telecommunications lines. The argument in favour of such a new tax was primarily based on the way that globalisation undermines traditional national tax bases. At the same time, the disincentive to the diffusion and use of new information and communication services could be assumed to be marginal, because generally speaking

these new services offer a new bundle of product or service characteristics (Cordell 1996).


## REFERENCES

Arnold, D., M. Arntz, T. Gregory, S. Steffes and U. Zierahn (2016), *Herausforderungen der Digitalisierung für die Zukunft der Arbeitswelt*, ZEW policy brief, Mannheim: Centre for European Economic Research.

Arthur, B. (2011), 'The Second Economy', *McKinsey Quarterly*, October, https://www.mckinsey.com/business-functions/strategy-and-corporate-finance/our-insights/the-second-economy.

Baran, P. and P. Zweezy (1996), *Monopoly Capital: an Essay on the American Economic and Social Order*, London: Monthly Review.

Bivens, J. (2017), 'You Want Faster Productivity Growth? Then Run a High-pressure Economy', interview by Jared Bernstein, *Washington Post*, 21 March, https://www.washingtonpost.com/posteverything/wp/2017/03/21/you-want-faster-productivity-growth-then-run-a-high-pressure-economy-an-interview-with-josh-bivens/?utm_term=.72d4fcf69674.

Bresnahan, T. F. and M. Trajtenberg (1992), *General Purpose Technologies 'Engines of Growth'?*, NBER Working Paper 4148, Cambridge, MA: National Bureau of Economic Research.

Brynjolfsson, E. and A. McAfee (2014), *The Second Machine Age: Work, Progress, and Prosperity in a Time of Brilliant Technologies*, New York: W. W. Norton & Company.

Cohen, S. and J. Zysman (1987), *Manufacturing Matters: the Myth of the Post-Industrial Economy*, New York: Basic Books.

Cordell, A. (1996), 'New Taxes for a New Economy', *Government Information in Canada [Information gouvernementale au Canada]*, 2(4), http://www.usask.ca/library/gic/v2n4/cordell/cordell.html.

David, P. (1990), 'The Dynamo and the Computer: an Historical Perspective on the Modern Productivity Paradox', *American Economic Review*, 80(2): 355–61.

David, P. and G. Wright (1999), *Early Twentieth Century Productivity Growth Dynamics: an Inquiry into the Economic History of Our Ignorance*, Economics Series Working Paper W33, Oxford: University of Oxford, Department of Economics.

Delaney, K. J. (2017), 'The Robot that Takes Your Job Should Pay Taxes, Says Bill Gates', *Quartz*, 17 February, https://qz.com/911968/bill-gates-the-robot-that-takes-your-job-should-pay-taxes/.

Devine Jr., W. D. (1983), 'From Shafts to Wires: Historical Perspective on Electrification', *Journal of Economic History*, 43(2).

European Commission (1996), *Building the European Information Society for us All: Intermediary Policy Report of the High-Level Expert Group*, Luxembourg: Office for Official Publications of the European Communities.

European Commission (1997), *Building the European Information Society for us All: Final Policy Report of the High-Level Expert Group*, Luxembourg: Office for Official Publications of the European Communities, http://aei.pitt.edu/8692/1/8692.pdf.

Flinders, K. (2017), 'AI and Robots Will "Create Political Instability" Until Humans Find New Occupations', *Computer Weekly*, 24 March, http://www.computerweekly.com/news/450415491/AI-and-robots-will-create-political-instability-until-humans-find-new-occupations.

Ford, M. (2015), *Rise of the Robots: Technology and the Threat of a Jobless Future*, New York: Basic Books.

Freeman, C. and L. Soete (1985), *Information Technology and Employment: an Assessment*, Brussels: IBM.

Freeman, C. and L. Soete (1987), *Technical Change and Full Employment*, London: Basil Blackwell.

Freeman, C. and L. Soete (1996), *Work for all or Mass Unemployment*, London: Frances Pinter.

Freeman, C. and L. Soete (1982), *Unemployment and Technical Innovation: a Study of Long Waves and Economic Development*, London: Frances Pinter.

Graetz, G. and G. Michaels (2015), *Robots at Work*, CEPS Discussion Paper 1335, London: London School of Economics, http://cep.lse.ac.uk/pubs/download/dp1335.pdf.

Guellec, D. and C. Paunov (2017), *Digital Innovation and the Distribution of Income*, NBER Working Paper 23987, Cambridge, MA: National Bureau of Economic Research.

Gurria, A. (2016), *Remarks at China Development Forum: Envisioning the 2016 G20 Summit in China*, Paris: Organisation for Economic Co-operation and Development.

Haskel, J. and S. Westlake (2017), *Capitalism without Capital: the Rise of the Intangible Economy*, Princeton: Princeton University Press.

Jahoda, M., P. F. Lazarsfeld and H. Zeisel (1932), *Die Arbeitslosen von Marienthal*, translated edition, *Marienthal: the sociography of an unemployed community* (2002), Piscataway, NJ: Transaction Publishers.

Jaimovich, N. and H. Siu (2012), *The Trend is the Cycle: Job Polarization and Jobless Recoveries*, NBER Working Paper 18334, Cambridge, MA: National Bureau of Economic Research.

Jenkins, C. and Barrie Sherman (1979), *The Collapse of Work*, London: Eyre Methuen.

Kaplan, J. (2015), *Humans Need Not Apply: a Guide to Wealth and Work in the Age of Artificial Intelligence*, New Haven, CT: Yale University Press.

Kharpal, A. (2017), 'Tech CEOs Back Call for Basic Income as AI Job Losses Threaten Industry Backlash', CNBC, 21 February, https://www.cnbc.com/2017/02/21/technology-ceos-back-basic-income-as-ai-job-losses-threaten-industry-backlash.html.

Millar, J. and D. Sutherland (2016), *Unleashing Private Sector Productivity in the United States*, OECD Economics Department Working Paper 1328, Paris: Organisation for Economic Co-operation and Development.

Neisser, H. (1942), 'Permanent Technological Unemployment: Demand for Commodities is not Demand for Labor', *American Economic Review*, 32(1), part 1: 50–71.

OECD (1994), *The OECD Jobs Study. Facts, Analysis, Strategies*, Paris: Organisation for Economic Co-operation and Development.

Rochet, J.-C. and Jean Tirole (2006), 'Two Sided Markets: a Progress Report', *RAND Journal of Economics*, 35(3): 645–67.

Soete, L. and B. ter Weel (eds) (2005), *The Economics of the Digital Society*, Cheltenham: Edward Elgar.

Soete, L. and R. Turner (1984), 'Technology Diffusion and the Rate of Technical Change', *Economic Journal*, 94 (375).

Solow, R. M. (1987), '"We'd Better Watch Out", review of Manufacturing Matters: the Myth of the Post-Industrial Economy, by S. S. Cohen and J. Zysman', *New York Times*, 12 July.

Tinbergen, J. (1975), 'Substitution of Academically Trained by Other Manpower', *Weltwirtschaftliches Archiv*, 111(3): 466–76.

# ENTREPRENEURIAL FINANCE IN THE ERA OF INTELLIGENT TOOLS AND DIGITAL PLATFORMS

## Implications and consequences for work

### Martin Kenney and John Zysman

**V**enture financing, a form of entrepreneurial finance, has played a central part in the story of the digital revolution. Indeed, Silicon Valley, the global centre of the venture capital industry, draws its name from the substrate of the contemporary semiconductor, which is the computational engine for all digital products. The continuing performance improvements characteristic of Moore's law provided ever new potentialities for new generations of start ups. While improvement in processing power was the core engine for this venture-capital-financed entrepreneurship, the new firms were not only in semiconductors, but also in layers in stack above the processor itself. There were semiconductor firms of various generations including Intel and AMD, Cirrus Logic, and even later NVIDIA. There were computer firms ranging from Tandem Computers to Sun Microsystems and Silicon Graphics on to Apple and Osbourne. As there were more computers, users wanted to network them together and with this came 3Com, Cisco and many other firms; all of which used semiconductor chips. In addition to semiconductor components, they needed disk drives, input devices, printers and many other devices – many of which were also pioneered in Silicon Valley. However, the most powerful development of all was the establishment of an independent software industry – the most successful was Microsoft, but there were many, many more, including Oracle, Adobe, Intuit and others successfully established in Silicon Valley. Eventually, these technologies were united in the internet, whose technologies were developed at CERN in Switzerland and the University of Illinois. At each stage in this development venture capitalists could be found who were willing to invest in the new firms (Kenney 2011). These entrepreneurial financiers had only one goal – to make capital gains. The vehicle for these capital gains was, quite simply, a firm whose product grew so rapidly that other investors would be willing to buy that firm, or buy equity in that firm, at massive capital gains multiples.[1]

Over the last two decades, we have been gradually moving into a phase in which technology has progressed to the point at which the ongoing digital revolution is resulting in a business environment within which platforms, intelligent tools and their application to manufacturing and services is becoming ubiquitous and even transformative. The rapid development and adoption of robotics and intelligent systems with self-learning algorithms are automating not only tasks associated with blue-collar work, but also less-routine tasks that have been considered knowledge-intensive (Brynjolfsson and McAfee 2012, 2014; Ford 2015).[2] This digitisation process seems to be inexorably diffusing into more sectors of economic and social life. Though there is a debate about the extent and speed of the transformation, much of this work will be reorganised on digital platforms and undertaken with digital tools. These developments are a backdrop for considering the role of finance in this process.

As we enter an era in which platforms and intelligent tools become important for the entire economic system, the computation-intensive automation of services and manufacturing is upon us. Moreover, given that this phase is transforming work and, dare we say, value creation, broadly, it is important to consider whether the firms born in this hothouse of entrepreneurship – motivated by capital gains, and driven to establish unassailable market positions – will also facilitate, let alone consider, the augmentation and promotion of the societal work force.

The ability of financial actors to fund firms introducing new disruptive digital technologies over relatively long periods of time, while experiencing large losses, is having a powerful impact on the relations and conditions of work and employment.[3] Suggesting that it is important to consider the role of finance in the growth of digital platforms does not mean we must engage with the larger question of the role of finance in the US economy or to enter into the more general debate over the financialisation of the US economy, though these are an important context for our essay (Davis and Kim 2015; Lazonick 2010). We focus on the implications of the enormous sums of venture capital (and private equity) available, permitting investors to provide massive sums of capital to firms with the intent of restructuring (or, in the current vernacular, disrupting) existing businesses or value chain organisation (Christensen 2013).

## FINANCE, THE TRAJECTORY OF TECH FIRMS AND CONSEQUENCES FOR WORK

Investment euphoria is not unique to the current era. Carlota Perez (2003), in Technological Revolutions and Financial Capital,[4] and William Janeway (2012), in Doing Capitalism in the Innovation Economy, have argued that because of the infrastructures built and technologies introduced during the investment euphoria, the political economy is permanently altered (Soskice and Hall 2001; Zysman 1983). The underpinnings of the current investment euphoria are important to consider. Financial conditions and start-up tools in this era permit a novel investment strategy that has real consequences for labour and work. The first element is that the cost of building digital 'tools', including platforms, has dropped dramatically. Cloud computing provides low-cost infrastructure for 'users' while vast libraries of open-source software are available online at repositories such as GitHub or SourceForge (Murray and Zysman 2011). Together they allow low-cost experimentation in the name of disruption, seeing what sticks and creates enough market position quickly to drive capital valuations. Sustainable market positions for these firms can be a concern for a later day.

The 'disruption' meme suggests that a new more efficient business model is being introduced to bypass the old-fashioned existing businesses. The automobile disrupted the horse-and-carriage business; digital search engines and digitisation of content displaced or altered library operations. In this narrative, disruption is positive; it compels existing businesses to adapt or vanish. For example, Amazon dramatically shrank the number of physical bookstores.

Of course, the ultimate question is: why should we care? If consumers gain and the disruptors benefit financially, who should complain? Certainly, Uber makes finding a ride in London easier for a visitor from San Francisco and vice versa. Google changes our attitude and approach to information. LinkedIn replaced the rolodex and the job board by transforming the manner by which professional connections are maintained.

This logic that progressive 'disruption' advances society comes with consequences, however. Let us note at least a few. As the newspaper business struggles, some have argued that investigative and international journalism is declining, and some argue that it has contributed to a decline in our democracy. Alternatively, others might argue that entirely new sources of information from outside the mainstream are now available allowing for new perspectives. If there is a problem, then perhaps a solution is to subsidise journalism with the result that it becomes dependent on the government, rather than private interests. Uber drivers lack protections, so perhaps we rejigger employment law.

What is particularly interesting is that the current financial euphoria is concentrated on funding platform economy firms. One of the characteristics of digital platforms is that they exhibit powerful network effects that often lead to winner-take-all outcomes

(Eisenmann, Parker and Van Alstyne 2006; Gawer and Cusumano 2008). It is the winner-take-all outcomes that allow the young firm to outpace its larger competitors and, if it is successful in the market, often establish a monopoly or near-monopoly position. For example, consider the position of Google in search, maps, YouTube and a variety of other services; Amazon in online retail; Facebook in social networks; eBay in online auctions; LinkedIn in professional networks; Yelp! or TripAdvisor in online reviews; OpenTable in restaurant reservation services; and the like.[5]

The start-up process in such winner-take-all environments assumes that the start up will initially be cash-flow negative as it grows and competes against other start ups and incumbents that are also seeking to restructure the new business space that the technology's progress has made possible. Such start ups begin by 'bleeding' money. Investors are wagering on the firm establishing a powerful market position – or what could be termed a 'proto-monopoly'. These firms are not expected to win via early, sustained operating profit but by absorbing operating losses during their growth phase financed by venture investment, with the aim of driving incumbents and other new entrants out of the market. Investors are increasingly comfortable with absorbing the exceptional losses, if convinced that it will be possible to lock in a position to generate proto-monopolistic profits and, by extension, enormous capital gains.[6]

Because many of the start ups must sustain operating losses over long periods, it is possible to question the narrowly economic, as much as the social benefit. Are the disruptions, if they are driven by extended losses, really justified as welfare generating? These firms are structured to pursue growth at all costs as they endeavour to achieve market domination. In one sense, this appears to be predatory, but it is also a natural outcome in many of these markets. For example, would the economy have been better off with 10 different incompatible personal computer or smartphone operating systems? Similarly, would the economy be better served with 10 search engines – moreover, technically in the case of search, there is learning from each search so ceteris paribus a search engine that attracts more searches is likely to enter a virtuous circle of improvement that is impossible for laggards to overcome. Importantly, operating losses with the goal of market dominance may also encourage business strategies of transgressing established marketplace and social rules, because locking in a winning position is everything.

Financing losses as a way of overcoming existing systems via social disruption and long-term operating losses forms a treacherous environment for incumbents that are judged by the profits they make. To illustrate, in its last annual report in 2017, Walmart had $486bn in sales and operating income of $23bn, while its greatest competitor Amazon in 2016 (last annual report) had $136bn and operating income of $4.1bn. However, though Amazon has grown significantly in the last year it still trails Walmart in profits and especially in income. And yet Amazon had a stock market valuation of $608bn, while Walmart had half the valuation at $301bn. Effectively, the stock market valued Amazon twice as highly as Walmart, despite Walmart having five times as much income. This stock market valuation allows Amazon to make far less profit, thereby allowing it to undercut competitors, which are forced to generate profits to keep investors satisfied.

The point is not to dismiss the enormous value that digital technologies and platform-based business have created. Rather, it is to interrogate the enthusiasm for backing entrepreneurial start ups, losses or not, and for seeking to turbo-charge their growth to the point that they become a so-called 'unicorns' – firms whose most recent venture capital round valued the young firm at more than $1bn (see below).

## THE DECLINE IN THE COST OF TECHNOLOGICAL AND BUSINESS EXPERIMENTATION

Over the past 20 years the cost of establishing a start up or experimenting internally has decreased dramatically. As important as the cost decline, incidentally, is how the abundance of software tools and cloud-based operations speeds the time from forming the firm to actually launching a digital service (Kushida, Murray and Zysman 2015). The reasons for this cost decline are numerous; a technical one is the secular decline in the cost of computation – a longstanding tendency encapsulated in the shorthand of Moore's law but far deeper than just the dynamics of semiconductors. It is evident that the economics of IT start ups have fundamentally changed. Previously, a start up had to purchase and build an entire IT infrastructure, which was a capital cost, and – as difficult – write original software for whatever product it was introducing. However, the emergence of merchant cloud-computing offerings allows a new firm to rent server capacity from a vendor, such as Amazon Web Services. What previously was a capital investment is now a variable cost, and capacity can be scaled up or down without any capital investment (Murray and Zysman 2011). Cost and time to market were further reduced by the availability of downloadable open-source software modules from sources such as GitHub. This open-source software eliminates the need to write code from scratch, thereby reducing cost, providing opportunities to customise, and avoiding vendor lock-in (Northbridge and Blackduck 2016). The availability of low-cost infrastructure and open-source software dramatically decreases the cost of establishing a new digital business. Thus the technical changes permit the entry of far more new firms than ever before and encourage internal experimentation in existing firms. Of course, being able to easily enter does not guarantee success – there can be many more experiments, with only a few survivors.

## ABUNDANT CAPITAL AND THE TOLERATION OF OPERATION LOSSES

The ample available capital and the belief that many industries are poised for disruption because of developments in information and communications technology (ICT) – such as big data, machine learning and the internet of things (which, with smartphones, are new classes of computers) – and the development of new business models have convinced investors that start ups offer the opportunity for great potential capital gains. This has resulted in an enormous flow of capital into private equity, of which venture capital is one type.

Not only is the sheer amount of capital available remarkable, but there has been a proliferation of start-up funding mechanisms (Arrington 2010). Let us begin with conventional venture capital firms. Before the internet bubble that began in the mid-1990s, traditional venture capital firms were the predominant funders of successful technology start ups (Kenney 2011). As the elite venture capital firms became more successful, many of them raised and managed mega-funds with $1bn or more in assets. These firms could no longer invest in early-stage firms, where an appropriate investment is $1mn or less simply because of the management time needed to ensure the investments were prudent.

The market gap created by the emergence of mega-funds evoked four institutional responses. First, a group of angels or 'super-angels' emerged easily able to invest up to a few million dollars in a firm's early stages, particularly in Silicon Valley (Manjoo 2011). Many of these angels were successful entrepreneurs who had already started a company that generated sufficient capital gains so that they could now invest in a new generation of entrepreneurs. Second, accelerators – which vet and then accept aspiring entrepreneurs, and then provide small amounts of capital and coaching in return for a small tranche of equity – emerged. Their goal was to assist in the growth of the entrepreneurs' idea to the point that they could 'graduate' and form a proto-firm, able to raise money from super-angels or venture capitalists (Radojevich-Kelley and Hoffman 2012). Third, a wide variety of digital platforms for crowdfunding have been established, ranging from Indiegogo and Kickstarter – where funds are contributed to a project, but the funders receive no equity – to other platforms, such as Angelslist – where only certified investors invest in return for equity (Belleflamme, Lambert and Schwienbacher 2014). Fourth, a proliferation of smaller, seed-stage venture capital firms has created a functional segmentation of the venture capital industry. An ecosystem of organisations and networks now exists to provide funding for entrepreneurial experiments made possible by the technological changes, reducing the cost of starting an ICT firm.

With the reduction in the capital necessary to enter a market and the increased number of channels for securing seed capital, more firms can be established, thereby increasing the number of experiments. If these experiments experience initial success as signified by rapid adoption of robotics, measured by the number of users or extent of use and not necessarily by revenue, access to far greater pools of capital is likely because, as we note, many of these digital markets have winner-take-all characteristics. It is imperative for the start up to grow as quickly as possible to occupy the space before other start-up competitors or an established firm can introduce a competitive product.[7] During this phase, profitability is not as important as growth that captures the market. At this stage, success demands even more capital as the start up grows as expenditures out-strip revenue growth. Angels and incubators can no longer provide the capital necessary for such growth, and thus the expanding start up must secure much larger investments from the big venture capital firms.

The entrepreneurial environment is particularly munificent today as venture capitalists have been raising huge sums for investment. Fundraising in 2014, 2015 and 2016 were the largest since 2006, with a total of $51bn raised by 314 funds in the US and Europe (Pitchbook 2017). Effectively, there is an enormous amount of capital searching for investment opportunities.

In the current environment, firms are resisting making an initial public stock offering, remaining private for longer periods. It is possible to secure the required funding, because there has been a remarkable growth of pools of available capital through the large private equity firms, some of which such as Blackstone are listed on public markets. In 2017, the private equity capital available for investment (so-called 'dry powder') equalled $739bn (Pitchbook 2017). This massive inflow into private equity and venture capital funds creates a need for fund managers to find opportunities with the promise of significant returns. The returns to investors in earlier platform firms tells investors that they can expect to earn similar returns in future precisely because platforms have network effects and can result in winner-take-all markets, with their concomitant monopoly dynamics. In the next section, we explore the proliferation of privately held start ups whose value is over $1bn – the so-called unicorns.

## THE RISE OF THE UNICORNS

The availability and low cost of capital, the technical changes, and the belief in the possibility of disruption has resulted in a remarkably large number of start ups that are not publicly traded, but whose valuation at the last private funding was $1bn or more. Silicon Valley venture capitalist Aileen Lee termed such firms after the rare mythical creatures 'unicorns' – a term that has now passed into common parlance. In 2013, Lee identified 39 US public and private firms that were founded between 2003 and 2013 that had achieved $1bn valuations in 2013. Remarkably, the number of unicorns grew quickly (Lee 2013). Verena Schwartz (2017) by combining a number of lists found that in February 2017 there were 267 unicorns worldwide. While the number of unicorns fluctuates, as do valuations, by 2018 the sheer number of unlisted firms with such a high valuation was remarkable.[8]

The point of this discussion is not to determine whether this is a bubble, but to examine a related phenomenon: the willingness of investors to fund firms that are either losing money or not making profits at such high valuations. The assumption is that eventually the firms will generate sufficient profits in the future to compensate for the lack of profits currently. There are both public and private firms without any or only minimal profits. While Apple, Facebook, Google and Microsoft have large profit margins, Amazon only barely breaks even. Other important public platform firms – Pandora, Blue

Apron, Snapchat and others – have never made a profit and have no discernible path to profitability. More significantly, nearly all of the unicorns appear to be losing money.

The amount of private equity available, much of it raised from pension funds, also has made it possible for firms to stay private longer and lose money longer. The firm Airbnb is interesting from this perspective because it was founded in 2009 and become profitable in 2016 – a long period of unprofitability that was funded by private equity. Given its growth and crossover into profitability, it would appear to be ideally suited for an initial public offering. However, in 2017, rather than going public, it raised $1bn capital at a $31bn valuation. The massive influx of capital allowed it to acquire a smaller competitor and continue to grow without offering stock to the public – the traditional venture capital exit strategy – or worrying about profitability.

The large number of private unicorns is remarkable and differs in an important respect from the dot.com boom from 1997 to early 2000, as during the dot.com bubble newly funded firms rushed to make an initial public offering. In the current period, now more common unicorns can remain private for a much longer period because they are able to raise capital privately. An ability to raise capital is vitally important, because a company with continuing influxes of capital can continue to offer its product or service without being profitable. This provides a tremendous advantage against incumbents already listed on markets, firms that under normal conditions are expected to generate profits.

## FINANCIAL WEAPONS IN DIGITAL MARKETS: CONSEQUENCES FOR LABOUR

We made our way through this complexity by focusing on investment and business strategies that rest on enduring operating losses. The ability to access enormous sums of capital or an elevated stock valuation provides the focal firm with a powerful tool for undercutting its rivals, as it can lower prices or even purchase its competitors, as the platform giants such as Facebook did with Instagram, WhatsApp and a host of smaller firms. The structure of competition is important not only for investors but also for labour. How firms compete can determine how much of what kind of labour is needed, who will deploy that labour, and where.

Establishing and contributing to the growth of start ups and internal firm experimentation by investors willing to incur long-term operating losses pose many questions. Rapid growth strategies by platform economy firms have, by implication, raised questions for government regulators in a wide variety of sectors, in practice an aggressive assault on regulatory boundaries, even as the labour platforms place significant and often effective wage pressure on parts of the workforce. Current strategies seem to suggest less attention is paid to developing the talents and ability of workforces or forming structures that support workers. The implications are profound.

In the case of Uber, Google Maps, a set of pricing and dispatching algorithms, and a smartphone app, for example, have transformed citizen drivers with limited knowledge of a locale into 'contracted' transportation providers, creating a compelling service. These new Uber drivers – freed from the constraints of a taxi being a public conveyance – put downward pressure on prices for all. Unfortunately, there is no single narrative here except for the ineluctable fact that platforms and intelligent tools are shifting the grounds on which all economic activities are undertaken. By extension, this suggests the two fundamental conditions in a capitalist society – labour and competition. Beyond knowing that these two conditions and everything built on them will shift, the implications are contingent and continue to evolve.

The consequences for labour will vary dramatically depending on activity and the evolution of the technology, and this will vary across applications and market segments, and indeed among firms. What appears common to all is that loss-driven market domination strategies that can generate capital gains without attaining even mid-term market sustainability appear certain to encourage strategies that will treat labour as a commodity whose cost is to be minimised rather than as an asset whose value can contribute to long-term competitive advantage for the firm and superior social outcomes.

## NOTES

1. The US economy gradually evolved to incentivise a capital-gains-driven system and, by extension, a turn away from a long-term, earnings-based system of corporate governance. The most important of these incentives was the dramatic lowering of capital gains taxes in the late Carter and early Reagan administrations. The lobbying effort was largely driven by American Electronics Association and the prime mover in Congress was Edwin Zschau, an entrepreneur who became a congressman from the district that included Silicon Valley. For a detailed discussion, see The Passage of the Investment Incentive Act of 1978 (Johnson 1980). There were other important initiatives such as loosening interpretations of the Employment Retirement Income Security Act, easing rules on granting stock options, and easing various rules on stock trading and listing.

2. For a detailed discussion see Arnold et al. this volume.

3. It was perhaps with the success of Yahoo! that venture capitalists came to realise that giving a service away for free would work, if one could convince advertisers that they could reach customers through the internet. For a discussion of this realisation, see 'On the 20th Anniversary – The History of Yahoo's Founding' (McCullough 2015). The discovery in 1994 by the elite venture capital firm Sequoia Capital that a free service could if successful in capturing the market generate enormous capital gains led to a rethinking of the economics of venture capital investment. The venture capitals were convinced that even with enormous losses a service could be monetised in some way, if the market was captured.

4. Our discussion draws on studies of investment euphoria, current studies of financialisation and the separate discussions about how differences in national financial systems influence the relations between business and state structure (Perez 2003).

5. We have seen similar dynamics in earlier digital industries with Microsoft in the personal computer operating system and office productivity software, Intel in personal computer microprocessors, Cisco in computer networking, and Oracle in relational databases.

6. We suggest that current antitrust and competition policy is completely unprepared to address the types of business strategies these small entrepreneurial firms use.

7. For the incumbent firm in an industry receiving the attention of the new entrants the challenge is daunting. Each of the entrants is likely to have a somewhat different business model. Thus, the incumbent faces not a single entrant with one model, but multiple entrants with different models. If any of these models shows any promise of success, then the venture capitalists will provide further funding for its growth. It is these multiple experiments and challenges that contribute to making the current environment so treacherous for incumbents. A further difficulty is that the new entrants may not challenge the incumbent across its entire business, but rather only certain particularly valuable parts of its business model, which if successful could relegate the incumbent to the commodity portions of its business.

8. Recent research suggests that the clauses in the financing contracts dramatically lower the true valuation of the most recent investment to such an extent that nearly half of the "unicorns they studied were not, in fact, worth $1 billion or more" (Gornall and Strebulaev 2017).

## REFERENCES

Arrington, M. (2010), 'VCs and Super Angels: the War for the Entrepreneur', *TechCrunch*, 15 August, https://techcrunch.com/2010/08/15/venture-capital-super-angel-war-entrepreneur/.

Belleflamme, P., T. Lambert and A. Schwienbacher (2014), 'Crowdfunding: Tapping the Right Crowd', *Journal of Business Venturing*, 29(5): 585–609.

Brynjolfsson, E. and A. McAfee (2012), *Race Against the Machine: How the Digital Revolution is Accelerating Innovation, Driving Productivity, and Irreversibly Transforming Employment and the Economy*, Lexington, MA: Digital Frontier Press.

Brynjolfsson, E. and A. McAfee (2014), *The Second Machine Age: Work, Progress, and Prosperity in a Time of Brilliant Technologies*, New York: W. W. Norton.

Christensen, C. M. (2013), *The Innovator's Dilemma: When New Technologies Cause Great Firms to Fail*, Cambridge, MA: Harvard Business Review Press.

Davis, G. F. and S. Kim (2015), 'Financialization of the Economy', *Annual Review of Sociology*, 41: 203–21.

Eisenmann, T. R., G. Parker and M. W. Van Alstyne (2006), 'Strategies for Two-sided Markets', *Harvard Business Review*, 84(10).

Ford, M. (2015), *Rise of the Robots: Technology and the Threat of a Jobless Future*, New York: Basic Books.

Gawer, A. and M. A. Cusumano (2008), 'How Companies Become Platform Leaders', *MIT Sloan Management Review*, 1 January, https://sloanreview.mit.edu/article/how-companies-become-platform-leaders/.

Gornall, W. and I. Strebulaev (2017), *Squaring Venture Capital Valuations With Reality*, Stanford University Graduate School of Business Research Paper 17-29, https://papers.ssrn.com/sol3/papers.cfm?abstract_id=2955455.

Janeway, W. H. (2012), *Doing Capitalism in the Innovation Economy: Markets, Speculation and the State*, Cambridge: Cambridge University Press.

Johnson, R. W. (1980), *The Passage of the Investment Incentive Act of 1978: a Case Study of Business Influencing Public Policy*, PhD dissertation, Harvard University.

Kenney, M. (2011), 'How Venture Capital Became a Component of the US National System of Innovation', *Industrial and Corporate Change*, 20(6): 1677–723, https://doi.org/10.1093/icc/dtr061.

Kushida, K. E., J. Murray and J. Zysman (2015), 'Cloud Computing: From Scarcity to Abundance', *Journal of Industry, Competition and Trade*, 15(1): 5–19.

Lazonick, W. (2010), 'Innovative Business Models and Varieties of Capitalism: Financialization of the US Corporation', *Business History Review*, 84(4): 675–702.

Lee, A. (2013), 'Welcome to the Unicorn Club: Learning from Billion-Dollar Startups', *Tech Crunch*, 2 November, https://techcrunch.com/2013/11/02/welcome-to-the-unicorn-club/.

Manjoo, F. (2011), 'How "Super Angel" Investors Are Reinventing the Startup Economy', *Fast Company*, 1 December, https://www.fastcompany.com/1715105/how-super-angel-investors-are-reinventing-startup-economy/.

McCullough, B. (2015), 'On the 20th Anniversary – the History of Yahoo's Founding', Internet History Podcast, 1 March, http://www.internethistorypodcast.com/2015/03/on-the-20th-anniversary-the-history-of-yahoos-founding/.

Murray, J. and J. Zysman (2011), *Cloud Computing: Policy Challenges for a Globally Integrated Innovation, Production and Market Platform*, Berkeley Roundtable on the International Economy, Berkeley: University of California, Berkeley.

Northbridge and Blackduck (2016), 'The Future of Open Source Survey Results', slideshare presentation, https://www.slideshare.net/blackducksoftware/2016-future-of-open-source-survey-results/.

Perez, C. (2003), *Technological Revolutions and Financial Capital*, Cheltenham: Edward Elgar.

Pitchbook (2017), *2017 PE & VC Fundraising Report*, Seattle: Pitchbook, https://pitchbook.com/news/reports/download/2017-pe-vc-fundraising-report?key=oOCJkjmyXX.

Radojevich-Kelley, N. and D. L. Hoffman (2012), 'Analysis of Accelerator Companies: an Exploratory Case Study of their Programs, Processes, and Early Results', *Small Business Institute Journal*, 8(2): 54–70.

Schwartz, V. (2017), *Determining Characteristics of Unicorns in Light of Different Profiles of "Money Burnt": Introduction to a New Matrix*, Master's thesis, Scuola Superiore Sant'Anna.

Soskice, D. and P. A. Hall (2001), *Varieties of Capitalism: the Institutional Foundations of Comparative Advantage*, Oxford: Oxford University Press.

Zysman, J. (1983), *Governments, Markets, and Growth: Financial Systems and the Politics of Industrial Change*, Ithaca: Cornell University Press.

# GENDER EQUALITY PROSPECTS AND THE FOURTH INDUSTRIAL REVOLUTION

Debra Howcroft and Jill Rubery

The prospects for gender equality arising from the fourth industrial revolution depend on current differences in the position of women and men in the division of both paid and unpaid work. Women in all societies are more involved in unpaid care work than men, though the amount of unpaid care work varies between countries and social classes according to family size, social norms and the availability of substitute services. Socio-economic differences mean that the immediate impacts from the fourth industrial revolution on employment and care work are likely to have gender-specific impacts. To trace the likely patterns of these effects, this chapter begins by outlining some potential outcomes, based on the assumption that there will be no significant change in employment regulation, social protection and gender equality arrangements. We also recognise that the fourth industrial revolution has the potential to facilitate social change; with this in mind, we outline a number of recommendations.

Given men and women lead unequal lives, debates on the fourth industrial revolution present a timely opportunity to propose a rethink of both the structures of employment and the forms of work. Therefore, the main focus of this chapter is to identify positive policy initiatives that could not only mitigate any immediate negative impacts but also harness the potential to make a positive step change towards gender equality. Here we should note that we would not expect to achieve progress through women-only adjustments to the world of work. Instead policies need to promote change on the part of men as well as women and to expand social support for care.

## PREDICTING THE IMMEDIATE IMPACTS OF THE FOURTH INDUSTRIAL REVOLUTION BY GENDER

While prediction is a hazardous exercise, we suggest focusing on four dimensions to identify the potential gendered impacts of the fourth industrial revolution:

- structural change
- change to the nature and quality of work
- change to the employment relationship
- change to access to work during the period of childbirth and childrearing.

First, structural change has been explored by Piasna and Drahokoupil (2017) looking at the transformation of occupational structures across Europe. They found examples of job loss in both male-dominated occupations such as construction and female-dominated occupations such as clerical work. There was also evidence of major gains in some male-dominated occupations (eg IT professionals) and in some female-dominated occupations (eg cleaners and helpers). This mixed pattern of growth is reflected in only a limited increase in the female share of all employment from 45% in 2008 to 46% in 2015. Segregation has also been changing but in complex ways, although the overall effect in the most recent period (2011–2015) is to upgrade women's occupational position. Nevertheless, most of the job growth for men and for women depends on what is happening in male-dominated and female-dominated jobs. As Rubery and

Rafferty (2013) explored in relation to the impact of recession and austerity, men are particularly vulnerable to changes in manufacturing and construction and women particularly vulnerable to changes in the public sector and private services. Arguably, future structural changes will be determined by not only technology but also the level and distribution of investment, the impact of subsequent job loss on consumer demands (particularly for private services) and the policies adopted towards the public sector, including whether to use technologies to simply reduce labour input or to assist staff to provide better care (Pritchard and Brittain 2015).

Trends in the second dimension, changes to the nature and quality of work for women, depend on three main factors: the pattern of displacement, the current and future patterns of recruitment by gender into different types of jobs, and of course the overall pattern of work reorganisation. If automation occurs mainly in relation to repetitive or routine tasks, then the content of women's jobs may improve on average. This is because, according to Piasna and Drahokoupil's (2017) research using the European Working Conditions survey (2015), women are more likely to be involved in repetitive work throughout the labour market (with the exception of clerical support workers) and are also less likely to report that they are doing complex tasks even with the same occupational group. This could thus raise the quality of women's jobs while reducing their number, but in fact repetitive jobs will not necessarily disappear first, as it may still be cheaper to use labour than machines when more disadvantaged groups such as women are employed on low wages. The big gains with automation may come from displacing high-paid male jobs, for example as financial analysts.

When considering women's future access to quality jobs, it should be noted that although there has been an historical tendency for women to be concentrated in repetitive work, recent trends uncovered by Piasna and Drahokoupil (2017) found women to be outperforming men in entering non-routine jobs requiring analytical or interpersonal skills. Not all trends are positive however. Women remain underrepresented in key growth areas such as jobs requiring science, technology, engineering and maths (STEM) knowledge and skills, accounting for 23% of core STEM occupations in 2017 (WISE 2017). This pattern persists despite women successfully moving into previously male-dominated areas such as life sciences and medicine. Their underrepresentation is particularly acute in the ICT sector, where levels of female employment are dropping (to 17% in 2017, from 18% in 2016), and where they tend to be concentrated in the lower-paid sectors (WISE 2017). Furthermore, retention is challenging as many women disappear within the first couple of years of entering the industry, with more leaving than are being recruited (Moore et al 2008). Recent reports of gender discriminatory practices in big-tech firms suggest there is little sign of improvement. This points to barriers to working in STEM – beyond those related to the education system – that may be deterring women from entering these fields.

Finally, what may matter most of all for the pattern of change in the quality of work for women is whether employing organisations favour designing out human interventions or using the human dimension to enhance competiveness or the quality of the service provided. For example a recent report on the retail sector (Tait 2017) outlined three possible competitive strategies in response to the fourth industrial revolution: squeezing the cost base, automating to efficiency or, the most promising, competing through connectivity, building on human skills as a basis for the survival of the high street and retail centres. This could, if adopted, lead to automation combined with reskilling rather than simple job displacement in retail, one of the sectors identified as most at risk from automation.

The third factor shaping the gender impact is the changing employment relationship, which can be expected to have gendered effects. The fourth industrial revolution marks a change from an open-ended agreement to sell labour time to one-off contracts for highly specified services and tasks (Bergvall-Kåreborn and Howcroft 2014), encouraging forms of dependent contractor and bogus self-employment. The gendered implications of these changes in the employment relationship are evident from women's disproportional representation in non-standard forms of employment and solo self-employment. Those working in the gig economy currently represent a relatively small share of the workforce,[1] but this type of employment is on the increase. Online platforms have international reach and may offer new opportunities to women with limited access to the formal economy, but gendered promises of freedom and flexibility are situated in a context where around 60% of the world's population – many of them women in low- and middle-income countries – still lack internet access (OECD 2017). While online platforms may appear to be gender-blind, research has revealed a gender pay gap (Adams and Berg 2017). Gender pay differentials operate regardless of feedback scores, experience, occupational category, working hours and educational attainment, which suggests gender inequality is embedded in the operation of platforms (Barzilay and Ben-David 2017) in ways that require further exploration.

A more significant trend than crowdwork is the rapid rise in solo self-employment. Women-run online entrepreneur firms predominate in Australia, Canada, the Philippines, the UK and the US (OECD 2017). Taking the UK as an example, we find that men outnumber women by more than two to one among the self-employed, but the number of self-employed women rose by three-quarters since 2001, with the increase in part-time self-employment rising even faster, at 88% (CRSE 2017). The majority of these self-employed have been found to have a stable income and to be independent – not working for a single client. However, around two-fifths are classified as low paid and one-fifth receive low or medium pay and are also insecure. While gig economy work and self-employment affect men as well as women, there are differences in the implications for women, particularly those who are carers. More men than women are undertaking gig economy work as an additional source of income to supplement the day job but when women are carers these jobs are likely to be those women's main source of income. Therefore the insecurity matters more to women, and a higher proportion of women's total working hours are likely to be unpaid. The International Labour Organization has estimated that those using platforms such as Amazon Mechanical Turk spend 18 minutes in every hour searching for work (Berg 2016). This is in contrast to the traditional employment contract where the employer pays for on-the-job-inactivity within the guaranteed working day (Supiot 2001).

The fourth dimension for gender equality concerns change in access to work over the period of childbirth and childrearing. There is the risk that if work becomes more fragmented with competition for each new task, much of the progress made by women in retaining access to employment through paid maternity leave may disappear. Across the European Union, almost half of self-employed women are not entitled to maternity benefits (OECD 2017). But, even if the state makes some provision, taking leave may be risky as access to work for the self-employed often depends on how good your last job was, so taking time out can be very costly. At the same time new technologies could potentially make it easier for employers to accede to requests for flexible working, thereby perhaps reducing the proportion of women pushed into self-employment or the gig economy after childbirth. Again the issue is not with the technology but the policies of employers.

If the outcome of the fourth industrial revolution is unemployment through displacement of workers, then individual employees' bargaining power may be reduced. This could make it more difficult to negotiate flexible working, particularly if this remains only a right to request, not a right in itself. This would have significant implications given that countries with the highest share of women working from home also have the highest rates of employment among women with children (OECD 2017). Furthermore, opportunities simply to work some of the time at home would not be sufficient to take into account caring responsibilities if very long total hours of work are maintained within a flexible but 24/7 economy. Indeed some employers may even consider the price for some limited autonomy over location and place to be willingness to be available outside standard working hours to meet the needs of the business or clients.

## RECOMMENDATIONS FOR CHANGE

Given the increasing attention being paid to debating the future of work, it is prescient to consider the possibility of a more gender equal world and sketch out alternatives. Future scenarios are neither inevitable nor predetermined, but depend on how society chooses to engage with technology. With this in mind, we offer a number of recommendations in the hope of opening up spaces of possibility and initiating wider debate.

If automation is to achieve the elusive higher productivity levels, this need not necessarily exacerbate inequality. Research shows increasing job polarisation by skill level in many Organisation for Economic Co-operation and Development (OECD) countries (Autor 2015), but differentiation is not inevitable. While Frey and Osborne (2013) paint a fairly woeful picture of the reduction of labour demand through automation, they neglect the impact on working hours. Rather than polarise those in work and those out of work, automation could facilitate a reduction in average working hours and the working year, generating more free time for all without reducing economic output or increasing unemployment.

For free time to be beneficial, a sufficient income is vital and so the implementation of reduced hours should avoid triggering concomitant salary reductions, at least for those at the low and middle end of the pay distribution. This would allow for a more equal distribution of wage work and income while providing the preconditions for a more equal sharing of care between men and women.

A woman's position in the labour market is inextricably linked to experiences in the home and the distribution of reproductive labour remains imbalanced. Reduced working time could enable more innovative approaches towards domestic, reproductive and care arrangements. New forms of flexible working – no longer subject to the whim of employers and with adequate social protection – could help normalise the dual roles of carers and earners in households, challenging expectations about who holds responsibility for paid and unpaid labour. Furthermore, while technology can help facilitate home-based working, to date this has primarily benefitted higher-status, male occupations, while women self-employed teleworkers experience a greater risk of work–life spillover (Hilbrecht and Lerob 2014). Rethinking the social relations of gender could transform home-based working to provide wider benefits for women.

Recent discussions on the future of work have enabled a revisiting of the societal value of care work (Srnicek and Williams 2016), so that high-status work is not simply associated with labour that is profitable for capital. Historically, domestic technology, including that related to physical and mental care, has been consistently marginalised due to an undervaluing of the feminine and the private sphere (Cockburn 1997). However, demographic changes and the impending crisis of care in many developed economies has led to an expansion of research into assistive technologies. These technologies have the potential to reduce the burden of care work with automation, but as with many innovations a seemingly smart technological solution also has the potential to generate negative and unintended consequences (Pritchard and Brittain 2015). For this reason, it is important to look beyond simply employing technology to compensate for the potential human shortfall and instead give due consideration to how it can be usefully employed to extend personal connectivity and stimulate social interaction. Engaging with users (older citizens) of the technology in participatory design practices may inform developers as to how this may play out in future scenarios.

Given the growing demand for STEM knowledge and skills, the issue of low representation of women workers needs to be addressed. This is significant given the lack of opportunity for women workers in an area that is likely to expand rather than shrink as a consequence of the fourth industrial revolution. It is particularly problematic if women have practically no voice in the design and development of major technological innovations, especially if these are perceived to be transforming the imagined future. Despite a number of initiatives, gender inequality is endemic to the ICT sector, so a fundamental re-orientation in the culture and organisation of work will be needed if we are to redress gender imbalances.

Increasing levels of non-standard forms of employment and precarious work has been intensified by digitalisation, leading to increasing fragmentation (Rubery 2015). Ostensibly, the emergence of platform-based working and 'gigs' may appear to benefit women, providing flexibility for those with care obligations and offering paid work for those weakly attached to the labour market. In reality, this is primarily characterised by low and intermittent pay, highly fragmented and routinised work tasks, unpaid time spent searching for tasks, as well as exclusion from social protection and employment standards. While platform-based working lies predominantly in the jurisdiction of big-tech companies, which are intent on generating capital, alternatives such as state-owned platforms could offer minimum guaranteed hours or income including financial compensation when work is not available at contracted times. Concurrently, adequate regulation is essential, and the state needs to step up and tackle the huge black hole in labour law so that platforms can no longer continue to facilitate exploitable work practices (Taylor 2017). If the future world of work is left in the hands of high tech monopolies that actively pursue tax avoidance and regulatory arbitrage, the prospects for gender equality appear bleak. It has never been more opportune for significant state interventions to shape technological futures.

## NOTE

1. The UK has the highest share of crowdworkers internationally at around 3% (ILO 2016).

## REFERENCES

Adams, A. and J. Berg (2017), 'When Home Affects Pay: an Analysis of the Gender Pay Gap Among Crowdworkers', https://ssrn.com/abstract=3048711 or http://dx.doi.org/10.2139/ssrn.3048711.
Autor, D. H. (2015), 'Why Are There Still So Many Jobs? The History and Future of Workplace Automation', *Journal of Economic Perspectives*, 29(3): 3–30.

Barzilay, A. R. and A. Ben-David (2017), 'Platform Inequality: Gender in the Gig-Economy', *Seton Hall Law Review*, 47(2).

Berg, J. (2016), 'Income Security in the On-Demand Economy: Findings and Policy Lessons from a Survey of Crowdworkers', Geneva: International Labour Office, http://www.ilo.org/wcmsp5/groups/public/---ed_protect/---protrav/---travail/documents/publication/wcms_479693.pdf.

Bergvall-Kåreborn, B. and D. Howcroft (2014), 'Amazon Mechanical Turk and the Commodification of Labour', *New Technology, Work and Employment*, 29(3): 213–23.

Cockburn, C. (1997), 'Domestic Technologies: Cinderella and the Engineers', *Women's Studies International Forum*, 20(3): 361–71.

CRSE (2017), *The True Diversity of Self-Employment*, London: Centre for Research on Self-Employment, http://www.crse.co.uk/sites/default/files/The%20true%20diversity%20of%20self-employment_0.pdf.

European Working Conditions Survey (2015), Eurofound, https://www.eurofound.europa.eu/surveys/european-working-conditions-surveys.

Frey, C. and M. Osborne (2013), *The Future of Employment: How Susceptible Are Jobs To Computerisation?*, Oxford: Oxford Martin School, https://www.oxfordmartin.ox.ac.uk/downloads/academic/The_Future_of_Employment.pdf.

Hilbrecht, M. and D. S. Lerob (2014), 'Self-Employment and Family Life: Constructing Work–Life Balance When You're "Always On"', *Community, Work & Family*, (17)1: 20–42.

ILO (2016), 'Non-standard Employment around the World', International Labour Organization, http://www.ilo.org/wcmsp5/groups/public/---dgreports/---dcomm/---publ/documents/publication/wcms_534326.pdf.

Moore, K., M. Griffiths, H. Richardson and A. Adam (2008), 'Gendered Futures? Women, the ICT Workplace and Stories of the Future', *Gender, Work and Organization*, 15(5): 523–42.

OECD (2017), 'Going Digital: The Future of Work for Women, Policy Brief on the Future of Work', Organisation for Economic Co-operation and Development, https://www.oecd.org/employment/Going-Digital-the-Future-of-Work-for-Women.pdf.

Piasna, A. and J. Drahokoupil (2017), 'Gender Inequalities in the New World of Work', *Transfer: European Review of Labour and Research*, 23(3), http://journals.sagepub.com/doi/abs/10.1177/1024258917713839.

Pritchard, G. W. and K. Brittain (2015), 'Alarm pendants and the Technological Shaping of Older People's Care', *Technological Forecasting and Social Change*, 93: 124–32.

Rubery, J. (2015), 'Change at Work: Feminisation, Flexibilisation, Fragmentation and Financialisation', *Employee Relations*, 37(6): 633–44.

Rubery, J. and A. Rafferty (2013), 'Women and Recessions Revisited', *Work, Employment and Society*, 27(3): 414–32.

Srnicek, N. and A. Williams (2016), *Inventing the Future: Postcapitalism and a World Without Work*, London: Verso.

Supiot, A. (2001), *Beyond Employment: Changes in Work and the Future of Labour Law in Europe*, Oxford: Oxford University Press.

Tait, C. (2017), 'At the Crossroads: the Future of British Retail', London: The Fabian Society, http://www.fabians.org.uk/wp-content/uploads/2017/01/FABJ4765_Retail_report_260117_WEB_.pdf.

Taylor, M. (2017), *Good Work: the Taylor Review of Modern Working Practices*, Department for Business, Energy & Industrial Strategy, https://www.gov.uk/government/uploads/system/uploads/attachment_data/file/627671/good-work-taylor-review-modern-working-practices-rg.pdf.

WISE (2017), 'Women in STEM Workforce 2017', Women into Science and Engineering, https://www.wisecampaign.org.uk/resources/2017/10/women-in-stem-workforce-2017.

# NO NEED FOR AUTOMATION ANGST, BUT AUTOMATION POLICIES

Daniel Arnold, Melanie Arntz, Terry Gregory, Susanne Steffes and Ulrich Zierahn

Technological change is increasingly turning the value chain into an automated and digitalised process. The digitalisation and automation of manufacturing processes is characterised by the use of increasingly autonomous systems and robots, as well as fully automated smart factories (Industry 4.0), which are interconnected with upstream and downstream business divisions. Similarly, service providers have been using intelligent software and algorithms on the basis of large volumes of data and web interfaces to digitalise and automate business processes. To this effect, businesses make use of big data analysis software, cloud computing systems or online platforms, to give but a few examples. In view of these technological developments – sometimes referred to as technologies of the fourth industrial revolution – an increasing number of concerns have been voiced in the public debate that this might lead to many jobs becoming redundant in the future. The idea of 'technological unemployment' is supported by a number of US studies which suggest that almost 50% of jobs are at risk of being replaced by new digital technologies (Frey and Osborne 2017). This raises a number of questions for both political decisionmakers and the general public: is it true that automation and digitalisation will result in major job losses? And if so, which jobs are at risk? In what ways are technological developments changing work processes and content? How will this affect qualification and skills requirements? Do we need to adapt in order to guarantee employee job security? This essay sheds some light on these questions.

## AUTOMATION RISKS SEEM TO BE OVERESTIMATED

Frey and Osborne (2017) investigated how susceptible are jobs to computerisation by asking experts how easily certain occupations could be automated in the next two decades. As a result they estimate that 47% of all US employees are in occupations that are at high risk of becoming automatable in the next 10 to 20 years. Applying the same methods to determine the automation potential of specific occupations in Germany and Europe yields similar results (Bonin, Gregory and Zierahn 2015; Bowles 2014). Hence, these findings subsequently spurred widespread automation angst and have sparked lively political debate public debate in recent years. However, there are good reasons to assume that these figures vastly overestimate the number of jobs that will actually become redundant due to technological advances in the next two decades.

First of all, usually, not all the tasks outlined in a job description can be automated to the same degree. In fact, though machines may take over certain tasks of any given job description, there are others that they cannot. Therefore, whether an occupation can be automated or not depends on how significant the type of tasks are that can be carried out by machines. Hence, even within the same occupation, the automation potential can vary greatly from job to job. An analysis of automation potential based on the actual task structure of individual jobs thus produces very different results (see Arntz, Gregory and Zierahn 2017). According to this analysis, the percentage of jobs in the US with a high automation potential (>70%) falls from 38% when applying Frey and Osborne's occupation-based approach to just 9% when looking at individual jobs (see Figure 4.1). One explanation for this significantly reduced automation potential is that many jobs involve tasks that are difficult to automate and that workers apparently specialise in different non-automatable niches within their profession. As a result, risk assessments that are based on occupational job descriptions for some representative workers do not sufficiently capture these non-automatable niches, and hence seriously overestimate the potential for automation. One potential reason for this result could be that workers increasingly shift their work towards tasks that complement these new technologies (Spitz-Oener 2006).

These findings also hold for many other Organisation for Economic Co-operation and Development (OECD) countries. In particular, the use of an individual job-oriented approach has shown that the automation potential of jobs in 21 OECD countries is far lower than previous studies would have us believe (Arntz, Gregory and Zierahn 2016), though the results vary from country to country. While 12% of jobs in Germany and Austria can be automated, the figure for Korea is only 6%. Even though the cause-and-effect

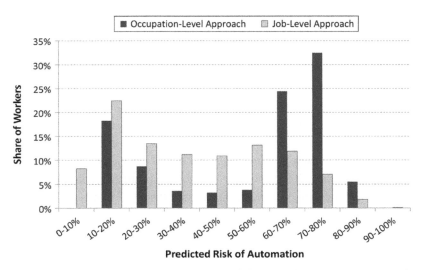

Figure 4.1 Automation potential on the US labour market. *Source*: Arntz et al. 2017.

relationship is yet to be sufficiently studied, the analysis suggests that countries with the lowest percentage of jobs that can be replaced tend to invest more in information and communications technology (ICT) and have a more communication-intensive workplace structure as well as a more highly educated workforce. Hence, there is some evidence that the automation potential has been exaggerated and that future potential for automation is actually lowest in the countries that have already undergone some adjustments through ICT investment and upskilling their workforce. Notably, these expert-based risk assessments also correspond more or less with subjective assessments of employees regarding technological change; according to a German survey, 13% of workers expect their job to be carried out by a machine within the next 10 years (Arnold et al. 2016).

## HURDLES TO DIGITALISATION LIMIT AUTOMATION POTENTIAL IN THE SHORT- TO MID-RUN

Although the automation potential may thus be much lower than is often claimed, around 1 in 10 jobs still seems to have the potential to become automated. Expecting an increase in unemployment of the same magnitude, however, would be much too simplistic a conclusion, since automation potential only reflects the technical potential for job displacement (see also Arntz, Gregory and Zierahn 2016; Bonin, Gregory and Zierahn 2015). For example, it is quite likely that it takes longer for these new technologies to be adopted by firms on a grand scale than is often asserted. Initial analyses based on the representative IAB-ZEW Working World 4.0 survey conducted in early 2016 have shown that although around half of German companies are using "technologies of the fourth industrial revolution", on average only 5% of all firm assets could be described as "production facilities 4.0" and only 8% as "electronic office and communications equipment 4.0" (Arntz et al. 2016b).

Some of the main hurdles faced by firms when implementing technologies of the fourth industrial revolution are the increasing cost of data protection and cyber security measures, the need for specific training for employees on how to work with new technologies, high investment costs, and an increased dependence on external knowledge and services (Arntz et al. 2016a). Apart from these hurdles, a number of regulatory, legal or social road blocks do not prevent the introduction of these new technologies, but they could slow their diffusion. Some of the obstacles will be overcome at some point. Social preferences for certain tasks to be carried out by humans rather than machines (eg in areas such as care services) may limit the adoption of new technologies even in the long run. This could be done by establishing technical standards for implementing networked manufacturing and liability issues surrounding self-driving cars.

## DIGITALISATION IS CHANGING JOBS BUT NOT REPLACING THEM

The implementation of new technologies does not necessarily lead to job losses if employees are increasingly carrying out tasks that are made more efficient by using new technologies without being replaced by these technologies (Acemoglu and Restrepo 2017; Autor 2015). This may also explain why only a third of the 13% of employees who believe their job could potentially be automated expressed concern over the security of their own job (Arnold et al. 2016). Since, from the perspective of companies, the use of new technologies goes hand in hand with increased work productivity as well as additional sales opportunities for new products and services (Arntz et al. 2016b), the effects of digitalisation on overall employment are not necessarily negative.

## TECHNOLOGICAL CHANGE CREATES MORE JOBS THAN IT DESTROYS

In order to make any concrete statement on the changes to overall employment over the course of digitalisation, we must consider both labour-saving and job-creating effects. From their initial empirical findings on the European level, Gregory, Salomons and Zierahn (2016) concluded that the net balance was previously on the whole positive. Figure 4.2 shows the corresponding aggregate effect of technological change in the period 1999–2010 on the labour demand of firms and dissects it into various causal factors. The lower limit is based on the assumption that only wage income leads to increased consumption in Europe, while the upper limit assumes that capital income also has a positive effect on the European economy through consumption. Overall, it appears that labour demand has increased as a result of recent technological change. The labour-creating effect of technological change thus seems to dominate the initial labour-saving effect. This is because the falling price of goods, together with increased consumption resulting from rising income levels, have led to an increase in labour demand in both the area of tradeable goods (this is an example of the positive product demand effect) and of non-tradeable services (this is an example of the positive product demand spillover effect). The latter effect is con-siderably stronger if capital income also contributes to consumption within Europe. This suggests that the effects of digitalisation on the labour market might also depend on how the profits of technological change are distributed and utilised.

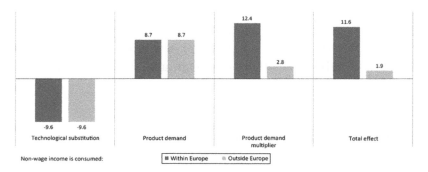

**Figure 4.2  Labour demand in Europe, estimated change (in millions of jobs) 1999–2010.** *Source*: Gregory, Salomons and Zierahn (2016).

## DIGITALISATION ALTERS QUALIFICATION AND SKILLS REQUIREMENTS

Even though overall employment is unlikely to drop significantly, this does not preclude massive structural changes. Jobs in IT and education are likely to benefit, whereas jobs in manufacturing industries where the use of machines and technical equipment is widespread will probably be hardest hit by staffing cuts (Wolter et al. 2015). This structural change will also lead to a change in qualification and skills requirements. Overall, the findings suggest that in the future jobs will be less physically demanding and instead more mentally demanding, as well as being more varied and complex. From the perspective of companies, job requirements will increase, particularly in the area of process expertise and interdisciplinary methods of working and transferable skills (see Figure 4.3). The latter primarily encompasses social skills (eg customer service) and creativity – in other words, skills where humans still have an advantage over machines. One of the side-effects of these developments, however, is an increasingly high mental strain on workers. Around two-thirds of employees believe that new technologies have

Scale: Proportion of firms that assume an increasing importance minus the proportion of firms that assume a decreasing importance.

**Figure 4.3  Increasing automation and changing skill requirements.** *Source*: Arntz, Gregory, Jansen and Zierahn (2016b).

led to increased workloads, with more and more tasks having to be completed at the same time (Arnold et al. 2016).

## TREND TOWARDS BOTH UP- AND DESKILLING

These changing skills requirements seem to be accompanied by an increased demand for better qualified workers even within occupations. According to the results of a survey conducted among German companies, the demand for qualifications is shifting as a result of digitalisation, particularly in the service sector, in favour of expert and specialist jobs (for workers with vocational training or further training on the job) and high-skilled jobs (for university graduates) and away from unskilled work (Arntz et al. 2016b). Employees have also begun to perceive this trend towards more highly skilled workers. In Germany, four-fifths of workers see a need to continuously develop their skills in order to keep up with higher job requirements (see Figure 4.4). Although this was observed across all qualification groups, the share of individuals seeking to upgrade their skills increases with the level of qualification. These changing skill and qualification requirements point to the new division of labour between man and machine in the near future. While machines take over tasks which are easier to programme and automate, human labour is mainly needed for less routine and skill-intensive tasks involving creativity and social interactions.

The trend towards more highly qualified workers is not seen everywhere, however. Companies in the manufacturing sector are reporting a polarisation of qualification requirements. Demand for both low-skilled and highly qualified workers has risen, to the detriment of workers with medium level technical qualifications – in other words, we are seeing a trend towards both higher and lower qualification requirements for workers. Indeed, 15% of workers in Germany reported that the skills and competencies required for their jobs had decreased over the past five years as a result of digitalisation

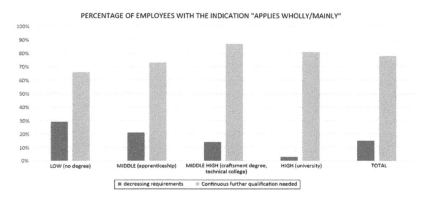

Figure 4.4   Competence requirements due to digitisation by education group, Germany.

(Arnold et al. 2016). Low-skilled workers in particular – around 1 in 3 – claim to have witnessed this sort of deskilling.

## FROM RISING POLARISATION TO RISING INEQUALITY?

Even though digital transformation is not expected to trigger any negative aggregate employment effects, it is still creating a fundamental shift in labour demand between different occupations and fields of activity. This will put increased pressure on workers, particularly low-skilled workers, to adapt. The share of low-skilled employees performing tasks with a high automation potential is significantly higher than among employees with high or medium level qualifications. Employees' subjective expectations regarding the likelihood of their job becoming automated are similarly distributed across the different education groups (cf. Figure 4.5). Recent studies suggest that the pressure to adapt is shifting from workers with medium level qualifications, who were hardest hit in the 1990s, to low-skilled workers (Arnold et al. 2016; Arntz, Gregory and Zierahn 2016; Wolter et al. 2015).

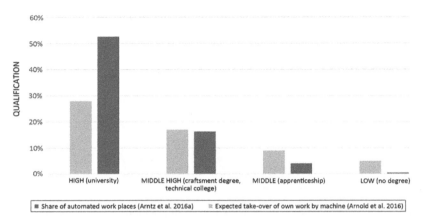

Figure 4.5    Automation potential and perceived threat from technological substitution by education groups.

As a result, the effect of digitalisation on the employment and wage structure may change. While it is highly qualified workers in occupations involving a high level of non-routine tasks who benefit most from an increasingly demanding work environment, as machines and algorithms are complementary to their work and increase their productivity, until recently, it was primarily workers with medium level qualifications in occupations characterised by a high degree of routine tasks who had reason to fear that their jobs might be replaced by machines. As a result, over the last two decades employment among highly qualified workers at the upper end of the salary distribution – and to a lesser extent among low-skilled workers at the lower end – increased, while employment growth in the middle was fairly weak. In this way, labour markets in western economies have experienced widespread job polarisation (Acemoglu and Autor 2011). If in the future, however, low-skilled workers come increasingly under pressure as simple non-routine tasks become more easily automated, a period of job polarisation in the recent past might be superseded by a period of increasing inequality.

## NEED FOR A COMPREHENSIVE POLICY RESPONSE

Overall, the challenges surrounding the digital transformation towards a Work 4.0 call for a policy approach that helps to unleash the full innovative and productive potential of this change, while at the same time ensuring that workers are not left out in the cold. In this regard, there are three key messages that can be derived from the research findings presented above.

First, workers' qualifications will have a central role to play. Continuous further training is important if workers are to meet the ever increasing skills requirements in many sectors. For this reason, many companies are intensifying their further training schemes and adapting the contents of their training courses. However, those whose jobs have the highest automation potential – low-skilled workers – actually see less of a need to continuously train and gain new skills than other, more highly qualified groups of workers. Corporate measures alone are not enough to combat a potential increase in inequality as a result of technological change. In addition, government programmes are needed to promote particular groups whose skill levels would otherwise fall further and further behind rising requirements. Moreover, these programmes should not only kick in once people have already lost their jobs; rather, they should be offered opportunities to gain higher qualifications alongside their current job that will help to keep them in stable employment.

Second, we can expect there to be a fraction of the labour force that is not in a position, and is unlikely to reach a position even through further training, to meet the growing demands of the labour market. Employment and income risks might increase for this group and will represent a challenge for social policy. Due to a lack of research, however, the extent of this challenge as well as any potential remedies remain underdeveloped.

Third, initial findings suggest that the aggregate employment effects of digital transformation depend, among other things, on how the profits of digitalisation are distributed and utilised. While increased wage income bolsters local consumption and thus creates new jobs, increased capital income might be less beneficial for the local economy. This raises the question of whether lower tax rates for capital income compared with wage income represent a disadvantage to the input factor labour and whether an adjustment of the relative tax burdens could lead to more positive employment effects of digital transformation.

## REFERENCES

Acemoglu, D. and D. Autor (2011), 'Skills, Tasks and Technologies: Implications for Employment and Earnings', in O. Ashenfelter and D. Card (eds), *Handbook of Labor Economics*, vol. 4, Amsterdam: Elsevier.

Acemoglu, D. and P. Restrepo (2017), 'The Race Between Man and Machine: Implications of Technology for Growth, Factor Shares and Employment', unpublished.

Arnold, D., S. Butschek, D. Müller and S. Steffes (2016), 'Digitalisierung am Arbeitsplatz: Aktuelle Ergebnisse einer Betriebs- und Beschäftigtenbefragung', Forschungsbericht im Auftrag des Bundesministeriums für Arbeit und Soziales und des Instituts für Arbeitsmarkt- und Berufsforschung, Berlin.

Arntz, M., T. Gregory and U. Zierahn (2016), *The Risk of Automation for Jobs in OECD Countries: a Comparative Analysis*, Social, Employment and Migration Working Paper 189, Paris: OECD.

Arntz, M., T. Gregory and U. Zierahn (2017), 'Revisiting the Risk of Automation', *Economics Letters*, 159: 157–60.

Arntz, M., T. Gregory, S. Jansen and U. Zierahn (2016a), 'Tätigkeitswandel und Weiterbildungsbedarf in der Digitalen Transformation', Studie des Zentrums für Europäische Wirtschaftsforschung (ZEW) und des Instituts für Arbeitsmarkt und Berufsforschung (IAB) im Auftrag der Deutschen Akademie der Technikwissenschaften (acatech).

Arntz, M., T. Gregory, F. Lehmer, B. Matthes and U. Zierahn (2016b), 'Arbeitswelt 4.0 – Stand der Digitalisierung in Deutschland: Dienstleister Haben die Nase Vorn', IAB Kurzbericht, 22.

Autor, D. (2015), 'Why Are There Still So Many Jobs? The History and Future of Workplace Automation', *Journal of Economic Perspectives*, 29(3): 3–30.

Bonin, H., T. Gregory and U. Zierahn (2015), *Übertragung der Studie von Frey/Osborne (2013) auf Deutschland*, Bundesministerium für Arbeit und Soziales, ftp://ftp.zew.de/pub/zew-docs/gutachten/Kurzexpertise_BMAS_ZEW2015.pdf.

Bowles, J. (2014), 'The Computerisation of European Jobs', blog, 24 July, Bruegel, http://bruegel.org/2014/07/the-computerisation-of-european-jobs/.

Frey, C. B. and M. Osborne (2017), 'The Future of Employment: How Susceptible are Jobs to Computerization?', *Technological Forecasting and Social Change*, 114: 254–80.

Gregory, T., A. Salomons and U. Zierahn (2016), 'Racing With or Against the Machine? Evidence from Europe', ZEW Discussion Paper, 16(53).

Spitz-Oener, A. (2006), 'Technical Change, Job Tasks, and Rising Educational Demands: Looking outside the Wage Structure', *Journal of Labor Economics*, 24(2): 235–70.

Wolter, M. I., A. Mönnig, M. Hummel, C. Schneemann, E. Weber, G. Zika, R. Helmrich, T. Maier and C Neuber-Pohl (2015), 'Industrie 4.0 und die Folgen für Arbeitsmarkt und Wirtschaft. Szenario-Rechnungen im Rahmen der BIBB-IAB-Qualifikations- und Berufsfeldprojektionen', IAB Forschungsbericht, 8.

# VALUE CREATION IN
# THE DATA-DRIVEN ECONOMY

Paul Hofheinz


It has been understood for centuries that society and the *economy* are linked. The 'base', as Karl Marx described it in his seminal depiction, provides a foundation for the 'superstructure' that sits on top of it (Marx 2014). But what happens when the base shifts? What occurs when the material foundation of the economy – the 'means of production', as Marx would have it – begins to change profoundly? Is the right policy response still to seize the 'commanding heights'? Or is it rather time to start retooling that society to sit more comfortably on top of an economy where the fundamental underlying value arises from completely unforeseen new processes and wealth is being created in a fundamentally different way?

I believe something like that is happening now, even if analysts sometimes struggle to cast the challenge in a way that sheds more light on the future being born than the past being left behind. The question policymakers face is not so much how to keep industry from disappearing, though this discussion is perennial and appeals can be found in most major political platforms at every major election. It is also a point of reference and a too-obvious-to-be-questioned explanation within the communities that have been devastated by industry's disappearance.[1] The issue is how do we prepare for and legislate for an economy where the social order will face a radically different set of challenges – problems that will themselves need to be mitigated with a radically different set of policies (Hofheinz 2017). The social structure has shifted already. In the old days men ran the world, but now there is more access, more opportunity. Is that a good thing? It depends on where you sit. But for the vast majority of people – particularly women, immigrants and, yes, the world's poor – this is a very good thing indeed (Sachs 2005).

So what, then, are the fundamental shifts?

## THE ECONOMY HAS BECOME DEMATERIALISED

First and foremost, the economy has become dematerialised (Haskel and Westlake 2017). It is no longer about making and shipping goods. It has become about producing and selling services (OECD 2017). Advanced manufacturers – at least the ones who understand the shift – are reacting cleverly and responding flexibly. Rolls-Royce, for one, no longer sells airplane engines. Instead, it sells guaranteed 'aviation hours' to the world's airplane manufacturers – and monitors the engines it leases with advanced analytics (Dinges et al. 2015). This is not a unique development. Companies worldwide are starting to see the goods they make as part of a larger set of services to offer. And those services, in turn, can be parsed, outsourced and spread around the world in unique combinations that make us a truly global economy, despite what the Brexiteers will tell you (Hofheinz and Mandel 2015). There is no 'little England' any more. The economy is truly global.

## IMPROVEMENT IN LIFE EXPECTANCY

Life expectancy has improved dramatically, with a consequent shift in the way public resources are spent and a major impact on the labour inputs available to the economy worldwide (Sachs 2005). Here, in 'industrial Europe', life expectancy has risen to 77.9 years for men and 83.3 years for women, up from a frighteningly low 25 years as recently as 200 years ago.[2] With improvements in lifelong healthcare and decreases in crippling infant mortality, the size of families has consequently also shifted, falling from an average of around 10 in Europe 200 years ago to 2.3 today (interestingly, almost two-thirds of European families are now one- or two-person households).[3]

This latter point is a radical shift as well: mothers are no longer stuck at home, essentially running small child-rearing businesses that would have defied the management capabilities of the men who deserted them each day for the factory floor. And the true revolution in our time is that the phenomenon is no longer limited to the developed world (Sachs 2005). With the notable exception of Africa, life expectancy has also risen dramatically in the developing world, an achievement that is not coincidentally contemporaneous with the rise of globalisation. This has brought literally billions of hardworking, relatively cheap and often extremely talented people into the global workforce.

## IMPROVEMENT IN ACCESS TO EDUCATION

Access to education has improved dramatically. Literacy rates are rising around the world and, guess what?, some of those who might not have learned to read in previous generations are fast becoming the world's best engineers. Five years ago, Massachusetts Institute of Technology agreed to let external students who followed a sophomore-level circuits and electronics course on the Institute's popular massive open online course (MOOC) to sit the final exam. The result was an explosion of good results. One of the recipients was Battushig Myanganbayar, a 15-year-old Mongolian boy, who earned a perfect score from his desktop in Ulan Bator.[4] More than 58 million people have participated in MOOCs since their advent some five years ago. Some of them are now covering Master's degree-level material.[5]

## SHIFT IN THE ECONOMIC 'BASE'

All of this is possible because of a dramatic shift in the economic 'base', to use the Marxist term. The internet made possible instantaneous, zero marginal cost communication – at the local as well as the global level (see Soete this volume). This has been an enormously empowering and disruptive influence – not just on politics, but on the social order that prevailed in some places for centuries. But it has other, more deep-seated, implications. Put simply, it has turned data into the economy's newest, most valuable vital asset (OECD 2015). Policymakers have struggled to find a suitable metaphor; data is the new economy's most important 'commodity', 'currency' and 'infrastructure', to use just three of the concepts to which it is most often (and somewhat misleadingly) compared. But data is really something else entirely. Data is data. Its use has its own logic, and its own requirements (Hofheinz and Osimo 2017). In a nutshell, data is how global businesses communicate across the vast spaces they now occupy. And it is the crucial raw material from which those companies – as well as governments and individuals – will come to new insights, develop and deliver new services and derive vital conclusions.

Everywhere you see the economy shifting. Financial service companies now derive more value from their ability to collect and learn from the data they gather than they do from the margins on routine financial transactions. Once obscure internet platforms have grown to be enormous global businesses, often offering excellent services for free in return for nothing more than the right to track how you use it. And now artificial intelligence (see Petropoulos this volume) is poised to take it to a higher level, holding out the possibility of automating more and more tasks with the knowledge internet platforms gain from the data we feed them (Hofheinz 2016).

## IMPLICATIONS FOR INDUSTRY

So what, then, are the implications for industry? First and foremost, industry in the developed world ignores these trends at its peril

(OECD 2017). Companies like Germany's vast Mittelstand (see Rahner and Schönstein this volume) are particularly affected. The world is big, hyper-competitive and horizontally connected. There is little nostalgia. Price is king, though quality can still command a premium, but it is important that that premium remains affordable and within reach. The developed world is both challenge and opportunity. It is a challenge because developing-world products and manufacturing techniques have risen so dramatically and remain relatively cheap. It is an opportunity because that rise gives developed-world manufacturers bigger and bigger markets to sell into.

The larger question is not can and will industry adapt – contrary to its reputation, European industry is more competitive than we give it credit for.[6] Rather, it is how we will deal with the dramatic social and political disruption that this brave new world gives rise to. First is rising inequality.[7] While global income disparities are falling, demonstrable and quantifiably rising inequality is the unwanted side effect at 'the local level' – which is how we now refer to the nation state in a sign of how much change these times have already brought. Put simply, the spread of digital technologies and the concurrent rise of the global economy created winners and losers. If enough of the losers feel the game is rigged against them – and many have come to that conclusion – the result will be a nasty form of protest politics, which threatens the prosperity on which so many countries and societies are based (Clinton 2017). Policy does make a difference. And decisions to dismantle democracy – as the Polish government is doing – or drop out of important global trade flows – as the British have foolishly decided to do – will be felt directly, and sooner than you think. The Roman empire did collapse, though few at the time of Julius Caesar's putsch could have foreseen the dark age that was to come.

There is something new, something truly ahistorical, about what is happening in the economy right now. It is the unforeseen shift in the way value is created (Hofheinz and Osimo 2017). More than is commonly perceived, the industrial economy was built on a model of strong property rights (including intellectual property) and the associated concept of individual accumulation of wealth.[8] It started with the great move towards enclosures in the 16th century – an effort to clear farmers from previously common land so that that land could be developed privately (until that time, the prevailing social order had been common, based mostly on unwritten feudal rights and duties, which tied owners and peasants together in patterns of shared responsibility for each other). But the trend continued with the rise of factories and the scientific and industrial explosion of the 18th and 19th centuries. This development was driven not by ever larger markets but by stronger – and more easily enforced – property rights than had existed before. Most notable was patents – a legal monopoly on innovation, which made science and scientific discovery extremely lucrative. But the notion of 'trademark' meant that companies could organise at scale. And accumulated capital – the ultimate private property – could be invested and reinvested. A strong legal environment with easily enforceable property rights allowed the returns to be reasonably assumed, accurately calculated and ultimately quite lucrative. The history of roughly 500 years can be summed up in these words: by and large it worked.

But the digital economy – with its heavy reliance on speed, flexibility and economies of scale – is pushing us towards a new, radically different logic. At the heart of the problem is data, a new kind of economic input, which not coincidentally has already become the new economy's most precious. Put simply, data is not worth much to the individuals who own or create it.[9] Data becomes valuable when it is combined. This is how we will find cures for cancer. This is how we will improve traffic in our cities. This is the area where large, industrial-scale services will be delivered with a level of personalised service that would have been unthinkable in the old days. And it is how the next, most advanced, innovation in our economy will be calculated and created.

And this has huge implications: society and the economy around it have a huge incentive to share their data with each other, putting it in larger and larger pools where the lucrative insights and brilliant innovations of the next phase of human history will come. We all have a very strong incentive to contribute to good economic outcomes. In the past, that meant being good consumers, holding down jobs and paying our taxes. It still means all of those things. But now it means pooling our data – the information about how we live, work, drive and play – so that new and more original insights can be generated. And as those insights are derived collectively, we have a strong incentive to make sure that the benefits are shared and apportioned collectively as well.

This is the true revolution. It won't be industrial. It won't even be digital. It will be social and political. And it will speak not just to the way we share wealth but also to the way we generate it. We stand on the cusp of an important decision: will we find and develop the social innovation needed to make the digital revolution a win-win-win for all? Or will we regress into our most atavistic politics, attacking and killing a system that has delivered uneven results, preferring to blind our neighbour's cows rather than giving sight to our own?

## SHARING MORE IN THE DATA-DRIVEN ECONOMY

And success is not guaranteed. The current wave of 'post-truth' politics is a dangerous lurch backwards. Rather than fixing a broken system, voters are choosing to smash the system itself. There are many reasons for this – including the fact that the pillars supporting that system have been poorly explained and were never widely understood. Many of the ideas floating around today – like universal basic income – are primitive, and would lead to poor social results if implemented. But they point in the right direction, and show that – in a crude way – people are thinking more or less correctly about the kind of change their future will require. One way or the other, the rise of a data-driven economy means that we will share more, which has implications on two levels: we will share more data about ourselves – with improved social outcomes that will be common and collective, and we need to find ways of sharing the wealth created in that process more equitably as well.

## USE NEW SYSTEMS TO SHARE DATA

Advanced economies need new systems for sharing data. Today, the area is blocked, still functioning under the old paradigm of individual property rights. Companies are hoarding data – sometimes even buying up other companies only for the data they own (Hofheinz and Osimo 2017). This is a fool's errand. Recent practice tells us that the average machine-learning trained machine will need as many as 10,000 to 100,000 times more data than single human workers will generate during the course of their professional life (Cutler 2017). This is well beyond the capacity of any one company to attain or provide. If the data economy is to be a success, we need common pools of data – a 'data commons', in other words, though this concept is still in its infancy (Hofheinz and Osimo 2017; OECD 2015). Under that scenario, companies will base their competition on the services they offer, drawing insight from common pools of data to which all will have access.

## MAKE DATA POOLS COMMON

If the data pools are common, the results should be more broadly socialised as well. Some of this will happen naturally. Cures for cancer will have broad and evident advances for all – though it will be important, when these advances come, to make sure that they are widely available. Improved traffic management in cities is a huge advantage to everyone as well, and data and the data-driven economy will play more than a small role here. The advent of ride-sharing technology like Uber will make the ownership of cars less necessary and the cities much cleaner.

## KEEP GLOBAL TRADE FLOWS OPEN

Global trade flows should be kept open. The challenge of managing the global economy within our own society should not become an excuse for shutting down the global economy itself. We need to find ways to preserve the benefits. There needs to be more concrete, credible and robust policymaking to take care of communities that have thus far been left behind.[10]

## FIGHT THE PRECARIOUSNESS OF THE DATA ECONOMY

The data economy is inherently precarious, but the effort to fight that precariousness should take the form of greater state-led social protection rather than greater requirements for social commitments from private-sector companies. The European social model grew up around a fairly simple concept – the best way to ensure social peace was to get companies to pay for it. The result is the highest non-wage labour costs in the world, a situation which is itself contributing to a hollowing out of good jobs in Europe, pricing them rather directly out of the market. This needs to stop. The global economy is too competitive – and European workers too expensive – to continue adding costs in the way we have added them over the years.

More recently, the most successful social-policy initiatives have had a common theme – freeing up companies to compete by taking the social burden onto the state. Towards that end, the best and most illustrative policy is still Denmark's 'flexicurity' model (Baily and Kirkegaard 2004, see Ilsøe this volume). It increased benefits to workers and lowered the direct requirement on companies to provide them. Legal severance was shortened to one week, for example. But the result was an explosion of new jobs, driving unemployment to 2.4%, down from the 12.4% that the government of Poul Nyrup Rasmussen inherited from his predecessor (Hendeliowitz 2008).

There are other policies which have performed a similar role: Obamacare makes it easier for Americans to switch jobs because their healthcare is no longer dependent on their employer. And the French have invented important new ways of spreading access to education over a lifetime with the compte personnel d'activité (personal activity account) (Hofheinz 2017, see Weber this volume).

Systems based on income tax credits, which provide incentives to work by offering top ups for those whose earnings are beneath a living wage, have proven enormously effective in the US and the UK. But these are merely the seeds of broader social changes that have yet to take hold. Put simply, in a rapidly globalising economy, it is no longer feasible to impose greater social commitments on companies in the form of requiring them to offer only full-time labour contracts or mandating expensive restructuring charges. The state must step in with a comprehensive set of policies designed to protect and empower workers in an economy based on flexibility and change. It must become the guardian of a radically rewoven social fabric. Above all new and innovative measures are needed to fight social challenges that are different from the ones that existed when the current system was conceived and implemented.

## PROVIDE GREATER ACCESS TO EDUCATION

Working life will unfold differently, too. Education is no longer something we can frontload; people will need access to it throughout their lives. Companies like General Assembly – with its short-term skills accreditation courses – and Udacity – with its 'vocational courses for professionals' – are showing the way. We must rethink the famous work–life balance as a triad of work–life–education balance, forever combining and recombining throughout what used to be called a person's 'working life'. The social system must support career patterns based on fast changing needs – that is what the world demands. And it would not require much more than a leap of imagination and a bit of education system retooling to provide it.[11]

## A DYSTOPIAN VISION AND ITS ALTERNATIVE

There is another future – a dystopian one – where technology becomes a weapon of oppression. The Chinese, with their

Communist Party-inspired social rating system, are dangerously close to this. And the Russians have shown a flair for mainstreaming their talent for 'disinformation', using it to disrupt their perceived enemies effectively, with unprecedented success. The Americans under Donald Trump are not far behind. In the US, efforts to fight inequality have been pushed radically backwards: an absurdly regressive tax reform, an internet where traffic is throttled, a blind eye towards police violence and the racial prejudice that remains America's greatest shame (see Kalleberg this volume).

We must counter this with an alternative vision. One where European industry has the tools it needs to succeed so it can continue to serve as a pillar for the world's most advanced social system. One where society itself feels that it is part of these exciting developments, with each of us making an important contribution. This outcome is not guaranteed. But it is not out of our reach, either.

## NOTES

1. A good example of this thinking is Marianne Cooper's very good study of family finances and risk management (Cooper 2014).

2. This is higher than in North America (where the equivalent figures are 76.9 and 81.6). The reasons for Europe's better performance are beyond the scope of this essay, but it is a fact worth noting. The European social model is delivering longer, healthier lives (Eurostat 2017a).

3. Around 40% of Europeans died before reaching adulthood in the 'pre-industrial era' (Eurostat 2017b).

4. Mr Myanganbayar was one of 350 of the 120,000 students who took the exam to make a perfect score (Pappano 2013).

5. The 58 million figure is for 2016 and comes from the very helpful 'By the Numbers: MOOCs in 2016' (Shah 2016). See also 'Master's Degree is New Frontier of Study Online' (Lewin 2013).

6. The euro area itself maintains a healthy monthly trade surplus with the rest of the world of €18.9bn, though much of that success is attributable to one country: Germany. As the global economy picked up steam, the trade balance with the rest of the world of the 28-member EU itself slid to a €0.3bn deficit in October 2017, down from a €2.4bn surplus a year before (Eurostat 2017c).

7. See World Inequality Report 2018 (World Inequality Lab 2018) and 'Inequality is a Threat to Our Democracies' (Wolf 2017a), a very good recent summary. The seminal work on this phenomenon is Capital in the 21st Century (Piketty 2014).

8. For a very good, early discussion of the policy implications posed by rise of intangible assets in the economy, see 'The Challenges of the Disembodied Economy' (Wolf 2017b).

9. The OECD tried to calculate the market value of individual data. The bottom line: the data people held about themselves was worth much less – companies were willing to pay much less for it – than the individuals themselves thought it was worth. Recent market-based transactions – such as the 2013 acquisition of Climate Corporation by Monsanto Corporation for $930 million – have demonstrated that the value of data rises considerably when it is aggregated (OECD 2015).

10. See especially the highly instructive account of a community left behind by globalisation – and the poverty of the policy response – in 'Are We Witnessing the Strange, Lingering Death of Labour England?' (Engel 2017).

11. By implication, efforts to make higher education 100% state funded, as US Senator Bernie Sanders has proposed, would be a step in the wrong direction. The crisis of rising costs for higher education is a real one. But the solution must be better, more broadly funded, higher education, with more resources, and less reliance on personal debt. Turning the state into the single payer would create the wrong incentives, and would hamstring the broader development that still needs to take place: the education system needs to be opened up. And this will require truly innovative financing models in which individual payments will surely play some part.

## REFERENCES

Baily, M. N. and J. F. Kirkegaard (2004), *Transforming the European Economy*, Washington: Peterson Institution.

Clinton, H. (2017), *What Happened*, New York: Simon and Schuster.

Cooper, M. (2014), *Cut Adrift: Families in Insecure Times*, Berkeley: University of California Press.

Dinges, V., F. Urmetzer, V. Martinez, M. Zaki, and A. Neely (2015), *The Rise of Servitisation: Technologies That Will Make a Difference*, Cambridge: Cambridge Service Alliance.

Engel, M. (2017), 'Are We Witnessing the Strange, Lingering Death of Labour England?', *Financial Times*, 10 February, https://www.ft.com/content/bcfe0106-edee-11e6-930f-061b01e23655.

Eurostat (2017a), *Mortality and Life Expectancy Statistics*, Luxembourg: Eurostat, http://ec.europa.eu/eurostat/statistics-explained/index.php/ Mortality_and_life_expectancy_statistics.

Eurostat (2017b), *Household Composition Statistics*, Luxembourg: Eurostat, http://ec.europa.eu/eurostat/statistics-explained/index.php/Household_composition_statistics.

Eurostat (2017c), 'Euro Area International Trade in Good Surplus €18.9 billion', *Eurostat Newsrelease Euroindicators*, 15 December, http:// ec.europa.eu/eurostat/documents/2995521/8541742/6-15122017-AP-EN.pdf/8eda7d75-6b12-4ed7-b6d1-f5902df6ab6d.

Haskel, J. and S. Westlake (2017), *Capitalism Without Capital: the Rise of the Intangible Economy*, Princeton: Princeton University Press.

Hendeliowitz, J. (2008), *Danish Employment Policy: National Target Setting, Regional Performance Management and Local Deliver*, Copenhagen: Danish National Labour Market Authority.

Hofheinz, P. (2016), *Artificial Intelligence and Machine Learning: Challenge and Opportunity*, Brussels: Lisbon Council.

Hofheinz, P. (2017), *Making a Progressive Future of Work*, London: Policy Network, http://www.policy-network.net/pno_detail.aspx?ID=62 20&title=Making+a+progressive+future+of+work.

Hofheinz, P. and M. Mandel (2015), *Uncovering the Hidden Value of Digital Trade: Towards a 21st Century Agenda of Transatlantic Prosperity*, Brussels and Washington DC: Lisbon Council and Progressive Policy Institute.

Hofheinz, P. and D. Osimo (2017), *Making Europe a Data Economy: a New Framework for Free Movement of Data in the Digital Age*, Policy Brief, Brussels: Lisbon Council.

Lewin, T. (2013), 'Master's Degree is New Frontier of Study Online', *The New York Times*, 7 August, http://www.nytimes.com/2013/08/18/education/masters-degree-is-new-frontier-of-study-online.html.

Marx, K. (2014), *A Contribution to the Critique of Political Economy*, Fairford: Echo.

OECD (2015), *Data-Driven Innovation: Big Data for Growth and Well-Being*, Paris: OECD Publishing, http://www.oecd.org/sti/ieconomy/ data-driven-innovation.htm.

OECD (2017), *The Next Production Revolution: Implications for Government and Business*, Paris: OECD Publishing, http://dx.doi. org/10.1787/9789264271036-en.

Pappano, L. (2013), 'The Boy Genius of Ulan Bator', *The New York Times*, 13 September, http://www.nytimes.com/2013/09/15/magazine/the-boy-genius-of-ulan-bator.html?pagewanted=all.

Piketty, T. (2014), *Capital in the 21st Century*, Cambridge, MA: Harvard University Press.

Sachs, J. D. (2005), *The End of Poverty: Economic Possibilities for Our Time*, London: Penguin.

Shah, D. (2016), 'By the Numbers: MOOCs in 2016', *Class Central*, 25 December, https://www.class-central.com/report/mooc-stats-2016/.

Wolf, M. (2017a), 'Inequality is a Threat to Our Democracies', *Financial Times*, 19 December, https://www.ft.com/content/47e3e014-e3ea-11e7-97e2-916d4fbac0da.

Wolf, M. (2017b), 'The Challenges of the Disembodied Economy', *Financial Times*, 28 December, https://www.ft.com/content/a01e7262-d35a-11e7-a303-9060cb1e5f44.

World Inequality Lab (2018), *World Inequality Report 2018*, Paris: The World Inequality Lab.

# SHAPING STRUCTURAL CHANGE IN AN ERA OF NEW TECHNOLOGY

## Robert D. Atkinson

In recent years an idea has spread, repeated at countless conferences around the world and in op-eds, tweets, books and reports, that we are in a fourth industrial revolution, more transformative than any change in human history, that will, among other negative effects, lead to massive job losses and unemployment. Indeed, it seems you cannot attend Davos, a G20 summit, or a TED talk – one organised by the media organisation TED (Technology, Entertainment, Design) – without hearing the warnings. Robots and artificial intelligence (AI) are coming to put most of us out of work, except for a growing number of 'gig economy' workers who cobble together a meagre income using internet platforms dominated by large US tech companies like Uber and Airbnb.

The 'fourth industrialists' are wrong. This next wave of innovation will be modest, but progressive, particularly by enabling an uptick in productivity that, with the right policies, will lift incomes for workers around the world. It is therefore time to think clearly and deflate the growing techno-panic before policymakers actually implement many progress-killing ideas like taxing robots and implementing a universal basic income.

To think clearly about technological transformations in the labour market, it is important to examine two factors:

- What will be the nature and pace of the next technology wave?
- What are its likely impacts on jobs, employment relationships, income inequality, job quality, firm disruption and labour market disruption?

This essay examines these questions and concludes that policymakers should ignore techno-Cassandras and instead embrace this next wave of innovation, while at the same time ensuring that workers are well equipped to prosper from it.

## WE ARE NOT FACING A FOURTH INDUSTRIAL REVOLUTION

Pundits use a variety of terms to refer to the supposed technological transformation that is currently under way: 'the Second Machine Age', 'the Rise of the Robots', 'the Coming Singularity' and others. But the term that has caught on the most is 'the Fourth Industrial Revolution', which was coined by K. Schwab, head of the World Economic Forum. He breathlessly writes, "We stand on the brink of a technological revolution that will fundamentally alter the way we live, work, and relate to one another. In its scale, scope, and complexity, the transformation will be unlike anything humankind has experienced before" (Schwab 2016).

If this were true, it might be cause for concern, for it suggests that history provides no guide to the present. But in fact, it is not true. First, the next innovation wave is not the fourth, it is the sixth. In Schwab's sweeping but shallow historical telling, the first revolution of steam power was in the late 1700s and early 1800s. Then came electric power in the early 1900s. Then a few years ago digital technologies. Now the fourth is upon us.

For historians of technology such periodisation makes little sense. Those who follow on the work of Joseph Schumpeter and who study technological long waves generally agree that there have been in fact five waves to date:

- the first industrial revolution of the steam engine in the 1780s and 1790s
- the second revolution of iron in the 1840s and 1850s
- the third revolution of the 1890s and 1900s based on steel and electricity
- the fourth revolution in the 1950s and 1960s based on electromechanical and chemical technologies
- the fifth of our present era based on information technology and communications technology (Atkinson 2005).

According to this periodisation, a sixth wave will emerge, likely grounded in AI, robotics and perhaps nanotechnology and biotechnology, but not before an intervening period of relative stagnation of perhaps as long as 20 to 25 years, a period the global economy appears to be currently suffering through now.

This more accurate periodisation points to several important conclusions. First, despite all the breathless talk about us being in the midst of a fourth industrial revolution, the next technology wave is not here yet and will not be for at least a decade. This, more than any other factor, explains the slowdown in global productivity over the last decade (Atkinson 2016). The current digital technology system has reached a spot on the 'S-curve' where it is difficult for it to continue to drive productivity at a robust rate.

Second, there is no reason to believe that this coming technology wave will be any different in pace and magnitude than past waves. Each past wave led to improved technology in a few key areas (eg steam engines, railroads, steel, electricity, chemical processing and information technology) and these were then used by many sectors and processes. But none completely transformed all industries. Within manufacturing, for example, each wave led to important improvements, but there were still many processes that required human labour.

The next wave, grounded in AI and robotics, will be no different. While it will no doubt affect many industries and processes, many will remain largely untouched: think of fireman, pre-school teachers, massage therapists and trial lawyers. Moreover, this technology will replace some workers, as all pasts waves have done, but they will also augment others. AI, for example, will not replace doctors, but it will help them make better diagnoses and treatment decisions. This is why the Information Technology and Innovation Foundation (ITIF) estimated that only about 8% of jobs were at high risk of automation by 2024, and why the McKinsey Global Institute estimated just 5% were at such risk (Atkinson 2017; Chui, Manyika and Miremadi 2015).

In response to this argument, 'fourth industrialists' tell us that computer systems with powerful artificial general intelligence (AGI) are just around the corner. For them AGI will eclipse the full range of human ability – not only in routine manual or cognitive tasks, but also where more complex actions or decision-making are involved. But there is about as much chance of AGI emerging in the next century as the earth being destroyed by an asteroid. As MIT computer science professor R. Brooks (2015, 111) puts it:

> The fears of runaway AI systems either conquering humans or making them irrelevant aren't even remotely well grounded. Misled by suitcase words, people are making category errors in fungibility of capabilities – category errors comparable to seeing the rise of more efficient internal combustion engines and jumping to the conclusion that warp drives are just around the corner.

To be sure, there is progress in AI, including in machine learning, but these are still and will remain discrete capabilities, not general (recognising fraud in financial transactions, for example).

This relates to the second important issue: the pace of change from the technologies. If the wave increased economy-wide productivity by 75%, but it took 30 years to do so, this would mean a modest annual rate of growth of less than 3%, on a par with past periods in developed nations where labour force adjustment proceeded apace. But if this happens over 10 years, it surely would mean a much faster rate of dislocation. And here again, without evidence, the 'fourth industrialists' assert that the coming pace of change will be unprecedented.

But past long-wave transformations have taken at least 30 years to work their way through developed economies. There are three reasons for this relatively slow pace. First, new technology systems do not emerge fully formed. Early versions are less advanced than later ones. We say this with the electric motor in the early 1910s, where it took decades for improvements in power, price and quality to enable electric motors to be transformative. Going forward we will likely see this pattern in autonomous vehicles. The best (and quite expensive) current autonomy technology is at what is referred to as level 3, where drivers are still necessary for many functions. Level 5 cars that are affordable – where the human can go on a long, complicated trip asleep in the backseat – are decades away. Second, even though new technologies are better than old, old technologies are usually not completely scrapped, at least until their value is significantly depreciated. Trucking companies, for example, will not suddenly toss all their expensive semis in the junk yard. Third, not all organisations are first-adopters. Some adopt early, most adopt in the middle after the technology is de-risked, and the rest late.

So, yes, there will be a next wave of innovation, but it will not be an unprecedented tidal wave of transformation, but rather a moderate increase in innovation that will hopefully kick in by at least the mid-part of the next decade and will likely take at least 20 years to diffuse through economies, leading to an increase in economy-wide labour productivity to at best 3–4% growth per year.

## MAJOR ISSUES OF CONCERN

Notwithstanding that the next wave of innovation will not be unprecedented, there still could be negative impacts that policymakers need to prepare for and seek to mitigate. However, there will also be benefits, something 'fourth industrialists' usually ignore. Most importantly, the next wave will raise productivity growth rates. European productivity has been growing at anaemic rates for years, and in the UK it has virtually ceased. Without productivity growth to create a 'bigger pie' there is no way for European living standards to increase, especially given that the working age to old person ratio will drop from 3.5 today to 2.2 by 2040. But this does not mean that there may not be some negative impacts from the next wave of innovation. However, most of these fears are unwarranted and the main one, job dislocation, can and should be addressed by smart policies.

## UNEMPLOYMENT

Let us start with unemployment. The 'fourth industrialists' claim that the next wave will lead to massive job losses. Yet academic studies, historical data and logic all suggest that increased rates of productivity growth will not lead to higher unemployment (Atkinson and Wu 2017; Miller and Atkinson 2013). If anything, higher productivity growth in nations has been associated with lower rates of unemployment. The reason is simple and ignored by 'fourth industrialists': companies invest in process innovation (innovations to boost productivity) to cut costs, and because of competitive markets, they pass the vast share of those savings on to consumers in the form of price cuts, and some to workers in the form of higher wages. This added purchasing power is not buried; it is spent, and that spending creates new jobs. This dynamic is the same if productivity grows at 1% a year or 5%. Moreover, higher productivity growth creates a 'rational exuberance' where consumers and businesses feel more confident, and spend and invest more, leading to even more growth and job creation. So, the bottom line, absent ill-advised policies such as universal basic income to pay people for not working, and higher unemployment from the next technology wave will not happen (Atkinson 2016).

## GOOD JOBS

Even if unemployment rates will not rise, many ask whether the new jobs from the next wave will be good ones. But for two reasons this is not the right question to ask. First, the new jobs created will be largely related to how people spend their new added income, which will likely be on things like education, personal services, hotels and other lodging, entertainment, insurance, air travel, new cars and trucks, and major appliances. Some of this will create good jobs (eg education), others not so good jobs (eg personal services).

Second, rather than fret about what industries and occupations are growing and shrinking, policymakers should focus on raising productivity. That some jobs pay more than others is because they are more productive. A main reason janitors are paid less than software engineers is because the latter's output per hour is much higher. Therefore, the most important question regarding the mix of jobs is whether the next innovation wave will raise productivity.

It will be even better if the next wave raises productivity more in lower-wage occupations. If it does, there will be relatively fewer workers employed in low-wage occupations and the wages of everyone, including the remaining low-wage workers, will increase. To see how, imagine that the next technology wave boosts productivity by 25% only for the bottom 25% of wage earners. In the US this would allow the tasks these workers currently do to be performed by just 23.4 million workers, instead of the current 31.2 million. That means 7.8 million workers freed up, and as the savings from lower prices are spent, they could be employed doing other work. Because the prices of goods and services produced by low-wage workers would fall, this spending would be distributed in the same shares as it is currently, with 12.9% going on goods and services produced by workers in the first wage quartile, 17.6% in the second, 27.2% in the third, and 42.3% in the fourth.[1] As a result, most of those 7.8 million workers would see a wage increase as they move to higher-wage jobs. So too would all other workers because the real prices of goods and services supplied by low-wage workers would now be lower.

## LABOUR MARKET STATUS

Even if most people will be working, 'fourth industrialists' warn that an increasing share of workers will be contingent workers, doing work through platforms of American tech giants. To be sure, such 'gig economy' work has grown in the last decade, but much of this has been a fall-out of the Great Recession, when full-time, permanent work was scarce compared with today. So even with the growth of Uber, Airbnb and other work-sharing platforms, in 2015 only about 600,000 people were employed this way. Moreover, the share of the US workforce that is self-employed is at an all-time low of less than 7% (US Bureau of Labor Statistics 2016). There is no reason to believe that self-employment will grow in the future (see Arnold et al. this volume).

## INEQUALITY

'Fourth industrialists' warn that the next wave of innovation will bring massive growth in inequality. There is no doubt that income inequality has grown in Europe and the US, although by considerably less than Thomas Piketty would have us believe (Rose 2014). But very little of this growth has been from occupational changes driven by technology. The Economic Policy Institute finds that inequality did not increase because jobs in middle-wage occupations were eliminated by productivity gains (Bivens and Mishel 2015). Rather, virtually all the increase was within occupations, with some individuals making winner-take-all incomes at the expense of other workers in the same occupation.

It is important to realise that this had nothing to do with technological productivity and everything to do with socio-political factors. To take an example from US pro basketball, income inequality in the National Basketball Association (NBA) did not grow because technology eliminated middle-skilled players, it grew because of political economy factors, such as the introduction of free agency that allowed the LeBron J. and Steph Currys of the world to make vastly more money than the NBA stars of the 1970s. As J. Rothwell showed in a study for the Brookings Institution, the one-percenters are largely professionals and financiers: 6% of the top 1% of earners are in the financial services industry, 7% in law, 7% are doctors, 7% work in hospitals, and 4% are dentists (Rothwell 2016). This growth in earnings inequality has nothing to do with productivity.

Not convinced, 'fourth industrialists' will say the future will be different, especially if the next wave of innovation impacts lower-wage occupations more than higher-wage ones. That indeed is likely to happen, as ITIF found that there was a modest (−0.38) correlation between the risk of a US job being automated and the levels of education needed for the occupation (Atkinson 2017). But this pattern of automation would actually reduce, not increase, inequality. One reason is that 40% of adult European employees report that they have higher skills than are required to perform their current job. (European Commission Skills Panorama 2014; McGowan and Andrews 2015). These workers are in jobs that require fewer skills than they possess, presumably for most of them because there are not enough high-skilled jobs in the EU economy to employ them. If the next technology wave has a larger impact on eliminating low-wage jobs, this would by definition mean that a greater share of jobs would be in middle and higher-wage employment. And many European workers now in low-wage jobs have more than enough skills to move into these jobs. More fundamentally, even with robust minimum-wage levels and tax-based redistribution measures, it is extremely difficult to raise significantly the after-tax income levels of people working in low-productivity, often low-skill-level, industries for the simple reason that wages cannot exceed the output of the worker. Automating low-wage jobs will lead to not only fewer low-wage jobs and more middle- and higher-wage jobs, but usually higher output per worker in the remaining workforce, so those workers' wages can more easily be increased.

This positive outcome depends on relative price declines from automating low-income jobs so that demand for goods and services grows. But 'fourth industrialists' say there will be no price reductions because all the savings will go to the increasingly fewer owners. Owners of capital will somehow no longer have to compete on the basis of price and will be able to make exorbitant profits, immiserating the proletariat. But this scenario of a few 'robot owners' making 'trillions' while the rest of us are unemployed strains credibility. The reality is that if one 'robot owner' jacked up prices and made massive profits, another robot owner would lower prices to gain market share, just as this process of competition has worked since the beginning of market economies (see discussion of competition and innovation in Atkinson and Lind 2018).

## BUSINESS DISRUPTION

While unemployment will not increase from the next wave of innovation that does not mean that there will not be modest or even significant rates of businesses disruption. Just as internet platforms today are disrupting a range of industries, including private transport, retail, lodging, and telephone and cable TV, one could imagine (and hope for) emerging technologies disrupting even more industries. For example, 'fin-tech' could disrupt the traditional banking industry. But progressives, more than people in other political camps, should understand that government's role is not to protect businesses from risk; it is to protect consumers from business opposition to change. For-profit businesses, big or small, are more than happy to reap the profit upside of success, but are all too quick to run to government to protect them from the downside of competitive loss. Progressives should focus not on protecting companies from technology-based disruption, which fundamentally helps consumers, but on helping workers make transitions to new employment. Uber, Lyft and other car services are a case in point today. Too many governments want to protect incumbent taxi companies at the expense of consumers who benefit from better and cheaper car services.

## WORKER TRANSITION AND DISLOCATION

Of the concerns 'fourth industrialists' raise, the only valid and important one is how to help workers adjust to the inevitably, albeit modest, higher rates of labour market churn that will be coming. It is important to note, however, that – at least in the US – the rate of labour market churn (defined as jobs created in occupations plus jobs eliminated in other occupations) has been at an historic low over the last two decades (Atkinson and Wu 2017). But as the next wave of innovation boosts productivity that rate is sure to increase somewhat.

One proposal to address this is the introduction of a universal basic income (UBI). Under this widely touted scheme, the state would somehow take money from somewhere and write monthly cheques to all adults, whether they are working or not, poor or rich. This allegedly would establish a stable floor on which everyone would build their own brighter future. This, however, is one idea progressives should loudly decry. UBI would lead to the very thing its advocates warn us technology will bring: large-scale unemployment as the government incentivises workers to be idle instead of helping pave pathways for those displaced by technology to find success in new jobs.

To be sure, the alternative should not be a return to the Hobbesian world of the 1800s when if a worker lost his job he was on his own. Progressives need to ensure that there is temporary income support for workers who lose their jobs through no fault of their own. On this score Europe is both better and worse off than the US. It is better in that it provides laid-off workers with more income support. It is worse in that at least in some European nations workers are eligible for unemployment income support for far too long, which not only encourages them to stay out of the labour market and have their skills atrophy, but by reducing the purchasing power of employed workers (who bear higher taxes), it reduces the demand for workers, leading to higher unemployment.

The lesson for Europe and the US is to copy the Nordic countries' flexicurity model, which ties benefits to proving that workers are either actively looking for work or are in a certified training programme. Progressives should also advocate for a system of lifelong-learning accounts similar to what France recently introduced while Emmanuel Macron was economy minister and Myriam El Khomri was labour minister. These accounts can be drawn down to pay for retraining throughout the working life (see Weber this volume). Progressives should also push to disrupt the traditional higher education system, which has become too expensive and too inflexible (Kennedy, Castro and Atkinson 2017).

These and other steps to ease transitions are important because if Europe is going to have any hope of its voters embracing change and innovation, governments needs to do more to reduce employment risk for workers. At the same time, if Europe is going to reap the benefits of the next innovation wave, the last thing progressives want to do is stoke people's unwarranted fears that their jobs are on the fourth industrial wave chopping block from all powerful 'Terminator-like' robots or support completely misguided policy proposals like taxing and regulating robots to slow their adoption. While slowing innovation runs counter to progressives' policy goals of ensuring a growing standard of living for workers, it also runs counter to their political goals. When centre-left parties have succeeded in Europe or the US they have done so when they stood for a vision of growth, widely shared, not limited growth with massive redistribution.

In short, the vision should be innovation, widely shared. And with the right policies the vision can very well become the reality.

## NOTE

1. This is based on the share of wage and salary income by quartile.

# REFERENCES

Atkinson, R. D. (2005), *The Past and Future of America's Economy: Long Waves of Innovation that Power Cycles of Growth*, Cheltenham: Edward Elgar.

Atkinson, R. D. (2016), 'Think Like an Enterprise: Why Nations Need Comprehensive Productivity Strategies', Information Technology and Innovation Foundation, May, http://www2.itif.org/2016-think-like-an-enterprise.pdf?_ga=2.112124294.382854264.1506957444-487073861 .1494271158.

Atkinson, R. D. (2017), 'Unfortunately, Technology Will Not Eliminate Many Jobs', *Innovation Files*, 7 August, https://itif.org/ publications/2017/08/07/unfortunately-technology-will-not-eliminate-many-jobs.

Atkinson, R. D. and M. Lind (2018), *Big is Beautiful: Debunking the Mythology of Small Business*. Cambridge, Mass, and London: MIT Press, forthcoming.

Atkinson, R. D. and J. Wu (2017), 'False Alarmism: Technological Disruption and the US Labor Market, 1850–2015', Information Technology and Innovation Foundation, https://itif.org/publications/2017/05/08/false-alarmism-technological-disruption-and-us-labor-market-1850–2015.

Bivens, J. and L. Mishel (2015), 'Understanding the Historic Divergence Between Productivity and a Typical Worker's Pay: Why It Matters and Why It's Real', Economic Policy Institute, http://www.epi.org/publication/understanding-the-historic-divergencebetween-productivity-and-a-typical-workers-pay-why-it-matters-and-why-its-real/.

Brooks, R. A. (2015), 'Mistaking Performance for Competence', in J. Brockman (ed.), *What to Think About Machines That Think*, New York: Harper Perennial.

Chui, M., J. Manyika and M. Miremadi (2015), 'Four Fundamentals of Workplace Automation', McKinsey & Company, November, http:// www.mckinsey.com/business-functions/digital-mckinsey/our-insights/ four-fundamentals-of-workplace-automation.

European Commission Skills Panorama (2014), 'Skills Under-Utilisation Across Countries in 2014', http://skillspanorama.cedefop.europa.eu/en/ indicators/skills-under-utilisation.

Kennedy, J., D. Castro and R. D. Atkinson (2016), 'Why It's Time to Disrupt Higher Education by Separating Learning from Credentialing',

Information Technology and Innovation Foundation, https://itif.org/publications/2016/08/01/why-its-time-disrupt-higher-education-separating-learning-credentialing.

McGowan, M. A. and D. Andrews (2015), 'Skill Mismatch and Public Policy in OECD Countries', OECD Economics Department Working Paper 1210, 28 April, http://www.oecd.org/eco/growth/Skill-mismatch-and-public-policy-in-OECD-countries.pdf.

Miller, B. and R. D. Atkinson (2013), 'Are Robots Taking Our Jobs, or Making Them', Information Technology and Innovation Foundation, http://www2.itif.org/2013-are-robots-taking-jobs.pdf.

Rose, S. J. (2014), 'Was JFK wrong? Does Rising Productivity No Longer Lead to Substantial Middle-Class Income Gains?' Information Technology and Innovation Foundation, http://www2.itif.org/2014-rising-productivity-middle-class.pdf.

Rothwell, J. (2016), 'Why Elites Want More Competition for Everyone Except Themselves', Evonomics, 2 April, http://evonomics.com/why-elites-want-more-competition-foreveryone-except-themselves/.

Schwab, K. (2016), 'The Fourth Industrial Revolution: What It Means, How to Respond', World Economic Forum, 14 January, https://www.weforum.org/agenda/2016/01/the-fourth-industrial-revolution-what-it-means-and-how-to-respond/.

US Bureau of Labor Statistics (2016), 'Current Employment Statistics, Employment Level – All Industries Self Employed, Unincorporated, and Total Non-Farm, All Employees'.

# B

# The changing face of work in the digital age

# THE IMPACT OF ARTIFICIAL INTELLIGENCE ON EMPLOYMENT

## Georgios Petropoulos[1]

Technological development, and in particular digitalisation, has major implications for labour markets. Assessing its impact will be crucial for developing policies that promote efficient labour markets for the benefit of workers, employers and societies as a whole.

Rapid technological progress and innovation can threaten employment. Such a concern is not new but dates back at least to the 1930s, when John Maynard Keynes postulated his 'technological unemployment theory' – technological change causes loss of jobs (Keynes 1937).

Technological innovations can affect employment in two main ways:

- by directly displacing workers from tasks they were previously performing (displacement effect)
- by increasing the demand for labour in industries or jobs that arise or develop due to technological progress (productivity effect).

Autor, Levy and Murnane (2003) stress that technology can replace human labour in routine tasks, whether manual or cognitive, but (as yet) cannot replace human labour in non-routine tasks. Goos and Manning (2007) argue that the impact of technology leads to rising relative demand in well-paid skilled jobs, which typically require non-routine cognitive skills, and rising relative demand in low-paid, least-skilled jobs, which typically require non-routine manual skills.

At the same time, demand for 'middling' jobs, which have typically required routine manual and cognitive skills, will fall. The authors call this process job polarisation. Acemoglu and Autor (2011) found similar results for the US, while Darvas and Wolff (2016) report such developments for a selection of EU countries: France, Germany, Italy, Spain, Sweden and the UK. In all these countries, the number of high-education jobs such as managers, engineers and health professionals is growing, while the number of middle-education jobs (clerks, machine operators, assemblers) is declining. By contrast, the number of low-education service occupations, such as shop workers, which are non-standard and difficult to replace by automation, is growing. A key conclusion is that technology was incorporated into the subset of core job tasks previously performed by middle-skill workers, causing substantial change. The quality of human capital also plays a crucial role. The ability of individuals to use the technological advances for the benefit of their work requires developing particular digital skills through well-designed policies. This underlines the importance of using appropriate instruments to ensure that workers are well prepared to harness the disruptive forces of digital technologies.

In the last decade platforms emerged that contributed to increased connectivity between individuals. For example, using this connectivity, peer providers of durable goods and services can trade online with individuals using collaborative economy platforms. A key common characteristic of collaborative economy models – despite a great deal of variety – is that they provide an economic opportunity for individuals and small enterprises to trade their under-used assets with other individuals through intermediaries that match supply and demand in an efficient way with the help of information technologies. In many cases, this opportunity to individual suppliers is only provided through collaborative platforms, as the supply of goods and services through other channels is subject to licensing and other regulatory barriers. Automation in shopping through ecommerce is another example, with the sector experiencing annual growth of 22% in Europe.[2] The benefits of information technologies increase demand for online retail goods and this in turn leads to an increased overall employment in retail.

However, looking ahead, a new wave of automation and advanced machine-learning techniques is on its way, in which intelligent machines will be increasingly capable of carrying out high-skill and possibly non-routine tasks. Moving from the efficiency gains in online trading to the extensive use of artificial intelligent systems in our industrial production, concerns about the potential displacement of labour emerge. The real question then becomes: which of the two labour market effects – displacement or productivity – will dominate in the artificial intelligence (AI) era?[3]

A first approach to answer this question is to examine the impact of technological breakthroughs on labour markets in previous industrial revolutions (Soete this volume). For example, the introduction of automobiles in daily life led to a decline in horse-related jobs, but new industries also emerged, with a net positive impact on employment. The automobile industry itself grew fast, creating many new jobs, but other sectors also grew because of the growing number of vehicles on the roads, and many new jobs in the motel and fast-food industries arose to serve motorists and truck drivers.

The Economist (2016) reports further case studies that show similar patterns. In general, past industrial revolutions suggest that in the short run the displacement effect may dominate. But in the longer run, when markets and society are fully adapted to major automation shocks, the productivity effect can dominate and have a positive impact on employment.

But how reliable is this approach? Researchers from the McKinsey Global Institute estimate that the disruption of society caused by AI is happening 10 times faster and at 300 times the scale of the industrial revolution of the late 18th and early 19th centuries, and is therefore having roughly 3,000 times the impact (Dobbs, Manyika and Woetzel 2015).

Moreover, the main engine of technological progress in the AI era is the continuous development of deep machine-learning techniques that use the function and complexity of the human brain as a model for design (see Petropoulos 2017b); for relevant definitions and analysis see Box 1. Machines are trained to be intelligent, which can have additional implications for the workforce.

## BOX 1. AN INTRODUCTION TO MACHINE LEARNING

Machine learning enables computer programs to acquire knowledge and skills, and even improve their own performance. Big data provides the raw material for machine learning, and offers examples that computer programs can use for 'practise' in order to learn, exercise and ultimately perform their assigned tasks more efficiently.

The idea of intelligent machines arose in the early 20th century. From the beginning, the idea of 'human-like' intelligence was key. Following Vannevar Bush's seminal work from 1945, where he proposed "a system which amplifies people's own knowledge and understanding", Alan Turing asked "Can a machine think?" In his famous 1950 imitation game, Turing proposed a test of a machine's ability to exhibit intelligent behaviour equivalent to that of a human.

In principle, machine learning follows Turing's recommendation of teaching a machine to perform specific tasks as if it were a child. By building a machine with sufficient computational resources, offering training examples from real world data and by designing specific algorithms and tools that define a learning process, rather than specific data manipulations, machines can improve their performance through learning by doing, inferring patterns and checking hypotheses.

At the core of this learning process are artificial neural networks, inspired by the networks of neurons in the human brain. A simple artificial neural network is organised in layers. Data is introduced to the network through an input layer. Then come the hidden multiple layers in which information is processed and finally an output layer where results are released. Each neuron within the network is connected to many others, as both inputs and outputs, but the connections are not equal. They are weighted such that a neuron's different outward connections fire at different levels of input activation. A network with many hidden layers can combine, sort or divide signals by applying different weights to them and passing the result to the next layer. The number of hidden layers demonstrates the ability of the network to detect increasingly subtle features of the input data. The training of the network takes place by adjusting neurons' connection weights, so that the network gives the desired response when presented with particular inputs.

The goal of the neural network is to solve problems in the same way that a hypothesised human brain would, albeit without any 'conscious' codified awareness of the rules and patterns that have been inferred from the data. Modern neural network projects typically work with a few thousand to a few million neural units and millions of connections. They are called deep because of the multiple intermediate hidden layers they have. However, deep neural networks are still several orders of magnitude less complex than the human brain and closer to the computing power of a worm.

Deep neural networks have proven very effective. There are several examples of games and competitions in which machines can now beat humans. By now, machines have topped the best humans at most games traditionally held up as measures of human intellect, including chess (recall for example the 1997 game between IBM's Deep Blue and the champion Garry Kasparov), Scrabble, Othello and Jeopardy! Even in more complex games, machines seem to be quickly improving their performance through their learning process. In March 2016, the AlphaGo computer program from the AI start up DeepMind beat Lee Sedol at a five-game match of Go – the oldest board game, invented in China more than 2,500 years ago. However, many of these machines are programmed to perform specific tasks, narrowing the scope of their operation. Humans remain superior in performing general tasks and using experience acquired in one task to deliver another.

A second approach would be to assess the risk of occupations and tasks to be automated in the next decades because of AI systems. Here the literature has focused on the feasibility of automating existing jobs given current and presumed technological advances (Arnold et al. this volume). Frey and Osborne (2013, 2017) famously claimed that 47% of US occupations were at risk of being automated "over some unspecified number of years, perhaps a decade or two" (Frey and Osborne 2017, 265). Bowles (2014) repeated these calculations for the European labour market, and found that on average 54% of EU jobs are at risk of computerisation. By contrast, Arntz, Gregory and Zierahn (2016, 2017) argue that a major limitation of Frey and Osborne is that they focus on deriving predictions over occupations as being threatened by automation rather than tasks. Their criticism is that in this way Frey and Osborne overestimate the automation risks. By using information on task content of jobs at the individual level they conclude that only 9% of US jobs are potentially automatable.

These studies can be viewed as feasibility tests on the potential impact of AI and focus on the displacement effect of automation. Assessing the impact of the productivity effect – the potential for new machines to increase employment – is much more challenging. Bessen's (2017) empirical research found that computer technology is associated with job growth that is particularly observable in non-manufacturing industries. At the same time there are potential sector spillover effects: as Acemoglu and Restrepo (2016) illustrate in their theoretical model, the aggregate labour market impacts of new technologies depend not only on the industries in which they operate, but also on adjustment in other parts of the economy. For example, other sectors and occupations might expand to absorb the labour freed from the tasks that are now performed by machines.

That would require adopting an equilibrium approach because what is technologically feasible does not necessarily correspond to the equilibrium impact of automation on employment and wages. For example, we need to take into account that firms' market strategies and investments are endogenous to technology shocks: Even if the presumed technological advances materialise, there is no guarantee that firms would choose to automate; that would depend on the costs of substituting machines for labour and how much wages change in response to this threat.

That brings us to the third approach of assessing the impact of AI on employment. A common characteristic of most of research papers that are moving towards this equilibrium approach is that all focus on one automated technology, the industrial robots and their impact on employment. This is because of the existence of good quality data on the penetration of industrial robots in the main industries in major economies around the world.

An industrial robot is defined as "an automatically controlled, reprogrammable, multipurpose manipulator programmable in three or more axes, which can be either fixed in place or mobile for use in industrial automation applications" (International Federation of Robotics 2016). Following this definition, a classification test would have required a clear answer to the following three questions:

- Does it have multiple purposes?
- Can it be reprogrammed to perform another task?
- Does it require a human control for performing its task?

While our coffee machine or the elevator at our home building does not pass this classification test, fully autonomous machines that do not need a human operator and that can be programmed to perform several manual tasks such as welding, painting, assembling, handling materials or packaging are classified as industrial robots.

Figure 7.1 presents the number of operational industrial robots per thousands of workers in China, the EU and the US. The EU so far has been the region with the most robots in operation, followed by the US while China is behind.

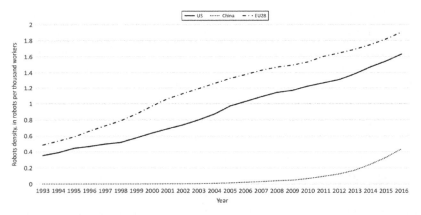

**Figure 7.1    Robot density in China, EU and US.** *Source*: Data from International Labor Organisation (2017), IFR (2016).

Figure 7.2 shows how the operational industrial robots per thousands of workers are distributed in different sectors in EU countries. So far, the EU automotive industry has introduced by far the most industrial robots in its production process, followed by the plastic and chemicals sector.

Graetz and Michaels (2015) estimate that between 1990 and 2005 the price of industrial robots in six major developed economies fell by approximately one-half or one-fifth if we adjust for the quality of robots. Moreover, between 1993 and 2007, the stock of robots per million hours worked increased by more than 150%, from 0.58 to 1.48, in 17 countries of the sample, leading to significant productivity gains. The study also finds that in these countries increased use of robots per hour worked from 1993 to 2007 raised the annual

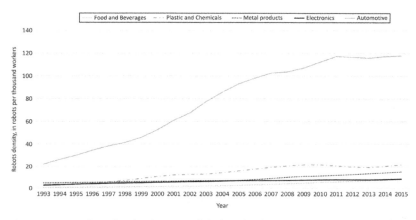

**Figure 7.2    Robot density in several industries in Europe.** *Source:* Datafrom EUKLEMS (2017), IFR (2016).

growth of labour productivity by about 0.37 percentage points. When considering an industry-country panel specification, they find that robots appear to reduce the share of hours worked by low-skilled workers relative to middle-skilled and high-skilled workers, they do not polarise the labour market, but appear to hurt the relative position of low-skilled workers rather than middle-skilled ones. Nevertheless, the use of robots per hour worked appears to boost total factor productivity and average wages. No significant impact on labour shares is found.

In a more recent study, Acemoglu and Restrepo (2017) used data in the post-1990 era to show that 1 additional robot per 1,000 workers reduces the US employment-to-population ratio by 0.18–0.34% and wages by 0.25–0.5%. When interpreting these results we should not forget that there are still few industrial robots in the US economy; if the spread of robots proceeds over the next two decades as expected by experts such as Brynjolfsson, McAfee and Ford, its aggregate implications for employment will be much larger (Brynjolfsson and McAfee 2012; Ford 2015). The novel element of their study is that they adopt a more regional approach than the industry-country panel approach of Graetz and Michaels (2015). As the labour force competes with robots for production, they exploit the heterogeneity in both local labour distribution across industries and national change in the use of robots to refine their results. They can therefore estimate the impact of industrial robots' penetration in local labour markets. Their negative result suggests that the displacement effect dominates the productivity effect of operation industrial robots. In addition, positive spillover effects are very modest. The employment effects of robots are most pronounced in manufacturing, particularly in industries most exposed to robots; in routine manual, blue-collar, assembly and related occupations; and for workers without a college education.

Dauth et al. (2017) repeat the empirical exercise of Acemoglu and Restrepo (2017) for Germany but they do not find any significant negative impact of robots. While industrial robots have a negative impact on employment in the German manufacturing sector, there is a positive and significant spillover effect as labour in the non-manufacturing sectors increases and overall counterbalances the negative effect.

The focus of these studies is on the impact of industrial robots on employment so far, without making any predictions for the future. These predictions would require the imposition of specific assumptions whose validity cannot be assessed with certainty.

While this allows for a more reliable assessment of the impact, we should keep in mind that the era of AI is in its early stages and the penetration of robots in our economy and industrial production is expected to significantly rise as a consequent of the rapid, ongoing technological progress. This suggests that existing studies using this third approach are able to capture only the onset of the AI era and not its full deployment. If indeed short-run and long-run effects are not in the same direction, these studies may only be able to capture some parts of the short-run effects.

Industrial robots are just one of the AI technologies that have been developed. At the forefront of the fourth industrial revolution will be a connected framework of machines that communicate with each other. Such connectivity is expected to be a major step forward, increasing the efficiency gains in AI markets and services. Completing a full economic framework for the impact of AI on labour markets before these new developments are deployed is a difficult task.

These future-facing studies do not reach a consensus over the potential impact of automation on labour markets. The fact that it is difficult to predict the exact impact of AI makes it complex to frame a policy response. But some society-level reaction is surely needed. It is therefore necessary to initiate an open consultation of all involved parties, to define our approach towards the AI era. This process should have several steps:

1. Ensure that society, and particularly policymakers, politicians and business leaders, understands what AI is and its potential for modern economies.
2. Define a framework of rules for the operation of machines and AI automated systems. These must go far beyond Asimov's famous three laws of robotics. The Civil Law Rules on Robotics proposed by the European Parliament can also motivate social dialogue about issues related to liability, safety, security and privacy in the coming AI era. Tegmark (2017) identifies numerous challenges on these matters, which should be addressed adequately. Adopting clear rules based on a good understanding of this new era could make the transition easier and mitigate potential concerns. However, adopting rules without good understanding and knowledge of how this new technology will be implemented (first step) would be counterproductive.
3. Design and implement those policies that will help us to accommodate new technology possibilities. Education and training programmes should be carefully redesigned so that they provide the right qualifications for workers to interact and work efficiently alongside machines and boost relevant digital skills. This might reduce potential displacement concerns as jobs typically consist of a number of distinct but interrelated tasks. In most cases, only some of these tasks are likely to be suitable for automation. By preparing human labour to interact effectively and efficiently with machines, we can maximise the productivity gains from the

interrelated tasks. That could potentially lead to the development of new jobs or occupations that will result from this cooperation and the advancements of the technology. Initiatives to prepare effectively human labour for this new era will require the close interaction of authorities and institutions with major technological firms which have both the knowhow and the capacity to contribute to the training. Improved instruments for job search assistance and job reallocation could also be beneficial and would mitigate concerns associated with the displacement effect.

However, we should not rush into a response (see Atkinson this volume). The time for policy will come, but at the moment we are still in the early stages of understanding the potential of AI and the various ways it might impact our economy. To deepen this understanding, we should promote further social dialogue among all the involved parties (researchers, policymakers, industry representatives and trade unions, politicians and so on). This is a vital first step to better grasp the challenges and opportunities of this new industrial revolution. And although we should not rush to conclusions, we should not adopt a passive attitude. We must act swiftly to assess and understand the implications of AI. The speed with which technology advances may introduce disruptive forces in the market earlier than some people expect.

## NOTES

1. This chapter is an updated version of my article 'Do We Understand the Impact of Artificial Intelligence on Employment?' published by Bruegel (Petropoulos 2017a). The superb research assistance by Nicolas Moës is gratefully acknowledged.

2. See Marcus and Petropoulos (2016) for further statistics and discussion.

3. AI refers to intelligence exhibited by machines. Hence, the AI era refers to that period in time in which machines equipped with deep learning techniques that are based on neural network architecture (see Box 1) will be able to perform tasks that require some form of intelligence, in an automatic way and without requiring human intervention.

# REFERENCES

Acemoglu, D. and D. Autor (2011), 'Skills, Tasks and Technologies: Implications for Employment and Earnings', in O. Ashenfelter and D. Card (eds), *Handbook of Labor Economics*, vol. 4, Amsterdam: Elsevier.

Acemoglu, D. and P. Restrepo (2016), *The Race Between Machine and Man: Implications of Technology for Growth, Factor Shares and Employment*, NBER Working Paper 22252, http://www.nber.org/papers/w22252.pdf.

Acemoglu, D. and P. Restrepo (2017), *Robots and Jobs: Evidence from US Labor Markets*, NBER Working Paper 23285, http://www.nber.org/papers/w23285.pdf.

Arntz, M., T. Gregory and U. Zierahn (2016), *The Risk of Automation for Jobs in OECD Countries: a Comparative Analysis*, Social, Employment and Migration Working Paper 189, Paris: Organisation for Economic Co-operation and Development.

Arntz, M., T. Gregory and U. Zierahn (2017), 'Revisiting the Risk of Automation', *Economics Letters*, 159: 157–60.

Autor, D., F. Levy and R. J. Murnane (2003), 'The Skill Content of Recent Technological Change: an Empirical Exploration', *Quarterly Journal of Economics*, 118(4): 1279–333, http://www.jstor.org/stable/pdf/25053940.pdf.

Bessen, J. E. (2017), *Automation and Jobs: When Technology Boosts Employment*, Boston University School of Law, Law and Economics Research Paper 17-09.

Bowles, J. (2014), 'The Computerisation of European Jobs', blog, 24 July, Bruegel, http://bruegel.org/2014/07/the-computerisation-of-european-jobs/.

Brynjolfsson, E. and A. McAfee (2012), *Race Against the Machine: How the Digital Revolution is Accelerating Innovation, Driving Productivity, and Irreversibly Transforming Employment and the Economy*, Lexington, Massachusetts: Digital Frontier Press.

Bush V. (July 1945), 'As We May Think', The Atlantic https://www.theatlantic.com/magazine/archive/1945/07/as-we-may-think/303881/

Darvas, Z. and G. B. Wolff (2016), *An Anatomy of Inclusive Growth in Europe*, Brussels: Bruegel, http://bruegel.org/2016/10/an-anatomy-of-inclusive-growth-in-europe/.

Dauth, W., S. Findeisen, J. Südekum and N. Woessner (2017), *German Robots: the Impact of Industrial Robots on Workers*, CEPR Discussion Paper DP12306.

Dobbs, R., J. Manyika and J. Woetzel (2015), *The Four Global Forces Breaking all the Trends*, London, San Francisco, Shanghai: McKinsey Global Institute.

Ford, M. (2015), *The Rise of the Robots: Technology and the Threat of Mass Unemployment*, London: Oneworld Publications.

Frey, C. and M. Osborne (2013), *The Future of Employment: How Susceptible Are Jobs To Computerisation?*, Oxford: Oxford Martin School, https://www.oxfordmartin.ox.ac.uk/downloads/academic/The_Future_of_Employment.pdf.

Frey, C. B. and M. A. Osborne (2017), 'The Future of Employment: How Susceptible Are Jobs To Computerisation?', *Technological Forecasting and Social Change*, 114: 254–80.

Goos, M. and A. Manning (2007), 'Lousy and Lovely Jobs: the Rising Polarization of Work in Britain', *The Review of Economics and Statistics*, 89(1): 118–33.

Graetz, G. and G. Michaels (2015), *Robots at Work*, CEPS Discussion Paper 1335, London: London School of Economics, http://cep.lse.ac.uk/pubs/download/dp1335.pdf.

International Federation of Robotics (2016), *Industrial Robots: Definition and Classification*. Frankfurt am Main: International Federation of Robotics.

Keynes, J. M. (1937), 'The General Theory of Employment', *Quarterly Journal of Economics*, 51(2): 209–23.

Marcus, J. S. and G. Petropoulos (2016), 'Cross-Border Parcel Delivery Prices: Intuitions drawn from the World of Telecommunications', paper for the 27th European Regional Conference of the International Telecommunications Society (ITS).

Petropoulos, G. (2017a), 'Do We Understand the Impact of Artificial Intelligence on Employment?', Bruegel blogpost, http://bruegel.org/2017/04/do-we-understand-the-impact-of-artificial-intelligence-on-employment/

Petropoulos, G. (2017b), 'Machines that Learn to Do, and Do to Learn: What is Artificial Intelligence?', Bruegel, 27 April, http://bruegel.org/2017/04/machines-that-learn-to-do-and-do-to-learn-what-is-artificial-intelligence/.

Tegmark, Max (2017), *Life 3.0. Being Human in the Age of Artificial Intelligence*, New York: Knopf.

The Economist (2016), 'Automation and Anxiety', *The Economist*, 25 June, http://www.economist.com/news/special-report/21700758-will-smarter-machines-cause-mass-unemployment-automation-and-anxiety.

# GAME-CHANGING TECHNOLOGIES FOR EUROPEAN MANUFACTURING

Enrique Fernández-Macías[1]

The manufacturing sector has always been at the forefront of technical innovation. Since the industrial revolution, its development has been punctuated by leaps driven by the successive introduction of radical technological breakthroughs. As a result, the growth of productivity in manufacturing has been consistently above that of other sectors, creating the structural foundations of the abundance of material goods currently enjoyed in advanced economies. But such a process of creative destruction also has a profoundly disruptive side, as reflected in the socio-economic difficulties historically faced by workers whose skills became obsolete by the introduction of new technologies, or by the existence of entire geographic areas scarred by the effects of industrial restructuring.

It is therefore important to identify the potential effects of disruptive technologies in the manufacturing sector at the earliest opportunity. This will help us to nurture these technologies to maximise the potential benefits, but also to minimise the wider social disruptions that they may provoke.

With these objectives, Eurofound (2018) recently carried out a detailed qualitative study of five technological breakthroughs, all of which are still in their infancy but have the potential to fundamentally transform the future of manufacturing in Europe. For each of these five technologies an international research team[2] identified and interviewed a number of key informants (mostly scientists and entrepreneurs, but also social partners and government representatives), and carried out regional and company case studies, in order to gather original information on the potential effects of these technologies on the production process, work and employment.

These were the five technologies studied:

- advanced industrial robotics (AIR) – involving machines designed to perform industrial tasks automatically, with high programmability and the capacity to interact with their environment thanks to the use of digital sensors
- additive manufacturing (AM) – involving digitally controlled devices that add layer on layer of material(s) to create objects from 3D digital models
- industrial internet of things (IIOT) – the use of connected sensors attached to different objects throughout the production process to feed live data to central computers
- electric vehicles (EVs) – vehicles whose main system of propulsion depends on (externally generated) electricity rather than fuel
- industrial biotech (IB) – the use of biological processes of living organisms for industrial purposes, drawing on recent scientific insights such as systems genomics and metabolomics.

The first three technologies (AIR, AM and IIOT) involve innovations in the manufacturing production process, and have a very wide applicability across most manufacturing sectors. In contrast, the other two technologies (EV and IB) concern innovations of specific products (and related processes), and have a more narrow applicability to particular sectors. All of them are in one way or another part of the ongoing digital revolution in manufacturing (sometimes labelled Industry 4.0), because they are either entirely driven by core digital technologies – microprocessors, internet, sensors, rendering devices and digital algorithms (AIR, AM and IIOT) – or largely facilitated by them (EV and IB).

## EFFECTS IN THE PRODUCTION PROCESS

If we visualise the typical value chain in manufacturing as a line going from research and development to (after-sales) services,[3] the impact of each of the technologies studied can be associated with some particular stages:

- AIR would have the biggest impact on (inbound and outbound) logistics and production, the core activities within the manufacturing process. Decades (or even centuries) of automation have already reduced the amount of labour input (and contribution to value added) of these activities in manufacturing, which limits the potential further impact of AIR in this sector (in contrast with the service sector, where the degree of automation is still low).
- IIOT can have a significant impact on all downstream stages in the manufacturing process, from inbound logistics to after-sales services. In core production activities, it can boost efficiency by massively increasing the transparency and control of the system. In marketing and services, it can expand significantly the range of possibilities because it allows for the maintenance of a remote connection to the final product.
- AM would have a significant impact on the upstream stages, especially research and development and design, but also on logistics and production. In many ways AM can be considered the most radical of the technologies studied, since it could theoretically collapse the entire manufacturing process into a single step (that of physically rendering a 3D model).

Since the other two technologies (EV and IB) are product rather than process innovations, they cannot be linked to a particular stage of the manufacturing process.

What are the potential effects of these technologies on the manu-facturing production process? According to the interviews and case studies carried out, they can be summarised around four key concepts:

- the increasing centrality of (digital) information
- mass customisation
- servitisation
- increased labour efficiency.

## THE INCREASING CENTRALITY OF (DIGITAL) INFORMATION

As previously mentioned, the five technologies studied are part of a broader trend of increasing diffusion and widespread application of digital technologies to all kinds of economic activity. As a result of these changes, information becomes the key source of value, with physical production itself becoming increasingly secondary. The clearest example of this effect is AM, which dematerialises the entire manufacturing process except for the final step of physically rendering a digital model. Similarly, it is the information provided by IIOT sensors (and the capacity to process that information) that can optimise manufacturing processes and add further services to the products, while AIR go beyond traditional robots because of their capacity to process autonomously information from their environment and interact with it.

## MASS CUSTOMISATION

In contrast with (pre-digital) Fordist mass production (which was very cost-effective but inherently rigid), these technologies open up the possibility for much more flexible production processes – thanks to algorithmic control and artificial intelligence (AI) – without compromising on cost effectiveness or standardisation. AIR are algorithmically controlled general-purpose machines that can be easily reprogrammed to carry out different tasks in production. In fact, with AI they can interact and respond autonomously to changes in their environment (see Petropoulos this volume). By interconnecting all objects of the production process under centralised algorithmic supervision, IIOT systems also increase the flexibility of the process without hampering standardisation. Real-time centralised control and interconnectivity allow a much faster reaction to problems, but also a relatively fast reprogramming of production in response to changes in demand or other factors. Finally, AM reduces the production process to a simple step, the 3D printing of the digital model, with remarkably few restrictions in the physical configuration of the resulting object but a high consistency in quality.

## SERVITISATION

The studied technologies tend to reduce the importance of production and logistics in manufacturing value added, while increasing that of research and development and design on the one hand and marketing and services on the other. IIOT in particular allows companies to maintain a line of communication and even control of the product after the sale, which facilitates the provision of after-sales services (the product can end up becoming just a platform for those services). In more general terms, these technologies involve the gradual replacement of manufacturing as traditionally understood (as the physical production of things) by a type of economic activity that is closer to the traditional concept of services. This process has become known as 'servitisation'.

## INCREASED RESOURCE EFFICIENCY

These technologies provide much richer information on every step and aspect of the industrial process as well as more precise control over it, which is likely to lead to a considerably more efficient use of materials and energy in production. This has the potential to provide big environmental benefits, and was identified by several interviewees as a potential driver for the adoption of these technologies in the future in Europe, in the context of growing environmental concerns.

When combined, the benefits of these technologies on the production process could multiply, so the use of any of these technologies in an industrial process makes the introduction of the others much more likely.

## EFFECTS ON WORK AND EMPLOYMENT

In the course of interviews carried out for this study, scientists, entrepreneurs and social partners confirmed that these changes to the production process were also likely to have an impact on work and employment.

The prognosis for employment numbers seems relatively clear: these technologies – particularly AIR, IIOT and AM, which cut across different processes and sectors – would have labour-saving effects, and could thus contribute further to a structural decline of employment in manufacturing that has been observed in most European countries for decades. In addition, structural changes in employment can be expected (see Arnold et al. this volume).

First, we are likely to see an upgrading of occupations. These technologies tend to reduce the amount of labour input necessary in production line work, but increase the amount of labour input required in (higher-skilled) engineering, such as design or research and development, and business tasks such as marketing or services. Second, the skills requirements of those occupations are also likely to change, most obviously requiring a higher level of information and communications technology (ICT) competence. Data analysis, network management and security are likely to become core skills for manufacturing occupations. In fact, several of the practitioners interviewed mentioned that an important challenge for the implementation of these new technologies in manufacturing is the difficulty of finding workers with the necessary hybrid skillset (combining mechanical engineering and ICT skills, for instance, or business management and big data analytics, etc.).

The typical working conditions of manufacturing are also likely to change as a result of the introduction of these technologies. It will probably contribute to a decline of repetitive and routine industrial work, as well as a reduction in the amount of hazardous industrial tasks (which could be increasingly performed by AIR, while the remaining risks can be minimised by the improved intelligence of IIOT). Industry 4.0 factories are likely to be safer, with more skilled workers carrying out less repetitive work.

But the experts interviewed also expressed concerns about the implications of these new technologies for the conditions of work in manufacturing, especially the degree of autonomy, privacy and control of future manufacturing workers (see Crouch his volume). Digital factories where all objects are equipped with connected sensors and where workers collaborate with advanced robots can easily become digital panopticons, where human operators feel permanently monitored and controlled. It seems difficult to maintain any sense of privacy at work if every object is observing you. And while management through algorithms and big data analytics can significantly improve the efficiency of manufacturing processes, it can also lead to work intensification and the stifling of any sense of autonomy for the remaining workers.

Therefore, as with the introduction of any other technological innovation in the economy in the past, there is some ambivalence over the potential consequences for work and employment of the five game-changing technologies studied. Within the European social model this can be addressed by social dialogue and collective bargaining at different levels, including the firms and establishments themselves where these technologies are introduced. As part of this study, information was also compiled on the role that social dialogue is having in this respect, and the results were not very encouraging. Social dialogue does not yet appear to be playing a major role – if any – in the introduction of Industry 4.0 technologies in Europe. The notable exception is Germany, where there has been an important debate with engagement of social partners and policymakers on the implications of Industry 4.0 on work and employment, around the concept of 'Arbeit 4.0' (see Rahner and Schönstein this volume). A similar debate between social partners and policymakers across Europe is needed.

## NOTES

1. This article summarises the Eurofound (2018) report Game-Changing Technologies in European Manufacturing – The Future of Manufacturing in Europe, written by the author together with Eleonora Peruffo, John Hurley, Elisabeth Packalen and Martijn Poehl. This study can be downloaded from https://www.eurofound.europa.eu/publications/report/2018/game-changing-technologies-in-european-manufacturing.

2. The five technology studies were conducted by Technopolis Group between May 2016 and July 2017 under the coordination of Martijn Poehl from Technopolis and the Eurofound research team.

3. A typical value chain would start with R&D and design, continue with inbound logistics, production and outbound logistics, and end with marketing and after-sales services.

# MASTERING THE DIGITAL TRANSFORMATION

*An inclusive robotisation agenda*

Monique Kremer and Robert Went

Over recent years there has been a lively debate in the Netherlands about robots and the potential consequences of digitalisation for society. 'Will robots ever take over our jobs?' was the front-page headline in the newspaper Algemeen Dagblad on 15 September 2015. 'Scared of the robots? There's good reason to be', wrote the daily NRC Handelsblad in March 2015 (Noort 2015). And the title of an item on Telegraaf TV was: 'Look out – the robots are coming!' In addition, the then minister for social affairs and employment, Lodewijk Asscher of the Partij van de Arbeid (PvdA), made a speech in which he expressed his concerns that robots and digitalisation could lead to a loss of employment opportunities.

There is a connection between the shrill headlines and recent research. The contentious study by Frey and Osborne (2013), which predicts that in 20 years' time 47% of all jobs in the US could be taken over by computers, was reproduced in the Netherlands by Deloitte (2014), with exactly the same alarming results.

But robots can be seen as fascinating and valuable in certain contexts. Google's self-driving cars have garnered innumerable television, newspaper and internet reports. Searches on the subject (on Google, naturally) turn up some 900 million hits. The use of robots in healthcare has also generated a lot of interest in the Netherlands. According to reports, the therapeutic robot seal Paro is brightening the lives of elderly people with dementia. These media reports consistently put a more positive spin on the future of work. 'Robot vacuum cleaner reduces workload' was a headline in the Algemeen Dagblad on 16 June 2015. A robot can also make a person's working life easier, and Minister Asscher gave examples of this, too.

At the Netherlands Scientific Council for Government Policy (Wetenschappelijke Raad voor het Regeringsbeleid; WRR), one of the key policy advising bodies to the Dutch government, we are working on a project that looks at the future of work. We have principally been considering two major trends – automation to do with robots and artificial intelligence (AI) and the increasing flexibilisation of our labour market – which require analysis and policies to ensure that we will all benefit from the new technology, and that benefits do not merely accrue to those who own the robots (Freeman 2015). In this chapter we present key elements of an 'inclusive robot agenda'.


## TECHNOLOGY WILL NOT SIMPLY HAPPEN TO US

Hardly a day goes by without news about professions that are in danger of being eliminated by 'robots' and algorithms, and by advancements in AI. There is a great deal of exaggeration and hype in such reports, because the development from a 'proof of concept' to the roll-out and diffusion of a new application on a scale that would have an impact on society would take a considerable amount of time and would involve a large degree of uncertainty. Furthermore, there is a lot of over-simplification, for example in the above-mentioned studies that predict the destruction of 20–30% of extant jobs or more (Frey and Osborne 2013). Jobs are bundles of tasks and it is very unlikely that everything done by a person will be taken over by a robot or an algorithm (see Arnold et al. this volume). In the near future, most workers will probably encounter changes in their work, to a greater or lesser extent. However, studies by the Organisation for Economic Co-operation and Development (OECD) and McKinsey & Company in which jobs were examined at the task level estimate that around 9% of jobs (10% in The Netherlands) may completely disappear in the next 20 years according to the OECD (Arntz, Gregory and Zierahn 2016, 33), and according to McKinsey & Company (MGI 2017) the figure may be less than 5%.

It is more important to note that the direction in which applications of new technology will develop is not set in stone, and is not necessarily predictable. Smarter machines can change our lives, but governments, companies, engineers, citizens and interest groups can influence such changes and help to determine how things may change. The impact of a technological innovation depends not only on a specific technology, but also more broadly on the way in which the introduction of any new technology is handled. Technology is a means to an end and not the end itself. In addition, new jobs will emerge and no one can predict with any accuracy what and where these new opportunities will be. McKinsey & Company (2017) has already presented a study positing that the Netherlands will be short of 100,000 people to do the new jobs created by the introduction of new technologies. For this reason, it is unnecessary and counterproductive, and also not in keeping with the available evidence, to frighten people about the prospect of robots coming to take our jobs.

'Too often technology is discussed as if it has come from another planet and has just arrived on Earth', wrote the late LSE professor Anthony Atkinson (Atkinson 2015; see also Mazzucato 2013 and Rotman 2015). Markoff (2015) describes wonderfully how two different schools of thought arose in the engineering community of the 1960s about the relationship between humans and computers and robots. In the AI school, the point is to replace people by machines, whereas in the intelligence augmentation school, the aim is to use computers to improve human learning and to drive human innovation (see Petropoulos this volume). These two schools of thought still exist alongside as well as opposite each other. Therefore, there is no predetermined path for the further development of robotics and AI.

Digital technology will not in itself transform the world. According to the World Bank (2016), for any major transformation to occur, it must be complemented by analogue factors such as legislation and regulation, institutions, skills and education. Technological revolutions reach deep into the social, political and cultural fabric of society, and put these under stress. They lead to conflict between different interests, visions and possibilities of how society might look and function. It is therefore necessary as well as possible to think about the opportunities that companies, engineers, trade unions, other interest groups, and citizens have to act, and about the role that governments should play in any putative technological revolution.


## DIGITALISATION AS A DISTRIBUTION
## PROBLEM OF WORK AND MONEY

In this context, it is important also to see digitalisation and robotisation as a distribution problem. There is evidence that digitalisation and its applications have had a different impact on the various segments of the labour market in the past few years. Graetz and Michaels (2015) studied the impact of industrial robots in 17 countries between 1993 and 2007, and concluded that in that period the introduction of robots (in the narrow sense of the word) was not reflected in a decline in employment. They state that there are distribution effects, with fewer opportunities for lower-skilled and intermediate-skilled workers.

The same observation can be found in research on the consequences of digitalisation and offshoring. In an international comparative study, Goos, Manning and Salomons (2014) show that in the period 1993–2006 there was 'job polarisation' – a gradually contracting middle segment in the labour market between x jobs and y jobs (see also Goos, Manning and Salomons 2009). This contraction appears to have been relatively limited for the Netherlands. Research by the Netherlands Bureau for Economic Policy Analysis (van den Berge and ter Weel 2015a; 2015b) also shows that in the last 15 years digitalisation has led to changes in the Dutch labour market, although these changes are limited when compared with many other countries. Jobs at the lower end of the middle segment are disappearing in the Netherlands, and the people who become unemployed as a result often end up taking new jobs on an even lower rung of the ladder. Jobs are also disappearing at the upper end of the middle segment, and many employees end up in jobs on a higher rung. The researchers conclude that a new dividing line has opened up between mid-level workers and those at the bottom and top of the income ladder.

Van den Berge and ter Weel also point out that job content and occupational activities are changing. Secretaries, who used to spend most of their working hours typing, answering the phone and distributing faxes, now have other duties, for example in relation to scheduling and project management. They conclude that the greatest changes are taking place within jobs (see also Chui, Manyika and Miremadi 2015). Studies involving data analysis are, of course, retrospective by nature. They help us to understand what has already happened, and we can learn a great deal from history. But no one knows whether the trends and developments of the past will continue into the future. There is no way of predicting whether technological advances will continue to have an impact on the middle segment (see Arnold et al. this volume). Algorithms and smart machines could just as easily pose a growing threat to jobs at the higher end of the labour market. Autor (2015), an authority on computerisation and the division of labour, does not expect the job polarisation trend of recent years to continue endlessly. Many jobs in the middle segment involve a combination of specific professional skills and basic skills such as literacy, numeracy, adaptability, an ability to solve problems, and applied common sense. Autor conjectures that such jobs cannot easily be divided into mid-level activities for machines and lower-level activities for people without a loss of coherence and quality.

It is not inconceivable that in the future a mismatch will arise between jobs and the skills and knowledge that many people possess. Therefore on the one hand workers must be allowed – and must want – to continue learning, including during work, in order to acquire new skills and knowledge so as to be able to remain in employment now and in the future. This requires space for, and the organisation of, 'learning by doing' and 'learning while you earn' (see Benhamou this volume). On the other hand, digitalisation should be adapted in favour of working people, and used to improve and simplify work. For example, care workers would have more time to talk to those they look after thanks to the role of robots and technological innovations in the home, and the hard physical work of road builders would be eased with the help of robots.

Throughout all these developments, digitalisation can increase economic inequality. 'A widespread application of the technologies of the second machine age creates a real chance of inequality increasing in the future', write van Est and Kool (2015) for the Rathenau Instituut, an influential Dutch thinktank in the field of science and technology, in a report for the Dutch House of Representatives. The impact will be felt both in equality of opportunities and equality of income and capital. In its aforementioned policy brief on job polarisation, the Netherlands Bureau for Economic Policy Analysis stated that "the rise of ICT since the 1980s has led to growing wage inequality between high-skill and low-skill workers and, recently, to a decline in employment and pressure on wages in the middle segment" (van den Berge and ter Weel 2015b; see also Kremer et al. 2014). What will happen to incomes in the future remains to be seen. What is certain, however, is that some people will benefit more from technological progress than others. In contrast, there will be people who will be worse off when new technologies are put into use.

Economists have been talking for some time about skill-biased technological change, which relates to technological innovations that benefit people with higher skills and education (see Aubrey this volume). A fairly recent discussion concerns capital-biased technological change, or technological innovation that is mainly advantageous to those who own robots (Cohen-Setton 2012; Krugman 2012). Richard Freeman (2015) states that robots and related technologies are growing more and more capable of taking over all sorts of workers' tasks, and that the economic position of labour versus that of capital is deteriorating as a result:

> Unless workers earn income from capital as well as from labour, the trend toward a more unequal income distribution is likely to continue, and the world will increasingly turn into a new form of economic feudalism. We have to widen the ownership of business capital if we hope to prevent such a polarization of our economies.

## MASTERING THE ROBOT: AN INCLUSIVE ROBOT AGENDA

In order to respond to the development of robots and AI, and to ensure that the associated benefits accrue to everyone in society, we need an 'inclusive robot agenda'. In this regard, the key word for us is 'complementarity'. This means that the aim should be not to try and replace as many people as possible with robots, but rather to make people more productive with the help of robotics. It is not a case of 'man *versus* machine', but 'man *with* machine'. In this regard, it is important to strive for inclusiveness. Although robots and other machines are getting smarter, technological advances and applications often turn out differently than expected and can proceed more slowly than is often predicted, and the costs and benefits of new technology are not automatically shared equally. For this reason, it is desirable for the government to encourage different parties to come together to seek out opportunities for co-creation. New applications should no longer be thought up by technicians and investors for people who then have to work with them, but instead all parties should develop such applications together. This is the first item in our proposal for an 'inclusive robot agenda'.

The second item in our robot agenda is that we must develop complementary expertise and skills at all levels of education. A good education is not in itself enough to anticipate the rise of increasingly intelligent machines. Accountants, physicians, lawyers and other highly educated professionals may see certain aspects of their work being taken over by robots some day in the future. Neither is technical training alone likely to be enough. The question that also concerns education should be: what aspects of work are typically human? Which tasks, relationships and responsibilities will continue to require the human touch, or will we specifically want to entrust (or continue to entrust) to people? That is why it is important to consider and identify complementary expertise and skills.

The third item relates to the ownership of work (see Crouch this volume). A common finding in studies about stress in the workplace, burnout and – on the positive side – work enjoyment and productivity is that autonomy or 'ownership' is good for productivity. The question we must ask is how we can get people and technology working together, and how people can become or continue to be masters of their own work (and of the robot). The emergence of 'digital Taylorism' and 'algorithmic management' increases the possibilities for tightly controlling and regulating work, thereby turning people into 'meat robots'. In a literature study for our WRR report, Mastering the Robot, economist Anna Salomons (2015) concluded:

> In summary, therefore, the digital revolution does not mean that our existing labour organisations and institutions, such as collective labour agreements, will become surplus to requirements. On the contrary, if employees are treated like robots, this will stand in the way of the productivity gains from the introduction of real robots.

The final item on the agenda that we are advocating concerns (new) distribution problems that can come into play if more robots and AI are used at work. Differences in income can increase if, as a result of further automation, large numbers of workers lose their jobs and either remain unemployed or find a new job at a lower level with lower income. Wealth gaps can widen if all the profits made from robots end up in the hands of the robots' owners. It will then become important to consider whether it is possible (and desirable) to make workers co-owners of robots and other machines, for example by means of a 'robot dividend' for all through a social wealth fund. And, finally, there will be people who cannot keep up in the robot society and who cannot be helped with an extra course or additional studies. It is impossible to predict who they will be. We do not know who will find themselves without work or who will need to be assisted from one job to the next. For this reason, we are in favour of a portfolio of several policy instruments for these groups (eg early retirement schemes, a form of basic income, government jobs), in order to help and support these people where necessary.

With these four agenda items, we can welcome robotisation and digitalisation with open arms, without a widening of the gaps between social groups. In this way, the workers can continue to master the robots.

## REFERENCES

Arntz, M., T. Gregory, and U. Zierahn (2016), *The Risk of Automation for Jobs in OECD Countries: a Comparative Analysis*, OECD Social, Employment and Migration Working Paper 189, Paris: OECD Publishing.

Atkinson, A. (2015), *Inequality: What Can Be Done?*, Cambridge MA and London: Harvard University Press.

Autor, D. (2015), 'Why Are There Still So Many Jobs? The History and Future of Workplace Automation', *Journal of Economic Perspectives*, 29(3): 3–30.

Chui, M., J. Manyika and M. Miremadi (2015), 'Four Fundamentals of Workplace Automation', *McKinsey Quarterly*, 29(3): 1–9.

Cohen-Setton, J. (2012), 'Blogs Review: Robots, Capital-Biased Technological Change and Inequality', blog, Bruegel, 10 December, http://bruegel.org/2012/12/blogs-review-robots-capital-biased-technological-change-and-inequality/.

Deloitte (2014), *Mogelijk 2 tot 3 Miljoen Banen op de Tocht: De Impact van Automatisering op de Nederlandse Arbeidsmarkt*, Deloitte, 1 October, https://www2.deloitte.com/nl/nl/pages/data-analytics/articles/mogelijk-2-3-miljoen-banen-tocht.html.

Freeman, R. B. (2015), 'Who Owns the Robots Rules the World', IZA World of Labor, https://wol.iza.org/uploads/articles/5/pdfs/who-owns-the-robots-rules-the-world.pdf.

Frey, C. and M. Osborne (2013), *The Future of Employment: How Susceptible Are Jobs To Computerisation?*, Oxford: Oxford Martin School, https://www.oxfordmartin.ox.ac.uk/downloads/academic/The_Future_of_Employment.pdf.

Goos, M., A. Manning and A. Salomons (2009), 'Job Polarization in Europe', *American Economic Review*, 99(2): 58–63.

Goos, M., A. Manning and A. Salomons (2014), 'Explaining Job Polarization: Routine-biased Technological Change and Offshoring', *American Economic Review*, 104(8): 2509–26.

Graetz, G. and G. Michaels (2015), 'Robots at Work', CEPS Discussion Paper 1335, London: London School of Economics, http://cep.lse.ac.uk/pubs/download/dp1335.pdf.

Kremer, M., M. Bovens, E. Schrijvers and R. Went (eds) (2014), *Hoe Ongelijk is Nederland?*, WRR verkenning 28, Amsterdam: Amsterdam University Press.

Krugman, P. (2012), 'Capital-biased Technological Progress: an Example (Wonkish)', *The New York Times*, 26 December, http://krugman.blogs.nytimes.com/2012/12/26/capital-biasedtechnological-progress-an-example-wonkish/?_r=0.

Markoff, J. (2015), *Machines of Loving Grace: Between Humans and Robots*, New York: HarperCollins.

Mazzucato, M. (2013), *The Entrepreneurial State: Debunking Public vs Private Sector Myths*, London: Anthem Press.

McKinsey Global Institute (MGI) (2017), *A Future that Works: Automation, Employment, and Productivity*, McKinsey & Company, https://www.mckinsey.com/~/media/McKinsey/Global%20Themes/Digital%20Disruption/Harnessing%20automation%20for%20a%20future%20that%20works/MGI-A-future-that-works_Full-report.ashx.

Noort, W. v. (2015), 'Bang voor de robots? Daar is ook wel reden toe', *NRC Handelsblad*, 30 March, https://www.nrc.nl/nieuws/2015/03/30/bang-voor-de-robots-daar-is-ook-wel-reden-toe-1482084-a704094.

Rotman, D. (2015), 'Who Will Own the Robots?', *MIT Technology Review*, 16 June, https://www.technologyreview.com/featuredstory/538401/who-will-own-the-robots.

Salomons, A. (2015), 'Hoe Robots Beter Kunnen Werken – en Wij Ook', in R. Went, M. Kremer and A. Knottnerus (eds), *De Robot de Baas: De*

*Toekomst van Werk in het Tweede Machinetijdperk*, WRR Verkenning 31, Amsterdam: Amsterdam University Press.

van den Berge, W. and B. ter Weel (2015a), 'De Impact van Technologische Verandering op de Nederlandse Arbeidsmarkt, 1999–2014', in R. Went, M. Kremer and A. Knottnerus (eds), *De Robot de Baas: De Toekomst van Werk in het Tweede Machinetijdperk*, WRR Verkenning 31, Amsterdam: Amsterdam University Press.

van den Berge, W. and B. ter Weel (2015b), *Baanpolarisatie in Nederland*, CPB Policy Brief, The Hague: Netherlands Bureau for Economic Policy Analysis.

van Est, R. and L. Kool (eds) (2015), *Werken aan de Robotsamenleving: Visies en Inzichten uit de Wetenschap over de Relatie Technologie en Werkgelegenheid*, The Hague: Rathenau Instituut.

World Bank (2016), *World Development Report 2016: Digital Dividends*, Washington DC: World Bank, http://www.worldbank.org/en/publication/wdr2016.

# WORKING IN THE GIG ECONOMY

## Insights from Europe

## Ursula Huws, Neil H. Spencer, Dag Sverre Syrdal and Kaire Holts

**M**ost European welfare systems have evolved from 20th-century origins. They have been modified over the decades to deal with changing circumstances such as the entry of many more women into the labour market, the growth of part-time working and the sorts of structural unemployment that require a reskilling of the labour force. But in essence they are grounded in a normative model of work that presupposes some more or less stable binary distinctions in the workforce. Workers, it is assumed, are either economically active or not (for example because of sickness or disability). If they are economically active, they are either in work or unemployed. If they are employed they are either self-employed or employees. Welfare systems are designed largely to provide benefits to those who are economically inactive (depending on circumstances) or unemployed. The unemployed are expected to engage in an active process of seeking work. A range of institutional arrangements have been designed to fit with these normative assumptions, including tax and national insurance regulations, employment legislation, education and training systems and the delivery of services. In an ideal world, in which all members of the adult population fit into these simple, mutually exclusive categories, there is a 'place' and an appropriate welfare package for everybody.

Unfortunately, in the 21st century, labour markets are diverging ever more sharply from this model, with growing numbers of workers falling into the cracks between these categories. On the one hand, they lack the kind of stable, long-term employment that is linked to solid benefits, such as pensions contributions, national insurance and (in some countries) rights to services such as health care and childcare. On the other, they are not actually unemployed and cannot claim unemployment benefit. They are neither 'genuinely seeking work' nor 'permanently employed' but occupying a precarious no man's land between the two, not knowing from one hour, day or week to the next if or when the next 'task' will come along to provide them with some income.

This chapter draws on evidence from surveys in the Austria, Germany, Italy, the Netherlands, Sweden, Switzerland and the UK that illustrate the extent of this kind of 'just-in-time' working (Huws et al. 2017) and discusses the implications of these developments for work and welfare in Europe in the future.

## CROWD WORK: SURVEYS IN KEY EUROPEAN COUNTRIES

These surveys were carried out at the University of Hertfordshire in collaboration with the European Foundation for Progressive Studies, UNI Europa and Ipsos MORI. Approximately 2,000 working-age adults were interviewed in each of the seven countries between January 2016 and April 2017.[1] The national surveys were complemented by in-depth interviews with crowd workers as part of an ongoing programme of research.

The context of the research was the strong policy interest in what is variously known as the 'sharing economy', 'gig economy', 'platform economy' or 'crowd work'. There had been an exponential growth of online platforms for managing work across Europe, but surprisingly little was known about the realities of gig work. Was it a liberating new form of self-employment or a new form of exploitation? How many workers were doing it? Who were they? What was the reality of their working lives? And what are the implications of these new realities for public policy in Europe?

These questions are important because crowd work is seen by policymakers as having strong positive potential, as well as carrying some risks. On the positive side, it has the potential to make a strong contribution to economic development and growth, especially in regions that are still recovering from the impact of the 2007–8 global financial crisis. It may also contribute positively to social innovation and entrepreneurship, allowing non-governmental organisations, individuals and small- and medium-enterprises to take advantage of the opportunities opened up by new technologies and the digital single market. On the negative side, trade unions, consumer groups and government bodies have expressed concerns about new risks to workers' rights, occupational safety and health and consumer safety. There are also concerns about how to apply existing regulations, such as those concerning tax and insurance and professional certification, in this new volatile context. More broadly, questions have been raised about the sustainability of new 'gig' work models, for example their ability to support a good work–life balance, long-term career development and income in retirement.

## THE EXTENT OF CROWD WORK

The research found that in each of the seven countries studied a high proportion of the population was using the internet as a means of gaining an extra income. In this context, the sale of labour was less important than some other form of income generation, such as selling or reselling goods online and only slightly more important than letting rooms to paying guests via online platforms. Nevertheless, a high proportion of the population reported having done some paid work found via an online platform (working 'virtually' from their own homes via an online platform such as Upwork or Clickworker; providing driving services via a platform like Uber, or working in somebody else's home for a platform like Helpling, MyHammer or TaskRabbit). The proportion reporting doing some crowd work was 9% in the UK and the Netherlands, 10% in Sweden, 12% in Germany, 18% in Switzerland, 19% in Austria and 22% in Italy. However the crowd work constituted a small proportion of total income for most respondents. It constituted more than half of all personal income for only 2.3% of the total sample in Austria, 3.5% in Switzerland, 2.5% in Germany, 5.1% in Italy, 1.6% in the Netherlands and 2.7% in Sweden and the UK – forming the main source of income for an average of 2.9% of the samples across all seven countries.

The majority of crowd workers combine 'new' forms of work for online platforms with more traditional types of casual work, such as working in bars or coffee shops, as well as using it to top up income from more regular full-time or part-time employment. In some cases, it is combined with other activities, such as studying or artistic work.

Crowd work must therefore be regarded as part of a broader spectrum of casual work, carried out, by and large, by the working poor, seeking any form of income they can find.

## EMPLOYMENT STATUS

In the policy debates about crowd work there is perhaps no question more vexed than that of their employment status. Many platforms insist that their workers are 'independent contractors', with the role of the platform simply being to mediate between workers and their clients. However legal experts frequently argue that the relationship of workers to the platforms is often a dependent one, and that the status of the workers should reflect this subordination (De Stefano 2016). Some recent legal judgments have supported this opinion, awarding 'worker' status to crowd workers but falling short of regarding them as 'employees'. Meanwhile, there have been proposals to create a new kind of legal status for crowd workers as 'independent workers' (Harris and Krueger 2015) or 'dependent contractors' (Taylor 2017).

Somewhat surprisingly, crowd workers in our surveys were most likely to describe themselves as employed full time, a status claimed by between 41% (in Italy) and 58% (in Germany) crowd workers. The proportion describing themselves as self-employed was rather low, ranging from 7% (in Italy) to 13% (in the UK). Follow-up interviews with crowd workers provided some insights into their working conditions.

While they typically valued the flexibility of crowd work, there were complaints about difficulty in communicating with platform personnel, the frequency with which changes were made, and the way that work was allocated and pay calculated. There were also complaints about unilateral arbitrary deactivations, whereby crowd workers suddenly found themselves unable to register for work, often with no explanation or warning and with no means to discuss the reasons with the platform personnel. Another major source of stress concerned customer ratings and the impossibility of challenging negative ratings.

The interviews with crowd workers also revealed a range of physical and psycho-social health hazards, some linked to working long and unpredictable hours, and reluctance to refuse work known to be dangerous for fear of receiving a negative customer rating. In some cases, crowd workers also reported social and criminal risks including sexual harassment, assault and tasks that involved errands relating to drug dealing and handling stolen goods.

## CONCLUSIONS AND POLICY IMPLICATIONS

We can conclude that crowd work cannot be regarded as a clearly defined and distinctive form of labour but forms part of a spectrum of rapidly changing and overlapping forms of just-in-time work, which draw to varying degrees on digital media for their management.

There is no clear definition of an online crowd work platform, with a fuzzy line between those websites that have developed specific applications for managing the interface between workers and clients (including the transfer of funds), platforms that advertise freelance postings, online directories and commercial listings sites. Similarly, workers shift constantly between different forms of casual work regardless of whether it is digitally managed.

It is thus almost impossible to isolate 'crowd workers' as a special category of worker. Rather, their existence draws attention to the inadequacy of the existing categorisations of work in the fluid and rapidly evolving labour markets of the digital age. This mismatch has introduced inconsistencies and ambiguities into the coverage of the accompanying regulations. While creating new opportunities for some, the resulting gaps in coverage have also left other workers unprotected and at risk.

One solution that is sometimes proposed is to develop new typologies: of companies, business models, patterns of work organisation, employment contract and labour; and new regulations to fit these typologies. This is a risky strategy for the following reasons:

- It may create rigidities that halt innovation in its tracks and give a permanent character to what may be transient forms.
- New regulations may be difficult to interpret, causing confusion and uncertainty for both employers and workers.
- There is a risk that the creation of new enterprise categories, employment categories or thresholds will have unintended consequences, for example encourage the development of contracts that skirt the boundaries of definitions (see Doellgast this volume). And if new employment categories are created, they may be used not just to provide some protection for workers who are currently unprotected but also to substitute for better existing provisions for regular employees.

For these reasons, we prefer a broader approach, which goes back to the underlying principles of the current regulations and legal frameworks in order to establish a clear basis for future regulation. This may imply creating new legal definitions of self-employment on the one hand and of subordinate worker status on the other.

There is also need for a fundamental rethink of welfare systems to make them compatible with the way labour markets work in a digitalised, globalised economy (see Palier this volume). In other words, a double-pronged approach is required, involving a reconceptualisation of employment regulation on the one hand, and of welfare systems on the other.

On the employment side, guidelines on the definition of self-employment for tax, national insurance and social protection purposes, as well as for determining employment status, must be clarified. This should take into account, among other things, whether workers have the right to:

• determine the price of the goods or services produced
• specify how the work will be done
• employ others to do the work
• retain intellectual property rights in their work outputs
• work for multiple clients and/or normally do so.

In cases where workers do not meet the above criteria, one solution would be to require that they are deemed to be subordinate workers as the default position. The onus of proof that this is not the case should rest with the employer rather than the worker.

Subordinate workers should be entitled to the same rights as other comparable temporary and/or part-time employees. Where they have another main job, the same rules should be applied as in any other secondary employment according to national regulations.

The status of platforms must also be assessed. If they are determining the wages and working conditions of subordinate workers are they not then employers? If they are putting workers in touch with other organisations who will then determine their wages and working conditions are they not employment agencies? It seems likely that some, if not all, online platforms that match subordinate workers with clients may fall within existing definitions of temporary work agencies or private employment agencies.

There is also a need to clarify workers' rights. These include a statutory minimum wage (in countries where this exists) and establishing a method to ensure equivalence with hourly rates for workers who are paid by the task, as well as a formula for including travel time, waiting time, preparation time and time spent bidding for new work. Other existing rights include paid holidays, sick leave, parental leave and compassionate leave, rights in the case of suspension or termination, and rights to call in labour inspectors, refuse dangerous work or other health and safety rights. New rights for workers should also be considered, for example in relation to data protection, the ability to challenge customer ratings and to bypass standardised app interfaces to engage in meaningful communication with employers and clients.

Reform of welfare systems may be even more challenging than the reform of employment regulation in the context of widespread 'just-in-time' working. Once it is accepted that the simple binary categorisation of jobseekers into those 'in work' and those 'seeking work' no longer fits the reality of flexible labour markets it becomes necessary to design a system that provides a minimum level of income security to prevent people falling into destitution while avoiding the creation of disincentives to work.

Given the diversity of welfare systems in Europe, there is no universal recipe for achieving this. The challenges will differ according to whether the existing welfare system is individually based (as in the Nordic countries) or household based; whether benefits are means tested; whether services such as health are provided universally as a right of citizenship or linked to sectoral, occupational or company-level collective agreements; whether care for the elderly and disabled is provided as a public service or by means of monetary assistance to individuals who buy these services in the market; and a host of other variables.

There is an urgent need for research on the ways in which each national welfare system addresses the needs of casual workers and their dependants, and the feasibility of alternative models. One idea which is increasingly proposed in this area is that of a basic minimum income. This idea is attractive to those who want to see a labour market in which workers can be moved from job to job unhindered by bureaucratic obstacles or costs to the employer and in which workers are free to move in and out of education and change their working hours flexibly to accommodate changing domestic caring demands. However critics point out that if such a scheme were to be paid for out of general taxation this would undo the principle that employers should contribute towards the cost of social welfare and could undermine the negotiation of benefits through collective bargaining. It could also raise difficult questions about who is entitled to such benefits, in the context of free movement of EU citizens and large-scale immigration from outside Europe. Clearly there is much to be done to redesign Europe's welfare systems to make them fit for the 21st century.

## NOTE

1. Additional funding was provided at a national level by Unionen in Sweden, the TNO Research Institute in the Netherlands, the Chamber of Labour (AK) in Austria, Ver.di and IG Metall in Germany, Syndicom in Switzerland and the Fondazione EYU in Italy.

## REFERENCES

De Stefano, V. (2016), *The Rise of the 'Just-In-Time Workforce': On-Demand Work, Crowdwork and Labour Protection in the 'Gig-Economy'*, Geneva: International Labour Office.

Harris, S. D. and A. B. Krueger (2015), *A Proposal for Modernizing Labor Laws for Twenty-First-Century Work: the 'Independent Worker'*, Brookings Institution Discussion Paper, 2015–10, Washington: Brookings Institution.

Huws, U., N. H. Spencer, D. S. Syrdal and K. Holts (2017), *Work in the European Gig Economy: Research Results from the UK, Sweden, Germany, Austria, the Netherlands, Switzerland and Italy*, Brussels and Hatfield: European Foundation for Progressive Studies, UNI Europa and University of Hertfordshire, http://www.feps-europe.eu/assets/9d13a6d2-5973-4131-b9c8-3ca5100f92d4/work-in-the-european-gig-full-report-pppdf.pdf.

Taylor, M. (2017), *Good Work: the Taylor Review of Modern Working Practices*, London: Department for Business, Energy & Industrial Strategy, https://www.gov.uk/government/uploads/system/uploads/attachment_data/file/627671/good-work-taylor-review-modern-working-practices-rg.pdf.

# THE PLATFORM ECONOMY

## Consequences for labour, inequality and the environment

## Juliet B. Schor

The current moment is a fateful one for the global community. We are witnessing a rise of authoritarian populism and the growth of anti-immigrant sentiment in many countries. Global temperatures are accelerating rapidly, bringing an intensification of dangerous impacts, such as melting permafrost, storms, wildfires and heat waves. Financialisation and the growth of extreme income and wealth concentration are destabilising societies that had relied on reasonable distributions of economic benefits. Democratic and other social institutions are under attack from these factors. Nuclear aggression is in the air.

In the midst of these perilous trends, studies of the 'sharing economy' may seem a bit beside the point. Companies such as Uber or Airbnb employ only very small fractions of the global workforce, and the sector as a whole only boasts a few real success stories. Yet the larger platform economy is but one part of another tidal wave that will be occurring around the world – rapid labour-displacing technological change. While the technological determinists who predict that artificial intelligence (AI) will wipe out massive numbers of the world's jobs in a short time are surely overstating future impacts (see Arnold et al. this volume), it is undeniable that technological advances in digitisation and AI are proceeding quickly, and that they will have far-reaching consequences, even if we do not fully understand them yet. There will be big changes in labour markets, and it is likely that technological displacement will contribute to the growth of extreme inequality. Societies that shift to large scale use of AI are likely to experience significant social pressures and even dislocation. Perhaps most importantly, the historic safety valve for absorbing displaced labour – GDP growth – is much harder to achieve in wealthy societies now.

While economists do not fully understand why, low growth appears to be a new but persistent feature of the global north. Furthermore, even if rapid growth were magically to reappear, meeting the massive emissions reductions that are now necessary to address climate change will be very difficult, if not impossible, in that context. Some scientists have been forthright enough to argue that rich countries need 10% annual reductions in emissions, a number that is far beyond the range of current experience, and one that is nearly impossible to square with continued growth (Anderson 2012). Thus, the fourth industrial revolution is likely to collide with political instability, threats to democratic institutions, and climate change. The platform economy, which represents a large-scale reorganisation of many kinds of work, is at the cutting edge of one type of technological transformation.

What exactly is this sector? Broadly, it represents a set of platforms that use algorithms to match buyers and sellers in a range of goods and labour services. There are both consumer and business-oriented platforms. Amazon's Mechanical Turk and Upwork are examples of the latter. This paper is concerned with the consumer-facing firms – in areas such as lodging, errands and tasks, durable goods rental and transportation.[1] These are the key features of these platforms:

• They use sophisticated logistics software (or algorithms) for matching and payment.

- Providers on the platforms are independent contractors (rather than employees).
- There are very low barriers to entry for providers on most platforms.
- Trust is achieved via crowdsourcing of ratings and reputational data, typically on both sides of the market.

There's a great deal of terminological dispute about the sector – with alternatives being collaborative consumption, sharing economy, on-demand economy and the gig economy. For reasons of space I will leave aside these disputes, which we have discussed elsewhere (Frenken and Schor 2017; Schor and Attwood-Charles 2017; Schor and Fitzmaurice 2015). There has also been a great deal of controversy about the sector, with supporters touting its efficiency and low cost and detractors claiming the platforms are exploiting workers, destabilising neighbourhoods, and acting illegally (Schor and Attwood-Charles 2017). While it is difficult to predict exactly how the sector will evolve, after conducting seven years of research (2011–2018), using a variety of methods, I am prepared to offer a number of findings, centring on three main issues.[2]

First, in contrast to frequent claims, platforms are less disruptors than reproducers of ongoing trends in labour markets. In particular, their impacts appear to be inequality-enhancing, rather than reducing, and racism appears to be endemic to their operation. Second, the growth of platforms is likely to be associated with rising carbon footprints, although this prediction awaits empirical testing. Finally, we ask whether the sector is sustainable, or whether its continued growth is contingent on a parasitic relationship to conventional unemployment.

## DISRUPTION OR REPRODUCTION?

Platform companies and many observers claim that this form of economic organisation represents a disruptive and novel way to organise economic activity. Others emphasise continuities with ongoing trends. For example, the de-institutionalisation of labour markets is a decades-long trend across OECD countries. In the US the trend towards what has been called precarious, or non-standard, labour has been observed since the 1980s. As noted above, platform work is nearly always organised via independent contracting. Does the emergence of the platform economy signal 'the end of employment', as some would have it (Sundararajan 2016), or is it an unsustainable way to organise labour markets, as others suggest? Our research on the everyday functioning of platforms provides insight into this question, and supports the latter interpretation (Schor et al. 2017). A main finding is that the model of independent contracting is difficult to sustain on its own terms because to achieve a viable model of labour management, platforms are 'free-riding' on conventional employment. Indeed, they have yet to show that their model works as a stand-alone. While the platforms claim that their providers prefer the independent contractor model, with the flexibility and autonomy that it provides, we find that this is true only for those who use the platform for supplemental earnings, rather than to pay their basic expenses.

It is important to remember that platforms have very low barriers to entry and attract a wide array of earners. While the companies do not release much data on their workforces, national surveys in the US, for example, find that less than 30% rely on their platform earnings as their means of subsistence. The vast majority have other sources of income. While this varies by platform, it remains a general rule almost everywhere (see Huws et al. this volume). Many in the supplemental earner category already have full-time jobs. Those in the partial-dependence category (some reliance on platforms to pay basic expenses) have significant alternative income. What we have termed 'dependent' workers rely solely on the platform. However, few in this group earn more than poverty wages. They experience extreme precarity, have less job satisfaction and autonomy, and are unlikely to persist if viable alternatives appear for them. If AI reduces conventional employment, we cannot expect the platform model to be a successful alternative without major changes to its methods of managing labour (see Petropoulos this volume).

## REPRODUCING INEQUALITY

Another main theme in the disruption–reproduction debate concerns inequality. Are platforms reducing wage inequality by providing new opportunities, particularly for less advantaged workers, as some claim (Fraiberger and Sundararajan 2015)? Or are they exacerbating existing patterns of privilege? While there is little question that platforms are offering new opportunities to the middle class, our research on the US suggests that these are mainly being taken advantage of by more privileged members (Schor 2017). We have argued that they are fostering an upward redistribution of opportunity and income within the top 80%; platform workers are disproportionately well educated, with majorities of college-educated providers on most platforms (Schor et al. 2017). In our qualitative work, we find that manual, often 'dirty' work, like housecleaning and driving, is being done by college-educated providers, who are displacing less educated workers. For example, TaskRabbit, Airbnb and Uber substitute for traditional housecleaning, hotel chambermaids and taxi drivers: as demand for the former expands, this has a negative impact on the latter. Chambermaids are unlikely to have apartments to rent on Airbnb. Although some taxi drivers have switched to ride-hailing apps, anecdotal evidence suggests their incomes plummet with the switch. Furthermore, many taxi drivers lack access to the latest vehicle models necessary for driving on platforms. Overall, we suspect that the additional income earned by high educated platform providers worsens the distribution between them and lower educated persons at the bottom of the income scale.

A second dimension of inequality is around race. In the US there is growing evidence that the platform economy is fostering racial discrimination, via the peer-to-peer structure of the exchanges. Every study we have seen confirms the existence of racially based discrimination. It is taking place on both sides of these platforms – customers are discriminating against providers and providers are discriminating against customers. In our research we find that in areas with high proportions of non-white residents, prices are lower, revenue is less and ratings are reduced (Schor et al. 2017). In an audit study, Harvard researchers found that Airbnb hosts were 16% more likely to refuse to rent to guests with African-American sounding names (Edelman, Luca and Svirsky 2017). This research received wide press coverage, a series of responses by the company, and attempts to create a new, 'noir' Airbnb for people of colour. Similarly, a field experiment of Uber and Lyft found that drivers cancelled on riders with African-American sounding names twice as often as riders with white sounding names and that African-American named customers had to wait longer. This study also found women were cheated more on these apps (Ge et al. 2016). A study of TaskRabbit found that Taskers were unwilling to provide services in areas with heavy concentrations of non-white residents (Thebault-Spieker, Terveen and Hecht 2015). Thus, on balance, it appears that rather than eliminating, or 'disrupting', racial inequalities, they are being transported into the 'sharing economy'.

## CHANGING CONSUMER PATTERNS

While there has been considerable criticism of platforms' labour practices, and of the impacts of Airbnb on the availability of housing and neighbourhood quality, there has been less debate about how these companies are affecting consumers. But here too there are worrisome impacts, especially over the longer run.

A key part of the appeal of the platforms is new services and low prices.[3] The benefits vary by platform: on Airbnb, much lower prices, local neighbourhoods and personalisation are key to consumer satisfaction. On Uber, factors include low prices, convenient payment, availability and ease of use. On TaskRabbit, middle-class consumers get middle-class providers, in contrast to the informal 'errands and tasks' market. For other services, such as the delivery of food or consumer goods, the platforms make 'servant labour' available at relatively low cost. These platforms allow middle-class and upper-middle-class consumers to access services previously reserved for the wealthy.

What of the worrisome trends? The most serious is environmental impacts. A major theme in the early years of the sharing economy was that these new services were more environmentally beneficial than existing businesses, in part because they were using 'idle resources'; Airbnb claimed it would reduce new hotel construction. Ride-sharing apps like Uber and Lyft were expected by many to reduce car ownership, increase the number of passengers per ride, and reduce carbon emissions. However, it has been difficult to assess these claims because the companies will not provide their data to independent researchers. But there are strong reasons to believe that platforms are increasing, rather than reducing environmental impacts, and especially climate emissions.

The evidence is hiding in plain sight: lower prices lead to more demand. In the lodging sector, cheap accommodation increases miles travelled and trips taken. Furthermore, Airbnb enables hosts to rent out their homes when they travel, so that lodging is essentially free. (We also find some hosts travel specifically to rent, to take advantage of price arbitrage – they can rent out their homes at a higher rate than the places they stay at.) Similarly, in the US ride-hailing apps appear to be taking people away from lower-carbon modes of transport. A recent study based on survey data finds that had there been no transportation app, 49–61% of ride-hailing trips would have either not been made at all, or been taken via walking, biking or transit (Clewlow and Mishra 2017). Furthermore, this study finds that there is no reduction in car ownership as a result of ride-hailing. The authors conclude that these services are likely to increase rather than reduce vehicle miles travelled. In the US, at least, if the transportation apps continue to grow it seems likely that they will further strain public transportation budgets by reducing ridership and weakening public support. This would have disastrous carbon consequences, as transportation is already the largest source of greenhouse gas emissions in the US and is a major contributor in many countries.

## HAS THE SHARING ECONOMY PEAKED?

In 2017, a research report suggested that growth in the US sharing sector had peaked (Farrell and Greig 2017). The torrid expansion of the previous few years appeared to be over. Platform incomes were even falling in some cities, labour turnover was extremely high (with more than half of all participants dropping out after a year), and the strengthening of the conventional labour market was reducing the pool of interested workers. While our research has found that employed workers are more likely to be satisfied on the platforms, this data also shows that they are less likely to stay. These findings suggest an obvious point that much of the discourse has failed to recognise: the platform economy remains tethered to the conventional labour market. The precarious model of independent contracting without benefits, protections or guaranteed income is unlikely to be preferred, except for those who can command superior market positions.

A number of other developments also suggest that the 'end of employment' future may be little more than fantasy. They concern the only two very large platforms in this sector: Airbnb and Uber. San Francisco recently enacted strong regulations to curtail Airbnb hosting, which has dramatically reduced the number of hosts who are eligible and registered. One report found that only 15% of hosts have registered (Brinklow 2017). Stricter regulations are being debated and enacted in cities around the world, and they will predictably reduce the growth of lodging platforms, particularly Airbnb. In the case of Uber, whose valuation recently dropped by one-third, the lack of a viable business model may be a more serious constraint than regulation. Independent analysis suggests that Uber will have lost $5 billion in 2017 and that passengers are paying only 41% of the cost of their rides, with Uber's investors subsidising the remainder in the hopes of achieving market domination (Smith 2016). However, competition in this market may be increasing. Furthermore, even if Uber were to best its competition, there is reason to believe consumers will balk at a more than doubling of fares, particularly since so many trips would not otherwise be taken.

## POLICIES FOR THE FUTURE

Our findings, at least to date, suggest that letting algorithms drive economic activity will further privilege the privileged. Furthermore, the platform sector fails to provide adequately for those without secure alternative sources of income, and exacerbates existing forms of social inequality. If we want to reap the benefits of platforms (and there are many) without this dark side, higher levels of regulation and new patterns of governance will certainly be necessary. Our research finds that platforms work best when workers have alternative means of support, and participate freely and without compulsion. One option is to reduce workers' dependency through broad social measures: stronger welfare support for the unemployed, a basic income, or more collective provisioning of basic needs could reduce desperation for platform providers with no other sources of income (see Palier this volume). Alternatively, platforms could be required to provide regular benefits and protections for workers who are essentially full-timers, who work over a certain number of hours a week. In that scenario, the independent contractor status would be reserved only for those who work below that threshold.

A second issue is that platforms must begin to monitor and take responsibility for their carbon impacts. The world cannot afford a dynamic new sector with a high carbon footprint. Commitments to data transparency are essential, in order to craft environmentally positive policies. Possibilities include carbon taxes on lodging (eg Airbnb) stays and ride-hailing services (eg Uber, Lyft and others). In many localities, platform companies are getting preferential regulatory treatment. In return they should commit to a strong sustainability agenda to control and reduce their environmental impacts.

Finally, platforms must tackle discrimination head-on. Racial discrimination in public accommodation has been outlawed in many societies. Consumers have legal rights to access to lodging, transportation and labour services. While the rise of a person-to-person alternative means of exchange has many beneficial aspects, it must not be allowed to re-inscribe racial and other forms of discrimination. Here what is required is a combination of legislation outlawing discrimination and new policies by the companies. Solutions include eliminating or de-emphasising pictures that show skin colour and company monitoring and punishment of discriminatory behaviour.

The 'sharing' or consumer-facing portion of the platform economy has proven to be an attractive option for consumers and many providers. To date, it has proven to be neither the earth-shattering innovation its proponents claim nor the absolute dystopia its detractors have asserted. However, negative impacts are already significant, and if it continues to grow, these harms will as well. To preserve the potential benefits, it will behove government at all levels to craft legislation and regulation that controls the impacts it is already having on labour, climate and public goods.

## NOTES

1. This is the portion of the platform sector typically referred to as the 'sharing economy'.
2. For more detail on our project, and copies of our papers, see: https://www.bc.edu/bc-web/schools/mcas/departments/sociology/connected.html.
3. There are also ideological, or 'moral' appeals that matter to users, as we detail in Domesticating the Market: Moral Exchange and the Sharing Economy (Fitzmaurice et al. 2018).

## REFERENCES

Anderson, K. (2012), 'Climate Change Going Beyond Dangerous: Brutal Numbers and Tenuous Hope', *Development Dialogue: What Next*,

3: 16–40, http://www.whatnext.org/resources/Publications/Volume-III/
Single-articles/wnv3_andersson_144.pdf.
Brinklow, A. (2017), 'Airbnb Says Online Registration Will Legalize
all SF hosts', *Curbed San Francisco*, 6 September, https://sf.curbed.
com/2017/9/6/16263986/airbnb-online-registration-san-francisco.
Clewlow, R. R. and Mishra, G. S. (2017), *Disruptive Transportation: the
Adoption, Utilization, and Impacts of Ride-Hailing in the United States*,
Davis, CA: Institute of Transportation Studies, University of California.
Edelman, B., M. Luca and D. Svirsky (2017), 'Racial Discrimination in
the Sharing Economy: Evidence from a Field Experiment', *American
Economic Journal: Applied Economics*, 9(2):1–22.
Farrell, D. and F. Grieg (2017), *The Online Platform Economy: Has
Growth Peaked?*, JP Morgan Chase Institute, New York City and Wash-
ington, DC: JP Morgan Chase Institute.
Fitzmaurice, C., I. Ladegaard, W. Attwood-Charles, L. B. Carfagna, M.
Cansoy, J. Schor and R. Wengronowitz (2018), 'Domesticating the
Market: Moral Exchange and the Sharing Economy', *Socio-Economic
Review*, forthcoming.
Fraiberger, S. and A. Sundararajan (2015), *Peer-to-Peer Rental Markets in
the Sharing Economy*, NYU Stern School of Business Research Paper.
Frenken, K. and J. Schor (2017), 'Putting the Sharing Economy into Per-
spective', *Environmental Innovation and Societal Transitions*, 23: 3–10.
Ge, Y., C. R. Knittel, D. MacKenzie and S. Zoepf (2016), *Racial and
Gender Discrimination in Transportation Network Companies*, NBER
Working Paper 22776.
Schor, J. and C. Fitzmaurice (2015), 'Collaborating and Connecting: the
Emergence of the Sharing economy', in L. A. Reisch and J. Thørgensen
(eds), *Handbook of Research on Sustainable Consumption*, 410–25.
Northampton, MA: Edward Elgar.
Schor, J. (2017), 'Does the Sharing Economy Increase Inequality within the
Eighty Percent? Findings from a Qualitative Study of Platform Provid-
ers', *Cambridge Journal of Regions, Economy and Society*, 10: 263–279.
Schor, J. and W. Attwood-Charles (2017), 'The Sharing Economy: Labor,
Inequality and Sociability on for-Profit Platforms', *Sociology Compass*,
Under Review.
Schor, J., W. Attwood-Charles, M. Cansoy, I. Ladegaard and R. Wen-
gronowitz (2017), 'Dependence and Precarity in the Platform Economy',
unpublished paper, Boston College.
Smith, Y. (2016), 'Can Uber Ever Deliver? Part One: Understanding
Uber's Bleak Operating Economics', *Naked Capitalism*, 30 November,

https://www.nakedcapitalism.com/2016/11/can-uber-ever-deliver-part-one-understanding-ubers-bleak-operating-economics.html.

Sundararajan, A. (2016), *The Sharing Economy: the End of Employment and the Rise of Crowd-Based Capitalism*, Cambridge, MA: MIT Press.

Thebault-Spieker, J., L. G. Terveen and B. Hecht (2015), 'Avoiding the South Side and the Suburbs: the Geography of Mobile Crowdsourcing Markets', in *Proceedings of the 18th ACM Conference on Computer Supported Cooperative Work & Social Computing*, https://dl.acm.org/citation.cfm?id=2675278.

# EMPLOYMENT AND REGULATION FOR CLICKWORKERS

Janine Berg and Valerio De Stefano

The aim of labour regulation is not only to protect workers from an unequal relationship of economic exchange (Deakin and Wilkinson 2005) but to grant employers managerial prerogatives to organise and direct their workers. Labour law ensures, however, that these prerogatives are not exerted in a way that is incompatible with workers' human dignity (Supiot 2011; see also Crouch this volume). Though the world of work has changed since the passage of the first labour laws over 100 years ago, the fundamental functions of this regulation – to provide minimum protections to working time regulations and earnings, to enable 'workplace democracy' by allowing workers' voice, as well as to protect health and safety – remain valid today.

It is often wrongly assumed that these regulations do not apply to work on platforms in the so-called gig economy, including to 'clickworkers' (Aloisi 2016). This is partly because the work is novel and, as a result, lawmakers, labour administration bodies and employers' associations and unions have failed to keep pace with this innovation (Dagnino 2016). But it is also the consequence of a business-driven narrative that, by overemphasising the allegedly new features of these forms of work, presents work on platforms as not suitable for existing labour regulations. An important element of this rhetoric is the use of buzzwords such as 'favours', 'rides' and 'tasks', rather than acknowledging that it is labour carried out by workers (De Stefano 2015). This rhetoric goes hand in hand with the practice common to many platforms of classifying workers as independent contractors (Prassl 2018).

Work on online labour platforms is diverse and includes those who perform 'clickwork' on 'crowdworking' sites as well as work undertaken locally through "work on demand via apps" (De Stefano 2015). On crowdworking sites, workers may complete small jobs or tasks ('micro-tasks' or 'clickwork') through online platforms, such as Amazon Mechanical Turk, CrowdFlower and Clickworker, or they may take on longer assignments in graphic design or data analysis from sites such as Upwork or Freelancer (Berg 2016). 'Crowdworkers' may access these platforms from anywhere in the world, so long as they have reliable internet connection, giving rise to a global competition for jobs in a sort of individualised international value chain. In work on demand via apps, workers perform duties such as providing transport, cleaning and home repairs, or running errands, but these activities are channelled and organised through mobile apps by companies such as Uber, TaskRabbit and Deliveroo (De Stefano 2015). The work is performed locally, despite the international presence of many of these companies (Aloisi 2016).

Representing platform-based work as a mere 'sharing of favours' conveys an image of the platform economy as a sort of parallel dimension, where chores are amateurishly carried out as a form of leisure or to earn 'pin money', and where labour protection and employment regulation are assumed not to be necessary. To give an example, when the bikers of foodora, a food delivery service, went on strike in Italy the managers of the company stated that working for foodora is only a means of earning some extra money 'for those who like to ride the bike' rather than a real job (Aloisi and De Stefano 2017). The reality, however, is different. For many of the people involved who labour on or through these sites, platform-based work is an indispensable source of income (see Huws et al. this volume; Schor this volume). In late 2015, the International Labour Organization (ILO) surveyed 'clickworkers' on two important click-working platforms: Amazon Mechanical Turk and CrowdFlower. More than one-third (40%) of the survey respondents indicated that crowdwork was their principal source of income, while the average time spent weekly on the platform was 30 hours. Half of the workers stated that they had crowdworked for more than 10 hours during at least one day in the previous month, and an impressive 40% of them also reported that they regularly worked seven days per week (Berg 2016).

Another common assumption driven by the mainstream narrative of platform-based work is that the workers are genuinely self employed. While there are some platforms that merely connect demand and supply of tasks between clients and independent service providers, there are many other instances where platforms do more than this, actively intervening in key elements of the work being provided (De Stefano 2015). Platforms often fix the price of the task and define its principal terms and conditions (Prassl 2018). In other cases, they enable the clients to determine these terms unilaterally, leaving workers unable to negotiate over them. The platform may define the details of the work, including instructing workers to wear uniforms, to use specific tools, or to treat customers in a particular way (Aloisi 2016).

Some platforms prohibit crowdworkers from subcontracting the completion of the task to other people. The general terms and conditions of Clickworker (2012) state:

> With respect to any project, Clickworker will exclusively mandate the clickworker who has submitted an offer to perform services relating thereto to consummate such project. Clickworkers are expressly prohibited from subcontracting or outsourcing projects to third parties unless this is expressly permitted by the terms of a project description.

Other platforms, such as CrowdFlower (2015), instead prevent the use of IT tools to complete tasks by banning the performance of any task with the use of Internet bots, web robots, bots, scripts, or any other form of artificial intelligence or otherwise attempt to obtain rewards from CrowdFlower without completing tasks as they are described.

Dictating how the work should be executed, including prohibiting the help of specific IT tools, is arguably a way of directing the performance of the work in a way that is not compatible with the purported self-employment status of workers. This is particularly the case when these ways of directing work are accompanied by stringent means of monitoring the execution of the work (see Crouch this volume). These forms of control vary greatly, spanning from the possibility of unilaterally determining the time required to complete a job to the use of technologies such as GPS or, in the case of virtual work, taking screenshots of the worker's screen to verify at any time their attendance to the given task.

In addition to these ways of interfering with the jobs done, many platforms have performance review systems that enable customers to rate the worker's performance. Ratings, in turn, are used to discipline the work, by limiting the ability of lower-rated workers to access jobs or excluding these workers from the platform (De Stefano 2015).

In platform work, therefore, practices are widespread that result in directing and controlling the performance of platform workers in fashions similar or even more stringent to what traditional employers would do. The management may be done through the terms of service, or it may be through an algorithm – so-called 'algorithmic management' – but it is still management. Indeed, it has been argued that "this often results in a determination of work that is so pronounced that it equals 'classical' personal dependency necessary for an employment relationship" (Risak and Warter 2015). Accordingly, when the platforms undertake these practices – or when they allow clients to take part in these forms of work management – the traditional legal tests used to determine the existence of an employment relationship could be met in platform work (Davidov 2016).

The arguments above call into question the mainstream rhetoric depicting platform work as a virtuous example of entrepreneurship, enabling people to 'be their own bosses' and freeing them from the control and hierarchy present in traditional employment or 'nine-to-five jobs' (using the 'straw-man' stereotypical term often used by platform-supporters to designate employment status). Presenting platform workers as a new class of independent micro-businesses and entrepreneurs could not be more misleading.

A convincing rebuttal of this rhetoric is provided in the landmark UK judgement that found two Uber drivers to be 'workers' under UK law. The tribunal dismissed as "faintly ridiculous" the notion that "Uber in London is a mosaic of 30,000 small businesses linked by a common 'platform'". Nor, according to the tribunal, does the company merely assist the drivers to 'grow' their businesses, since "no driver is in a position to do anything of the kind, unless growing [their] business simply means spending more hours at the wheel". The judge also found that, through the rating system, the platform subjected drivers to "what amounts to a performance management/disciplinary procedure", going beyond what is allowed in coordinating independent self-employed workers who act in the performance of their own business.[1] This is also perfectly coherent with the late-2017 judgment of the Court of Justice of the EU observing,

> Uber determines at least the maximum fare by means of the eponymous application, that the company receives that amount from the client before paying part of it to the non-professional driver of the vehicle, and that it exercises a certain control over the quality of the vehicles, the drivers and their conduct, which can, in some circumstances, result in their exclusion.[2]

At a closer look, therefore, it is evident that rather than the 'new' fourth digital revolution, platform work is simply 21st-century casual work rebranded. New technologies may be used to channel and organise work activities, but it is still about work executed by human beings and under the control of other people, in exchange for compensation. Indeed, 'gig work' needs to be considered along with broader trends of casualisation of the labour market in developed countries such as the spread of zero-hour contracts and on-call work (Freedland and Prassl 2017). These forms of work – in turn – closely resemble casual labour arrangements that were typical at the outset of industrialisation and are still a prominent feature of labour markets in developing countries (De Stefano 2016a).

As most platform work is currently unregulated – or rather self-regulated by the platform – it is characterised by a lack of job security and few, if any, labour protections. Moreover, while those in traditional casual work arrangements – such as day labourers, dock workers and agricultural farmhands – are at least paid by the day, those working in the platform economy are paid by the task at hand, be it riding a client from one place to another, delivering food around the city or translating texts on the internet. The Uber driver, the 'Turker' on the Amazon Mechanical Turk or the foodora worker must continuously search for work, monitoring their computer screens or smartphones for work opportunities. Indeed, the ILO survey shows how crowdworkers averaged 18 minutes looking for work for every hour working (Berg 2016).

Even when jobs span a few hours or a few days, the worker needs to be continually searching for new jobs; 90% of workers in the survey reported that they would like to be doing more work than they are currently doing, citing insufficient work and low pay as the reasons they were not (Berg 2016).

The lack of protection for workers, the casual nature of the work and the management and control practices put in place by the platforms all demonstrate the need to regulate platform work. The current model of platforms' self-regulation does not guarantee decent working conditions and risks putting responsible businesses out of the market. Indeed, unless the authorities acknowledge that workers should not be denied protection just because they work for platforms, they will continue to have an advantage over traditional business. There is therefore a risk of a deterioration in working conditions going much beyond platform-based work (Prassl 2018).

Opportunities for regulation are not scarce, as platforms purport. To begin with, the technology that has allowed parcelling and distributing work to 'the crowd' can also be used to regulate the work and provide protection to workers. Technology can monitor when workers are working, when they are searching for work, and when they are taking breaks. For example, Upwork, the online freelance marketplace, offers its clients the option of paying by the hour, as it can monitor the workers by recording their keyboard strokes and mouse clicks and taking random screen shots. Uber expects drivers always to have the app on, which can track drivers' whereabouts including their downtime.

This same technology can thus also be used to ensure that workers earn at least the minimum wage or ideally to regulate the wage agreed collectively by the workers and the platform. If labour protections are put in place, then platforms will have the incentive to re-organise work to limit search time. Technology and better organisational design can help to minimise search time, improving efficiency for all (Berg 2016). The technology can also be used to facilitate payment of social security contributions.

In addition, technology could be put in place to allow workers' contributions to be recognised outside the platform. Currently, if a young Indian college graduate works on Amazon Mechanical Turk after leaving university, but then after a few years decides she would prefer a job in a physical office, she has no way of showing that she did the work for Amazon Mechanical Turk, or taking her star rating with her. This is true of other platforms as well – whether Uber, Upwork or TaskRabbit. Certainly there are technological fixes that can be instituted, allowing for more open markets and free mobility of labour.

Needless to say, a strong push towards better regulation and policies to support platform work would also be provided by union action (see Doellgast this volume). Platform workers have shown the will to organise collectively through either grassroots organisations or traditional labour unions (Aloisi and De Stefano 2017). These efforts, however, may be materially hurdled by current regulatory limits banning self-employed workers from joining unions or engaging in collective bargaining, lest they be in breach of antitrust law and risk heavy sanctions (De Stefano 2016b). For instance, very recently an ordinance passed by the city of Seattle allowing collective bargaining for ride-hailing platforms such as Uber was challenged in court by businesses groups, and the Federal Trade Commission, the US antitrust authority, officially expressed the view that the ordinance should be nullified and collective bargaining banned for these workers (Miller 2017). Recognising freedom of association and the right to collective bargaining as fundamental and universal rights applying to all workers, as mandated under the international standards of the ILO (1998), would already represent an enormous step forward in giving protection to platform workers.

Another important step forward would be to include platform workers in strategies aimed at bettering the conditions of casual workers, with whom they share important dimensions of risk, as argued above (Aloisi, De Stefano and Silberman 2017). In particular, extending the regulation aimed at guaranteeing a minimum number of hours of work to be paid, taking into account the average number of hours worked over a reference period, as it is the case for zero-hour workers in the Netherlands, could be considered (ILO 2016). The same can be said for the regulation banning exclusivity clauses for these types of work, as it is currently mandated under the UK regulation of zero-hour work.

While it is easy to become enamoured by the glitz and convenience of apps and the myth that we have broken from our past, we need to remember that these platforms are merely providing another way of mediating work – driving and running errands, or carrying out data entry or audio transcription online are not 'new'. Technology is key for progress, we need good regulation to ensure that the technology is used responsibly and contributes to social wellbeing and not used to unravel the gains from the hard-fought battles to improve worker's rights. Otherwise, technology will not take us into the future, but instead return us to the past.

## NOTES

Janine Berg is senior economist at the ILO in Geneva, Switzerland. The views in this article are her own and do not necessarily reflect those of the ILO. Valerio De Stefano is BOF-ZAP research professor in the faculty of law at Katholieke Universiteit Leuven.

1. For further information see the Employment Tribunal *Mr Y Aslam, Mr J Farrar and Others* v *Uber*, case numbers 2202551/2015, from 28 October 2016. This judgment was appealed by Uber, but in November 2017 the Employment Appeal Tribunal upheld the decision given in the first instance. For further information on the appeal, see Employment Appeal Tribunal, *Uber B.V. and Others* v *Mr Y Aslam and Others*, UKEAT/0056/17/DA, 10 November 2017.

2. For further information see the case file C-434/15, *Asociación Profesional Elite Taxi* v *Uber Systems Spain* (2017).

## REFERENCES

Aloisi, A. (2016), 'Commoditized Workers: Case Study Research on Labour Law Issues Arising from a Set of "On-Demand/Gig Economy' Platforms"', *Comparative Labor Law & Policy Journal*, 37.

Aloisi, A. and V. De Stefano (2017), 'App contro app, così i precari sfidano i padroni della gig-economy', *Pagina 99*, 3 March, http://pagina99.it/2017/03/03/gig-economy-sindacato-lavoretti-diritti-deliveroo-foodora-uber-amazon/.

Aloisi, A., V. De Stefano and S. Silberman (2017), 'A Manifesto to Reform the Gig Economy', *Pagina 99*, 29 May, http://www.pagina99.it/2017/05/29/a-manifesto-to-reform-the-gig-economy/.

Berg, J. (2016), 'Income Security in the On-Demand Economy: Findings and Policy Lessons from a Survey of Crowdworkers', Geneva: International Labour Office, http://www.ilo.org/wcmsp5/groups/public/---ed_protect/---protrav/---travail/documents/publication/wcms_479693.pdf.

Clickworker (2012), 'General Terms and Conditions (Clickworkers)', https://workplace.clickworker.com/en/agreements/10123?_ga=2.4686711.578681291.1519481227-880470536.1519481227.

CrowdFlower (2015), 'CrowdFlower Master Terms of Service', https://www.crowdflower.com/legal/.

Dagnino, E. (2016), 'Labour and Labour Law in the Time of the On-demand Economy', *Revista Derecho Social y Empresa*, 6: 43–65.

Davidov, G. (2016), 'The Status of Uber Drivers: a Purposive Approach', *Spanish Labour Law and Employment Relations Journal*, http://www. labourlawresearch.net/sites/default/files/papers/The%20status%20 of%20Uber%20drivers%20A%20purposive%20approach%20copy.pdf.

Deakin, S. and F. Wilkinson (2005), *The Law of the Labour Market*, Oxford: Oxford University Press.

De Stefano, V. (2015), *The Rise of the 'Just-in-Time Workforce': On-Demand Work, Crowd Work and Labour Protection in the 'Gig-Economy'*, Bocconi Legal Studies Research Paper 2682602.

De Stefano, V. (2016a), 'Casual Work beyond Casual Work in the EU: the Underground Casualisation of the European Workforce – and What to Do About It', *European Labour Law Journal*, 7(3): 421–41.

De Stefano, V. (2016b), . 'Non-standard Work and Limits on Freedom of Association: a Human Rights-Based Approach', *Industrial Law Journal*, 46(2): 185–207.

Freedland, M. R. and J. Prassl (2017), *Employees, Workers, and the 'Sharing Economy': Changing Practices and Changing Concepts in the United Kingdom*, Oxford Legal Studies Research Paper 19.

ILO (1998), *ILO Declaration on Fundamental Principles and Rights at Work*, Geneva: International Labour Office, annex revised 2010.

ILO (2016), *Non-standard Employment Around the World*, International Labour Organization, http://www.ilo.org/wcmsp5/groups/public/---dgreports/---dcomm/---publ/documents/publication/wcms_534326.pdf.

Miller, C. (2017), 'FTC and Uber Align to Stop New Seattle Law for Ride-Hail Drivers', *The Recorder*, 6 November, https://www.law.com/therecorder/sites/therecorder/2017/11/06/ftc-and-uber-align-to-stop-new-seattle-law-for-ride-hail-drivers/?slreturn=20180109104042.

Prassl, J. (2018), *Humans as a Service: the Promise and Perils of Work in the Gig Economy*, Oxford: Oxford University Press.

Risak, M. and J. Warter (2015), 'Decent Crowdwork: Legal Strategies Towards Fair Employment Conditions in the Virtual Sweatshop', paper for the Regulating for Decent Work 2015 Conference, http://www. rdw2015.org/uploads/submission/full_paper/373/crowdwork_law_ RisakWarter.pdf.

Supiot, A. (2011), *Critique du Droit du Travail*, Paris: Presses Universitaires de France.

# C

# Labour relations and the welfare state in the digital age

# REDEFINING LABOUR RELATIONS AND CAPITAL IN THE DIGITAL AGE

## Colin Crouch

**S**ome observers argue that artificial intelligence (AI) and other forms of extreme automation will make most human labour redundant; and – more chillingly for the kind of people likely to read what they say – they suggest that it will be many highly skilled jobs that will be most threatened by this process. Were these predictions to be true, the first negative consequence would be a collapse in demand, since, if there are no (or few) skilled workers, there is little labour income, and therefore no demand for all those products that AI is eager to make for us to buy. There could be two alternative responses to this, precedents for both of which exist. First, and likely to be favoured by banks, is a vast growth in consumer credit to enable all these redundant people to carry on spending, unsecured credit funded by a near infinite regress of secondary markets. We had an experiment in this approach, mainly to deal with the stagnation of US labour incomes over the turn of the century. The regress turned out to be considerably short of infinite, leading to the crisis of 2008. This does not mean that the experiment will not be repeated; to some extent the British economy is repeating it at the time of writing. Its sustainability will always be highly doubtful, but unsecured credit is likely to remain an important, dangerous element of any rich capitalist society experiencing difficulty in sustaining a high volume of employment income.

The alternative approach is for workers, or rather non-workers, to be paid an income funded by taxation. Proposals for this, and even some experiments, exist in the increasingly popular idea of a basic or citizen's income. Again we have some real experience of this, as unemployed, disabled, the elderly and other people unable to work have long received non-work incomes of this kind. As they might tell basic income advocates, such incomes are at the mercy of political opinion, and can become the target of considerable criticism from those who do work and pay the taxes that fund those who cannot or do not. This vulnerability would become even more severe if a shrinking number of working people was being called on to pay the taxes needed to fund them. This approach to the problem is not likely to be as popular with business and politics as extended unsecured credit, as the latter at least brings short-term banking profit; it is also likely to be no more sustainable, though considerably less dangerous.

In the circumstances it is probably more constructive to share the assumption that economists usually make: that human beings will always find things to do for each other; and that if technology replaces some activities, they move on to find other things to do, usually making use of those very technologies. This is the history in the *longue durée* of the relationship between human work and technology. It is objected that this time is different, because now it is highly skilled work that is affected. That is however at least in part a result of how we retrospectively view those skills that technology replaces. The art of making highly elaborate copies of religious texts that dominated the work of many monks in the centuries before printing seems to us now to have been a laborious process of copying. But at the time it was one of the most skilled activities in a society where very few could read and write, let alone produce beautiful texts with primitive implements. Much the same could be said of the skills of medieval architects, who had to work out calculations of stresses and strains in materials with extraordinary skill and ad hoc judgement, with none of the established knowledge that enabled such tasks to become routine, first by using textbooks, and then in the late 20th century by using computers. Technology did not make architects redundant, but enabled them to move on to different activities. The list of examples can be extended across the centuries and sectors of the economy.

Rather than skill levels, it is types of work that are affected differentially by technology. In general, people working in professions that require some quality of human interaction to be performed, whether psychiatrists or waiters, are likely to be more robust in the face of the digital challenge than those requiring either repeated manual operations or those forms of intellectual effort that have little need for human interaction.

If this starting point is accepted, we can address the question of labour and capital relations in the digital age by making the following assumptions:

1. There will be considerable upheaval as old jobs are destroyed by technology and new ones created. There is nothing new about this, but previous historical episodes – such as the initial industrial revolution – were accompanied by considerable distress and conflict. That will be repeated. Also, the speed of change and therefore the repetition of successive waves of shock and responses to it can be expected to intensify.

2. Digitalisation will continue the present trend for information technology to place increasing powers of monitoring, surveillance and control into the hands of the managers of labour. The character of jobs, how they are performed, and with what skills, will increasingly be defined by these managements.

3. This shift of ever more discretion over the conduct of work tasks from practitioners to managers will apply even if the workforces involved have the appearance of being independent contractors. Indeed, it is intensified control that facilitates the current trend to self-employment, the so-called gig economy and other forms of precarious work relations. Until the growth of contemporary

information technology, workers could be most effectively controlled by bringing them together in one observable space; employers had little choice but to make them employees. If they can be managed at vast distances, there is little reason to do that.

4. Even though we should expect new jobs to replace old ones, there will be prolonged intermediate periods of adjustment, when old jobs are disappearing, but entrepreneurs have not yet discovered new ways of taking advantage of the labour that is available. While this is occurring, unemployment among certain kinds of workers and their skills must be expected to rise. During these periods there will be surpluses of labour. This will shift the balance of power in the employment relationship towards employers and capital. We have been observing a similar process, resulting from globalisation, for some decades now.

5. This last point will lead to intervals of deficient mass demand, which will also be negative for capital. However, in the early stages a shift to capital's advantage will produce more income inequality between capital and most forms of labour apart from senior management, producing increased dependence of producers on markets for luxury rather than mass-consumption goods and services. These may themselves be quite labour-intensive, as luxury products are usually characterised by high labour inputs, partially reversing the overall trend to the replacement of labour. This process is likely in turn to stimulate increased labour demand. We are already to some extent living in an economy of this kind, with employment in important luxury niches accompanying otherwise growing mass production (Khan 2015; Silverstein and Fiske 2003).

6. Finally, we should assume that employers in sectors where IT is part of the core business will continue their current practice of locating themselves fiscally in the most benign jurisdictions. As IT spreads to more activities and sectors, ever more firms will be able to do this. Indeed, many firms now claim that they do not have a geographical location. Taken together with point 3, digitalisation is producing a world of firms that have no location

and do not employ the people who work for them. This breaks long-established assumptions of public policy, especially over taxation, firms' responsibilities towards workers, and the financing of non-wage labour costs.

Digitalisation therefore seems set to continue certain recent trends: a growth in various kinds of precarious jobs, rising inequality, and increasing managerial surveillance power, with employers increasingly able to avoid making any contribution to workers' various employment risks (from health and safety to social insurance). This combination has two particular sets of implications for employment relations: the erosion and perhaps collapse of the concept of the employee as a figure with associated rights and duties, and growing power asymmetries between those who control work and those who carry it out.

## REDEFINING THE EMPLOYMENT RELATIONSHIP

From the point of view of economic theory, labour is just another commodity; when it is unemployed it is no different from any other piece of unsold stock waiting on a shelf. Thus, the main reason that firms give for using various forms of non-employees is the flexibility it gives them to match labour supply to demand; it is inefficient to have workers hanging around with nothing to do while being paid. They therefore want to take advantage of the control possibilities afforded by digitalisation to dispense with the idea of the standard employee, to whom they have responsibilities to provide ongoing work. They are therefore inventing (sometimes re-inventing) such categories as the gig economy, temporary work, casual work, jobs with highly flexible hours (at their extreme, zero-hour contracts), and false self-employment. We shall here use the general term 'non-employees' to bring together all these categories. Being a non-employee might work well for workers having no need for stability, such as students, actors between roles, people just wanting a few hours of paid work from time to time. However, if people can find only such work when they are trying to buy, or pay high rent for, a home, or build a family, or equip a house, unpredictability and extreme fluctuation in income brings high negative externalities of flexibility. The commodity 'labour' needs to reproduce, to restore itself and to consume. When it gets angry it can be troublesome. The more that employers insist on labour being flexible, the more difficult they make it for workers to achieve the stability that much non-working adult life requires. No matter how neoliberal they want to be in their economic policies, governments, even undemocratic ones, cannot ignore these irritating characteristics of human labour. In the last analysis they pick up many of the costs of these externalities.

The changes being wrought by digitalisation are intensifying the degree of disturbance that people face in their working lives, producing a crisis of stability at least as important as that of the depressions of the 1920s and 1930s. It will however be increasingly difficult to tackle these problems through social insurance systems funded partly by employers' contributions – a reasonable approach, requiring firms to bear the costs of the externalities they generate, along with workers themselves and government. How can this be done when firms have no fiscal location in the country where the work takes place, and where the workers are not their employees?

There is also a growing imbalance between the fiscal position of those firms and sectors that can choose their physical location, and those that simply cannot. Taxation is distorting investment patterns across sectors and across sizes of firms. For these and other reasons, corporate taxation will have to shift from an employment or head-office location base to a sales base. A firm might threaten to de-locate from a country because of its high taxes on the locus of production, but it will not refuse to sell goods to a country with high sales taxes. This raises important issues, because sales taxes are regressive. On the other hand, if economists are right to argue that most corporate taxes are eventually reflected in prices, then the overall effect might not be much different. The issue requires detailed investigation and goes beyond our current concerns, but we can here signal a need for action if the security needs of an increasingly unsettled working population are not to be neglected.

Because digitalisation greatly increases companies' ability to use non-employees, firms like Uber complain that critics of its employment practices are standing in the way of technological advance, but there is nothing new about these work forms in themselves. In the early industrial revolution a very common form of employment in the textile and clothing industry was the 'putting out system'. Women worked in their own homes producing items, with the finished goods being collected on behalf of the entrepreneur from time to time. The reappearance of this primitive employment forms is partly driven by IT and AI, because remote and digitalised communications systems make it possible to control large numbers of people without giving them employee status. But technology neither determines nor originates the form of work contract; it could be deployed to make life more, not less, secure for the workforce.

If firms are using non-employment in order to evade obligations owed to employees, then by making a sharp distinction between dependent employment and self-employment the legal system is accidentally giving them bad incentives. The key concept needs to become the use that an organisation makes of labour, rather than its formal relationship to it. There are already precedents for this. If one employs an independent contractor to carry out tasks on one's premises, one has certain obligations, for example to maintain a safe working area. The range of these provisions should be extended so that, for example, if a so-called self-employed restaurant-food delivery worker falls off her bike, the firm that had contracted her to make the delivery should be legally responsible for any unreasonable risks they imposed on her (eg excessively heavy loads, insufficient time to make journeys safely) and for subsequent sick pay – though of course if it was her own bike she would still be responsible for any defects in it that led to the accident.

Often firms' search for extreme labour flexibility conflicts with the most efficient use of labour. Workers' productivity is enhanced if firms have an incentive to invest in their skills and prolonged experience. This is unlikely to be done for non-employees, who are usually seen as having no long-term future with the firm. The best approach to this problem would be a per capita tax on the 'use of labour', additional to social insurance taxes. Firms providing true formal employment contracts to the workers they use would be completely exempt from this tax. This would reverse current negative fiscal and regulatory incentives. Also exempt would be firms that use non-employment contracts, but accept various liabilities towards the workers concerned: health and safety, guarantees of working hours, provision of training, payment of social-security contributions. To provide flexibility, there could be a tariff of tax reductions for different items in such a list. There would also be exemptions for firms below a certain size and for contracts for very small numbers of hours. The tax needs to be set at a rate such that those firms using non-employment primarily to avoid responsibilities have an incentive to use at least certain elements of a formal employment relationship. If, with extreme digitalisation of managerial control, non-employment before long becomes the norm for work relations, the fiscal and labour law obligations needed to accommodate it would already be in place.

## SURVEILLANCE AND CONTROL

The second major way in which digitalisation will change employment relations is through the intensified control it offers to managers to control workers in their performance of tasks. One can hypothesise two extreme forms of management–worker relationship. In the first scenario, management has complete confidence in the professional skill and ethic of the workers, such that it allows them complete discretion in their performance of tasks, a discretion removed only when there is evidence of poor practice. This is obviously the preferred system for workers; for employers it also represents a prime facie efficient system, as monitoring costs are kept very low. However, the employer faces considerable moral hazard, as it has little chance to check on avoidance of tasks, inefficient use of time and poor quality work. The other extreme is one of zero trust. Management assumes that workers will cheat, waste time and work inefficiently at every opportunity. They are therefore constantly monitored and allowed little discretion in how they perform their tasks. Workers do not like such a system, but employers avoid moral hazard. Monitoring is costly, but they may believe that these costs are recouped by the efficiency gains. There is however another cost to both employer and workers: workers who are not trained to use discretion are incapable of responding to deviations from routine, and likely to work without commitment.

AI and IT make possible cheaper and more extensive monitoring, increasing employers' incentives to shift to the zero trust model, including its extension to so-called 'professional' forms of employment, in particular in education, health and care services. This has been accompanied by a major increase in the ratio of managers to professional staff, but digitalisation can be expected to automate much of the monitoring task itself: managers are themselves workers likely to present moral hazards to the owner. Professional athletes already have their heart rate, food intake, etc. constantly monitored. We should expect this kind of activity to expand to secure more managerial control over the movements and behaviour of workers, not just while they are at work, but all the time. Some of these extensions might be generally welcomed; we should all appreciate having the alcohol levels of surgeons and airline pilots monitored. But others might be experienced as very irksome with little benefit for customers or the general public.

It is impossible to imagine that workers would ever have equivalent means to monitor the conduct of managers. The overall result of digitalisation will therefore be a major increase in the power of the latter over the former. This intensifies a need, already developing over recent years of relative labour surplus, for workers at all levels to have easy access to trade union representation. This is something that unions and workers need to fight for themselves, or it would

not be authentic, though governments should certainly be expected
to create a level playing field for unions, for example, by making
it illegal for employers to take measures to impede their activities.

This will need to be unionism with a different emphasis from that
to which we have become accustomed. Unions are usually perceived
to be mainly concerned with securing wage rises, but individual
and collective grievance handling, an important but less prominent
aspect of their work, will become increasingly important with intensified managerial control and the growth of non-employment. They
will also have to learn how to represent the interests and attract the
membership of non-employees; like labour law, unions need to dis-
card the distinction between employees and other kinds of worker.
To represent the disaggregated workers of the digitalised economy,
they will have to abandon the tendencies of decades to base their
local organisations in large workplaces, partly returning to old
methods of town organisation, but mainly using social media and
websites. Much of this already happens, but a major extension of it is
desperately needed. Groups like the Independent Workers' Union of
Great Britain, representing growing numbers of gig economy workers, need to be brought fully into the union fold.

Another old practice that will need reviving is for unions to see
themselves as interested and expert in their members' professional
capacities. This was fundamental to the original craft unions, and
even more so to the 'professional associations' representing the
highly skilled non-manual occupations. These latter used to stand
aloof from the trade union movement; today they are more fully
integrated, but in the process have lost much of that earlier professional role. If workers of various kinds are to combat the spiral into
low-trust, low-discretion total monitoring, they will need representatives trying to push the border back, regaining the ability of workers to win trust through respect for their skills. Unions can do this
by participating in training, and by themselves winning increased
discretion for the majority of workers by exercising various forms
of professional discipline over the poorly performing. Critics of the
concept of 'post-Fordism' have long pointed out that Fordism, in the

sense of detailed managerial control over workers' movements, has only just arrived for teachers, medical practitioners, care workers, lawyers and others in similarly skilled occupations (Crowley et al. 2010). There are today considerable grounds for solidarity, or at least for sharing a joint priority, on the balance between control and merited trust among working people at all levels of the occupational structure, including managers themselves.

How we establish the right to be trusted and therefore not have our every movement under permanent surveillance will become a major theme of politics in a digital age, applying to citizens' relations with police and security services as much as employees' and non-employees' relations with management. Governments and employers will be completely seduced by the possibilities of total surveillance. But they may become sensitive to arguments about the importance of discretion to efficiency, the bad morale and resentment produced by monitoring, and the serious trade-off that exists between it and trust, saving us from the digital age finally bringing reality to all those mid-20th-century dystopias of totally monitored lives.

## REFERENCES

Crowley, M., D. Tope, L. J. Chamberlain and R. Hodson (2010), 'Neo-Taylorism at Work: Occupational Change in the Post-Fordist Era', *Social Problems*, 57(3): 421–47.

Khan, O. (2015), 'Luxury Consumption Moves East', *Journal of Fashion Marketing and Management*, 19(4): 347–59.

Silverstein, M. J. and N. Fiske (2003), 'Luxury for the Masses', *Harvard Business Review*, 81(4): 48–57.

# REBALANCING WORKER POWER IN THE NETWORKED ECONOMY

## Toward collective regulation of outsourced and precarious work

### Virginia L. Doellgast

Inequality is on the rise across the global north. Pay for top earners is growing at a much faster rate than for middle- or low-income workers, and in-work poverty rates are increasing as more new jobs are low-wage and insecure. Meanwhile, welfare states are being rolled back and labour unions are losing members and influence, widening the gap in access to social rights and voice at work. These two sets of trends are weakening democratic institutions via the concentration of economic and political power. Democracies are sustained by checks and balances to prevent the interests of a small group from taking priority over those of the majority. They progress through debate and compromise to identify and advance common interests. The challenges of combating inequality and extending democracy are thus tightly linked, and at root about returning a larger share of power and voice to workers.

In this chapter I will argue that strong labour unions are crucially important for promoting more equal distribution of power within economies being reshaped by the fourth industrial revolution, and by extension are central to saving the democratic institutions that are threatened by extreme inequality. I propose two broad policy solutions aimed at rebalancing union power vis-à-vis employers: establishing more encompassing forms of social and collective regulation that close existing legal loopholes; and supporting union organising and bargaining across companies linked through contracting relationships. In the following sections I review evidence from three sources that support these proposals. The first is a comparative international study of call centre work, the Global Call Center Project, based on surveys and case studies in 17 countries (Batt, Holman and Holtgrewe 2009). The second is a 10-country study of restructuring and job quality in European and US telecommunications firms (Doellgast, Sarmiento-Mirwaldt and Benassi 2016). The third is the edited book Reconstructing Solidarity, which analyses comparative case study findings from nine industries and occupations across 15 European countries (Doellgast, Lillie and Pulignano 2018).

## HOW OUTSOURCING UNDERMINES WORKER POWER AND DRIVES GROWING INEQUALITY

The example of call centres shows how a combination of technological change, market liberalisation and firms' changing organisational strategies have weakened unions and driven growing inequality. In the 1990s and early 2000s, it became easier and cheaper to answer calls far from the customer, distribute calls to different locations and workers, and more accurately predict how many calls would come in at any particular time. At the same time, new technologies have been used to intensify performance monitoring through continuous capture of key strokes, screen shots and voice recordings. Call centres today are extremely efficient and the work they perform is easily moved to regions and countries with lower wages and higher unemployment than the areas and countries they service. Meanwhile, a multinational industry of subcontractors has taken over a growing share of call centre work from banking, telecommunications and retail firms facing a cost squeeze from liberalisation and globalisation of once protected markets. These subcontractors route calls across locations worldwide, with centres serving customers in the global north from both domestic and lower cost locations in the global south – for example, in India and the Philippines (English), Northern Africa (French) and Latin America (Spanish, Portuguese).

Call centres thus show in an extreme form trends we can observe across the economy: jobs are highly mobile and easily offshored, worker performance can be intensively monitored and tightly controlled, and employers outsource a large portion of work to often non-union subcontractors expected to compete on low cost and high flexibility. What are the effects of these trends on workers? First, we found that call centre subcontractors had significantly lower pay and worse conditions than those working in call centres in other industries. Studies based on the Global Call Center survey showed that typical wages of subcontractors were on average 18% lower than for in-house (non-subcontracted) call centres, a gap that shrunk only marginally when controlling for skills, size and other variables (Batt, Nohara and Kwon 2010). In our 10-country study, we found even larger gaps in pay between nearly identical call centre jobs in telecommunications firms and in their subcontractors, with 20–50% lower pay in some countries (Doellgast, Sarmiento-Mirwaldt and Benassi 2016). Subcontractors also had worse working conditions: they used more part-time and temporary workers, had higher turnover rates, monitored workers more intensively, and invested less in training (Batt, Holman and Holtgrewe 2009; Doellgast, Holtgrewe and Deery 2009). Thus, as a growing number of call centre jobs move out of traditional industries like banking and utilities and into independent subcontractors, they are becoming lower quality and lower paid.

A second, more indirect, effect of outsourcing is to make it more difficult for workers in unionised workplaces to hold on to past gains. Companies often compare costs and flexibility between their own workers and their subcontractors' workforce or with conditions or collective agreements in the call centre industry. Managers can easily threaten to outsource more jobs if unions or works councils do not agree to lower wages, more monitoring, or more flexible working practices. We found that these kinds of threats led to major concessions aimed at stopping or reversing outsourcing in 4 of our 10 telco company cases (Doellgast, Sarmiento-Mirwaldt and Benassi 2016). Not coincidentally, these were all cases with large pay differences between internal and outsourced call centre workers, and with low union coverage of subcontractors.

Outsourcing thus drives down job quality not only through market-based competition but also through the effects of this competition on workers' bargaining power. Studies looking at other industries show similar political dynamics and outcomes associated with outsourcing: in low-wage service jobs, among higher skilled professionals, such as government workers, as well as in manufacturing and construction (for a review of this research, see Doellgast, Lillie and Pulignano 2018, 7–10 and 18–21). Worker representatives are more restricted in the kinds of strategies they can use to represent their members' interests in better pay and improved working conditions when they are told the only option is to be as cheap and flexible as subcontractors. These challenges are most severe, however, where subcontractors are able to bypass the stronger collective agreements or minimum legal conditions covering in-house workers in traditional industries.

## THE VICIOUS CIRCLE OF EXPANDING PRECARIOUS WORK

Outsourcing is one kind of strategy that can reduce costs and increase flexibility through moving work to a separate firm with different pay and conditions. Firms can also adopt non-standard arrangements such as agency, freelance and marginal part-time contracts. These often have similar effects in making work more short term and unpredictable, as well as less likely to be covered by collective bargaining or benefits – for example, unemployment insurance, parental leave, pensions and further training. In our book Reconstructing Solidarity we argue that the expansion of these different forms of precarious work can be traced to a negative feedback dynamic or vicious circle linking growing gaps in union agreements and employment protections with the breakdown of broad, inclusive forms of worker solidarity – both of which shape employer and union strategies (Doellgast, Lillie and Pulignano 2018).

After the second world war, western European countries had the most success in extending decent conditions and pay across the workforce. First, inclusive institutions were critical for stopping the spread of precarious work. These institutions include welfare state protections, labour market legislation and collective agreements that cover all workers. Workers with weaker bargaining power are less likely to be precarious where they are covered by the same protections and benefits as those workers with stronger bargaining power. These institutions have to be built, and typically that has happened through social and labour movements grounded in inclusive solidarity – based on forming common cause across workers with different identities (eg based on gender, ethnicity and class) and labour market power (eg based on skills and collective organisation). This kind of inclusive solidarity is necessary for workers and citizens to support inclusive institutions such as solidaristic welfare states; and encourages unions to take into account diverse worker groups in its organising and bargaining strategies. Meanwhile, where there is less precarity in a labour market, inclusive solidarity is easier to build and sustain. It is less likely one group of workers will scapegoat another group of workers or want to deny them benefits when they are all under the same collective agreement and social safety net.

Today, it is becoming easier and cheaper across Europe to avoid legal and negotiated protections by outsourcing work or hiring workers on more precarious, short-term contracts. This has two effects: employers find creative ways to escape from past obligations to their workers, making work feel more insecure for those in both permanent and non-standard jobs; these employer strategies have a further effect of undermining solidarity across the workforce. It is difficult to build collective action where workers are on different contracts or based in different subsidiaries or subcontractors. These divisions are often heightened where more precarious workers are also from different racial or ethnic groups. The call centre and tele-communications studies cited above found evidence of both kinds of effects, which were most severe in countries like the UK, the US, Germany and Denmark, where management could easily escape collective bargaining or introduce different terms and conditions across the workforce.

## POLICY SOLUTIONS TO PRECARIOUS WORK

How do we reverse the vicious circle of expanding precarity to rebalance political and economic power within our increasingly unequal societies? Across the country and industry case studies in Reconstructing Solidarity we found many examples of union campaigns focused on organising precarious workers and improving pay and conditions across the workforce. Those that were successful shared a common focus on sustaining or building inclusive institutions and mobilising inclusive forms of worker solidarity – including solidarity within the labour movement itself. Our research findings across the three projects suggest two sets of policies at the national or European level that provide some measure of support for union efforts in both areas.

First, more encompassing social and collective regulation are needed to close existing legal loopholes. The most obvious thing that governments can do to level the playing field is to make it more difficult for companies to exit social arrangements. It seems that the opposite trend is more common, with the EU and its member states including a widening array of potential loopholes to give companies flexibility in how they apply social protections. For example, the UK's legislation requiring equal treatment of agency workers included a clause known as the 'Swedish Derogation', which allowed temporary staffing agencies to be exempted from the requirement of equal treatment on pay provisions if they offered an agency worker a permanent contract of employment and paid the worker between assignments. When the legislation was first introduced, the UK's incumbent telecommunications firm BT (formerly British Telecom) was employing 4,000 agency employees, who began earning up to 20% more pay. However, its staffing agencies immediately began to exploit the pay-between-assignments loophole in the legislation, and by 2013 this had become the default contract for this group of workers, allowing agencies to pay their workers between £2 and £4 less per hour than similar permanent workers (for more detail, see Doellgast, Sarmiento-Mirwaldt and Benassi 2015).

There are several examples in our book of successful campaigns to close these kinds of loopholes, often led by unions. Chiara Benassi and Lisa Dorigatti (2018) compared union campaigns to fight precarious agency work in the German and Italian metal sectors. In Germany, agency work was substantially deregulated in the early 2000s, making it easy and cheap for metalworking companies to hire large numbers of lower-wage agency workers. Works councils first cooperated with these changes to save their companies money. However, they soon noticed that their members were being replaced by this cheaper workforce, and were forced to make local concessions on pay and conditions to protect their jobs. IG Metal responded with the campaign Besser Statt Billiger [Better Not Cheaper] – which sought to encourage works councils to regulate agency work in similar ways at the local level. Meanwhile, they used the campaign to build a stronger sectoral agreement on agency work and to push for stronger national regulations, both of which took the pressure off local works councils for concessions. Today agency jobs in the German metal sector are better paid, there are more pathways to permanent jobs, and these workers are more integrated into local works councils.

An important lesson from IG Metal's experience is that collective action was most successful when it targeted both legal reforms and building more solidaristic bargaining within existing collective agreements. This leads to our second point.

Collective agreements should be extended not only within traditional industries, but across companies and their subcontractors and staffing agencies. This is an important complement to legislation that closes exit options and loopholes – to counter the negative effects that outsourcing and agency work often have in breaking apart coordinated bargaining. Here I can give an example from my comparative research on European telecommunication firms. In a paper with Chiara Benassi and Katja Sarmiento-Mirwaldt, we asked why after telecommunications markets were liberalised, Austria and Sweden developed coordinated collective bargaining across large employers and their subcontractors, while Germany and Denmark experienced increasingly disorganised bargaining. We also asked what effects these different paths had for pay and working conditions in the sector (Benassi, Doellgast and Sarmiento-Mirwaldt 2016). Findings showed that inequality across in-house and subcontracted jobs were lower in the Austrian and Swedish cases in large part because bargaining structures brought together different groups of workers linked together across firms' networks of subcontractors and staffing agencies. For example, I interviewed a network technician who had worked for TeliaSonera in Sweden. She had been transferred to a subcontractor as part of a major outsourcing of all of TeliaSonera's technician services in the 2000s. She was then laid off and rehired through a temporary agency. However, she remained a member of the same union, and continued to be covered by strong collective agreements. Her pay had stayed largely at the same level throughout these moves and her agency paid her 90% of her normal salary when she was not placed on an assignment. In contrast, workers outsourced from Denmark's former state-owned telco provider, TDC, experienced dramatic downgrading of pay and conditions as they were moved to firms with weaker union agreements covered by often competing labour unions.

This example suggests that countries differ significantly in how well existing collective bargaining institutions are able to adjust to the challenges of more fragmented, networked production models that link workplaces across organisational boundaries. Governments in Austria, Finland and France, to give only three examples, are considering legislation (at the time of writing in early 2018) that would give firms more flexibility to exit industry-level agreements or to further decentralise bargaining to the workplace level. This would weaken unions' capacity to continue to coordinate bargaining even at industry level, much less to extend these institutions across firms linked together in subcontracting relationships but formally located in different industries. Public policy instead should seek to strengthen supports for inclusive institutions that help to establish increased bargaining coordination at the level of these production networks. These would be most effective at the European level, given the growing integration of firms across European markets.

## CONCLUSIONS

Growing inequality undermines solidarity and makes it more difficult to use our political institutions to engage in meaningful debate about the goals that firms and governments should pursue. Growing support for far-right political parties in Europe is evidence that inclusive forms of solidarity are breaking down, replaced by more exclusive group identities often based on a narrowly defined nationalism. Taking measures to support increased collective worker voice within firms and industries is central to combating inequality and its associated social problems. History suggests that proposals for strengthening collective regulation are unlikely to be advanced unilaterally by governments without significant pressure from social and labour movements. There is a certain Catch-22 to proposing reforms to strengthen unions when the political will for those reforms requires strong unions in the first place. But the point is still worth making: effective democracies need mechanisms for workers to participate in decisionmaking within firms and industries, and unions are the actors with the most obvious capacity and experience to take on this role. If we are serious about sustaining our democratic institutions, we should seek to strengthen collective bargaining institutions through extending them across our economies.

## REFERENCES

Batt, R., D. Holman and U. Holtgrewe (2009), 'The Globalization of Service Work: Comparative Institutional Perspectives on Call Centers, Introduction to a Special Issue of ILRR', *ILR Review*, 62(4): 453–88.

Batt, R., H. Nohara and H. Kwon (2010), 'Employer Strategies and Wages in New Service Activities: a Comparison of Co-ordinated and Liberal Market Economies', *British Journal of Industrial Relations*, 48(2): 400–35.

Benassi, C., V. Doellgast and K. Sarmiento-Mirwaldt (2016), 'Institutions and Inequality in Liberalizing Markets: Explaining Different Trajectories of Institutional Change in Social Europe', *Politics & Society*, 44(1): 117–42.

Benassi, C. and L. Dorigatti (2018), 'The Political Economy of Agency Work in Italy and Germany: Explaining Diverging Trajectories in Collective Bargaining Outcomes', in V. Doellgast, N. Lillie and V. Pulignano (eds), *Reconstructing Solidarity: Labour Unions, Precarious Work, and the Politics of Institutional Change in Europe*, 124–43, Oxford: Oxford University Press.

Doellgast, V., U. Holtgrewe and S. Deery (2009), 'The Effects of National Institutions and Collective Bargaining Arrangements on Job Quality in Front-Line Service Workplaces', *ILR Review*, 62(4): 489–509.

Doellgast, V., K. Sarmiento-Mirwaldt and C. Benassi (2015), 'Union Campaigns to Organize Across Production Networks in the European Telecommunications Industry: Lessons from the UK, Italy, Sweden, and Poland', in J. Drahokoupil (ed.), *The Outsourcing Challenge: Organizing Workers Across Fragmented Production Networks*, 177–98, Brussels: ETUI.

Doellgast, V., K. Sarmiento-Mirwaldt and C. Benassi (2016), 'Contesting Firm Boundaries: Institutions, Cost Structures, and the Politics of Externalization', *ILR Review*, 69(3): 551–78.

Doellgast, V., N. Lillie and V. Pulignano (eds) (2018), *Reconstructing Solidarity: Labour Unions, Precarious Work, and the Politics of Institutional Change in Europe*, Oxford: Oxford University Press.

# COLLECTIVE ACTION AND BARGAINING IN THE DIGITAL ERA

Cécile Jolly

Digitalisation is transforming the nature of work in Europe and around the globe. On the one hand digitalisation could provide new and less arduous job opportunities, increased autonomy for workers, greater scope for collaborative working between people in different countries, and the dissemination of greater levels of skills development and training. On the other hand, digitalisation could threaten existing jobs, increase the extent of precarious work with little social protection, blur the boundary between work and family, and weaken collective labour relations.

These changes present a major challenge for actors including trade unions, employers' organisations and governments, in collective bargaining, forming and implementing labour regulations, and reforming social insurance coverage for the new, emerging forms of employment. Since the invention of the microprocessor in 1971 computing capacity has exponentially transformed work and society, but as Carlota Perez (2004) has pointed out the socio-institutional framework has been slower to adapt to the pace of innovation, and political actors are still 'catching up'. Labour relations are one of the pillars of the post-war socio-institutional framework, but how is social dialogue adapting to the new conditions of growth and work?

Drawing on a number of recent embryonic initiatives to regulate these changes collectively and by examining the growth of non-standard and gig employment I argue that the digital transformation requires a new form of social dialogue that is yet to be designed.

## THE EMERGING TRANSFORMATION OF SOCIAL DIALOGUE IN THE DIGITAL AGE

Technological change in the workplace is occurring across many types of industries. The trend is not new for trade, finance and tele-communication but the pace is accelerating, and platforms are now disrupting sectors that are traditionally less exposed to international competition such as transport and hotels. These changes are difficult to manage when jobs are at risk and when changing skill requirements are unclear. For employers' representatives and unions, fear and uncertainty for the future do not augur well for the establishment of a constructive dialogue; in many cases neither managers nor employees are fully aware of the impending consequences. Although 7 in 10 Europeans agree that robots and artificial intelligence can 'steal people's jobs', a majority (53%) say their job could not be done at all by a robot or artificial intelligence while more than 4 in 10 (44% ) think that it could (European Commission 2017).

Established channels of social dialogue and institutional frameworks of labour relations inside companies or at the sectoral level are not well adapted to addressing these topics. The subject of negotiations, as well as the bargaining timeline, do not match the reality of technological change, as the impact of digitalisation on jobs and skills is not easy to anticipate, and their impact can be highly varied depending on the sector in question. The dialogue needs to be conducted continually across a number of cross-cutting issues such as jobs, skills, quality of working life and personal data protection. However, social dialogue is more often organised on a regulated fixed timeline, and considers a limited range of specific topics. Traditionally working hours and wages formed the pillars of collective bargaining, while today working conditions, organisational and skill transformations are key. But there is no such thing as a mandatory social negotiation about the digital transformation in collective bargaining.

Nevertheless, some recent initiatives developed at company level illustrate the growing awareness of the negative effects of telework and information-and-communication-technology-facilitated mobile work (Messenger et al., 2017). To address the problems of 'hyper connectivity' some recent radical initiatives can be found. For example, in Germany, Volkswagen blocks email sent outside working hours and Daimler-Benz sends automated 'out of office' messages on behalf of those on holiday who receive emails, with the contact details of an alternative staff member. These measures are intended to protect employee's work–life balance (BBC 2014). In France reforms to labour law introduced in 2016 established a new 'right to disconnect' from out-of-hours work emails or phone calls. The specific terms and conditions whereby employees can 'switch off' have to be negotiated by the social partners at company level (BBC 2016). Similar initiatives have been identified in Spain in a company-level collective agreement between union and employer representatives at the insurance company AXA, which recognised the right to turn off company phones or not to answer work-related calls out of working hours in 2017 (EurWORK 2017a).

A number of collective agreements have been implemented on the insecurity associated with teleworkers in Austria, Belgium, Denmark, Germany, Greece, France, Italy, Luxembourg and Spain (see Doellgast this volume). These company-, industry- or national-level agreements are derived from the European framework agreement on telework in 2002 (Welz and Wolf, 2010). However, such achievements, along with a number of collective agreements that deal specifically with the overall effects of digitalisation on the labour market, are relatively rare. Many social partner representatives are engaged in informal dialogue on the social impact of digitalisation at national level (eg in Germany, France, Netherland, Luxemburg and Sweden), and these issues are discussed through formal negotiations (on working conditions and restructuring plans, for example) or informal ones, essentially at company level. But they have rarely led to mutual commitments or framework agreements at the company, industry, national or European levels.

The first company-level agreement on digital transformation signed at Orange constitutes an exception to this, and is an example worth considering in some detail. Orange, one of the most prominent French multinational telecommunication companies, signed an agreement with social partners to prevent 'over-consumption' of digital tools, foster digital skills, develop new collaborative way of working, and protect the personal data of workers. As another example, the former public railway company Deutsche Bahn and the Railway and Transport Union (Eisenbahn- und Verkehrsgewerkschaft; EVG) announced in 2016 the start of negotiations for a new collective agreement in order to address mobile work issues and how digitalisation is affecting occupational profiles in the sector (see Rahner and Schönstein this volume).

Despite some progress, much remains to be done to address the social impact of digital technology in the collective bargaining process. Employers and employees need each other: employers need technological change to be accepted, employees have to adapt their skills and working conditions to be protected to avoid marginalisation or job loss. But to manage this change collectively requires explanation and assessment of the likely consequences, some experimentation and a new framework on the cross-cutting issues that require more protracted dialogue, but this new form of dialogue is yet to be designed and comprehensively implemented.

## INTEGRATING NON-STANDARD FORMS OF EMPLOYMENT INTO EXISTING COLLECTIVE BARGAINING FRAMEWORKS

Collective action and bargaining is also needed, not only inside the boundaries of companies that hire employees on open-ended contracts, but also for more vulnerable workers including part-timers, those on fixed-term contracts or those in self-employment, who receive a relatively low income, and casual workers. Not all self-employed workers are in a precarious employment situation, for example lawyers. Nevertheless, Vermeylen et al. (2017) estimate that almost a quarter of European self-employed workers are vulnerable or are in 'concealed', bogus, self-employment. Many self-employed workers do not have the same levels of social protection as salaried employees. Technology is not the only driver of change, but has indeed facilitated the growth of non-standard forms of employment as automation and product standardisation permits a fragmentation of jobs into tasks that can be outsourced. As a consequence intermittent salaried and self-employed workers are not easily subsumed into the established institutional framework of labour relations and social protection.

First, the development of non-standard forms of employment undermines the ability of trade unions to organise and represent the most vulnerable workers. Created to be the voice of salaried blue-collar workers – the proletariat – trade unions are often reluctant or ill-adapted to defend the new proletariat of temporary workers and the precariously self-employed (see Kanjuo-Mrc ela this volume). Their presence inside the boundaries of companies is counterbalanced by the trend to use teleworkers or to employ non-standard forms of employment outside the core workforce. Faced with this trend a growing number of European trade unions are offering services and support to self-employed workers to help them deal with the contractors and to protect themselves (for example when dealing with legal issues, occupational health and insurance) (EurWORK 2017b).

This commitment is relatively new and growing steadily. It can ultimately lead to negotiating pay or late payments on behalf of a particular group of self-employed workers, for example musicians, actors or freelance journalists. But in these cases the arrangements may be scrutinised by competition authorities that are concerned with preventing price-fixing cartels. Trade unions are also often engaged in a struggle to limit the extent of temporary contracts or bogus self-employment. However, this kind of commitment may give the impression of disregarding self-employed or temporary workers whose interests are not well represented by the traditional trade unions. For some young people working in sectors with a disproportion number of casual workers, trade unions may be seen as 'old-fashioned' and out of date, so that many unions yet have a lot to learn about engaging with young people (Vandaele 2017).

Second, self-employed workers may not identify with the employers' organisations that are part of the system of labour relations. As subcontractors to larger firms, they may in fact share more similarities with an employee. Most of the new self-employed workers are not in traditional self-employed occupations that are regulated by strong professional associations such as craftsmen, doctors or lawyers. Instead, they often have jobs related to communication, design, corporate consulting, homecare and other services, and they may not even regard themselves as a manager or an employer.

## NEW FORMS OF UNIONISM FOR NEW TYPES OF WORKERS

Two kinds of new organisations dedicated to non-standard forms of employment are emerging: associations or unions dealing specifically with a legal status on the one hand, and specialised trade unions that exclusively organise the self-employed on the other.

Labour law has indeed encouraged, or minimised, the risks of non-standard forms of employment by creating new legal forms of employment status. For example, 'casual entertainment workers' in France, 'economically dependent self-employed' in Spain, and 'para-subordinates workers' in Italy. However, this has raised controversy as it was seen as undermining prevailing pay and working conditions. At the same time, new forms of organisation dedicated to these non-standard forms of employment have been created.

'Casual entertainment workers' in France are salaried employees who have more social benefits than other casual or temporary workers. This category was created to foster domestic production. However, employers' representatives have opposed this because the special unemployment scheme for entertainment workers is paid by general social insurance contributions[1] (Coquet 2010), while trade unions have opposed it because it discourages the hiring of employees on an open-ended contract. A temporary workers' collective (*collectif des intermittents*) has organised demonstrations and advocacy to defend workers' interests (Sinigaglia 2012).

A new legal status for 'the economically dependent self-employed' and 'para-subordinated workers' has been introduced in Spain and Italy to transform undeclared work into formal employment. This kind of worker is self-employed but has access to some of the employees' social rights such as severance pay or unemployment insurance, and costs are met by the main employer or buyer. Alongside this development an association of autonomous workers, affiliated with the biggest unions, has been established and is dedicated exclusively to defending these new types of 'economically dependent self-employed' workers, and the 'para-subordinated' workers'.

In countries where unions and social protection are weak, other organisations are dealing with these new forms of self-employment. Freelance associations have been created in the US (2001), Canada (2008) and the UK (2017). Their schemes to protect freelancers focus on issues such as late payments, with ambitions to offer stipends for sick pay or other social protection, including healthcare, income security and insurance.

Neither the self-employed branches of trade unions, for example, the United Services Trade Union (Vereinte Dienstleistungsgewerkschaft; ver.di) in Germany, nor the self-employed organisations and temporary workers' collectives, are able to negotiate collective agreements that deal specifically with the self-employed or employees with fixed-term contracts. In the majority of EU member states, collective bargaining is reserved for the regulation of the employment relationship between employers and trade unions, and it takes place either at sector or industry level. There is sometimes collective bargaining for specific occupations in certain sectors including construction, broadcasting and journalism, where self-employed trade union members have shaped their respective industries for decades, as they have done for example in the UK. But this is not usually the case in sectors where there have been new forms of employment created by the fourth industrial revolution. Exceptions to this are workers who find employment through temporary work agencies. Most EU15 countries have sector-level bargaining for temporary agency work, with the UK constituting the exceptional case, where this does not occur. At the European level this 'triangular' form of employment itself is recognised as an industry, for which sectoral social dialogue has taken place since 2000. But the lack of a trade union organisation for agency workers remains a key problem in the regulation of the sector by the social partners.

## CONCERNS RAISED BY THE ON-DEMAND AND GIG ECONOMY

Although changes in labour relations have been relatively slow, the rise of the on-demand and gig economy has given birth to new forms of collective action and bargaining at a rapid pace because it increases flexibility for workers at the risk of creating greater job insecurity. It raises questions about the definition of employment status and employment rights (Gierten 2016), and ultimately challenges the suitability of the current employment law framework in addressing the needs of people working outside the traditional employment model.

Technology has facilitated new business models that are based on matching sellers and buyers of goods and services: even if the latter are delivered by workers (physically or digitally), the platform is not formally the employer, although it may control the production process or prices, as happens for example with Uber or Deliveroo.

The employer's accountability for securing decent working conditions and social rights is in fact transferred to platform workers themselves, who perform their tasks as independent contractors. Online platforms have allowed often casual and unstable work to be parcelled and distributed to 'the crowd', breaking it into microtasks, with relatively low pay. As pointed out by Berg (2016) and the ILO (2016), gig work needs to be considered along with broader trends in the casualisation of the labour market, such as the spread of zero-hour contracts and the growth of bogus self-employment (see Berg and De Stefano this volume). Last but not least, the on-demand economy challenges existing welfare models. Platforms pay low contributions for social protection and corporate tax, which in turn affects the social insurance coverage of the people who do this work.

The spread of labour platforms, as opposed to other market places where assets are traded, has involved considerable opposition in European countries, ranging from an Uber ban[2] to taxation or regulation, court cases at the national or European level (relating to worker status or the license to operate) and strikes of workers or contractors. The platforms that intermediate taxi or delivery services (for example, Uber or Deliveroo) and crowdsourcing micro-tasking platforms like Mechanical Turk and CrowdFlower have attracted the most attention. The workers who perform these types of tasks are mostly low skilled, and though platforms are offering them opportunities to work, the pay is often relatively low. But there is also evidence that platform work may increase inequality rather than reduce it as higher-skilled push lower-skilled workers out of jobs (see Schor this volume). They have been backed strongly by European trade unions, fulfilling their traditional role of defending the most vulnerable and securing better working conditions. First, drivers and deliverers using apps and crowdworkers have been federated, despite their distance from each other, with the help of trade unions, citizens and technology. The sharing of common interests and experiences has thus encouraged crowdworkers to join together. In the same way, high-skilled workers, such as freelancers, tend to be federated professionally.

Second, new forms of collective action have emerged. Protest movements among the platform's workers have used technology to gather and inform other workers on a large scale, as smartphones and the internet are their professional tools. Crowdworkers are using the rating system of platforms to assess the contractors' conditions of payment and report bad payers. In business-to-customer services, workers call on consumers and citizens to support their claims. The support of the potential client in protest campaigns has been seen in the US in the Walmart workers' campaign (Hocquelet 2014) and in the UK recently in the McDonald's zero-hour contracts campaign.

Third, trade unions do not only support the claim of the workers' platforms, they also create unionised groups in the transport industry and are beginning to negotiate directly with the platforms. However, it is difficult to establish labour relations with platform organisations as they are not recognised as an employer, and are not part of an industry and therefore have no collective representation. Thus the workers' platform has no legal representation through formal channels. Trade unions can mediate conflict, however, as seen for example in France. While unions were part of the initial protest against Uber, they then participated in mediation that finally contributed to establishing a dialogue with the company to protect vulnerable drivers. In Germany, IG Metall has signed a voluntary agreement with German platforms to provide standard wages and working conditions, and German, Austrian and Swedish unions have launched an online review platform Fair Crowd Work, which provides reviews and ratings on working conditions at different online labour platforms based on surveys with workers. These examples clearly illustrate how the gig economy can provide an opportunity to reshape labour relations and modes of action.

Safeguards are needed to accompany the transformation of work in order to maximise opportunities for all workers while minimising risks (see Palier this volume). Collective bargaining, alongside labour law and welfare state provisions, is one of the tools to protect against the negative effects of the casualisation of labour. To that end, collective bargaining needs to be adapted to the accelerated pace of technological change, non-standard forms of employment and the gig economy. As work is taking place in many non-standard locations, and not only inside the boundaries of companies, social dialogue cannot be limited to selective groups of standard employees. Furthermore, new business models such as platforms and the large-scale use of outsourcing have significantly disrupted established business models, industries, activities and occupations. Yet collective agreements are still based on traditional concepts of the firm and the standard worker. The question that needs to be addressed is whether it is necessary to rethink how industry-level negotiations can cope with new economic realities or whether, on the contrary, new activities should be incorporated into existing communication channels. Furthermore, is it necessary to go beyond the scope of the occupation to negotiate pay and working conditions by tasks, or do we need to reassess the combination of tasks and skills that are performed by workers? Obviously there is no one-size-fits-all solution. Recent initiatives to regulate labour relations collectively can be seen as a source of renewing and updating existing arrangements, while maintaining the core principles and functions of social dialogue – to promote better conditions of work and economic growth through consensus-building in the world of work.

## NOTES

1. 'Casual entertainment workers' account for 0.8% of the employees covered by the French social security system, 3.4% of the employees indemnified by the social security and 5.9% of unemployment benefits.
2. UberPop, a version of Uber that lets people give rides without holding a licence, has been suspended in France, the Netherlands, Finland, Sweden and Hungary. Transport authorities in London have revoked Uber's licence and threatened to ban the service.

# REFERENCES

BBC (2014), 'Should Holiday Email Be Deleted?', BBC News, 14 August, http://www.bbc.co.uk/news/magazine-28786117.

BBC (2016), 'French Workers Get "Right to Disconnect" from Emails Out of Hours', BBC News, 31 December, http://www.bbc.co.uk/news/world-europe-38479439.

Berg, J. (2016), *Income Security in the On-Demand Economy: Findings and Policy Lessons from a Survey of Crowdworkers*, Geneva: International Labour Organization.

Coquet, B. (2010), 'Workers in the Entertainment Industry: an Advantageous but Questionable Unemployment Insurance Scheme', *Futuribles Journal*, 367.

European Commission (2017), 'Attitudes Towards the Impact of Digitisation and Automation on Daily Life', https://ec.europa.eu/digital-single-market/en/news/attitudes-towards-impact-digitisation-and-automation-daily-life.

EurWORK (2017a), 'Spain: AXA Recognises Workers' Right to Turn Phones Off out of Working Hours', EurWork, 9 October, https://www.eurofound.europa.eu/observatories/eurwork/articles/spain-axa-recognises-workers-right-to-turn-phones-off-out-of-working-hours.

EurWORK (2017b), 'Trade Union Extends Membership to Self-Employed Workers', EurWork, 14 October, https://www.eurofound.europa.eu/observatories/eurwork/articles/trade-union-extends-membership-to-self-employed-workers.

Gierten D. (2016), *New Forms of Work in the Digital Economy*, Paris: OECD Publishing.

Hocquelet, M. (2014), 'Grande distribution globale et contestations locales: les salariés de Walmart entre restructurations discrètes et nouvelles stratégies syndicales', *Travail et Emploi*, 137(1): 85–103.

ILO (2016), *Non-Standard Employment around the World*, Geneva: International Labour Organization.

Messenger, J., O. Vargas Llave, L. Gschwind, S. Boehmer, G. Vermeylen and M. Wilkens (2017), *Working Anytime, Anywhere: the Effects on the World of Work*, Dublin: European Foundation for the Improvement of Living and Working Conditions.

Perez, C. (2004), 'Technological Revolutions, Paradigm Shifts and Socio-Institutional Change', in E. Reinert (ed.), *Globalization, Economic Development and Inequality: an Alternative Perspective*, 217–42, Cheltenham: Edward Elgar Publishing Limited.

Sinigaglia J. (2012), *Artistes, intermittents, précaires en lutte: retour sur une mobilisation paradoxale*, Nancy: Presses universitaires de Nancy.

Vandaele, K. (2017), 'How Can Trade Unions in Europe Connect with Young Workers?', in J. O'Reilly, J. Leschke, R. Ortlieb, M. Seeleib-Kaiser and P. Villa (eds), *Youth Labor in Transition*, New York: Oxford University Press.

Vermeylen, G., M. Wilkens, I. Biletta, A. Fromm, A. Parent-Thirion and R. Rodriguez Contreras (2017), *Exploring Self-Employment in the European Union*, Dublin: European Foundation for the Improvement of Living and Working Conditions.

Welz C. and F. Wolf (2010), *Telework in the European Union*, Dublin: European Foundation for the Improvement of Living and Working Conditions.

# BRITISH WORKER'S RIGHTS AFTER BREXIT

## Kate Bell

> We should go into those [EU] renegotiations with a clear agenda: to root out the nonsense of the social chapter – the working time directive and the atypical work directive and other job-destroying regulations.
>
> —Boris Johnson, May 2014

Almost four long years ago, as David Cameron was attempting to negotiate concessions that might persuade Britain to stay within the EU, Boris Johnson felt free to rail from the backbenches against the EU's provisions that protect working rights. Johnson is now on the front bench, and the negotiations are about the terms on which we will leave. But the rhetoric has not changed. Just before Christmas 2017 Boris Johnson was back briefing papers that Britain would aim to scrap the directive that has given British workers more paid holidays, more paid breaks and safe limits on their working hours (Moore 2017).

Scrapping the working time directive is a convenient shorthand for a deregulatory agenda in which Britain would compete on an ultra-flexible model, with fewer rights for working people, and a freer hand for business. Proponents of this approach argue that Britain's economic problems – a vicious cycle of low investment, low productivity and falling wages – stem from a social model, imposed by Europe, that is holding back competitiveness.

But as Britain has edged closer to the deregulators' dream over the past few years, with the rise of hyper-flexible contracts, poor enforcement of rights, and a seemingly permanent wage freeze, the weaknesses of this model have become clear. And there is now increasing evidence to suggest that a more successful economy rests not on embracing insecurity, but in tackling it.

## THE UK IN CONTEXT

Before looking at what lies behind the failings of the British economic model, and how these failings might be addressed in a post-Brexit world, it is worth placing the UK's performance in its international context.

First, the good news – the UK remains pretty good at delivering jobs, with the employment rate at its highest level since 1975. The importance of that should not be underestimated, but unfortunately it is a small bright spot in an otherwise gloomy landscape. For working people, the gloom is most evident in their pay packets. Real wages in the UK fell for eight consecutive months last year, and are still well below the level they reached before the start of the financial crisis of 2008. UK real pay growth in 2018 is expected to be the lowest of any country in the Organisation for Economic Co-operation and Development (OECD).[1]

Wage falls are having a real impact on living standards; in recent polling for the Trades Union Congress (TUC), one in eight workers said they had to skip meals to make ends meet (TUC 2017b). This year, household unsecured debt is set to be higher than ever before – with TUC analysis of the Office for Budget Responsibility (OBR) figures showing a rise to a record £13,900 per household in 2017 (TUC 2017c). And while consumer demand has been the mainstay of the British economy in recent years, the Bank of England predicts that "consumption growth is projected to remain subdued in the near term, reflecting continued slow real income growth and the ongoing adjustment to the past squeeze in real income growth" (Bank of England 2017, 10).

The failure of the UK to deliver on the quantity of reward for work is reflected in the decline in job quality within many parts of the labour market. Key risks associated with work have been increasingly transferred to working people, while any financial rewards from flexibility have been accrued by employers.

Too many employers have sought to manage the financial risk that comes from the inability to guarantee a constant demand for a product or service by employing workers on contracts in forms of employment – whether 'zero hours', casual or agency work, or bogus self-employment – that offer flexibility for the employer at the expense of pay and certainty for the employee. And because these contracts often come with lower pay and fewer rights and protections, the risk of being unable to work because of sickness or caring responsibilities is also transferred to working people.

These trends are not unique to the UK, but they are exacerbated here. Research for the TUC carried out by the National Institute for Economic and Social Research found that the UK had the largest increase in the number of self-employed workers for any EU country from 2008 to 2015, and the third largest increase in the number of temporary workers for any EU country over the same period. The research also pointed out that temporary workers elsewhere in the EU tend to have stronger protections and greater job security than in the UK (Hudson and Runge 2017).

It is important to note that the rise of greater job insecurity is not all about technology. Online platforms have reduced the transaction costs associated with breaking work up into smaller tasks, and contracting workers on a piece work basis – as high-profile employment rights cases taken by unions, including at Uber, have shown. But we found that it is in traditional professions, including hospitality, residential care, and education, that insecurity is rising fastest (TUC 2017d).

And while 'automation', 'the gig economy' and 'job insecurity' are often linked together, if we were relying on robots to explain the rise of insecurity at work we should expect UK jobs to be more secure than our neighbours, not less. As the OECD recently pointed out, automation in the UK is lagging; the UK came last in an international league table of 'industrial robot density'. France, a country with a similar level of industry to the UK, has 80% more robots (OECD 2017).

In the deregulators' version of Britain's economic woes the relatively lax labour market regulation, and lack of labour market institutions that help explain our weak wage growth and high level of job insecurity, should be helping Britain to out-produce and outgrow our European neighbours. But Britain's productivity problem is well known; the amount we produce per hour of work has flatlined for a decade. And Britain's performance is not just bad in historical terms but when placed in its international context; output per hour worked in the UK in 2016 was 15.1% below the average for the rest of the G7 advanced economies.[2]

This is already feeding through into lower growth. The OECD forecast UK GDP growth in 2017 at 1.5% compared with 2.4% in the euro area, and in 2018 these figures are expected to be 1.2% and 2.1% respectively (OECD 2018). Analysis of the UK's poor performance over the last year has focused on the impact of the vote to leave the EU. But many of these trends were in place before the referendum. The trend since 2010 was already for weaker growth, with average GDP growth averaging 2.0% in the last seven years, well below the longer-term average of 2.7%.[3] It is hard to look at those figures and not think that something is going wrong with the UK economy.

## REVERSING THE TELESCOPE

In the deregulatory model of the world, it is the hyper-flexible nature of Britain's labour market that needs to be extended, and will power us to a better future outside the EU. But there is increasing evidence that it is this very flexibility – and the insecurity that comes with it – that helps explain at least part of Britain's productivity problem, and the slow growth and low wages that accompany it.

In one sense the link between insecurity and poor productivity is pretty intuitive: people who know when they will be working, that their rights will be respected, and that they do not have to show up for work when they are ill, are more likely to be able to work effectively and efficiently when at work. But the quantitative evidence also suggests that there is a link between insecurity and productivity. Research commissioned by the TUC from the Learning and Work Institute found a reasonably strong correlation between those sectors where there has been a rise in insecure work, and those which had lower productivity (Bivand and Melville 2017).

Correlation of course does not necessarily imply causation, but the findings chime with a range of other evidence, which shows that businesses that demonstrate they value their staff are more productive. This also links closely to another longstanding British problem – the lack of investment in workplace training.

A recent report from the Institute for Public Policy Research showed that employer investment in continuing vocational training per employee in the UK is half the EU average and investment in training and learning per UK employee fell by 13.6% per employee in real terms between 2007 and 2015 (IPPR 2017). Government spending on adult skills and further education has also been cut sharply – a recent analysis by the House of Commons Library identified a cut of 41% in the adult skills budget between 2010/11 and 2015/16 (Foster 2017).

The OECD draws a clear link between Britain's poor skills performance and the level of insecure work, by highlighting the fact that in the case of zero hours contracts "there is less incentive for training participation by the worker and training provision by the employer, given the lower attachment and temporary nature of the contract, [and] hindering the productivity of low-skilled workers" (Zwart and Baker 2017, 27). Recent TUC research confirmed that far from forming a stepping stone into a better paid job, workers in casual employment were almost five times more likely to drop out of work altogether as those in permanent jobs (Newsome et al. 2018).

We can see more evidence that the British model's failure to value the workforce may lie at the heart of some of our productivity problems when considering workplace voice. Here yet again the UK lags behind. In a recent poll of 3,000 workers conducted for the TUC, over two-fifths of workers said that big changes at their workplaces are undertaken without consultation. A fifth said that staff suggestions for how to do things differently were routinely ignored. A recent survey of nearly 7,500 workers found that while 87% agreed with the statement "I am keen to embrace technology and maximise its benefits", 73% agreed that technology would improve productivity, and less than 1 in 4 (24%) said that their employer gave them a say in how technology effects their work.[4] In a league table of workforce participation across Europe, the UK comes second from last.[5]

Again, it is intuitive why voice at work might be associated with higher productivity. There are numerous instances of suggestions for product and process innovation that have come from the workforce; for example, a suggestion from a British Airways employee is saving the airline £600,000 in fuel (as well as reducing the company's emissions). The suggestion was to make the planes lighter by descaling the toilet pipes; it is easy to see why this suggestion was more likely to come from the shop (or in this case plane) floor than the boardroom.

The OECD highlights skills mismatches as a critical problem for the UK (see Aubrey this volume), stating that "a misalignment between the skills that workers possess and those that are used in their work can constrain innovation, limit the adoption of new technologies and ultimately restrict productivity improvements" (Zwart and Baker 2017, 20). If no one asks the workforce about how their skills are being used, it is hard to identify where these mismatches can exist.

And at an economy-wide level, we know that collective voice is critical in maintaining workers' ability to convert productivity improvements into wage growth, and to protect their wages and conditions at times of industrial or technological change. As evidence from the International Monetary Fund to the International Labour Organization shows, countries with higher levels of collective bargaining coverage have had higher levels of wage growth (IMF 2017) and lower levels of wage inequality (Hayter 2015).

## POST-BREXIT INSECURITY?

What does this mean for the UK's economic model when we finally leave the EU? For a start, it suggests that a race to the bottom in workers' rights is unlikely to deliver the results – higher growth and productivity – that its advocates profess to want. That is one of the reasons why the TUC has consistently advocated staying inside the single market as the best way to protect workers' rights, as well as to protect the many jobs of our members that are linked to 'frictionless trade' with the EU. While we know that the single market and customs union are not perfect, the TUC's analysis (2017f) clearly shows that they are far better for workers' jobs and rights than any other trade models that exist.

Getting the right Brexit deal is vital for securing workers' rights and jobs. But delivering a more productive economy, with greater security and pay for working people, involves looking at where the UK model is going wrong now. It may come as no surprise that the TUC believes that starts with ensuring that working people have more of a say in the decisions that affect their lives. Unions have been critical to stemming the tide of insecure work in the UK, fighting for the rights of workers from Sports Direct to Pimlico Plumbers. And recent research from Norway seems to support the intuition that union membership – and the greater job security that comes with it – can raise productivity. Looking at a sample of Norwegian firms between 2001 and 2012, this research found that increases in union density led to substantial increases in firm level productivity, as well as in wages (Barth, Bryson and Dale-Olson 2017).

Achieving similar increases in union density in the UK requires unions to innovate, reaching out to more young workers, particularly

in the private sector. Turning round the decline in union membership in recent years is a significant challenge. But legislation could
help too – in particular, by giving unions access to workplaces to
tell people about the benefits of joining a trade union. And it is
welcome that there's an increasing debate starting – at international
and national level – about how to extend the benefits of collective
bargaining more widely, with the recognition that workers' collective power provides a bulwark against increasing inequality.

The importance of worker voice in raising productivity, encouraging workplaces to develop the skills of their staff, and ensuring
that working people get a fair share of the rewards from business,
is likely to increase as we face the challenges that are posed by
changes in technology. The questions asked by those encountering
new forms of work and employment are often ones of distribution,
including the distribution of risk when platform companies seek to
fragment the employment relationship, the distribution of rewards
when increasingly large technological monopolies are able to mop
up consumer markets, and the distribution of work itself if robots are
able to fulfil more of the tasks that employers are currently willing
to pay workers to undertake. Ensuring that that distribution is fair
requires workers to have a source of collective power and representation – exactly what unions aim to provide.

That does not mean that we do not need government action as
well. The TUC's Great Jobs Agenda sets out the legal changes we
need to provide a higher floor for employment rights in the UK,
including new rights for workers not currently considered to be
'employees', and new rules to ensure that employers who need to
offer variable shifts are required to give their workers fair notice, or
face a penalty if they fail to do so. Even the most fervent advocates
of flexibility cannot think that it is right that over half of workers
on zero hours contracts say that they have had their shifts cancelled
with just 24 hours' notice (TUC 2017e).

And we know that the long period of spending restraint in the UK
has restrained growth. Philip Hammond's autumn 2017 budget got
the rhetoric right when he stated that the "key to raising the wages of

British workers is raising investment – public and private" (Financial Times 2017). But his plans were disappointing. The average spend across the OECD on investment is 3.5% of GDP. The budget announced an extra £7bn spread across the life of this parliament. But that gets us to just 2.9% of GDP (in 2020 and 2021) – just a notch up from the 2.6% in 2016 (going back down to 2.8% in 2022). It may come as no surprise that the OBR described the boost to growth provided in this as 'modest', and it is clear that a more ambitious strategy – aiming for the OECD average of 3.5%, at least – is needed.

At present, the UK's economic model is failing to deliver on what most people want – for people to be able to hold on to a decent job, with wages that you can expect to increase at least in line with the cost of living, and to receive fair treatment from your boss. The challenges of Brexit and changing technology provide a chance to think again about how those expectations can be met. But while providing collective voice may be an old response it is not an outdated one. In the TUC's 150th year, we will be working hard to prove that trade unions have as much to offer workers in the 21st century as they did those in the 19th.

## NOTES

1. See TUC analysis of OECD data (TUC 2017a).
2. See the Office for National Statistics (ONS) statistical bulletins on international comparisons of UK productivity (ONS 2017).
3. This average is taken from 1956, when the ONS series of quarterly figures begins.
4. See the Smith Institute report on employees' perspectives on productivity jointly commissioned by Prospect; the Union of Shop, Distributive and Allied Workers (USDAW); the Broadcasting, Entertainment, Communications and Theatre Union (BECTU); Community; the Association of Teachers and Lecturers; the First Division Association, formerly Association of First Division Civil Servants (FDA); and the Society of Radiographers (Smith Institute 2016).
5. See the UK's position in the European Trade Union Institute's European Participation Index (Vitols 2010).

# REFERENCES

Bank of England (2017), *Inflation Report: November 2017*, London: Bank of England, https://www.bankofengland.co.uk/-/media/boe/files/inflation-report/2017/nov.pdf.

Barth, E., A. Bryson and H. Dale-Olson (2017), *Union Density, Productivity and Wages*, IZA Discussion Paper 11111, Bonn: IZA Institute of Labor Economics.

Bivand, P. and D. Melville (2017), *What is Driving Insecure Work? A Sector Perspective: Report to the Trades Union Congress*, Leicester: Learning and Work Institute.

Financial Times (2017), 'Autumn Budget 2017: The chancellor's speech', *Financial Times*, 22 November, https://www.ft.com/content/d0e520be-cf6b-11e7-b781-794ce08b24dc.

Foster, D. (2017), *Adult Further Education Funding in England since 2010*, House of Commons Library Briefing Paper 7708, London: House of Commons Library.

Hayter, S. (2015), 'Want to Tackle Wage Inequality? Shore Up Collective Bargaining', blog, Work in Progress, International Labour Organization, 3 March, https://iloblog.org/2015/03/03/want-to-tackle-inequality-shore-up-collective-bargaining/.

Hudson, N. and J. Runge (2017), *International Trends in Insecure Work: a Report for the Trades Union Congress*, London: National Institute of Economic and Social Research.

IMF (2017), *Recent Wage Dynamics in Advanced Economies, Drivers and Implications*, Washington: International Monetary Fund, http://www.imf.org/en/Publications/WEO/Issues/2017/09/19/world-economic-outlook-october-2017.

IPPR (2017), *Another Lost Decade: Building a Skills System for the Economy of the 2030s*, London: Institute for Public Policy Research.

Johnson, B. (2014), 'You Kip If You Want To – But Only One Party Can Offer Real Change', *The Telegraph*, 18 May, http://www.telegraph.co.uk/news/politics/10839796/You-kip-if-you-want-to-but-only-one-party-can-offer-real-change.html.

Moore, J. (2017), 'Burnout Britain Looms as Gove and Allies Plan to Axe Working Time Directive', *Independent*, 18 December, http://www.independent.co.uk/news/business/comment/burnout-britain-looms-as-gove-and-allies-plan-to-axe-working-time-directive-a8116381.html.

Newsome, K., J. Heyes, S. Moore, D. Smith and M. Tomlinson (2018), *Living on the Edge: Experiencing Workplace Insecurity in the UK*, London:

Trades Union Congress, https://www.tuc.org.uk/sites/default/files/insecure%20work%20report%20final%20final.pdf.

OECD (2017), *OECD Economic Surveys, United Kingdom Overview*, Paris: OECD Publishing.

OECD (2018), *OECD Economic Outlook and Interim Economic Outlook*, Paris: OECD Publishing.

ONS (2017), *Statistical Bulletin: International comparisons of UK productivity (ICP), first estimates: 2016*, Newport: Office for National Statistics.

Smith Institute (2016), 'The Productivity Puzzle': a View from Employees, London: The Smith Institute, http://www.smith-institute.org.uk/wp-content/uploads/2016/03/240316-Productivty-at-work-presentation-final-1.pdf.

TUC (2017a), *UK to be Bottom of the Wage Growth League in 2018, TUC Head to Warn in New Year Message*, London: Trades Union Congress, https://www.tuc.org.uk/news/national/uk-be-bottom-wage-growth-league-2018-tuc-head-warn-new-year-message.

TUC (2017b), *One in Eight Workers Are Skipping Meals to Make Ends Meet*, London: Trades Union Congress, https://www.tuc.org.uk/news/1-8-workers-are-skipping-meals-make-ends-meet-tuc-mega-poll-finds.

TUC (2017c), *Household Debt Will Reach Record High in First Year of New Government, Says TUC*, London: Trades Union Congress, https://www.tuc.org.uk/news/household-debt-will-reach-record-high-first-year-new-government-says-tuc.

TUC (2017d),*The Gig Is Up: Trade Unions Tackling Insecure Work*, London: Trades Union Congress, https://www.tuc.org.uk/research-analysis/reports/gig.

TUC (2017e), *Great Jobs with Guaranteed Hours*, London: Trades Union Congress, https://www.tuc.org.uk/sites/default/files/great-jobs-with-guaranteed-hours_0.pdf.

TUC (2017f), *Putting Brexit to the test: How do Britain's Brexit options perform against the TUC's tests?*, London: Trades Union Congress, https://www.tuc.org.uk/brexitoptions.

Vitols, S. (2010), 'The European Participation Index (EPI): a Tool for Cross-National Quantitative Comparison', European Trade Union Institute, https://www.worker-participation.eu/content/download/.../EPI-background-paper.pdf.

Zwart, S. and M. Baker (2017), *Improving Productivity and Job Quality of Low-skilled Workers in the United Kingdom*, OECD Economics Department Working Paper 1457, Paris: OECD Publishing.

# WHY ADAPTIVE TECHNICAL SKILLS SYSTEMS ARE NEEDED TO CAPITALISE ON THE TECHNOLOGICAL REVOLUTION

## Challenges for the UK

### Thomas Aubrey

As governments try to work out how best to respond to the pending technological revolution, countries with adaptive and localised technical skills systems are more likely to be able to capitalise on the opportunities ahead. For the UK, this poses a number of challenges as its underdeveloped technical skills system has been one of the reasons behind the persistent productivity lag since the early 20th century.

Analysis by the Centre for Progressive Capitalism across the UK indicates that the technical skills system is already failing to meet current demand from employers: hundreds of thousands of well-paid technical roles are proving extremely difficult to fill because of the lack of appropriate technical qualifications. This inability to meet current demand indicates that the UK is not well placed to adapt to future demand as a result of the pending technological revolution.

## HEADLINES VS REALITY

The technological improvements that machines have helped introduce have been central to the long-term rise in living standards, as evidenced by the near doubling of average life expectancy since the late 19th century in advanced economies. Improvements in productivity as a result of digitisation and machine learning are expected to continue to bring down the cost of manufactured goods. But they could also result in falling costs for legal and financial services as basic data processing functions become automated and outsourced. Such productivity improvements could provide huge benefits to society as legal and financial products become affordable to many people for the first time.

But these improvements will disrupt the workplace, leading to concerns about the future of jobs. Predictions that the machines are coming for everyone's job are as old as the development of technology itself. The Abbot Johannes Trithemius wrote a tract in praise of scribes highlighting concern that the printing press would put monks out of the business of writing books. Such stark warnings make great headlines, but often the reality is less dramatic.

Despite the concerns raised by Trithemius on the future of scribes, the scribal industry continued to prosper for decades, which was long enough for the existing scribes to make a living while enabling young apprentices to learn a new trade. Some scribes also made a successful transition to become printers, while others found new jobs as type designers.

According to the consultancy McKinsey & Co, in the next phase of expected technological development less than 5% of all jobs are likely to become redundant as a result of new technology over the next few decades (Manyika et al. 2017). Some functions will be automated in most jobs, though, with around a half of the activities currently performed by people being automated. More than 60% of the tasks involved in data collection, data processing and predictable physical work are expected to be automated.

So how should governments respond to the potential upheaval in the workplace arising from increased automation, digitalisation and artificial intelligence?

Central to such a response should be ensuring that a technical skills system can adapt to changing technology and the associated technical skills. There will be a challenge to ensure that workers whose time is freed up from undertaking repetitive processes will have the skill sets to provide greater value added. It is critical that young people entering the workforce are provided with training that continues to have value in the work place. And an appropriate retraining system will be needed for the few who will lose their jobs outright to enable them to return to the workplace with more up to date and relevant technical skills. Hence, getting the skills system right and ensuring it can adapt to changing technology is the foundation of future productivity growth.

For countries such as Austria and Germany, which have strong and local technical skills institutions with employer engagement, this is likely to be somewhat easier than for countries like the UK, which has a more centralised and weaker technical skills systems and is likely to face significant challenges as a result.

## TECHNICAL SKILLS AND PRODUCTIVITY

Productivity can be thought to grow as a result of two distinct forces: capital deepening and total factor productivity (TFP). Capital deepening occurs when the flow of physical capital services rises faster than hours. TFP is the residual which reflects technical change, improvements in the delivery of services, the organisation of production, and the rise in skill levels.

The general approach to growth accounting from Robert Solow's pioneering work is that labour augmenting technological progress leads to capital deepening because it enhances the marginal productivity of capital. This implies that rises in TFP are largely responsible for rises in capital deepening. Some recent estimates suggest that TFP growth explains three-quarters of all capital intensity (Madsen 2010), so a more technically sophisticated workforce applies innovations to their production processes, thus driving new capital investment and increased output per employee (see Soete in this volume).

Long-run data analyses suggest that the UK has floundered on both TFP and capital deepening (Broadberry and O'Mahony 2004). As capital deepening and TFP are both partly related to the capability of a firm's workforce, understanding the technical skills base of the UK economy may shed some light on this.

During the postwar period Britain suffered from its inability to implement a technical skills system. Too few students attained an upper secondary level of education and pupils had a lower average length of time in school than those in other countries (De la Fuente and Doménech 2012; Hansen and Vignoles 2005). In addition, the UK has a lower level of ongoing training conducted in the workplace than other economies.

Although Britain has finally caught up in the years of schooling it provides, the level of upper secondary attainment[1] – a reasonable proxy of a technical skills base – still remains low compared with other countries. Even today this issue can be seen in the OECD data education attainment figures (Figure 17.1).

In recent years, British governments have begun to realise the scale of the issue. For example, Alison Wolf, author of the Wolf Report commissioned by the government, stated that "as a society we are failing at least 350,000 of our 16- to 18-year-olds, year on year" (Wolf 2011, 52). A society and a skills system that is failing for so many will struggle to deal with the threats and opportunities brought on by the pending technological revolution.

## UKCES 2015 EMPLOYER SKILLS SURVEY

According to the UKCES 2015 Employer Skills Survey, 32% of all vacancies for jobs requiring core technical skills were difficult

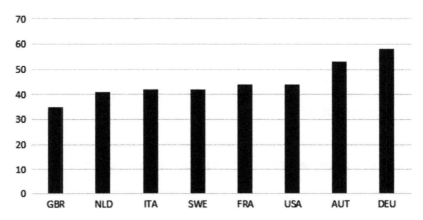

Figure 17.1    Percentage share of attainment of upper secondary education in seven EU countries and the US, 2016. *Source*: OECD (2018).

to fill because the employer could not find applicants with the appropriate skills, qualifications or experience (UKCES 2016). This is significantly more than for other types of vacancies. Core technical skills are defined as those skills needed to perform roles that typically require a minimum of level 3 qualifications from a further education college linked to a specific technical profession.

The Centre for Progressive Capitalism estimates that in 2016 there were around 320,000 core technical job vacancies in the UK that were difficult to fill because of skills shortages, including in firms having access to the pan-European labour market. Crucially, those in these roles are well paid with salaries of £35,300 – more than two and a half times the living wage of £13,100.

Tackling this shortfall for technical skills will not only bring significant benefits for productivity, but it is also crucial for raising living standards. The centre estimates that if the UK addressed these shortages, workers would get an aggregate wage increase of over £7bn. Furthermore, it would start to reduce the large numbers of people on the living wage, which is estimated to be around 2.3 million employees.

Given the expectation that the freedom of movement of labour into the UK from the EU will be curtailed as a result of Brexit, resolving this issue should be an even higher priority. In particular, plugging the gap for technical skills would particularly help manufacturers and the construction sector, which are most affected by the lack of technical skills.

## CHALLENGES WITH TECHNICAL EDUCATION

The key challenge with the UK skills system is to stabilise the constant flux it has suffered from over decades. This has led to a system with more than 21,000 qualifications, many of which have limited value for employers. Only 17% are at level 3 – equivalent to A level – and above.[2]

Moreover, there has been a lack of consistency of institutional development at the local level between firms, colleges and local government to facilitate adaptive processes. Such institutions have gone through constant upheaval compared with other countries, which have maintained some level of stability through time. This has been set against a culture of over-centralisation with many, if not most, decisions related to local economic development taken at the centre rather than in the regions. In addition, too few students are taking courses that lead to well-paid, technical roles, and in some cases too many students are taking courses leading to less well-paid, self-employed roles.[3]

The positive news is that there is now a consensus in the UK across both major political parties that there needs to be a greater focus on technical education. The government is introducing a streamlined set of 15 technical routes, which aims to strengthen the quality of qualifications and link courses to potential careers.

The immediate challenge for these nascent local institutions is that there remain significant technical skills shortages right across the economy. Not only are these shortages constraining the ability of British businesses to expand and increase productivity, but they are also leaving too many people on low wages.

## SUPPORTING LOCAL ECONOMIES TO RESOLVE SKILLS MISMATCH

In order to support local economies to resolve this skills mismatch, the Centre for Progressive Capitalism has developed a skills mapping system to provide local economies with a detailed mismatch of the supply and demand for technical skills. This analysis has already highlighted some major issues that will need to be resolved if local economies are to be able to capitalise on current and future opportunities. Figure 17.2 shows the core technical job vacancies that employers struggle to fill by sector.

The centre has also undertaken a number of detailed regional analyses, which have highlighted some specific mismatches. One area in the Midlands faces an annual undersupply of close to 1,000 electricians. Conversely there remains an oversupply of fitness instructors of more than 1,200. Another fast-growing technology region had a potential undersupply of nearly 1,500 non-graduate digital roles, preventing firms from expanding. And one local economy, which

**Figure 17.2　The percentage share of UK core technical job vacancies difficult to fill because of skills shortages, 2016.** *Source*: Centre for Progressive Capitalism estimates based on analysis of UKCES Employer Skills Survey 2015 data (Norman 2017).

still has a manufacturing base, had a shortfall of over 3,000 technical engineering and manufacturing roles. Again, there remains an oversupply of courses in areas such as sports and fitness instructors as well as beauticians.

One major challenge with the current skills system is that there is insufficient information for school leavers to understand whether demand is increasing or decreasing for certain occupations to help them make an informed career decision. This information and coordination failure too often results in school leavers opting for courses that do not lead to well-paid jobs or a viable career.

Central government needs to devolve skills policy and support the development of local institutions to ascertain the local mismatch between supply and demand for individual technical skills. This information needs to become central to the local careers advisory service to make clear to students where the opportunities are in the local economy. In addition, each devolved area needs to be able to measure how well it is doing to resolve these shortfalls through time.

## GREATER CO-OPERATION ACROSS THE KEY STAKEHOLDERS

The UK government appears to understand that this will require greater cooperation across the key stakeholders, hence the announcement of its intention to work closely with the Confederation of British Industry and the Trades Union Congress is to be welcomed. But for this to truly work, it needs to be implemented at the local level, and for a highly centralised country like the UK, this remains a significant challenge.

Although devolution is now making greater cooperation a real possibility, particularly with the development of metro mayors and combined authorities, many parts of the country still have not developed robust local structures that are coterminous with a functional economic area.

The British government needs to ensure that local enterprise partnerships working jointly with local authorities and colleges have sufficient resources to analyse and measure technical skills mismatches. The government in its industrial strategy white paper announced its intention to introduce skills advisory panels to produce rigorous analysis of the current and future supply and demand for skills (HM Government 2017). These panels will be rolled out and integrated into mayoral combined authorities and local enterprise partnerships to inform the analysis that feeds into local industrial strategies.

As long as these panels are sufficiently funded and are able to provide a continuous update of potential skills shortages this will be a major step forward, particularly if this information really is able to have a meaningful influence over the provision of local education and training.

As devolution proceeds, central government must take care not to overburden these new institutions. For example, further education colleges have to not only provide a world-class technical education but also pick up the pieces for students who were unable to get a basic education at school. This dual purpose is likely to remain a major hindrance if the objective is to create a world-class, adaptable technical education system.

## POLICY FOCUS AND ADAPTABILITY

Trying to forecast the technical skills of the future is mostly unhelpful. Technology changes in unpredictable ways. Furthermore, even if the technology develops as expected, businesses may decide not to use it if it is still cheaper to use labour. Hence the policy focus needs to be on adaptability and responsiveness to changing employer demand, rather than on second guessing what employers might want.

As firms begin to introduce new technology it will become clearer to companies what kind of skills they will have a greater need for. This information needs to be provided to colleges to help them with course design. Furthermore, local government needs to ensure it is investing in courses to build on these technological shifts and continually assess the capacity of existing courses. This in turn is likely to require more investment, as technical courses tend to be more expensive to run. Crucially, the growth in these new opportunities needs to be clearly signposted to students.

The UK government needs to prioritise supporting the development of robust and mature local skills systems across the country over the course of this parliament. If this is achieved, then not only will the economy be far more productive following an improvement in the technical skills mismatch, but it will be better able to support those already in the workforce looking to upskill, and those whose jobs may be displaced.

As the UK embarks on leaving the EU, the pressure to get this right is critical given the increasingly subdued economic outlook, and the curtailment of the freedom of movement of labour. The key to success is in adaptation. Local economies that have built up robust, mature skills ecosystems will be in a far better position to adapt and respond to the opportunities that technological change brings. This is critical if a society is to provide individuals with good jobs and fulfilling careers.

## NOTES

1. Upper secondary education typically follows completion of lower secondary schooling.

2. See Lord Sainsbury's Post-16 Skills Plan and independent report on technical education (Department for Education and Department for Business, Innovation and Skills 2016).

3. Results of Centre for Progressive Capitalism private reports are summarised in various skills articles at http://progressive-capitalism.net/category/skills/.

## REFERENCES

Broadberry, S. and M. O'Mahony (2004), *Britain's Productivity Gap with the US and Europe*, Coventry and London: University of Warwick and National Institute of Economic and Social Research.

De la Fuente, A. and R. Doménech (2012), *Educational Attainment in the OECD, 1960–2010*, Madrid: BBVA, https://www.bbvaresearch.com/KETD/fbin/mult/WP_1220_tcm348-357479.pdf.

Department for Education and Department for Business, Innovation and Skills (2016), *Post-16 Skills Plan,* Cm 9280. https://www.gov.uk/government/uploads/system/uploads/attachment_data/file/536043/Post-16_Skills_Plan.pdf.

Hansen, K. and A. Vignoles (2005), 'The United Kingdom Education System in a Comparative Context', in S. Machin and A. Vignoles (eds), *What's the Good of Education?: the Economics of Education in the UK*, 13–35, Princeton: Princeton University Press.

HM Government (2017), Industrial Strategy: *Building a Britain fit for the future*, Cm 9528. https://www.gov.uk/government/uploads/system/uploads/attachment_data/file/664563/industrial-strategy-white-paper-web-ready-version.pdf.

Madsen, J. B. (2010), 'Growth and Capital Deepening since 1870: Is it all Technological Progress?', *Journal of Macroeconomics*, 32: 641–56.

Manyika, J., M. Chui, M. Miremadi, J. Bughin, K. George, P. Willmott and M. Dewhurst (2017), *A Future that Works: Automation, Employment and Productivity*, San Francisco, Chicago, Brussels, New Jersey, London: McKinsey Global Institute.

Norman, A. (2017), *The skills challenge: turning rhetoric into reality*, London: Centre for Progressive Capitalism. http://progressive-capitalism.net/2017/11/skills-challenge-turning-rhetoric-reality/.

OECD (2018), *Adult education level*, Paris: OECD. https://data.oecd.org/eduatt/adult-education-level.htm.

UKCES (2016), *Employer Skills Survey 2015: UK Results*, UK Commission for Employment and Skills, https://www.gov.uk/government/uploads/system/uploads/attachment_data/file/525444/UKCESS_2015_Report_for_web__May_.pdf.

Wolf, A. (2011), *Review of Vocational Education: the Wolf Report*, London: Department for Business, Innovation & Skills.

# THE POLITICS OF SOCIAL RISKS AND SOCIAL PROTECTION IN DIGITALISED ECONOMIES

## Bruno Palier

**W**hen looking at the economic changes and technological revolution under way throughout much of Europe, many debates focus on the fragmentation of the labour force and the 'Uberisation' of employment: traditional forms of employment giving way to forms of working where there are armies of independent workers who are detached from any work contract and often paid on the basis of tasks performed. For many, this has marked the demise of traditional labour relations and stable work contracts. Our economies and societies are confronted with a long-term dualisation trajectory, which is being exacerbated by the processes of digitalisation. Not all forms of employment will be subject to 'Uberisation', but this process is part of the movement towards dualisation, which is forcing apart labour market insiders and outsiders in an ongoing process that amplifies trends that have been detectable since the 1980s.

To address the challenges posed by increased dualisation and a more fragmented labour market, policymakers and researchers need to identify the nature of these trends, and consider whether they create new social needs and at-risk groups. One can identify new economic cleavages between the winners in the knowledge economy (the productive and 'creative' types) and the losers, whose purpose is increasingly to provide low-paid services to the winners.

These challenges emphasise the need to build a new social contract between these two groups. Winners need to understand the need to protect losers by sharing the profits that are generated by both groups. Such a social contract requires renewed forms of social protection that must be embedded in the different types of welfare state regimes that prevail in Europe.

## NEW RISKS?

Social insurance systems in the 20th century were designed to address the needs of people working, for the most part, in a mass industrialised economy that was responsible for generating millions of permanent jobs in Europe after the second world war, until the mid-1970s. In the 21st century, employment is becoming less routine, less stable and for many less well paid, in part because of the process of digitalisation that is under way.

On the employers' side, digital platforms do not act like traditional employers, and do not bear any collective responsibility for the protection of employees, as they had done in the 20st century. However, the erosion of this erstwhile responsibility of employers towards their employees is not due to, nor specific to, 'platform capitalism'. Employers are increasingly relying on atypical jobs, and governments tend to favour the development of atypical jobs in order to fight unemployment (Palier and Thelen 2010), for example by promoting zero-hour contracts.

In most Organisation for Economic Co-operation and Development (OECD) countries since the early 1970s average unemployment levels have increased by 5–10 percentage points, stabilising at 5–15% since the 1980s. The share of atypical employment (part-time and fixed-term combined) in the overall OECD workforce has grown to around 10%, and in some countries to as high as 25–35%, of all employment today (Emmenegger et al. 2012).

Contemporary labour markets are characterised by an increase in precarious employment; this is particularly evident in what has happened to the youth labour market in the decade following the economic crisis of 2008. This increase in precariousness is particularly important in the platform economy. Stable long-term employment with a single employer is no longer the norm for many workers, and unemployment or underemployment is far from being a rare or exceptional situation for workers. The 'norm' on these platforms is a form of 'pseudo-independence' ('dependent self-employed'), where freelancers and 'auto-entrepreneurs' are paid by performing a series of fragmented tasks at different stages of their working life.

These labour market trends are not specific to the platform economy, nor anything new. There have always been independent workers and self-employed people. Specific social protection schemes have been developed over centuries for such social groups, for example in the agricultural sector, and among shopkeepers, architects and notaries. In labour markets, outsiders such as low-paid workers, part-timers, temporary workers or the unemployed are traditionally badly covered by existing social protection schemes even if they are not based in the platform economy. However, since the 1990s, in some countries (eg the Nordic countries and the Netherlands) a number of measures have given women and part-time workers basic social-security coverage, rather than excluding them as was often the case in the past. However, young workers, especially in southern Europe, have often been excluded from social protection and entitlements, or – especially in recent years – the age thresholds for qualifying for such protection have increased.

Workers in four types of atypical employment situations are poorly covered by traditional social insurance systems:

- women, who in general are more likely to be in part-time employment, have staggered hours and earn lower wages than men
- 'precarious', often unskilled, workers who move between very short-term contracts

- independent workers, sometimes with erratic incomes, often considered micro-entrepreneurs
- those living partly on 'supplementary' income by performing micro-tasks, on-demand services or offering services through Airbnb or other platforms.

Many of these workers are far more insecure than people with open-ended contracts and access to full social insurance. There is an increasing dualism between individuals who have comprehensive social protection coverage, and those who rely on modest (largely means-tested) public provision, merely designed to tackle poverty, if any.

Some societal groups are overrepresented as outsiders in all countries studied, including Belgium, France and Germany: women, young people, the low-skilled, immigrants and second generation migrant workers, in particular if they are employed in the services sector. These groups have higher unemployment rates than average, are more likely to be in atypical employment, and more likely to be poor and to suffer from the insufficient social rights outlined above (Emmenegger et al. 2012).

Automation and digitalisation are expected to disrupt the organisation of employment. This is likely to aggravate some problems and inequalities that already exist, which leaves many workers worse off than before. Some traditional social policy challenges will persist, such as healthcare, pension provision and care for the elderly, but at a new level. Other challenges will also emerge. For example, housing in many big cities is becoming increasingly unaffordable for large proportions of the population. Paradoxically, digitalisation is also associated with some large platform companies such as Airbnb putting major pressure on the limited housing stock in some major cities.[1] Such platforms can also increase pressure on the availability of long-term affordable housing, as landlords prefer to rent property as short-term lets. The extent of this trend has resulted in attempts to regulate and ban some of these developments (Oltermann 2016). The greatest challenge, however, will be to deal with the consequences of increasing intermittent forms of employment.[2]

## NEW POLITICAL CONFLICTS AND CLEAVAGES

Structurally, the transformation of the labour market is creating new social and economic divides that may in turn give rise to new political cleavages. It is well established by many labour market economists that during the 1990s and 2000s there was a polarisation of employment in western labour markets (Autor and Dorn 2013; Goos and Manning 2007). Goos and Manning (2007), among others, argue that this has been due to technological changes rather than to globalisation. Job polarisation correlates with technological progress.

What is striking about these changes is the number of middle-class, especially lower-middle-class, jobs that have been disappearing. This is because routinised tasks can be replaced by machines. Those most targeted by this transformation are therefore not merely those in the least qualified jobs (already having low pay, and weak levels of social protection), but those having mid-skilled, middle-class jobs as well.

This trend is likely to have profound social and political consequences, as our democracies and welfare states are made for and rely on the middle class. First, these trends undermine the fiscal basis of the traditional welfare state (since most of its contributors and beneficiaries belong to the middle class). Second, this polarisation of jobs is constructing a new form of class divide, and the emergence of a widening gap between winners and losers in the knowledge-based economy.

The widening gap in incomes and job quality is evident with knowledge-based jobs, and interpersonal services that are on the rise in the digitalised, knowledge-based economy.

Literature on labour market polarisation identifies an increase of badly paid, so-called 'unskilled' or 'non-productive' jobs. These are interpersonal, face-to-face jobs whose development is partly linked to intermediation platforms, in fields such as logistics (eg Amazon, Deliveroo), transportation (eg Uber), restaurant, hotels (eg Booking.com, TripAdvisor), home helpers and personal services (eg Yoopala, TaskRabbit). These jobs are associated with low pay, bogus self-employment, short-term contracts, part-time work and low levels of social protection (Peugny 2016).

The economic literature on the polarisation of the labour market does not question the fact that they are bad jobs because they are regarded as low-productivity jobs occupied by low-skilled people. The only indicator of the low productivity of jobs is the fact that they are low paid, which – according to orthodox neoclassical economic theory – reflects the fact that the productivity is low. However, it might be that more and more people have to compete for these low-paid interpersonal services jobs as a consequence of the displacement of mid-skilled employment.

Against the backdrop of a polarised labour market a new form of social polarisation is forming, with the emergence on the one hand of an internationalised 'creative class', with global connections, living in the heart of global urban centres (Andreotti, le Galès and Fuentes 2015), and on the hand a class of people at their service (Morel 2015) – to take care of their children, to care for them, to serve them in restaurants, to transport them (by taxi or Uber), to build or renovate their homes, to educate their children, and to provide healthcare to them and elderly relatives.

This becomes clear by taking into account professions where employees are paid less than 1.5 times the French minimum wage that developed over the 1990s and 2000s in France, according to Catherine, Landier and Thesmar (2015, Table 8). Many of these jobs are in the services sector. They are more frequently held by women, and include maternal assistants, family workers, nurses, self-service workers, nursing aides, restaurant staff and domestic workers.

Along with the polarisation of the labour market another new social cleavage is taking shape between so-called 'productive' people with very high wages and 'non-productive' people whose jobs are concentrated in the services sector. This brings with it new forms of social domination in the knowledge economy. This relationship of domination depends not so much on owning the means of production but rather on possessing human capital, knowledge and creativity.

This cleavage partly overlaps with a gender divide, insofar as many low-paid services jobs are mainly occupied by women. Feminist studies have shown that the specific competences associated with these jobs were traditionally regarded as 'inferior' or 'feminine' skills (Howcroft and Rubery this volume). This phenomenon of social polarisation stemming from these changes in the labour market and in gender relations is further reinforced by the increasing phenomenon of homogamy, where people from the same educational and social milieu are increasingly likely to be in contact to work together and to marry each other. As a result there has been a concomitant polarisation of household types between the work-poor, where no member of the household works, and the work-rich, where at least two members are employed, alongside a decline in the traditional breadwinner model (Esping-Andersen 2009).

## CONCLUSION: A NEW CLASS ALLIANCE FOR RENEWED SOCIAL PROTECTION?

If one wants to renew social protection for the fourth industrial revolution one needs first to overcome the new cleavage that has emerged between those working in highly paid sectors, and those working in low-paid services. This cleavage is growing with a disproportionate increase in resources and security concentrated on one side of modern society, and a growth of low-paid, precariousness and new social risks concentrated on the other.

Instead of trying to take advantage of the increasing gaps, the winners could perhaps realise that there is a need to share out the benefits of the knowledge-based economy better, and to expand social protection to precarious workers. Improving social conditions today is not necessarily about increasing the level of existing protection for typical jobs (and thus reversing the trend towards retrenchment), but about including and protecting better those people working in so-called 'atypical' employment, as this form of employment has become more and more common in the lower-paid sectors. For instance, one should provide improved social protection for part-time and temporary workers, and promote equal pay (as women are more frequently in low-paid, part-time and short-term employment than men). Imposing equal pay rules would improve the fate of these outsiders (Rubery and Grimshaw 2014).

These new social situations might be covered by existing and adjusted codes, statuses, reformed assistance benefits and existing and improved social protection schemes. Three main families of solutions are currently contemplated to face these challenges, which may correspond to the three types of welfare regimes:

- implement a universal unconditional basic income
- improve existing social protection schemes for independent workers
- introduce the flexicurity model, which guarantees high levels of minimum income and universal rights to social services and publicly financed training to all.

## A UNIVERSAL BASIC INCOME: A GENUINELY LIBERAL SOLUTION

In the US and Europe there is a renewed debate on the development of a universal basic income. From Milton Friedman to Philip Van Parijs, there has long been a great variety of reasons put forward to justify introducing an unconditional basic income: to fight poverty, to simplify social protection systems by providing a single benefit for all, to increase access to social benefits, to remove unnecessary bureaucratic elements of the welfare state, to fight non take-up of benefits due to complex procedure and stigmatisation, and to guarantee freedom to choose to work or not.

The rise of the platform economy and the ensuing precariousness of work with intermittent income provides another source of argument. More and more luminaries from the digital economy (such as Elon Musk) argue in favour of implementing a universal basic income. As yet there has been no systematic enquiry into how the promotion of a basic income scheme can be linked with the emergence and development of the platform economy, but one source of development of this debate is the 'digital' community. See for instance My Basic Income (www.mybasicincome.org).

Recently, there have been various experiments in introducing a basic income (in Finland and the Netherlands, for instance). When hearing the arguments put forward in favour of these experiments one is struck by the fact that 'liberal' arguments (in the European sense – those of Milton Friedman) largely predominate. Financial constraints, and the desire to replace existing social benefits (and their associated bureaucracies), have led to the proposal that a relatively low basic income should be handed out to everyone, financed mostly through income tax. Hence, an expansion of a simple negative income tax credit is the most widely discussed proposal. Since this has already been developed in many countries, especially the US and the UK, one does not see how it could change the current problems of poverty and precariousness that are developing in these countries.

## IMPROVING THE SITUATION OF INDEPENDENT WORKERS: A BISMARCKIAN SOLUTION

The growth of independent work with new forms of self-employment and dependent contractor status presents a challenge in many jurisdictions with regard to how this employment relationship is governed and what forms of social protection accrue to this status.[3] The main concern is to improve the access and level of social protection for these 'independent' workers. Countries usually base independent workers' social protection on a mix of universal rights (such as access to basic healthcare or a minimum income) and professional protection to be associated with specific schemes and social contributions. The challenge for governments and policymakers is to provide a specific scheme with relatively low protection (proportional to the contribution capacity of the new independent workers, which is usually relatively low). Notably, this new scheme would not protect against the risks associated with intermittence – successive periods of activity and inactivity.

## DEVELOP AND FINANCE SOCIAL RIGHTS AND SOCIAL SERVICES FOR ALL: THE FLEXICURITY MODEL

Flexicurity is a popular model for social policy in the Nordic countries (particularly in Denmark) and the Netherlands. Flexicurity is the separation of the provision of benefits from work. If the government can guarantee citizens' access to healthcare, housing, education and training, and a universal basic income without regard to employment status, those citizens will be protected, even though they are not necessarily typically salaried workers. This should allow the government to deregulate labour markets, leaving decisions about hiring and firing employees to firms and employers in accordance with economic logic. In this way, government social policy does not just compensate for occasional market failures, but works alongside markets to help sustain a flexible, well-trained, highly productive workforce. Such a framework provides good protection for working people whatever their status.[4] The challenge is to guarantee there are sufficient resources to finance these policies, to ensure that new independent workers and platforms pay their taxes.

Further research is needed to understand the content and politics of such diverse proposals, and their differing capacity to address the main challenges that have been created by the digital revolution in the realm of work. One can however already observe that amid the various proposals encountered in all countries, these three types of solutions to the challenges created by the digital revolution echo the existing three types of welfare regimes – the liberal, conservative and social democratic variants (Esping-Andersen 1990). The provision of a (low) universal basic income could be the 21st century form of a liberal welfare regime. The improved social insurance for independent workers aimed at including the workers of the platform economy is closely connected to the conservative corporatist type of welfare regime. Guaranteeing universal access to childcare, education, training and social services to all, including atypical workers, is typical of the social democratic way of providing welfare.

## NOTES

1. There is a paradox that although the digital economy should enable people to work from anywhere, there is ever more aggregation of resources and people in 'global cities' (see Moretti 2013).

2. For a detailed analyses of these trends see OECD Employment Outlook and yearly European Commission: Employment, Social Affairs and Inclusion review (especially 2016 and 2017).

3. For France see a very detailed report on these issues by Haut Conseil du financement de la protection sociale (2016).

4. Analyses of quality of jobs or income inequalities continue to place the Nordic countries in the group of best performing countries, even in the category of 'polarisation' of work (Peugny 2016).

## REFERENCES

Andreotti, A., P. le Galès and J. F. M. Fuentes (2015), *Globalised Minds, Roots in the City: Urban Upper-middle Classes in Europe*, Chichester: Wiley Blackwell.

Autor, D. and D. Dorn (2013), 'The Growth of Low-skill Service Jobs and the Polarization of the US Labour Market', *American Economic Review*, 103(5): 1553–97.

Catherine, S., A. Landier and D. Thesmar (2015), *Marché du travail : la grande fracture*, Paris: L'Institut Montaigne, http://www.institutmontaigne.org/res/files/publications/Etude%20M.he%CC%81%20du%20travail_f%C3%A9vrier2015.pdf.

Emmenegger, P., S. Hausermann, B. Palier and M. Seeleib-Kaiser (eds) (2012), *The Age of Dualization: the Changing Face of Inequality in Deindustrializing Societies*, New York: Oxford University Press.

Esping-Andersen, G. (1990), *The Three Worlds of Welfare Capitalism*, Cambridge: Polity Press.

Esping-Andersen, G. (2009), *The Incomplete Revolution*, Cambridge: Polity Press.

Goos, M. and A. Manning (2007), 'Lousy and Lovely Jobs: the Rising Polarization of Work in Britain', *The Review of Economics and Statistics*, 89(1): 118–33.

Haut Conseil du financement de la protection sociale (2016), *Rapport: la protection sociale des non salariés et son financement*, Paris: Haut Conseil du financement de la protection sociale, http://www.securite-sociale.fr/IMG/pdf/hcfips_rapport_sur_la_protection_sociale_des_non_salaries_et_son_financement_tome_1.pdf.

Morel, N. (2015), 'Servants for the Knowledge-based Economy? The Political Economy of Domestic Services in Europe', *Social Politics*, 22(2): 170–92.

Moretti, E. (2013), *The New Geography of Jobs*, New York: Mariner Books.

Oltermann, P. (2016), 'Berlin Ban on Airbnb Short-Term Rentals Upheld by City Court', *The Guardian*, 8 June, https://www.theguardian.com/technology/2016/jun/08/berlin-ban-airbnb-short-term-rentals-upheld-city-court.

Palier, B and K Thelen (2010), 'Institutionalizing Dualism: Complementarities and Change in France and Germany', *Politics & Society*, 38(1): 119–48.

Peugny, C. (2016), 'L'évolution de la structure sociale dans quinze pays européens (1993–2003): quelques éléments sur la polarisation de l'emploi', *Notes et Documents de l'Observatoire Sociologique du Changement*, 2016(1), http://www.sciencespo.fr/osc/sites/sciencespo.fr.osc/files/nd_2016_01.pdf.

Rubery, J. and D. Grimshaw (2014), 'The 40-year Pursuit of Equal Pay: a Case of Constantly Moving Goalposts', *Cambridge Journal of Economics*, 39(2): 319–43.

# THE WORLD OF WORK IN 2030

## Four scenarios

## Salima Benhamou

In setting out how the organisation of work might evolve by 2030, this chapter outlines four potential scenarios. The aim of these four scenarios is not to predict trends, but rather through extrapolating from existing organisational paradigms to identify some of the key challenges for policymakers arising from the future of work (Benhamou 2017).

Drawing on a significant body of management and employment research we distinguish between two traditional models capturing the organisation of work, referred to as 'Taylorian' and 'simple', and two modern models, which emerged during the mid-1980s, referred to as 'learning' and 'lean' organisations (Valeyre et al. 2009). Each one has a different set of impacts on the quality of jobs, work contracts, working conditions, management, income levels and the capability of firms to maintain a good rank in the global market (European Commission 2015).

Traditional organisations referred to as Taylorian and simple have in common a very limited degree of worker autonomy. Jobs involve repetitive and highly fragmented tasks, there is a low level of learning on the job and strong, hierarchical supervision. The work process is less formalised in the simple model.

In more modern learning organisations workers are often multitasking and autonomous, and can influence the decisionmaking process of the firm. They receive regular training within and outside the firm and use technology to improve work processes. This model is very well developed in Scandinavian countries and is progressing in Germany and Austria. Learning organisations seem to offer more job stability and better quality employment (permanent contracts, higher skills development, better work conditions and better relationships with hierarchy) than other organisations. They also have a high level of performance in innovation and productivity due to highly participative management practices (Lorenz and Valeyre 2006).

In lean production, workers are more controlled by machines or customer needs than in learning organisations. This 'controlled autonomy' is due to a stronger process of work standardisation and high norms of quality imposed by the firms or expected by the clients. Lean production is also characterised by a high diffusion of high performance working practices (just-in-time, zero waste, deadline compliance and quality circles) oriented mainly towards high quality of products and high rationalisation of production costs. The Japanese carmaker Toyota is seen as a pioneer in introducing this mode of organisation, which also 'revolutionized' the automotive industry (Womack and al. 1991). Lean production can lead to significant productivity gains by optimising the production process. However, these gains are often obtained at the expense of deteriorating working conditions, for example stress caused by work intensification. The main differences between lean production and learning models are the learning dynamic at work and the degree of autonomy that are stronger in learning organisations than in lean ones.

Using these four organisational paradigms as a guide to inform our prospective consideration of imagining the organisation of work in 2030 we identify four scenarios:

- greater development of learning organisations
- new virtual learning organisations

- the super-interim model
- a new age Taylorism.

Each is outlined and discussed in turn, with the aim of identifying key policy challenges for the future.

## SCENARIO I: TOWARDS A GREATER DEVELOPMENT OF LEARNING ORGANISATIONS

Will learning organisations progress in 2030 and replace the low performance organisations? And will high-quality jobs be accessible to the majority or limited to a minority of workers? France has a relatively low proportion of employees working in private-sector modern learning and lean organisations – around half compared with over two-thirds of employees in Europe (European Commission 2015). Only 30% of French employees work in learning organisations, with France ranked 17th among the EU 28, and very far behind the Nordic countries, where 55–60% work in these organisations. Although the learning model offers a number of advantages for both workers and firms, it has not been so easy to put into practice.

In this scenario, we can imagine a massive diffusion of learning organisations in France and across Europe. For example, the health care sector is projected to grow considerably due to longer life expectancy (Blanpain and Buisson 2016), and this will generate demand for more care assistants. Domestic care givers who tend to work in rather simple organisations could in the future be integrated into learning organisations. Through a process of collecting information about the people they care for this could contribute to the whole value chain optimisation process and potentially improve the quality of these low status jobs.

The switch from simple to learning organisation in health is already well documented in many advanced economies such as Canada, the Netherlands, Sweden and the US, with the recent emergence of high performance health organisations, commonly known as the learning healthcare system (NHS Confederation 2016; Savitz et al. 2014). These structures are based on multidisciplinary care provided to patients. All the staff are integrated within one organisation and involved in maintaining patients' health and wellbeing. They combine an intensive use of information technology and have an approach that emphasises lifestyle and prevention. It is easy to imagine that the likes of domestic assistants, physical training or health mental coaches, social workers, cleaning staff and clerical healthcare professionals will play a crucial role in maintaining the general health of the population. They will be integrated into a common training programme with the administrative executives and medical and nursing staff, in order to develop and share an organisational culture based on the idea that each member plays a key role and that global performance relies on the interdependence of all jobs. Their integration into learning organisations will give them a higher value in the job market (better job stability, skills development, mobility), which would be promising for a sector that will be one of the main source of jobs in France by 2030 (France Stratégie and Dares 2015).

## SCENARIO 2: NEW VIRTUAL LEARNING ORGANISATIONS

Global competition is set to intensify by 2030, particularly in goods and services with high added value (ESPAS 2015). Faced with a more complex and unstable environment, firms should become more reactive and adaptable. Such a context favours flexible organisations that are able to rationalise labour, equipment and infrastructure costs. Firms will prioritise organisational models that allow them to generate innovative goods and services rapidly in order to differentiate themselves from their main competitors in the global market. Other important trends are already at work: the emergence of big data with a capacity for analysing and collecting data, the development of robotisation and automation, and the spread of information and communication technology. These will radically change work organisations by facilitating collaborative work between people located in all four corners of world. The possibility of rapidly connecting non-physical resources could be a major challenge for firms by 2030, maybe more so than building up in-house skills.

Collaborative virtual platforms based on computer systems give workers access to resources and tools that facilitate collaborative and remote working. They can be used to manage projects, organise knowledge (methods, problems solving, information data) and improve innovation processes. They have important organisational consequences because they lead to a 'burst' into different services: research and development, management, marketing, production, while connecting them to virtual working places. Firms can then minimise the costs of infrastructure, skills acquisition and information collection. They facilitate interactions between workers and clients around a specific project and allow greater externalisation at an unprecedented level, with few transaction costs. If necessary, it is easier to draw on external skills or on small teams within the firm, which constitute an important source of flexibility for businesses (eg Local Motors Labs, Lego or Nike).

The collaborative virtual platform shares some organisational characteristics with the learning organisation, especially the mode of coordination where information and communication are decentralised. In these virtual working places, the 'workers' and the enlarged community do not communicate through the hierarchy anymore but with those who possess the information. Just as with the learning organisation model, the collective working community requires strong autonomy and flexibility. Roles involve a higher level of cognitive tasks and require more sophisticated individual and collective training. Firms are emerging that are entirely dematerialised and deterritorialised (eg InnoCentive). Workers do not need a desk, because the platform follows them wherever they are. By 2030, this model could spread across a great number of sectors, with high value-added tasks. More generally, this mode of work shared can amplify the diffusion of new forms of learning organisation in the economy.

## SCENARIO 3: THE SUPER-INTERIM MODEL

In this scenario, which we refer to as 'super-interim', technological and organisational progress could improve working conditions for low-skilled workers by integrating them within highly skilled teams. Conversely, these factors could increase the prevalence of simple models in the form of an ultra-flexible 'super-interim'. Based on powerful and very rapid communication networks, this model would become widespread within sectors that have peaks of very short duration demand; as a result we might see the end of the single employer, single contract model, which is already being eroded (UKCES 2014).

This scenario would lead to a two-tier society, with a well-integrated techno-elite and a techno-proletariat assigned to low value-added jobs. The organisational choice depends largely on the available workforce: if social inequalities increase, firms could adapt their work organisation to an abundant and low-skilled workforce, as with digital platform models such as Uber. The conditions associated with the standard employment contract involve recruitment processes and are regulated by employment law. In an 'Uberised' world of platform employment workers are considered to be independent contractors, although this is being legally disputed. These forms of employment call into question the functioning of the labour market as we know it today. During the same day, an individual could spend two hours gardening for a first employer, then two hours as a waiter in a restaurant for a second employer, then an hour as a taxi-driver, and so on (The Economist 2015). In this scenario, workers would not be linked to a single employer but to several employers. They would not need to limit their availability to a single company. From an optimistic perspective flexibility would be a two-way process: every individual could choose the most suitable employer, working schedule and attractive offer.

This scenario would lead to parts of the labour market undermining established forms of employment status and the creation of ultra-simple organisational forms. Each individual would be their own subcontracting firm and would sell their own work on these platforms. Competition between individual 'subcontractors' would be strong. The training and mobility opportunities in this context would be very limited. This platform model could expand rapidly insofar as it can be replicated in many low-skilled jobs subjected to peak hours of activity. Joining a platform does not require any knowledge or specific skills, all you need is a computer or a smartphone.

## SCENARIO 4: A NEW AGE TAYLORISM

The fourth possible scenario explores a new age of Taylorism, in which the revolution in automation and technology could radically change the method of production, disrupting the world of manufacturing as we know it (see Fernández-Macías this volume). For example, each worker would perform tasks at home. This is comparable to the 'putting out system' used in the early stages of the industrial revolution, when workers produced goods in their own homes (Thelen 2004).

Key trends point in this direction: increasing digital diffusion, increased competition, the gap between a minority of high-skilled workers and a majority of low-skilled workers. Against the background of these trends a new type of 'collaborative' platform is emerging where people can find work remotely making relatively simple micro-tasks with low added value. This is a 'production platform' rather than a 'super-interim' service platform. One of the first was created by Amazon.com's subsidiary in 2005: Mechanical Turk. 'Little hands' are connected to make micro-tasks that the more advanced computer programs cannot make, like identifying objects in pictures, translating text fragments and classifying pictures by categories. The principle is always the same: producing 'peripheral' tasks achievable remotely by low-skilled individuals. The model is reminiscent of the scientific management conceptualised by Taylor, based on fragmented and repetitive tasks but with one difference: hierarchical control does not exist in the same way anymore (see Crouch this volume), and surveillance and control become virtual through algorithms.

This model may affect young people, the unemployed or retirees, who can work at anytime and anywhere, if they possess a computer. These 'neo-workers' are just 'contributors' spending a few minutes or hours performing tasks for firms that outsource their services through simple production platforms. Workers could use these platforms as their main source of income or to supplement it (see Huws this volume). If this model of work organisation were to become widespread, a sub-proletariat could emerge, exacerbating social divisions within the labour market and society more generally. On the one hand there would be individuals doing jobs with high added value, capable of taking advantage of the new technology; on the other hand, the rest would execute low-value tasks remotely, without social rights or the prospect of career development, unless policymakers design policies to prevent this happening.

## DIVIDED OR INCLUSIVE SOCIETY? CHOOSE YOUR MODEL WISELY

The evolution of these four organisational models are illustrative scenarios. It is likely that these models will coexist by 2030, as they currently do. Firms and industries will not adopt a single work organisation model but will choose a combination or range of models that suits them best according to their competitors, business environment and supply chains. Some changes are positive. For example, some low-skilled jobs in the personal services sector (domestic health workers) that are not highly valued today could be better paid in the future. Simple platforms could, paradoxically, be used in the fight against tax evasion and fraud, which is currently common in low-skilled work sectors. These platforms allow us to know who does what, when and at what rate.

In any event, these scenarios raise important challenges. Many scenarios mentioned here point to a high risk of social polarisation. Countries that will benefit most from these changes will be those that are best able to promote high performance models. Countries that have the most developed learning organisations achieve more desirable socio-economic outcomes. Nordic countries are examples to follow in this field. There two main issues at play here: on one hand, education and constant training; on the other, mitigating the risks of social fragmentation and the lack of guarantees of fundamental workers' rights, especially in social protection.

In the future, the job market will demand a high level of adaptability and autonomy from each person (see Aubrey this volume). The keys to success will have less to do with mastering basic skills than with the ability to integrate and create new technical and soft skills. Teamwork and collecting information regardless of where it comes from, sharing it and coordinating different skills will be crucial. Countries with an inclusive education system also tend to have the most learning organisations and are more innovative and competitive than other countries, with strong socio-economic outcomes. The scenarios described here show that more inclusive structures can lead to better performing organisations. In contrast, the scenarios that point to highly polarised organisations rely on the presence of a highly qualified elite alongside a much larger group of workers with no or low qualifications. Where there is a massive spread of learning organisations, one might imagine companies being encouraged to invest in professional training. In spite of this, in the new age Taylorism and ultra-flexible organisations, there is a risk that firms will pull out from training or will only invest in ultra-specialised training, which leaves little chance of mobility for workers. In this case, the state will have to provide a flexible system of training for a large number of workers. The main goal is to facilitate the development of learning skills that make it easier for workers to change fields and apply for higher qualified jobs than those they currently hold.

Another major challenge for the state is to mitigate the risk of social fragmentation. The social security system is based fundamentally on the notion of the status of salaried workers with stable jobs. Today, employers and employees contribute during a given period and employees (or ex-employees for jobs seekers and retired workers) can access social security. These scenarios suggest that the status of salaried workers could gradually diminish. A trend in this direction has been pointed out by the International Labour Organization (ILO 2015). We also know that people with non-standard jobs (with interim, independent, part-time and short-term contracts) receive the lowest income. The current model was valuable in a world where long-term contracts were the norm and not the exception (see Doellgast this volume).

Several institutions need to redefine their role and missions. Trade unions, for instance, have played a major role ensuring social cohesion and improving working conditions. But this 'model' was conceived in a context where the Taylorian model was predominant in which workers, gathered in a same place, shared the same conditions. How will trade unions adapt to a new context marked by a dispersed work environment (see Jolly this volume)?

To address these challenges, we need trade unions, the state and civil society to engage in a dialogue, engaging with one another in order to anticipate the risks and opportunities for the workers of tomorrow. Changes of an unprecedented scale may transform society as much as the industrial revolution did in its own time. Today, the debate about the future of work seems to be principally focused on disruptive technology, robotisation or artificial intelligence. But organisational transformations could have more impact on the future, and these are, of course, directly influenced by disruptive technologies, but not necessary determined by them. These evolutions will provide new opportunities but also present substantial challenges. Depending on whether these changes are ignored or well anticipated, they could foster social and political instability, or construct a better and more inclusive future.

## REFERENCES

Benhamou, S. (2017), *Imaginer le travail en 2030?: quatre types d'organisation du travail à l'horizon 2030*, Paris: France Stratégie.

Blanpain, N. and G. Buisson (2016), 'Projections de population à l'horizon 2017: deux fois plus de personnes de 75 ans ou en plus qu'en 2013', Insée Première 1619.

European Commission (2015), *Employment and Social Developments in Europe 2015*, Brussels: Directoire-Generale of Employment, Social Affairs and Inclusion, European Commission.

European Strategy and Policy Analysis System (EPSAS) (2015), Global Trends to 2030: Can the EU meet the challenges ahead? Brussels: EPSAS, http://ec.europa.eu/epsc/sites/epsc/files/espas-report-2015.pdf.

France Stratégie and Dares (2015), *Les métiers en 2022: rapport du groupe prospective des métiers et qualifications*, Paris: France Stratégie and Direction de l'animation de la recherche, des etudes, et des statistique.

ILO (2015), *World Employment and Social Outlook: the Changing Nature of Jobs*, Geneva: International Labour Organization.

Lorenz, E. and A. Valeyre (2006), 'Organizational Forms and Innovative Performance: a Comparison of the EU 15', in E. Lorenz and B.-A. Lundvall (eds), *How Europe's Economies Learn: Coordinating Competing Models*, 109–39, Oxford: Oxford University Press.

NHS Confederation (2016), *New Care Models and Prevention: an Integral Partnership*, London: NHS Confederation, http://nhsproviders. org/resource-library/reports/new-models-of-care-and-prevention-an-integral-partnership.

Savitz, L. A., B. C. James, P. Briot and S. Barlow (2014), 'International Trends in Healthcare and Health in Insurance Reform: the Intermountain Way', *Journal de droit de la santé et de l'assurance maladie*, 2014(1): 31–40.

The Economist (2015), 'The Future of Work: There's an App for that', *The Economist*, 3 January.

Thelen, K. (2004), *How Institutions Evolve: the Political Economy of Skills in Germany, Britain, the United States and Japan*, Cambridge: Cambridge University Press.

UKCES (2014), *The Future of Work: Jobs and Skills in 2030*, London: UK Commission for Employment and Skills.

Valeyre, A., E. Lorenz, D. Cartron, P. Csizmadia, M. Gollac, I. Miklos and C. Mako (2009), *Working Conditions in European Union: Work Organization*, Dublin: European Foundation for the Improvement of Living and Working Conditions, https://www.eurofound.europa.eu/sites/default/files/ef_publication/field_ef_document/ef0862en.pdf.

Womack, J., D. Jones and D. Ross (1991), *The Machine that Changed the World: the Story of Lean Production*, New York: Harper.

# Part II

# Comparing digital discourses

# A

# High digital density EU countries

# DENMARK

## Progressing the voluntarist approach

### Anna Ilsøe

With a digitally connected population and heavy public investment in digitising government services, Denmark is considered a 'digital frontrunner' (McKinsey & Company 2017), and well prepared for economic and labour market changes associated with the fourth industrial revolution (Eurostat 2015a, 2015b). It is estimated that job content and skill requirements could change for up to 40% of the current workforce (McKinsey & Company 2017), and non-standard employment and self-employment is on the rise (Ilsøe 2017). Jobs will change in form and content – how fast is still unclear.

The Danish labour market is mainly regulated via collective agreements negotiated between member based organisations – labour unions and employers' organisations (Due et al. 1994). This voluntarist approach still stands at the core of the system, with legislation playing only a limited role. Reform is primarily initiated through union–employer negotiations, but it can also occur through one side taking unilateral action, or tripartite cooperation, with government typically taking a leading role (Ebbinghaus 2002; Mailand 2008).

Therefore adjustments to the evolving digital economy depend on initiatives by Danish social partners – especially trade unions and employers' organisations. However, whether this will work in practice is the subject of debate. Some scholars believe the voluntarist model has potential for governing the digital economy in a sustainable way (eg Söderqvist 2017): changes resulting from the fourth industrial revolution call for rapid and incremental adjustment close to the individual company and worker – something that regulation via legislation does very poorly. Regulation via negotiated agreements often results in more flexible and efficient rules.

Others highlight that it will be much more difficult for workers and companies to organise in the digital economy. If unions and employers' organisations have fewer members and less bargaining power, how can they negotiate agreements (De Stefano 2016)? The share of solo self-employed (self-employed without employees) and marginal part-timers has been increasing in the Danish labour market, now respectively accounting for 5% and 10% of the workforce (Ilsøe et al. 2017; Larsen and Ilsøe 2016). It is difficult for unions to organise these workers, and new digital platform companies are less likely to join employers' organisations because they often rely more on the self-employed than employees, so their total wage bill is low (Ilsøe and Madsen 2017).

In this chapter I will argue that it is possible to adjust to the fourth industrial revolution in Denmark via the voluntarist model of labour market regulation, but that it will be necessary to develop a Danish model 2.0, where unilateral and tripartite initiatives play a larger role alongside traditional bipartite negotiations.

## MEASURING THE SIZE OF THE FOURTH INDUSTRIAL REVOLUTION – WHERE, WHAT AND WHOM

The two main trends in the fourth industrial revolution – automation and the rise of digital platforms – have been debated among social partners in Denmark and in the media, especially since autumn 2016. Reports of automation leading to job losses and loss of job functions in the US have received increasing attention during this period (Chui, Manyika and Miremadi 2015, 2016; Farrell and Greig 2016). Furthermore, international digital platforms like Airbnb, Uber and Upwork have become very active in Denmark, while Danish-owned digital platforms such as GoMore, meploy and Worksome have also emerged.

Digital automation is a reality for many working Danes, but there are major variations across sectors, documented in a large 2017 study on the digitisation of work conducted by Statistics Denmark, involving 18,000 Danes (Ilsøe and Madsen 2017).

Half of all working Danes experience what can be characterised as office automation: they use computers or devices at work and said 'yes' in answer to at least two of the following three questions:

- Do you use computers most of your working hours?
- Do you use programs to handle large amounts of data?
- Do you use the internet or an intranet?

In the information, communication, finance and insurance industries more than 8 in 10 working Danes, including clerical support staff, report that they work in automated offices.

In addition, 1 in 5 working Danes experience machine automation: they rely on computerised machines such as robots or scanners at work. In the industry, mining, quarrying, energy, supply, agriculture, forestry and fishing sectors this number increases to 1 in 3. Those reporting that their working environment has been automated are particularly likely to have been given new types of tasks in their job within the last year. Therefore, these groups might be in particular need of education or further training due to digital automation.

The use of digital platforms for work is still relatively limited in Denmark (Ilsøe and Madsen 2017). 2.4% of Danes aged 15–74 – equivalent to 100,000 people – earned money via digital platforms in 2016/2017. Just 1% earned money through a labour platform such as Upwork or Worksome, and 1.5% earned money via a capital platform such as Airbnb or GoMore. The majority of those who obtained an income via digital platforms earned less than DKK25,000 (€3,330) annually before taxes. Earnings via platforms are therefore primarily a supplement to other sources of income such as salaried work, student allowances, pensions, unemployment benefits or social assistance.

Different groups of Danes earn money via labour platforms and capital platforms – very few have earnings from both types of platforms. Of the Danes supplementing their income with earnings from labour platforms, there is an overrepresentation of young, low-paid, low-skilled, unemployed immigrants and workers with temporary contracts. They are typically either newcomers to the labour market or are having difficulty gaining a foothold in it. They might consider digital labour platforms as a stepping stone to regular employment, but there have been several cases demonstrating that it can be difficult for these groups to combine such work with government support. The main problem seems to be that they work and earn too little as self-employed people to be entitled to various forms of support from the welfare state.

By contrast, high-skilled and high-earners across different age groups are overrepresented among Danes supplementing their income with earnings from capital platforms. This may be because you have to own something before you can rent it out via a capital platform. Those who are well established with educational credentials and jobs are more likely to be home and car owners. The main challenge regarding capital platforms in Denmark is tax collection. Normally, Danish tax authorities receive information on various sources of income automatically, but capital platform users must report income themselves, and the rules on this are not completely clear – especially regarding car rental.

## SOCIAL PARTNERS: UNILATERAL OR TRIPARTITE RESPONSES?

While social partners in Germany and Sweden had participated in at least eight large tripartite commissions on digitalisation and labour market issues by 2016 (including 'Industrie 4.0' and Digitale

Plattformen in Germany as well as Digitaliseringskommissionen and Taxiutredningen in Sweden), such initiatives arrived later in Denmark but many finally took off in 2017 (Ilsøe 2017); see Table 20.1.

The government initiated a disruption council called Partnership for Denmark's Future, with 32 members from Danish social partners, chief executive officers from a number of larger companies, entrepreneurs, academics and representatives from other areas of society.[1] It meets bimonthly from spring 2017 to summer 2018 at one-day conferences, with talks, presentations of new analyses and company visits.

The most important tripartite initiatives in 2017 have been the negotiation and conclusion of two agreements – one on further training and one on unemployment benefits (see Table 20.1). The purpose of the former, concluded in October 2017, was to adjust training to the needs of an increasingly digitalised workplace, particularly for those in the secondary sector. However, trade unions organising high-skilled workers have been critical of the agreement (Danish Confederation of Professional Associations 2017). As our survey demonstrated, workers in knowledge-based services experience a high degree of office automation and are often confronted with new tasks at work. These groups might need further training to maintain their employability on the labour market.

The government also initiated a working group to examine the Danish unemployment insurance system. It currently differentiates sharply between self-employed and wage earners, but more and more Danes are combining the two forms of employment. In May 2017, a new agreement was reached drawn from some of the recommendations from the working group. It allows both sources of income to be reported at the same time and to be combined when calculating entitlement to benefits, and individuals can decide whether an income is reported from self-employment or a job. It is expected to be implemented on 1 July 2018, and many observers have emphasised the potential the agreement holds for platform workers. As our survey showed, these workers often combine different sources of

Table 20.1 Social partner responses to digitalisation of the labour market in Denmark.

| Arena | Unions | Employers'organisations |
|---|---|---|
| Unilateral arena | Analyses and reports, media appearance<br>Political project<br>Dialogue with government departments and political parties<br>Responses to EU strategies<br>Pension scheme for union members (PFA, PKA) – including freelancers, 2016<br>Freelancer networks<br>Dialogue with European and international unions | Analyses and reports, media appearance<br>Political project<br>Dialogue with government departments and political parties<br>Dialogue with European forums and employers' organisations |
| Tripartite arena | Tripartite cooperation on education and further training<br>Roundtable at Copenhagen municipality<br>Government strategy on sharing economy, 2017<br>Disruption council, 2017–2018<br>Union-led conference on platform economy<br>Union-led expert panel on platform economy, 2017 | Tripartite cooperation on education and further training<br>Roundtable at Copenhagen municipality company forum<br>Debates at Denmark's political festival on Bornholm 2016–2017<br>New tripartite agreement on unemployment benefits, 2017<br>New tripartite agreement on further training, 2017 |
| Bipartite arena | Informal contacts to employers' organisations<br>Contacts to new digital employers | Informal contacts to unions |

Source: Ilsøe (2017); table updated in November 2017 via additional interviews.

income, and income received via the labour platforms is often too little to bring an entitlement to unemployment benefits in itself.

There have been unilateral innovative responses to the digitalisation of the labour market (see Table 20.1). The largest Danish pension company, PFA Pension, has created a pension scheme called PFA MedlemsPlus for members of 15 different unions representing workers in both the private and public sectors who are not covered by collective agreements. The pension scheme is very attractive for groups such as the solo self-employed as it includes many of the same elements and benefits (eg insurance and low administrative costs) as the labour market pension schemes that form part of most collective agreements in Denmark. The pension fund PKA has created a similar scheme (PKA Privat) together with nine unions mainly representing workers in the public sector.

There have been no significant bipartite responses to the most recent developments in digitalisation of the labour market. This is perhaps not surprising: many of the adjustments required as a result of automation, such as in training, include many actors like further training centres, which are governed by tripartite cooperation in Denmark (Mailand 2008).

Those finding work on digital platforms are often solo self-employed, rarely unionised and difficult to organise. Unions often struggle to negotiate bipartite agreements for these groups as competition laws prevent fixed prices across companies. There are exceptions – for instance the Albany judgement, where the EU court approved the negotiation of a collective agreement on pensions for independent workers (ECJ 1999). However, it seems that negotiations on topics like pay will be much more difficult for such workers. Therefore, unilateral initiatives like the pension scheme for union members not covered by collective agreements seems to be a more realistic first avenue to attract, organise and protect solo self-employed – including platform workers. If these or similar schemes encourage them to organise, perhaps this can ultimately lead to collective agreements for solo self-employed.

## CLOSING REMARKS

When creating voluntarist responses and solutions to the challenges and opportunities that digitalisation brings to labour markets in the western world, a change in the balance between unilateral, bipartite and tripartite initiatives may be required within the Danish model. In other words, we need to accept the gradual development of a Danish model 2.0.

The Danish model of labour market regulation is founded on bipartite initiatives, and negotiations and collective agreements are still the core instrument in this voluntarist model of labour market regulation. However, the nature of digitalisation might require additional emphasis on both unilateral and tripartite initiatives. The former can mobilise and organise the solo self-employed, while the latter can help coordinate adjustments to the education system. Without union members, a voluntarist model cannot exist, and without necessary adjustments to the education system a voluntarist model can lose its legitimacy. This emphasises the responsibility of individual organisations to consider adequate initiatives on their own and the responsibility of the government to consider necessary tripartite processes and initiate them in time. Whether or not this will ultimately prepare the foundations for further bipartite responses it is too early to say, but the potential is there.

## NOTE

1. For more information see Disruptionrådet at https://www.regeringen. dk/partnerskab/.

## REFERENCES

Chui, M., J. Manyika and M. Miremadi (2015), 'Four Fundamentals of Workplace Automation', *McKinsey Quarterly*, 29(3): 1–9.
Chui, M., J. Manyika and M. Miremadi (2016), 'Where Machines Could Replace Humans – and Where They Can't (Yet)', *McKinsey Quarterly*, 30(2): 1–9.
Danish Confederation of Professional Associations (2017), 'Trepart: Vores Ambitioner var Højere', press release, 29 October, http://www. ac.dk/politik/tvaergaaende-politiske-emner/trepart-vores-ambitioner-var-hoejere.aspx.

De Stefano, V. (2016), 'Introduction: Crowdsourcing, the Gig-Economy and the Law', *Comparative Labor Law & Policy Journal*, 37(3): 461–70.

Due, J., J. S. Madsen, C. S. Jensen and L. K. Petersen (1994), *The Survival of the Danish Model: a Historical Sociological Analysis of the Danish System of Collective Bargaining*, Copenhagen: DJØF Publishing.

Ebbinghaus, B. (2002), *Varieties of Social Governance: Comparing the Social Partners' Involvement in Pension and Employment Policies*, Cologne: Max Planck Institute for the Study of Societies.

ECJ (1999), *Albany International BV v Stichting Bedrijfspensioenfonds Textielindustrie*, European Court of Justice judgement of 21 September 1999, C-67/96, ECLI:EU:C:1999:430, http://curia.europa.eu/juris/liste. jsf?language=en&num=C-67/96.

Eurostat (2015a), 'Information Society Statistics – Enterprises', http://ec.europa.eu/eurostat/statistics-explained/index.php/Archive: Information_society_statistics.

Eurostat (2015b), 'Information Society Statistics – Households and Individuals', http://ec.europa.eu/eurostat/statistics-explained/index.php/ Archive:Information_society_statistics.

Farrell, D. and F. Greig (2016), 'Paychecks, Paydays, and the Online Platform Economy: Big Data on Income Volatility', Washington DC: JPMorgan Chase Institute, https://www.jpmorganchase.com/corporate/ institute/document/jpmc-institute-volatility-2-report.pdf.

Ilsøe, A. (2016), 'From Living Wage to Living Hours – the Nordic Version of the Working Poor', *Labour & Industry*, 26(1): 40–57.

Ilsøe, A. (2017), 'The Digitalisation of Service Work: Social Partner Responses in Denmark, Sweden and Germany', *Transfer*, 23(3): 333–48.

Ilsøe, A. and L. W. Madsen (2017), *Digitalisering af arbejdsmarkedet: Danskernes erfaring med digital automatisering og digitale platforme*, Copenhagen: Faos.

Mailand, M. (2008), *Regulering af arbejde og velfærd : mod nye arbejdsdelinger mellem staten og arbejdsmarkedets parter*. Copenhagen: Jurist- og Økonomforbundets forlag.

McKinsey & Company (2017), *Shaping the future of work in Europe's 9 digital front-runner countries*, October. https://www.mckinsey.com/ global-themes/europe/shaping-the-future-of-work-in-europes-nine-digital-front-runner-countries.

Söderqvist, F. (2017), 'A Nordic Approach to Regulating Intermediary Online Labour Platforms', *Transfer: European Review of Labour and Research*, 23(3), 349–52.

# FINLAND

## Teaching old dogs new tricks

Jenni Karjalainen

The fourth industrial revolution has created a big buzz in Finland and elsewhere and digitalisation, in particular, has become the new phrase for renewal in politics and public policy. Still, technology is only one of many transformations changing modern economies. We are living in an era where economy and societies are in constant motion: markets, jobs, technology, climate, geopolitics, personal relationships and the way in which people communicate and interlink. There is no way of stopping change, nor should we neglect it.

Adapting to this change has been easier for conservative parties because the fourth industrial revolution offers vast opportunities for businesses. Governments are exploring how to best attract young talents and the most thriving businesses to boost their own nation state. Consequently, the solution of the centre-right in Europe is straightforward: ever more deregulation, more flexible labour markets and a more favourable business environment.

For progressive parties the digital transformation has been challenging greater challenge. They do not want to stop change or become the luddites of the 21st century, but at the same time struggle to provide solutions that would embrace this tech revolution while mitigating social risks of people and workers and the more vulnerable of society.

In this article, I will discuss Finnish labour market policies and develop ideas about how the system can better adapt to the change at hand. My main argument is that upskilling, training and education have to be taken far more seriously. I also present solutions on how Finland can make use of its long tradition of tripartite labour market cooperation. On the one hand, my argumentation rests on economic foundations: without a skilled workforce there will be no innovations, no growth and no tools to preserve the welfare state. On the other hand, I see upskilling as the most prominent tool to keep society together. Without a workforce fit for the digital transformation our democratic institutions are at risk of failure because the populist surge has proven what it might mean when progressives do not adapt to new realities but fail to manage and shape change.

## THE LONG TRADITION OF TRIPARTITE CO-OPERATION AND CONSENSUS

Since the end of the second world war, tripartite cooperation and consensus have been at the forefront of the Finnish labour market policy credo. For decades, Finns have believed that giving organised employer and employee organisations great power means that they will also bear great responsibility. Tripartism has not merely been seen as a labour market policy, but a key factor in building Finland's competitiveness and innovation landscape.

A high organisation rate on both the employee and employer sides of the table has long been a cornerstone of the Finnish labour market system.[1] Framework agreements on income were most often made on a national scale between employees, employers and the government. These national agreements covered not only pay rises, but also social security reforms and taxation.

Society was developed through close cooperation between employers' organisations, trade union confederations and the government, regardless of its political colour.

The Finnish system worked surprisingly well even when the world outside changed. First came the free flow of capital that coincided with the fall of the Soviet Union. Then came globalisation, outsourcing and so-called atypical forms of employment. The Finnish model struggled, but survived. The latest grand social reform negotiated by the social partners was the pension reform of 2014 that came into force in 2017. It rose the retirement age linking it to life expectancy and stabilising employers' and employees' insurance contributions far into the future.

Even though the Finnish labour market system has been challenged before, it is now faced with the deepest crisis in its history. There are many voices questioning the democratic foundations of 'cabinet decisionmaking' by social partners. For many employers' organisations, profitmaking and influencing decisionmaking have become more than negotiating terms of employment with trade unions.

In Finland the current government took office in May 2015 with an agenda that showed a drastic change of course in labour market policy. Already after the elections, before his actual nomination, the prime minister, Juha Sipilä, had called for a 'social contract' with employer and employee organisations, aiming at moderate wage formation and more flexible labour markets. The first attempt did not pay off and in the early fall of 2015 the idea of the social contract in its original form was abandoned.

In September 2015, the Sipilä government announced that it would one-sidedly push through a legislative package that would lengthen working time, cut sick leave payments and the length of annual leave and holiday bonuses, and weaken workers' status in local agreements. The government was to introduce binding legislation that reduced the social partners' right to collective bargaining. In the Finnish consensus-oriented tradition, the manoeuvre was completely unheard of; it was an aggressive offensive against workers and their rights. Trade unions were quick to point out that the proposed restrictions to free collective bargaining went against not only the national tradition, but also the conventions and regulations of the International Labour Organization (ILO) and EU.

After months of uproar, the government was forced to step back. Employers seemed to acknowledge that the government would not be able to pull its grandiose initiative through and therefore quickly switched their orientation back into negotiation mode.

The end result of this process was the exceptional 'competitiveness pact' signed by national social partners and the government in February 2016. It included a wage freeze for 2017, a 24-hour extension in annual working time without remuneration, reduced holiday pay for public sector employees, and a transfer of a part of employers' social security liabilities to employees. Once again, Finnish trade union confederations showed great responsibility, negotiating instead of striking – only this time by signing an historical agreement that weakened employee conditions.

This turmoil came with a high price in form of labour market relations. Hardline employers' organisations took advantage of the disorder. For example, Forest Industries, the organisation of highly profitable forestry companies, abandoned its central organisation, the Confederation of Finnish Industries. The Federation of Finnish Enterprises, a small and medium-sized enterprise (SME) lobby and an outsider to the traditional social dialogue, started aggressively pushing forward its own initiatives for further labour market liberalisation. Also on the trade union side, radical tones gained ground. In the aftermath of the labour market dispute, the Confederation of Finnish Industries changed its statute to restrict its mandate on wage negotiations so that in the future organised Finnish employers could only negotiate social reforms at the national level – leading to cuts in social security.

The biggest price was paid in lost trust between the social partners and the government. Employers, for their part, have started to play with two sets of cards. When the government is acting according to their will, they support it. But if the government is unable or not willing to follow employers' will, they turn to negotiate with trade unions. Mistrust is palpable, and the situation far from good for society as a whole.

Now the unions are starting a labour market round without the support of confederations. The latest uncoordinated wage negotiation round in Finland took place in 2007/08 and resulted in very large across-the-board wage increases, largely unrelated to individual firm productivity performance. Time will tell whether upcoming rounds will provide better results.

## THE EMERGING LABOUR MARKET MODEL

Finland has historically been competitive in manufacturing, especially in forest, metal, engineering and ICT industries. New sectors, making use of new technologies, are currently emerging, such as gaming, clean-tech and biotechnology. The changing industrial landscape is also reflected in labour market relations. Whereas workers used to be, and still are, highly organised in factories, trade union membership in SMEs and services is declining. Modern sectors, such as programming and the gaming industry, have largely chosen to stay outside the traditional labour market pattern.

Traditional labour market policy has started to lose its appeal: all the old golden rules of negotiation, wage-setting mechanisms and tripartite cooperation are increasingly perceived as being out of date. National industrial policy has become almost nonexistent. In the belief that free markets will provide the best results, all governments since the 1990s have avoided making clear decisions or strategies on industrial policy.

The fourth industrial revolution shapes production and societal processes: networks replace closed corporative blocks, value chains become increasingly complex and big data is the key resource in the internet age. From the labour market point of view, digitalisation reflects globalisation in many important ways. They are both borderless phenomena that affect all aspects of human life everywhere – and are therefore very difficult to manage. Collective agreements and regulations are mainly agreed on at the national level, while businesses are increasingly global.

For a long time national labour market politics have mainly focused on wage formation, purchasing power and earning-based social security. In the emerging new world these are all still important, but not enough to tackle the new challenges. Education and training, throughout a career, are becoming even more central than they have been so far.

For years, Finland has been aiming for a 72% employment rate. We are only now starting to understand that this goal might be impossible to reach if we do not take education and (re)training far more seriously.

The current government has at least tried to find some solutions to the changing nature of industrial landscape and work, however. The most prominent effort is led by Mika Lintilä, minister of economic affairs, who took office in early 2017 and promised to work out an action plan for renewing industry – something that industrial trade unions have long been asking for.

The original plan on industrial strategy soon transformed into one concentrating on artificial intelligence. The minister reasoned that AI has become a core element of digitalisation and that therefore Finland needs to be at the forefront in developing its own national programme. The objectives set out for the steering group, nominated in May 2017, were to find new key measures that best support the use of AI and robotics in companies in Finland to survey the changes AI and robotics will bring to workplaces, and to support the possibilities in the use of data.

The interim report published by the ministry of economic affairs and employment and the steering group in October 2017 lists eight "key principles for taking Finland towards the age of AI" (Finnish Ministry of Economic Affairs and Employment 2017):

- enhancing business competitiveness with artificial intelligence (AI)
- using data in all sectors effectively
- safeguarding quick and easy AI adoption

- ensuring top-level expertise and attracting top-experts
- making "bold decisions and investments"
- building the world's best public services
- establishing new models of collaboration
- making Finland a frontrunner in AI.

As the above list shows, one key principle level, working life issues and especially themes that would have given anything tangible to workers or the people, were conspicuously absent. The steering group, and more importantly the subgroup on working life operating under the steering group, is however still continuing its work. Some of the preliminary information on the group's work looks promising and will hopefully provide a pathway for the next government programme.

First, the working group does not think that the current industrial revolution is as big a rupture as is often seen. This notion bridges the gap between digi-evangelists and end-of-work doomsdayers. The group has listed several filters that tone down technological change on a societal level: ethical, social, institutional, economic and legal, and administrative. Earlier it has been estimated that in Finland some one-third of workplaces might vanish with digitalisation (Pajarinen and Rouvinen 2014). Now it seems that these numbers were overestimated. The transformation will affect more tasks that are possible to automate, and the number of complete occupations at risk of disappearing could be approximately 9% (Arntz, Gregory and Zierahn 2016; see also Arnold et al. this volume).

Second, the group has been brave enough to touch on delicate issues such as earnings-related social security, which it sees on the one hand as a guarantee for greater labour market mobility, but on the other hand as a system that causes negative incentives.[2]

Third, and most importantly, the working group has paid attention to lifelong learning, training and upskilling. It has also acknowledged that responsibility and costs need to be shared between government, worker and employer.

## THE WAY AHEAD FOR POLICYMAKERS

The Finnish labour market model has been called both rigid and stabilising. Both points of view ring true. In the emerging new labour market model, we have to create a model that combines both features: a labour market that is resilient and supportive of retraining opportunities. In order to succeed in this process industrial policy is essential.

More and more often we hear stories of companies laying off employees because of outdated skill sets. When a specific technology is driven out of markets, the same happens to workers using this technology.

The skills challenge is huge even among employees with higher education. In June 2016, the Finnish Union of Professional Engineers published a survey conducted among its unemployed members. The results were shocking: 24% of unemployed engineers, all with higher education and many with long careers, did not believe that they would find a job again. For those over 60 years, it was 60%. The main reason for unemployment, according to respondents, was an inadequate skill set, one that was either outdated or ill-suited to the employment opportunities in their area of residence.

The situation is more difficult for people with inadequate literacy, numeracy and digital skills. Musset (2015) estimates that in Finland 600,000 adults lack these skills. If skills development is not up to date with technological change, the result will be growing inequality. Without an effective education framework we are not able to foster innovations nor wealth.

What we would need is a complete revolution in education, resulting in the equivalent of universal education. A degree is not enough: reskilling and upskilling is needed throughout the whole career (see Aubrey this volume).

Schwartz et al. (2017) have studied different actors' capability to live up to technological change. In technology, the rate of change is extremely high, and some individuals are able to cope with it. Businesses are slower adapters than individuals. The lowest capability to live up to the change seems to be in the field of public policy.

The complex interaction of globalisation, technology and welfare means that alleviating poverty on the political left or boosting business on the right is not enough. We have to be able to see change and be bold enough to use our political imagination for ways to tackle it.

Finnish decisionmakers should use the old Finnish tripartite labour market system to work together on the future world of work. Even The Economist, a business magazine, has pointed out that trade unions should have a significant role in shaping the education system (Palmer 2017).

The reasoning for this is straightforward. First, trade unions have an industry-wide view of themes that may not be available to smaller employers. Second, skills will accompany people throughout their working lives, which may become increasingly important in a world of rising self-employment. This is exactly what the Union of Professional Engineers in Finland, among several other unions, is intending to do. We provide members with career counselling and organise workshops with issues ranging from 'CV clinics' to negotiating techniques and labour law. At the same time we constantly collect data of our members trying to improve inform policymaking in the areas of employment and industrial strategy in the digital future.

Lifelong learning needs to become a reality instead of a mere slogan. Especially educational structures must be completely transformed to support genuine lifelong learning. To succeed in this task, we need coordinated efforts to bring together employees, employers and providers of education.

## NOTES

1. Finland's organisation rate has been in decline for some 20 years. Estimates for the current organisation rate differ between 60% and 75%.

2. Negative incentives of unemployment benefits are a widely discussed and often a very politicised theme. The political right often sees it as passivising, while the left stands firmly against the weakening of unemployment

benefits. In Finland employees are entitled to an earnings-related unemployment benefit that lasts for 400 days, if the unemployed person has been working for eight months or more before becoming unemployed.

## REFERENCES

Arntz, M., T. Gregory and U. Ziehran (2016), *The Risk of Automation for Jobs in OECD Countries: a Comparative Analysis*, Social, Employment and Migration Working Paper 189, Paris: Organisation for Economic Co-operation and Development.

Finnish Ministry of Economic Affairs and Employment (2017), *Interim Report on Artificial Intelligence*. TEM Publications 41/17, Helsinki: Finnish Ministry of Economic Affairs and Employment.

Musset, P. (2015), *Building Skills for All: a Review of Finland*, OECD Skills Studies, Paris: Organisation for Economic Co-operation and Development.

Pajarinen, M. and P. Rouvinen (2014), 'Computerization Threatens One Third of Finnish Employment', *ETLA Brief*, 22, Helsinki: Research Institute of the Finnish Economy.

Palmer, A. (2017), *Special Report on the Future of Work: Learning and Earning*, London: The Economist.

Schwartz, J., L. Collins, H. Stockton, D. Wagner, B. Walsh, B. Pelster, R. Attra, S. Garr, B. Kaunert, P. Lowes, C. Manning, S. Rogers, D. Schatsky, N. Sloan and J. Bersin (2017), *Rewriting the Rules for the Digital Age: 2017 Deloitte Human Capital Trends*, London: Deloitte University Press.

# SWEDEN

## Will history lead the way in the age of robots and platforms?

### Fredrik Söderqvist

The digitalisation debate in Sweden has become a debate over the future of the 'Swedish model'. Given the current trajectory in most developed countries, the future of work looks bleak. As large sections of the labour market look set to be displaced by automation, the workforce must either reskill in order to keep up with the quickening pace of structural change, or face a future of precarious work, perhaps by finding that work via low-paid digital labour platforms. For a country with ambitions of inclusive growth and a generous welfare state, much is at risk. If the bleakest scenario materialises, Swedish institutions, developed and guarded by the country's trade union movement, will have failed to maintain a long-standing tradition of successfully mitigating the adverse effects of creative destruction on the labour market.

The challenges ahead will require action from Sweden's trade union movement and its counterparts. Job polarisation, as described by Acemoglu and Autor (2011), will need to be met with reforms to enable workers to upskill, so the labour market can keep up with demand for new skillsets in an increasingly digital economy. The growing importance of digital platforms and their algorithms in our societies may become a challenge as platform business models spread across sectors, resulting in the partial automation of the employer. For a country with 90% collective bargaining coverage, if labour platforms are to be regulated successfully it will be necessary to integrate existing collective agreements into these digital platforms.

In this essay I will briefly discuss these two challenges and how they might be met by Swedish trade unions. Given Sweden's high rate of collective bargaining coverage, and the strength of the country's unions and labour market institutions, finding solutions to these problems may 'only' require tweaks and adaptations of existing systems. The ideas presented below may appear overly optimistic. However, as Sweden's labour traditions and institutions may be severely disrupted by the challenges ahead, solution-oriented approaches are perhaps the only option.

## A TRADE UNION MOVEMENT RESILIENT TO STRUCTURAL CHANGE[1]

Swedish (and Nordic) trade unions are possibly the greatest proponents of structural change in the world. This may be explained through the institutional history of Sweden's labour market, which developed in the wake of the conflict-ridden early 20th century, into the largely codetermined labour market regime of today.

During the 'golden era' of Swedish labour relations (or *Saltsjöbadsandan* stretching from the mid-1930s to the early 1970s) many of the institutions on which union acceptance of Schumpeterian creative destruction depend were developed. These were modelled on the ideas of the economists Gösta Rehn and Rudolf Meidner of the Swedish Confederation of Trade Unions (Landsorganisationen i Sverige) (LO 1951). The Rhen–Meidner model combined active labour market policies, a general welfare state, solidary centralised wage bargaining, and restrictive macroeconomic policy, in order to achieve full employment, price stability, fair wages and high economic growth. In practice sectors dependent on low-cost labour became unprofitable as centralised wage bargaining increased pay across all sectors. Instead of protecting low-paid, labour- intensive industries, the trade unions proposed supporting displaced workers to migrate to more productive sectors through active labour market policies. The embrace of creative destruction, by promoting labour market mobility, was conditional on the safety-net institutions set up in order to mitigate the adverse effects of structural change to their members.

Institutions mitigating structural change were further developed in the 1970s when white-collar trade unions and employers' associations signed the first structural change mitigation agreements, or *omställningsavtal*. These agreements formalised the trade unions' positive stance on technology-driven rationalisations, as long as employers helped finance mitigation efforts. At the time, there was a sense that the state-run active labour market regimes were not sufficiently oriented towards white-collar professionals. The mitigation agreements created the first job security councils – essentially private unemployment offices owned by employers' associations and trade unions, with a focus on white-collar professionals. Similar mitigation agreements have since been added to cover most of the labour force, and the job security councils have become very successful in helping redundant workers retrain and find new employment (OECD 2015).

Although many aspects of the original Rhen–Meidner model have been altered, abandoned or later revived over the past 60 years, central aspects pertaining to reskilling remain. The 'Swedish model' is not a static or stable concept, but one that is constantly evolving and adapting to prevailing conditions in the labour market. As most of the Swedish labour market regime is regulated by contracts, collective bargaining parties are relatively unconstrained to solve challenges deemed important for a well-functioning and competitive labour market.

# INCORPORATING LIFELONG LEARNING
# INTO THE SWEDISH MODEL

Reports on the number of jobs displaced by the ongoing process of digitalisation range from somewhat alarming – 7% of Swedish workers are at high risk of being automated according to Arntz, Gregory and Zierahn (2016) (see also Arnold et al. this volume) – to utterly dismal – half of all jobs in Sweden according to Fölster (2014). The debate seems to have created a consensus that further reforms are needed to reduce the skills gap caused by this structural change. For a trade union movement that has spent decades trying to convince legislators to invest in lifelong learning, the challenge of digitalisation has finally pushed the issue higher up the agenda (see Karjalainen this volume).

As in most countries, institutions that mitigate the effects of structural change for the individual are reactive. Access to unemployment insurance and job security councils is normally granted after redundancy has taken place. Successful lifelong learning reforms will need to push existing institutions to take proactive measures.

Given the growing complexity and specialisation of the labour market, efforts will need to be focused on the individual. First, taking time off to retrain or upgrade skills will need to be financially viable for working people. Second, if the financial barrier is overcome, for example through the creation of individual competence accounts or funds, institutions must support individuals to make sound investments in their human capital. Here, the state will need to play a pivotal role in a number of areas, such as giving universities a mandate to include skill upgrading in their educational offerings, and provide skill validation, so that work–life experience is better taken into account in completing academic courses or programmes.

Successful lifelong learning reform would result in a higher proportion of workers making regular investments in their human capital to keep up with demand within the labour market. If the adaptations made by these institutions are successful in changing attitudes and behaviour, upskilling may become more career-oriented, rather than geared towards an individual's current job. Opportunity-based labour turnover may therefore increase, creating upward pressure on wages, to the benefit of union members, and improving matching in the labour market over time, benefiting firms.

There have already been attempts to incorporate lifelong learning into existing mitigation agreements, but these have failed in negotiations because of disagreements over costs (employers have wanted significantly reduced employment protection in exchange). However, given the increased prominence of the digitalisation debate, there are likely to be further attempts in the near future.

## PLATFORM WORK AND THE ALGORITHM-BASED EMPLOYER

Related to the challenges presented by automation is the sudden rise of digital labour platforms, which may complement or replace the traditional role of the employer in leading and directing work within a firm (see Schor this volume). Examples also show that technology may be used to circumvent regulation, including those related to the labour market.

The economic literature on digital platforms (including labour platforms) mainly focuses on the economic opportunities and efficiency gains made possible with platform-based business models. Platforms are economic agents that facilitate transactions and interactions between its users. In order to be successful in these functions, platforms must gain a critical mass of users. If a platform attains a sufficient base network, this may help attract even more users, so platforms display significant economies of scale. If the users give away data when using the platform, the data may be used to further improve the functions of the platform. As a consequence, inter-platform competition is often oligopolistic in developed platform markets, with high barriers to entry (see Hagiu and Wright 2015; Rochet and Tirole 2003; The Economist 2016).

If platforms are marketplaces "where people and businesses trade under a set of rules set by the owner or operator" (The Economist 2016), what happens when the actions of a platform owner or operator have an adverse impact on its users? If a platform market is characterised by duopolistic competition, for example, there may be few alternatives for labour suppliers. If a handful of platforms become the de facto marketplaces for large parts of the economy, and thus critical infrastructure in market economies, how should regulators act in order to promote fair competition?

Digital platforms play a critical role in an increasingly connected society. When ranking the world's highest valued publicly traded companies we often see Apple, Alphabet (formerly Google), Microsoft, Facebook and Amazon at the top – firms that own and operate multi-sided platforms. The highest valued privately owned company is Uber, a labour platform.

Since its founding in 2009, Uber has quickly become the largest facilitator of taxi services in the world. As of June 2017, Uber had facilitated over 5 billion trips (Holt, Macdonald and Gore-Coty 2017). Apart from disrupting the taxi industry, the company's advanced digital platform has shown that the traditional role of the employer to lead and coordinate work can now be undertaken by an algorithm, capable of organising work for a highly decentralised workforce.

Uber has been particularly influential in that it has created a highly imitable model, which entrepreneurs have attempted to apply across various industries, and it may prove to be the first incarnation of an advanced, algorithm-based employer.

However, in the past year, a cascade of scandals has tarnished Uber's tech-glossy reputation. Among the labour-related scandals, we have seen hire-and-fire practices parallel to day labour (one-sided price setting and driver terminations through an opaque rating system), blacklisting ('blackballing'), the misclassification of labour, and company stores (dysfunctional car leasing schemes). It appears to be corporate culture built on purposefully breaking rules and regulations in order to gain competitive advantages over its competitors, with the end goal of reaching an international (self-driving) taxi monopoly (Thiel 2014).[2]

Platforms imitating Uber's business model often adapt a similar attitude towards their labour force (misclassification). Getting to grips with the undesirable aspects of these platforms involves dealing with the preconception that platform labour must be bogus self-employed, precarious, gig work.

A labour platform may be seen as an organisational tool that employers can use to connect its service providers with customers more efficiently. If the platform dictates the terms and conditions of the transactions it facilitates sufficiently, then the platform is not a free market consisting of independent contractors, and should be classified as an employer. The boundaries considered in Coase's (1937) firm, regarding whether one is working in a free market or within the confines of a firm's planned economy, are pertinent not only in discussing the shortcomings of platform economies, but in most labour markets where precarious work and bogus self-employment cause social and economic inequality.

In Söderqvist (2016, 2017), I present a so-called Nordic approach to regulating labour platforms. It first involves integrating platforms into existing sectoral collective bargaining regimes. Here, defining employer status is key; this has not yet been a major issue in Sweden, where most service platforms have accepted employer status within our existing labour standards.[3] Second, we are exploring ways to make collective agreements easier to integrate and more compatible with the platform firms' software, in essence developing digitalised versions of existing collective agreements. This may sound complicated, but needn't be in practice if the process is carried out at a small scale. Sitting down with platform programmers and discussing how best to incorporate important aspects of collective agreements or labour codes is one way of doing this. From such talks, standards or best practices can be developed that may be used by other firms under the same or similar agreements.

This concept can be taken further by making similar adaptations outside the regulatory reach of traditional collective bargaining. The idea is that the social partners take a more active role in adapting and creating new standards in areas of relevant regulation, in order to make them better able to integrate into digital business models. To accomplish this, we propose the creation of a social-partner-owned institution where digital regulatory standards can be developed with a more holistic perspective, closer to market forces, so platforms, unions and national regulators develop novel digital regulatory standards in cooperation. The hope is to provide better digital regulatory standards, closer to market forces than would be possible if regulators take a piecemeal approach to adapting to the rise of labour platforms.

Recognising that such platforms could make a significant positive contribution to the Swedish economy if regulated properly, these proposals would have unions take a proactive approach, focusing on migrating existing regulation rather than attempting to stall the implementation of productivity-enhancing technology. If playing by the rules is made easy for firms with platform-based business models, then the often-heard arguments lambasting the sclerotic regulations of 'the old economy' will ring hollow. If, as Lawrence Lessig (1999) eloquently stated, "code is law", regulators will need to gain influence over the code. To do so efficiently firms may need to devote more resources towards building sustainable and competitive business models.

## CONCLUSION

I have presented solution-oriented approaches to dealing with some of the challenges faced by the Swedish trade union movement in the years ahead. Although the proposals may seem overly optimistic, our tradition, and the long-term survival of our institutions, leave Swedish trade unions with little choice other than to act. The approaches proposed here depend on the ability of capital, labour and politics to engage in constructive dialogue over common challenges. Such a commonsense approach may be difficult in a political discourse where trade unions are not seen as legitimate representatives of the labour force. Getting to grips with the rise in income inequality, democratic polarisation and capital gains capturing an ever-increasing share of economic surpluses, involves fixing fundamental shortcomings of capitalism pertaining to bargaining power. The Swedish example shows that complicated issues within the labour market may be solved at the bargaining table, given that bargaining power between labour and capital is relatively equal. If more countries recognise the key role of trade unionism in solving the challenges ahead, then the transition to the new digital economy may prove less turbulent.

## NOTES

1. For more on the history and development of Swedish labour market institutions see for example Erixon (2010) and Swenson (2002).
2. Continual updates about Uber controversies can be found on the website http://www.uberscandals.org.
3. However, there are unresolved complications as to who should be seen as the employer.

## REFERENCES

Acemoglu, D. and D. Autor (2011), 'Skills, Tasks and Technologies: Implications for Employment and Earnings', in *Handbook of Labor Economics*, vol. 4, 1043–171, Elsevier.

Arntz, M., T. Gregory and U. Zierahn (2016), 'The Risk of Automation for Jobs in OECD Countries: a Comparative Analysis', OECD Social, Employment and Migration Working Paper 189, Paris: OECD Publishing.

Coase, R. (1937), 'The Nature of the Firm', *Economica*, 4(16), 386–405.

Erixon, L. (2010), 'The Rehn-Meidner Model in Sweden: its Rise, Challenges and Survival', *Journal of Economic Issues*, 44(3), 677–715.

Fölster, S. (2014), *Vartannat Jobb Automatiseras*, Stockholm: Stiftelsen för Strategisk Forskning.

Hagiu, A. and J. Wright (2015), 'Multi-sided Platforms', *International Journal of Industrial Organization*, 43, 162–74.

Holt, R., A. Macdonald and P.-D. Gore-Coty (2017), '5 Billion Trips', press release, Uber, 29 June, https://www.uber.com/newsroom/5billion-2/.

Lessig, L. (1999), 'Code is Law', in L. Lessing, *Code and Other Laws of Cyberspace*, 3–8, New York: Basic Books.

LO (1951), *Fackföreningsrörelsen och den Fulla Sysselsättningen*, report to the Landsorganisationen i Sverige Congress, Malmö: translated by A.-B. Framtiden.

OECD (2015), *Back to Work: Sweden – Improving the Re-employment Prospects of Displaced Workers*, report by the Directorate for Employment, Labour and Social Affairs, Paris: OECD Publishing.

Rochet, J.-C. and J. Tirole (2003), 'Platform Competition in Two-Sided Markets', *Journal of the European Economic Association*, 1(4), 990–1029.

Söderqvist, F. (2016), *Plattformsekonomin och den Svenska Partsmodellen*, Stockholm: Unionen.

Söderqvist, F. (2017), 'A Nordic Approach to Regulating Intermediary Online Labour Platforms', *Transfer: European Review of Labour and Research*, 23(3), 349–52.

Swenson, P. (2002), *Capitalists Against Markets: the Making of Labor Markets and Welfare States in the United States and Sweden*, Oxford: Oxford University Press.

The Economist (2016), 'The Emporium Strikes Back: Platforms Are the Future – but Not for Everyone', *The Economist*, 21 May, https://www.economist.com/news/business/21699103-platforms-are-futurebut-not-everyone-emporium-strikes-back.

Thiel, P. (2014), 'Competition is for Losers', *The Wall Street Journal*, 12 September, https://www.wsj.com/articles/peter-thiel-competition-is-for-losers-1410535536.

# THE NETHERLANDS

## The sectoral impact of digitalisation on employment and job quality

Maarten Keune and Fabian Dekker

In the Netherlands, as in the rest of the world, an energetic debate is under way on the potential impact of digitalisation on the labour market and welfare state. The importance of digitalisation in the Dutch public debate is demonstrated, among other things, by the heightened attention it has received in the key Dutch advisory bodies. At the end of 2016, the Socio-Economic Council, the key institution of the Dutch neo-corporatist model, published its study *Mens en Technologie: Samen aan het Werk* (Humans and Technology: Working Together) (SER 2016a). A year earlier the Scientific Council for Government Policy published *De Robot de Baas: de Toekomst van Werk in het Tweede Machinetijdperk* (The Robots in Command: The Future of Work in the Second Machine Age) (Went, Kremer and Knottnerus 2015). In the same year, the Rathenau Institute published a report commissioned by the parliament titled *Werken aan de Robotsamenleving* (Working on the Robot Society) (van Est and Kool 2015).

Digitalisation has also become a major subject at the collective bargaining tables across the labour market. On the one hand, this heightened attention reflects the impact digitalisation has been having on the Dutch economy and labour market in recent years and the need to deal with its economic and social implications. On the other hand, it reflects worries about the possible negative outcomes digitalisation may have on the number and quality of jobs, inequality and welfare, and the desire to influence this process through public and private policy. Although the new Dutch government is trying to reap the benefits of the fourth industrial revolution by investing in digital technologies and cybersecurity (VVD et al. 2017), there is no explicit policy agenda centred on technological innovation.

In this essay we will discuss the impact of digital technologies in the Netherlands, with a focus on its varied effects in the different sectors of the economy, and point out how new social policies and related interventions can overcome some of the possible negative consequences brought by technology.

## WORK IN THE DIGITAL AGE

New technologies, including physical and social robots, artificial intelligence, driverless cars, cloud computing and data analytics, have a big impact on employment in Europe. Well-known commentators like Elon Musk, Bill Gates and Stephen Hawking as well as policymakers are worried that intelligent and more powerful machines will eventually take over most of the existing jobs (see also Frey and Osborne 2013). The most routinisable jobs are most at risk of automation (Acemoglu and Autor 2011; see also Arnold et al. this volume). However, most studies and scenarios largely neglect the creation of new jobs, goods and services brought about by new technology. Furthermore, most jobs are a so-called 'bundle of tasks' that can't all be automated that easily. For example, consider the work of mental health workers which depends considerably on complex problem solving and social skills. Only humans have the power of social empathy, which is extremely difficult to automate (Colvin 2015). Notwithstanding these limitations, new technology is fundamentally altering the nature of work. We will briefly reflect on what technology means for job markets, with a focus in particular on the Netherlands as an example of an open economy with a rapid increase in information and communications technology (ICT) investments since 2000 (OECD 2016).

New technologies, such as ICT and the adoption of computers, have triggered a process of job polarisation across many European labour markets (Goos, Manning and Salomons 2014; van Est and Kool 2015). Many jobs, mostly routine and middle-skilled but also certain low-skilled jobs, are being replaced by ICT and other technologies. This trend can be seen in many European countries (see Figure 23.1). The Netherlands has also experienced automation of many routine middle-skilled jobs, such as in banking, insurance and other financial service providers, or low-skilled jobs in warehousing, though less than most other EU countries. Jobs at the lower end of the labour market distribution remain relatively stable, however, due to a growing demand for new services and a declining number of low-skilled workers, while high-skilled jobs can more easily complement the introduction of new technology (Dekker and van der Veen 2017).

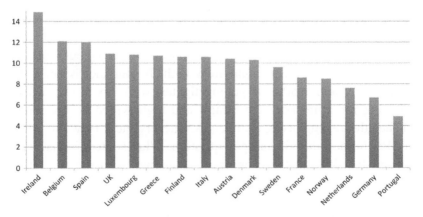

Figure 23.1 Percentage decline in occupational employment shares in middle-wage occupations (16 EU countries, 1993–2010). *Source*: Author.

While new technology sometimes substitutes (middle-skilled) employees and sometimes complements (high-skilled) employees, it may also affect the nature of the employer–employee relationship. Online platforms, such as Uber, Airbnb and TaskRabbit, already disrupt existing business models and enable companies quickly to adjust the size of their (flexible) workforce. In the Netherlands, 12% of all adults report that they have earned money through the platform economy as a self-employed worker at some point (see Huws et al. this volume). The rise of this so-called 'gig economy' poses important questions and challenges concerning the protection and regulation of new groups of 'crowdworkers' (TNO 2016). These concern, above all, the often high insecurity and low quality of jobs and limited access to social security, particular for the rapidly growing group of (dependent) self-employed (see Schor this volume). Various types of flexible employment already accounting for 35% of the Dutch labour market, and this is likely to increase further as the platform economy grows.

New technology is fundamentally changing labour markets, but the future extent of possible job losses, labour market polarisation and the rise of the 'gig economy' is still unclear. The same is true for the quality of jobs, which may deteriorate if the present trend continues but which can also be safeguarded through public or collective interventions (Went, Kremer and Knottnerus 2015). Indeed, the future development of the labour market is not an autonomous process and can be steered by politics and collective labour market actors. At the moment, unemployment in the Netherlands is low and the Dutch labour market is getting tighter, with labour shortages emerging for a number of medium- and high-skilled occupations (IT, healthcare, engineers, technicians, teachers, etc.). How this will develop in the future is an open question. What is clear is that the demand for skills in the economy is changing, with digital skills becoming ever more important across occupations.

The next section focuses on an important but less studied dimension of digitalisation, which is key to understanding its immediate impact: how the process varies across sectors.

## A SECTORAL PERSPECTIVE

The complex and diverse effects of digitalisation are underlined when we take a sectoral perspective. Here we will provide some examples of the impacts of digitalisation on the number and quality of jobs in different sectors in the short and medium term. In some sectors, such as banking, digitalisation leads mainly to jobs losses. Automation and the increased use of internet banking have destroyed many mid-level jobs at both headquarters and closing bank branches. Employment in the three largest banks in the Netherlands has declined by some 40,000 jobs and further cuts are foreseen for the immediate future.

Another example is the graphic design industry. Here digitalisation has reduced the demand for printed materials and improved the capacity of companies and individuals to do their own design work, mainly hitting printing personnel and low- and medium-skilled graphic designers. As a result, employment in the sector declined from 45,000 jobs in 2004 to 24,000 jobs in 2014 (UWV 2016a). At the same time, graphic design is providing more opportunities for highly skilled designers (UWV 2016a), which is in line with the skill-biased technological change hypothesis.

In other sectors digitalisation leads to employment growth, although with varying levels of quality. One example is the IT sector, where employment has increased following growing demand for IT services throughout the economy. According to the UWV (2016b), the sector has created some 25,000 additional jobs since 2013. Moreover, these are generally high-quality jobs, making a positive contribution to the labour market. Employment has also grown in various types of distribution activities related to e-commerce and the platform economy, including parcel delivery and food delivery (like Deliveroo, foodora or ThuisBerzOrgd.nl). Here, though, jobs are often of low quality, characterised by high insecurity, low earnings and lack of social protection and disability insurance. Employers in this sector follow a low-cost, high-flexibility strategy to the detriment of the workers. They often want only self-employed workers to cut costs by avoiding, among other things, contributions to the social security system, and to transfer much of the employer risk onto the shoulders of these workers. A case in point here is Deliveroo, which recently announced that it wants to transform all 1,750 employment contracts into self-employment arrangements. This led to the first protest march of Deliveroo workers; they objected to this plan, demanding permanent contracts and the establishment of a works council to give employees influence on company policy.

In other sectors, digitalisation does not necessarily have an effect on the number of jobs but rather on the quality of jobs. A key example here is the health sector. A recent study on digitalisation in Dutch healthcare shows that digitalisation is a priority policy area in the sector, but not with the objective to reduce costs or employment (Het Digitale Landschap 2016). A survey among care professionals shows that the three major objectives of digitalisation in health are to provide tailor-made care, to reduce the administrative burden for healthcare workers, and to be able to react quicker and more accurately to care demands. Such forms of digitalisation then allow healthcare workers to dedicate more of their time to patients and to provide better care. It is also likely to improve the quality of their jobs. Similar observations can be made in the education sector (Onderwijsraad 2017).

These sector-by-sector perspectives demonstrate that in the short and medium term digitalisation can lead to job creation as well as job losses, and to increases as well as decreases in job quality. An effective response to digitalisation would therefore include a strong sectoral component. In the Dutch context, where most sectors are covered by collective agreements, discussions between trade unions and employers' organisations should play a key role.

## A LONGER-TERM POLICY PERSPECTIVE

What long-term role should policymakers play in the context of digitalisation? With future developments so uncertain, they should define a set of principles and goals concerning the process of digitalisation. For example, digitalisation should be at the service of society; it is not an end in itself and should therefore abide to certain conditions. Most importantly, it should not result in declining job quality and increased inequality. It should only take place in a context in which workers' rights are protected for everyone who works, income distribution is fair and social protection is available to all. Following such principles, politicians can monitor this process and, where needed, adjust it.

Translating such principles into policy first of all involves guaranteeing workers' rights, including decent wages and secure employment for platform workers, including the self-employed. This requires an adjusted definition of what a worker is and of the relationship between platform workers and their employers. This issue is currently being debated in the Netherlands but has not yet been resolved. Platform workers, and all others confronted with digitalisation, should get a say in company policy through works councils and/or collective bargaining.

Second, the welfare state will also need reform to adapt to these challenges (see Palier this volume). Many self-employed people lack access to unemployment benefits, disability insurance and pensions. For many this is a choice, but there is a growing group of the self-employed, including those involved in the platform economy, for whom it is a matter of prohibitive costs. The welfare state should be adapted to include the self-employed in these three areas of social security. The respective costs could be carried by the companies through social contributions, as with employees. This will prevent self-employment leading to precarious work and high-income insecurity. An alternative approach is reforming the tax system. For example, all generic fiscal incentives and tax allowances for the self-employed in the Netherlands could be used for social security coverage instead.

Third, education and training will be crucial components of the policy response (see De Franceschi this volume). Digital skills should become part and parcel of educational programmes where this is not yet the case, to prepare students properly for the future. For those already in work, the lifelong learning principle should be taken much more seriously than it is today. Dutch enterprises and public organisations pay lip service to the issue but only provide limited training and retraining efforts (SER 2016b). Training is organised along sectoral lines, through specific training funds, making it more difficult for workers to get training for new occupations (Dekker and van der Veen 2017). This is especially problematic for workers in sectors where employment is declining because of digitalisation, for workers on flexible contracts, who need more but get less training than workers on permanent contracts, and for the (dependent) self-employed, who do not have access to collectively organised training at all. In light of this, increasing training efforts for all workers and overcoming the sectoral division of the funding and delivery of training should be a priority in a rapidly evolving labour market.

Finally, there is the issue of inequality and income distribution. According to some predictions, digitalisation may lead to strongly increasing inequality because of the concentration of ownership of algorithms, platforms and robots, and strong negative employment effects (see Crouch this volume). If this is the case, questions should be asked about private ownership of the means of production and the extent to which income generated by private enterprises corresponds to their owners. Collective ownership or technology taxes may be a way out of such dilemmas. Some of these issues may not be solvable within national borders and may require a coordinated effort in the context of the EU or the World Trade Organization.

## REFERENCES

Acemoglu, D. and Autor, D. (2011), 'Skills, Tasks and Technologies: Implications for Employment and Earnings', in D. Card and O. Ashenfelter (eds), *Handbook of Labor Economics*, Vol. 4, 1043–171, Amsterdam: Elsevier.

Autor, D. (2015), 'Why Are There Still So Many Jobs?', *Journal of Economic Perspectives*, 29(3): 3–30.

Colvin, G. (2015), *Humans Are Underrated: What High Achievers Know That Brilliant Machines Never Will*, New York: Penguin.

Dekker, F. and R. van der Veen (ed.) (2017), *Het Midden Weg?*, Delft: Eburon.

Frey, C. B. and M. Osborne (2013), *The Future of Employment: How Susceptible are Jobs to Computerisation?*, Oxford: Oxford Martin School.

Goos, M., A. Manning and A. Salomons (2014), 'Explaining Job Polarization: Routine-Biased Technological Change and Offshoring', *American Economic Review*, 104(8): 2509–26.

Het Digitale Landschap (2016), *Het Digitale Landschap van de Zorg in 2016*, Amsterdam: Het Digitale Landschap, https://hetdigitalelandschap.nl/wp-content/uploads/2016/03/HDL-Onderzoeksrapport-Zorg-V7.pdf.

OECD (2016), *OECD Economic Surveys: Netherlands 2016*, Paris: OECD Publishing.

Onderwijsraad (2017), *Doordacht Digital: Onderwijs in het Digitale Tijdperk*, The Hague: Onderwijsraad. https://www.onderwijsraad.nl/upload/documents/publicaties/volledig/Doordacht-digitaal-a.pdf.

SER (2016a), *Mens en Technologie: Samen aan het Werk*, The Hague: SER.

SER (2016b), *Toekomstgericht Beroepsonderwijs*, Den Haag: SER.

TNO (2016), *Nieuwe Schatting van de Omvang van de Nederlandse 'Gig Economie'*, The Hague: Nederlandse Organisatie voor Toegepast Natuurwetenschappelijk Onderzoek, https://www.tno.nl/media/7841/2016-22_factsheet_netherlands_platform_economie.pdf.

UWV (2016a), *Grafische Sector onder Druk door Verdergaande Digitalisering*, The Hague: Uitvoeringsinstituut Werknemersverzekeringen, https://www.uwv.nl/overuwv/pers/persberichten/2016/grafische-sector-onder-druk-door-verdergaande-digitalisering.aspx.

UWV (2016b), *Arbeidsmarktprognose 2016–2017*, The Hague: Uitvoeringsinstituut Werknemersverzekeringen.

van Est, R. and L. Kool (ed.) (2015), *Werken aan de Robotsamenleving: Visies en Inzichten uit de Wetenschap over de Relatie Technologie en Werkgelegenheid*, The Hague: Rathenau Instituut.

VVD, CDA, D66 and Christenunie (2017), *Vertrouwen in de Toekomst: Coalition Agreement 2017–2021*, The Hague: Volkspartij voor Vrijheid en Democratie, Christen-Democratisch Appèl, Democraten 66 and Christenunie.

Went, R., M. Kremer and A. Knottnerus (ed.) (2015), *De Robot de Baas: de Toekomst van Werk in het Tweede Machinetijdperk*, WRR-Verkenning 31, The Hague: WRR.

# B

# Medium digital density EU countries

# BELGIUM

## Reinvigorating the self-regulated labour market model[1]

## Patrizia Zanoni

The academic debate on the Belgian platform economy is still only at its very beginnings. Scientific interest is slowly emerging from an intermittent yet increasing debate on the platform economy – more often called the 'sharing', 'collaborative', 'peer-to-peer' or 'on-demand' economy (Drahokoupil and Fabo 2016) in the press – mainly reporting cases of conflicts between large, international, platform-organised companies such as Uber, Airbnb and Deliveroo and trade unions or public authorities. At the time of writing (January 2018), Deliveroo bike couriers are striking in Brussels against the company's imposition that they work as self-employed for €5 gross per delivery, after Deliveroo's recent unilateral termination of the contract with SMart, a platform-based organisation which had negotiated a collective deal for its members working as bike couriers (Kilhoffer and Lenaerts 2017).[2] Only a few weeks ago, taxi drivers were taking to the streets against the Taxi Plan of the socialist minister of mobility of the Brussels region, redrawing existing legislation to 'modernise' the taxi sector, which is expected to lead to the regularisation of Uber.

The media coverage suggests that existing Belgian federal law regulating the 'sharing or collaborative economy' – '*deeleconomie*' in Dutch and '*économie collaborative*' in French, which entered into force on 1 March 2017, has not resolved the controversy. Introduced to "support and give more freedom to a growing group of mini-entrepreneurs" (De Croo 2016), this legislation sets a fixed taxation rate of 10% for individuals working on a registered platform of up to €5,000 per annum. Previously the tax rate was 33% on activities in the sharing economy. The law foresees that the tax, which will be levied by the platform itself, only applies to individuals offering services occasionally, as opposed to those offering them professionally. These individuals will still need to register as self-employed. It thus creates a third employment status, in addition to employee and self-employed. The law was passed only a few days after the European commission's plea for national legislation that would aim at eliminating barriers in the sharing economy, yet at the same time avoiding the imposition of "cumbersome legislation on platforms" (European Commission 2016). This latter point had been advocated by 11 EU member states in an open letter to the commission a few months earlier (UK et al. 2016).

The law clearly echoes the main arguments of the EU communication that the economic growth potential, estimated between €160bn and €572bn(!) depending on the sources, can be attained only by taking the sharing economy out of the 'grey' legal zone in which it is currently operating. At a historical time of stagnating economic growth, a sector whose revenues doubled between 2014 and 2015 (Vaughan and Daverio 2016), the sharing economy is presented as a unique opportunity to enhance Europe's competitiveness. Accordingly, the platform economy is seen as an occasion to "simplify and modernise market access requirements. [. . .] to relieve operators from unnecessary regulatory burden [. . .] and to avoid fragmentation of the Single Market" (European Commission 2016: 7).

The language of both Belgian law and the EU communication obscures what is at stake with the platform economy. It is not only the organisation of work in specific sectors but the entire institutional tradition of labour market self-regulation between social partners that historically stands at the core of the Belgian labour market and society as a whole. Although the platform economy still represents only a small share of the total economy, it has rapidly become the dominant business model in specific sectors, indicating that this is only the start of what is to become a fourth industrial revolution. If this were the case, then the key question is, as stressed by Söderqvist (2016, 2017a, 2017b), how do we integrate the platform economy into our social welfare model, a self-regulated labour market model collectively negotiated between employers and trade unions?

This chapter links the challenges posed today by the platform economy to the long-term debate on the flexibility of the Belgian labour market to foster inclusion. Flexibility has been increased through the direct intervention of the state therefore breaking the tradition of self-regulation. I argue that the platform economy, while posing a great challenge, might paradoxically offer a historical occasion for capital and labour to (partially) realign their interests and reinvigorate self-regulation. I will conclude by proposing policy actions to strengthen workers' rights in the platform economy.

## THE PLATFORM ECONOMY DEBATE AS A SHOWCASE OF THE CRISIS OF BELGIAN SELF-REGULATION

Belgium is a European country with strong collective bargaining institutions at the national, sectoral and company levels, and with one of the highest collective bargaining coverage rates in the EU (96%), a high and stable union density of over 50% (ETUI 2017), and 76% of employees work for an employer that is organised (European Commission 2011). The self-regulating Belgian system has increasingly come under pressure because of technological changes, European enlargement, the global financial and economic crisis and, more recently, the shift of national politics to the right. Since the mid-1990s, various governments have intervened to 'modernise' labour market institution. In July 1996, the law on the promotion of employment and preventative measures to safeguard competitiveness was adopted. The law sets a ceiling – the so-called 'wage norm' – for collectively negotiated wage growth based on the expected average increase of the labour cost in France, Germany and the Netherlands, Belgium's main trading partners (Van Oycke and Van Gyes 2017). The government intervened directly setting maximum wage increases in 1997–1998, 2005–2006 and 2011–2012, and froze all salaries between 2013 and 2015. Next to wage moderation, the legislator has changed the labour law to increase flexibility. The last initiative is the law on feasible and agile work passed on 5 March 2017, which foresees among others the calculation of working hours annually (maximum nine hours per day and 45 hours per week), the possibility for temporary agencies to employ workers with contracts for an indefinite period, and changes in the regulation of joint employment of workers by small companies through an 'employers' grouping plan'. Of particular importance in this context is article 79, which allows night work for logistical and support services linked to e-commerce (Federal Public Service Employment, Labour and Social Dialogue 2017).

A key argument used in support of containing labour cost increases and enhanced flexibility is the argument of inclusion: this 'modernisation' of the labour law would allow historically excluded groups to enter the Belgian labour market. The following statement by Jan Denys, the director corporate communications and public affairs of Randstad Belgium, a prominent voice in the public debate about labour market issues, is instructive:

> To answer the question where we have to go with our labour market policy, we should start from the current performance of the Belgian labour market. Overall, it is not good relative to the European context, and certainly not if we want to brand ourselves as a 'top region'. In this country, *too few people work, above all those above 50, the youth, people with a migration background and low-skilled women.* The transition between unemployment to work is one of the lowest in the

EU. A stronger proof of a malfunctioning labour market cannot be given. At the same time, job security is one of the highest. *This points to a strong insider-outsider labour market model.* [. . .] The big challenge for our policy-makers is to adapt our labour market institutions to the changing conditions with as baseline: *from job security to work security.* This can be achieved through more flexibility (deregulation) but also re-regulation for instance concerning training (Denys 2013, emphasis added).

An analogous, if more explicit, reasoning was formulated by Hein Knaapen, global director of human resource management at ING [Internationale Nederlanden Groep], who in the wake of an announced lay off of 3,500 employees in the Belgian branch, publicly lamented the 'petrified' nature of the Belgian (and the Dutch) labour market(s):

[The] open-end employment contract is increasingly protected. And then you achieve the opposite of what you want to. It boils down to the fact that young people and minorities get less and less hired. As in the current system, you cannot lay anyone off (Tanghe 2016).

Also scholars pleading for deregulation commonly argue that current workers' rights are incompatible with the inclusion of young and elderly in the labour market. Ive Marx, one of the leading Belgian experts on poverty, recently stated:

There is a too large group of low-educated people, often with a migration background, without a job now [. . .] This is a key main cause of poverty. Therefore, we have to get rid of the rigid regulation of our labour market (Wauters 2016).

The discursive mobilisation of inclusion unveils the continuity between the current debate on platform-based work and the longstanding debate on labour costs and flexibilisation. Indeed, the inclusion potential of platform-based work does not only feature prominently in the EU communication but is also acknowledged in recent trade union initiatives:

The collaborative economy generates new employment opportunities, generating revenues beyond traditional linear employment relationships, and it enables people to work according to flexible arrangements (European Commission 2016, 11).

Platforms for work that can be completed remotely and delivered online (such as Upwork, Freelancer.com, Amazon Mechanical Turk, CrowdFlower, and 99designs) offer economic opportunities that might not otherwise be available to some workers. They allow, for example, workers with responsibilities that prevent them from leaving home, workers in rural areas, workers with disabilities, and workers in 'developing' countries the potential to earn income by working online (ETUI and IGM 2017).

## THE PLATFORM ECONOMY: A HISTORICAL OPPORTUNITY TO REINVIGORATE SELF-REGULATION?

While trade unions and employers typically hold contrasting views on whether labour cost moderation and labour flexibilisation represent an adequate recipe to create a more inclusive labour market, their analysis of digitalisation and the sharing economy appears more aligned, as suggested by a recent report of the National Labour Council and the Central Council for the Economy (CNT and NAR 2017). Focusing on commercial digital platforms the report emphasises that a level playing field is a necessary condition for fair competition. It also criticises the optimistic rhetoric leading to insufficient control of fiscal fraud and expresses serious reservations about the provisions of the law on the sharing or collaborative economy, including the raise of tax-free annual income to €6,000. The text points to the many risks regarding unfair competition, equal treatment, work organisation, social protection, fiscal income and social security balance. Significantly, the social partners unanimously invite the government to consult the inter-professional and directly concerned sectoral social partners to assess the involved risks before working out the implementation, reaffirming their own role in the regulation of the Belgian labour market.

A few days after the report's release, the president of the Neutraal Syndicaat voor Zelstandigen [Syndicat Neutre pour Indépendants], Christine Mattheuws, called the rise to €6,000 per year "a poisoned chalice" for Christmas, warning that unfair competition will drive a number of self-employed out of business. It would also lead to an estimated loss for the social security fund of about €200mn a year (Mattheeuws and Nouten 2017). This reaction reveals that interests of 'classical' employers might not necessarily overlap with firms operating a digital platform model, especially in the eventuality that the former get the bill of those that are unwilling to pay. This possibility is also highlighted by the question provocatively asked by Chris Serroyen, the head of the research unit of the Christian-democratic trade union ACV: "Why should people keep working full-time if they can make as much as €500 a month without any social security contribution?" (Trends 2017). Pulling individuals outside the formal labour market represents an alarming scenario for both employers' and employees' representatives, at a time of economic recovery and increasing labour shortage due to the massive retirement of the baby-boomers and an enduring skill mismatch.

These statements point to the predatory nature of platform-based firms, which extract value from labour whose cost of social reproduction they do not pay (Bhattacharya 2013). Therefore the organisation of work through algorithms coordinating spatially dispersed labour does not only posit huge organisational challenges to trade unions, which have historically organised workers territorially, from workplaces, sectors and, in some cases, communities. It also poses important problems to other firms and the state. When a platform-based business model enables a firm to circumvent existing collectively negotiated rules, it builds a competitive advantage based on the evasion of institutional accountability towards the community of firms and of citizens. In particular, it externalises the cost of social reproduction of labour to individual workers, their families, other firms operating within existing institutions, and the state providing services to endow individuals with the skills that make them productive. The diffusion of platform-based firms is likely to accelerate the

tendency towards an ever more fundamental crisis of social reproduction characterising contemporary global capitalism (Leonard and
Fraser 2016).

The spectre of predatory capital taking over ever larger shares
of the economy could represent a motivation for social partners to
recover and innovate the Belgian tradition of self-regulation. Various
actors, ranging from trade unionists to academics and representatives
of the cooperative world, are today calling for 'a new deal' (Graceffa
and de Heusch 2017). Whatever that deal might look like, there
should be awareness that workers' inclusion without protection is no
option, as it will induce an ever more deep crisis of social reproduction, undermining the Belgian economy in the longer term.

## WHERE TO GO FROM HERE?

There is ample agreement on the union front that platform-based
work should at once allow a larger amount of workers not only to
access paid work, but also entitle them to analogous rights as those
associated with 'traditional' employment. The Frankfurt paper on
platform-based work launched about a year ago by nine trade unions
notes that the first International Workshop on Union Strategies in the
Platform Economy was convened to discuss, among other matters:

> the role of unions and other worker organizations in realizing the
> promise of platform-based work to provide labor market access to
> large groups of previously excluded people, including workers in
> 'developing' countries, and to offer all workers unprecedented free-
> dom and flexibility in their working lives – while retaining elements
> of the 'traditional' employment relationship hard won in the last two
> centuries of labor struggle, such as:
>
> • minimum wage
> • the reasonable expectation to earn a living in a 35- to 40-hour work
>   week
> • affordable access to health care

- compensation in case of injury on the job
- integration into national social protection systems such as social security
- legal protection from discrimination, abuse, and wrongful dismissal, and, crucially
- the right to organise, take collective action, and negotiate collective agreements;

that is, in summary, the role of worker organisations in realizing the promise of online labor platforms to make 'good work' available to many more people (Arbeiterkammer et al. 2016, 2–3).

Granting platform-based workers these rights would enable them to have access to sufficient means – directly and indirectly, through higher wages, insurance, but also access to welfare services – to ensure their own social reproduction. Primarily, this is in their own interest, but also, importantly, in the interest of capital, which crucially relies on labour for capital accumulation.

Many politically meaningful initiatives surrounding platform-based work are emerging. Here, I focus on three types of action that I believe are important for Belgium: fostering collective organisation of platform workers through inclusive union strategies, leveraging platform technology to foster firm compliance, and performing counter-narratives of firm accountability towards society (Crouch this volume).

## FOSTERING THE COLLECTIVE ORGANISATION OF PLATFORM WORKERS THROUGH INCLUSIVE UNION STRATEGIES

Platform-based workers should be allowed to organise and conduct collective bargaining, independent of their status as employees or self-employed. Belgian trade unions should consider diversifying their strategy to stimulate the collective organisation of platform workers. At the international level clickworkers establish internet-based forums, such as turkernation.com, to exchange information and network across borders. In Belgium, the platform-based SMart has in the past negotiated an agreement for platform workers for Deliveroo. In Vienna, bike couriers for the app-based restaurant delivery service foodora recently formed a work council with the support of the Austrian transport and services union Vida (Kuba 2017). These different experiences should be considered as potential complementary strategies by the Belgian unions, such as the transport union Belgische Transportarbeiderbond (BTB), to organise bike couriers to get better working conditions. An algorithm that offers better working conditions and does not discriminate needs to be negotiated, to echo De Stefano (2017).

More fundamentally, the platform economy offers the opportunity to rethink the modalities of union action, tackling in novel ways issues of representativeness, internal democracy in decisionmaking, and 'network syndicalism'. These issues have been on the trade union agenda since the early 1990s, when the first references of 'diversity' – in terms of the socio-cultural, socio-economic and political shifts – and challenge of keeping internal cohesion were included in congress documents (Martens et al. 2001). To the extent that historically subordinated groups in the labour market and in society at large are overrepresented in the platform economy, and this latter's potential to include them represents a key ideological argument, as I have argued above, trade unions should attempt to envision new modalities of operating to increase their own inclusion. The inclusion of the most vulnerable groups is in no way ancillary to trade unions, but rather of strategic importance in order to be able to defend the labour class as a whole.

## LEVERAGING DIGITAL TECHNOLOGIES TO ENFORCE FIRMS' COMPLIANCE

It has been observed that platforms cannot only be used to control workers, but also, potentially, to enhance law enforcement. For instance, if platform-based companies were forced to share the data they hold about their workers with labour inspectorates and trade unions, the application of labour laws could be greatly facilitated (Fabo, Karanovic and Dukova 2017). The Swedish Unionen analogously proposes to embrace an algorithm to foster firms' compliance with the law. Söderqvist argues that trade unions should switch to a 'facilitation' mode: "If we want platforms to play by the rule, we have to make the rules more easily available to them" (Söderqvist 2016, 2017b). This entails in the first place requiring algorithms to become more transparent, so that they can be programmed according to the provisions stipulated through collective agreements, rather than to bypass the rules (UNI Global Union 2017). Second, union action should thus further be directed at making these firms comply more easily by incorporating the collective agreements in their algorithm, such as a taxation code. If controlled externally, platform mediation has the potential to actually lead to increased, rather than lower compliance.

## FOSTERING A COUNTER NARRATIVE OF FIRM ACCOUNTABILITY

Last, but certainly not least, at a historical moment of crisis of the Belgian social model, the solid grip of the centre-right parties in Belgian politics, and the complete disarray of the left, I believe there is a need for the unions to promote strong counter-narratives to the dominant neoliberal, celebratory discourse of the 'sharing, collaborative economy'. The recovering economy and the shortage of key skills present opportunities to improve the weakened image of the Belgian trade unions in the eyes of public opinion (especially in the north of the country). This one condition that that they become proponents of an alternative discourse emphasises firm responsibility and accountability for labour's social reproduction and towards society at large. Reflecting the diversity of workers' socio-demographic and work status constituencies, this narrative

can no longer be centred on the re-affirmation of existing workers'
rights (for those workers who have them), but necessarily needs to
prefigure novel arrangements that extend rights and protections to
workers who have historically been left outside and now risk being
included as the cheapest labour (Schor this volume).

## NOTES

1. I would like to thank Marco Rocca for his feedback on an early draft
of this text.
2. Following a parliamentary inquiry by a socialist MP, the Christian-
democratic federal minister of employment is currently conducting an
investigation into the legality of this unilateral decision by the employer to
change the terms of employment.

## REFERENCES

Arbeiterkammer, ÖGB, HK, IG Metall, International Brotherhood of
    Teamsters Local 117, Service Employees International Union and
    Unionen (2016), 'Frankfurt Paper on Platform-Based Work: Proposals
    for Platform Operators, Clients, Policy Makers, Workers, and Worker
    Organizations', Copenhagen, Frankfurt, Seattle, Stockholm, Vienna and
    Washington: Arbeiterkammer, Austrian Trade Union Federation, Dan-
    ish Union of Commercial and Clerical Workers, German Metalwork-
    ers' Union, International Brotherhood of Teamsters Local 117, Service
    Employees International Union, and Unionen.
Bhattacharya, T. (2013), 'What is Social Reproduction Theory?', *Socialist
    Worker*, 10 September, https://socialistworker.org/2013/09/10/what-is-
    social-reproduction-theory.
CNT and NAR (2017), *Diagnose van de Sociale Partners over Digi-
    talisering en Deeleconomie – Uitvoering van het Interprofessioneel
    Akkoord 2017–2018*, Brussels: Conseil National du Travail and Natio-
    nale Arbeidsraad (National Labour Council and Central Council of the
    Economy), http://www.cnt-nar.be/RAPPORT/rapport-107-NL.pdf.
De Croo, A. (2016), 'Kamer Keurt Nieuwe Regeling Deeleconomie Goed',
    press release of Alexander De Croo, deputy prime minister and minister

of development cooperation, Digital Agenda, Telecom and Postal Services, 30 June, http://www.decroo.belgium.be/nl/kamer-keurt-nieuwe-regeling-deeleconomie-goed.

De Stefano, V. (2017), 'Negotiating the Algorithm: Technology, Digital(-ized) Work, and Labour Protection "Reloaded"', *Regulating for Globalization*, 7 December, http://regulatingforglobalization.com/2017/12/07/negotiating-algorithm-technology-digital-ized-work-labour-protection-reloaded/.

Denys, J. (2013), 'Arbeidsmarkt Flexibiliseren? Misschien. Moderniseren? Zeker en Vast', *Knack*, 27 June, http://www.knack.be/nieuws/arbeids-markt-flexibiliseren-misschien-moderniseren-zeker-en-vast/article-opinion-83127.html.

Drahokoupil, J. and B. Fabo (2016), *The Platform Economy and the Disruption of the Employment Relationship*, ETUI Policy Brief, Brussels: European Trade Union Institute.

ETUI (2017), *Belgium: Key facts*, Brussels: European Trade Union Institute, http://www.worker-participation.eu/National-Industrial-Relations/Countries/Belgium.

ETUI and IGM (2017), *Call for Comments: Paying Minimum Wage on Online Labor Platforms*, Brussels and Frankfurt: European Trade Union Institute and IG Metall (German Metalworkers' Union), http://minwage.platformwork.org/en.html.

European Commission (2011), *Industrial Relations in Europe 2010*, Luxembourg: Publications Office of the European Union.

European Commission (2016), *Communication from the Commission to the European Parliament, the Council, the European Economic and Social Committee, and the Committee of the Regions: a European Agenda for the Collaborative Economy*, COM(2016) 356 final, Luxembourg: Publications Office of the European Union, https://ec.europa.eu/transparency/regdoc/rep/1/2016/EN/1-2016-356-EN-F1-1.PDF.

Fabo, B., J. Karanovic and K. Dukova (2017), 'In Search of an Adequate European Policy Response to the Platform Economy', *Transfer: European Review of Labour and Research*, 23(2): 163–75.

Federal Public Service Employment, Labour and Social Dialogue (2017), *Wet betreffende Werkbaar en Wendbaar Werk*, Brussels: Federale Overheidsdienst Werkgelegenheid, Arbeid en Sociaal Overleg, http://www.werk.belgie.be/defaultNews.aspx?id=45797#.

Graceffa, S. and S. de Heusch (2017), 'Reinventing the World of Work', *Transfer: European Review of Labour and Research*, 23(3): 359–365.

Kilhoffer, Z. and K. Lenaerts (2017), *What Is Happening With Platform Workers' Rights? Lessons from Belgium*, Brussels: Centre for European Policy Studies.

Kuba, S. (2017), 'Foodora Couriers Found Works Council', *Fair Crowd Work*, 28 April, http://faircrowd.work/2017/04/28/deutsch-oesterreich-foodora-fahrer-gruenden-betriebsrat/.

Leonard, S. and N.Fraser (2016), 'Capitalism's Crisis of Care', *Dissent*, fall 2016, https://www.dissentmagazine.org/article/nancy-fraser-interview-capitalism-crisis-of-care.

Martens, A., G. Van Gyes, and P. van der Hallen (ed.) (2001), *De vakbond naar de 21ste eeuw Syntheserapport.* Programma 'Toekomstgericht sociaal-economisch onderzoek': Federale Diensten voor Wetenschappelijke, Technische en Culturele Aangelegenheden, Leuven: Hoger instituut voor de arbeid.

Mattheeuws, C. and S. Nouten (2017), 'Federale Regering Wijzigt Amper iets aan Onbelast Bijverdienen: Vergiftigd Kerstgeschenk voor heel wat Ondernemers', Neutraal Syndicaat voor Zelfstandigen, 9 December, http://www.nsz.be/nl/pers/detail/federale-regering-wijzigt-amper-iets-aan-onbelast-bijverdienen-vergiftigd-kerstgeschenk-voor-heel-wat-ondernemers.

Söderqvist, F. (2016), presentation at Sime Conference 2016, Stockholm, video, 11:23, https://www.youtube.com/watch?v=f2mlLlcAPeo.

Söderqvist, F. (2017a), 'How to Unite Unions, Platforms and Government Through Algorithms?', filmed September 2017 at the World Interdisciplinary Network for Institutional Research conference, Utrecht, video, 10:43, https://www.youtube.com/watch?v=We3LV-xD9ok.

Söderqvist, F. (2017b), 'International Platforms vs Swedish Unions: How do Digital Platforms fit the Nordic Labour Model? Who is Responsible for What?', filmed April 2017 at Earnings on Demand Industry Talk, Stockholm, video, 03:20, https://www.youtube.com/watch?v=JFCQlM5RzlQ.

Tanghe, N. (2016), 'Personeelsbaas ING Keihard voor eigen Bankiers', *De Standaard*, 20 October, http://www.standaard.be/cnt/dmf20161020_02529633.

Trends (2017), 'Économie collaborative: syndicats et employeurs sabotent les plans du gouvernement', *Trends*, 10 October, http://trends.levif.be/economie/entreprises/economie-collaborative-syndicats-et-employeurs-sabotent-les-plans-du-gouvernement/article-normal-736291.html.

UK, the Czech Republic, Poland, Luxembourg, Finland, Sweden, Denmark, Estonia, Latvia, Lithuania and Bulgaria (2016), 'Joint Letter to the Vice-President of the European Commission Andrus Ansip', London,

Prague, Warsaw, Luxembourg City, Helsinki, Stockholm, Copenhagen, Tallinn, Riga, Vilnius and Sofia: UK, the Czech Republic, Poland, Luxembourg, Finland, Sweden, Denmark, Estonia, Latvia, Lithuania and Bulgaria, https://www.gov.uk/government/uploads/system/uploads/attachment_data/file/513402/platforms-letter.pdf.

UNI Global Union (2017), 'Global Union Sets New Rules for the Next Frontier of Work: Ethical AI and Employee Data Protection', *UNI Global Union*, 11 December, http://uniglobalunion.org/news/global-union-sets-new-rules-next-frontier-work-ethical-ai-and-employee-data-protection.

Van Oycke, J. and G. Van Gyes (2017), 'Collective Bargaining', in *Working Life in Belgium*, Dublin: Eurofound, https://www.eurofound.europa.eu/printpdf/country/belgium?section=2.

Vaughan, R. and Daverio, R, PwC UK (2016), Assessing the size and presence of the collaborative economy in Europe', https://publications.europa.eu/en/publication-detail/-/publication/2acb7619-b544-11e7-837e-01aa75ed71a1/language-en

Wauters, J. (2016), 'Armoede-Expert Verdedigt Regering: Harde Ingrepen Zijn Nodig', *De Morgen*, 17 October, http://www.demorgen.be/politiek/armoede-expert-verdedigt-regering-harde-ingrepen-zijn-nodig-b15419fa4/.

# UK

## *Preparing for the digital revolution*

## Olivia Bailey and Andrew Harrop

One hundred years ago the British Labour party described itself as 'the party of the producers' in its first ever constitution (Webb 1918). It was founded to fight for good jobs, full employment, and a strong welfare state. Over the past century the party has had to find new ways to achieve those goals as the nature of work has changed. In particular, from the 1960s onwards, helping to build a skilled workforce and to create opportunities for workers have become as important for the Labour party as protecting workers from exploitation.

Today, globalisation, demographic change and the advent of transformative new technologies all mean that the British labour movement must once again find new ways to fulfil its founding purpose. It must renew collectivism in an era of fragmentation and insecurity, and ensure there is widespread access to the opportunities that new technological advances can provide.

The political consequences of inaction are plain to see. The Brexit vote was, at least in part, a roar of anger from parts of the UK that felt left behind by the pace of change, and Labour's popularity among working-class voters has been on a downward trajectory over the last two decades (Evans and Tilley 2017).

Technological change could provide the opportunity for a transformation of our labour market. It could grow productivity, raise wages and create more rewarding employment opportunities for people. But it could also lead to unemployment, insecurity and increasing numbers of workers stuck in low-paid, low-skilled jobs. The UK's path is not in the hands of the markets or the gods; it is a matter of political choice.

## THREE KEY TRENDS

Experts have warned that the fourth industrial revolution could bring the 'rise of the robots' and a precipitous collapse in employment. But this stark prognosis has not yet materialised and it is far from clear that it will. The UK employment rate is at an all-time high, and while flexible work is on the rise the number of people in full-time work has not shrunk. Most people in the UK are satisfied with their work, with a recent Fabian Society study showing that 8 out of 10 workers in the UK find their work to be "interesting and enjoyable" (Tait 2016). The overall volume of jobs may not be a concern, but there are three key trends which must be addressed for the challenges of technological change to be met effectively: low productivity and stagnant pay, growing inequalities, and the changing labour market.

## LOW PRODUCTIVITY AND STAGNANT PAY

The most stubborn challenge for the future of work is low productivity: productivity growth in the UK has consistently been ranked the second slowest in the G7 group of rich countries since 2010 (PWC 2017). Wages have stagnated because of this low productivity, with real wages still below their pre-crisis peak. Far from the pace of innovation and technological change being too fast, as many have predicted, the UK's record on productivity suggests that it is actually far too slow, with the exception of a small minority of firms.

In the absence of rising productivity, the most important policy driver for pay increases is the statutory wage floor. This fell in value after the financial crisis in 2008, but since 2015 the Conservative government has been steadily raising the minimum wage for workers over 25 towards 60% of median hourly earnings. The Low Pay Commission has predicted that the proportion of the workforce who will be covered by the national minimum wage and national living wage will rise from 5% in 2015 to 14% in 2020 (Low Pay Commission 2016). This has led some commentators to discuss the adoption of 'one wage' towns and sectors, where employers benchmark pay against the minimum wage and often remove differentials between different types of worker (Bell 2016). The Office for Budget Responsibility (OBR) expects that the higher wage floor will modestly reduce employment, but it is hoped that it may also push employers to invest in skills and new business processes.

## INEQUALITY

Over the last 20 years overall income inequality in the UK has remained high but stable, with all but the very rich fairing equally well before the crisis and equally poorly ever since. The last Labour government (2007–2010) succeeded in helping low-income households to keep up with middle and upper-middle income groups through three main policies: a welfare to work programme, the introduction of the statutory minimum wage and the expansion of in-work benefits. Together this led to a significant fall in child poverty (Joyce and Sibieta 2013). In 2010/11, 18% of children in the UK – some 2.3 million in total – came from households that had incomes that were lower than 60% of the median rate of disposable household income before housing costs, and 27% – some 3.6 million children – came from households that had incomes that were lower than 60% of the median rate of disposable income after housing costs. Compared with 2009/10, this is a fall of two percentage points in before housing costs – affecting some 300,000 children, and a fall of two percentage points in after housing costs – affecting some 200,000 children (DWP 2012). Since 2010 the Conservative-led governments have steadily eroded social security for working-age families and a significant increase in child poverty is now expected over the next five years (DWP 2017, Table 4.1).

In the UK economy there have been growing inequalities in household wealth, male earnings, regionally and for generational cohorts (Blundell et al. 2017). One of the most pronounced inequalities is the uneven geographical distribution of new opportunities, with House of Commons Library analysis suggesting that cities have recovered twice as fast as towns following the economic crisis (Harari and Ward 2018). A recent report from Future Advocacy, a research institute, found that the UK's former industrial towns, which are still struggling with the previous period of industrial change since the 1970s, are likely to be disproportionately affected by the increasing digitisation of jobs, given the nature of employment that dominates in these areas (Future Advocacy 2017).

Significant demographic shifts have been brought about by internal migration throughout the UK, with small towns and villages losing more than a million young people to cities and urban centres in search of work and education over the past three decades (Hurst 2017). This divide is in danger of becoming even more pronounced, with the new, skilled and creative jobs that are arriving being concentrated in cites, and low-paid, low-productivity jobs being the primary option for long-term employment everywhere else.


## A CHANGING LABOUR MARKET

While the robots are not yet at our door, far-reaching changes can be observed in the UK labour market. The number of people worried about losing their jobs has been rising steadily since the turn of the century, and there has been an upturn in insecure work (Gallie et al. 2013). The number of people on zero hours contracts has risen nearly five-fold since the turn of the millennium, and the number of agency workers is approaching 1 million, accounting for nearly 3% of the overall UK workforce in 2016 (Harrop and Tait 2017). There has also been a significant rise in the number of the self-employed, who now make up a record 15% of the UK workforce, and in the share of workers who are employed part-time, up by 1.2% since 1997. This rise in part-time employment has been accompanied by an increase in the number of people who say that they want to work more hours than they currently do – up by almost 1 million since 2007 (Taylor 2017).

But what might the future hold? Is a collapse in UK employment just over the horizon? Studies have certainly warned that automation is likely to affect a significant number of jobs in the UK. The OECD estimates that 9% of jobs are directly at risk. Although Osborne and Frey (2013) put the figure at an alarming 47% for the US labour market, most economists seem to think that the lower end of this range is more likely (see Arnold et al. this volume). Studies suggest that workers with low and middle incomes are at the greatest risk of displacement through automation, with Deloitte estimating that UK jobs that pay less than £30,000 a year are five times more vulnerable to displacement than jobs paying over £100,000 annually (Dellot 2017a).

We can already see the impact of the new wave of automation in some parts of the UK economy, with machines and automated systems replacing humans in the delivery of a wide range of routine tasks. Even if enough jobs are generated to replace all those lost, it seems likely that technological advancement will bring about a significant dislocation of jobs and skills. There are still clear skills shortages in the UK economy, particularly in high-skill occupations, but there is also a problem of excess skills capacity in other areas (see Aubrey this volume). This dislocation could further increase earnings inequality if intermediate occupations are replaced by more high- and low-skill jobs.

## THREE CHALLENGES FOR POLICYMAKERS

The British labour market is changing, and the labour movement must change with it. Without a strong, progressive policy agenda, technological change could result in a rise in insecurity and inequality. There are three priorities that policymakers must tackle in order to obviate the worst effects of these challenges: create more good jobs, take concerted action to prevent exploitation at work, and renew the social security system.

## CREATE MORE GOOD JOBS

The first challenge for progressives is to ensure that the opportunities of the fourth industrial revolution are available to everyone. A new strategy must focus on geographic inequality in the UK, fair pay and skills, and creating an environment in which productive new businesses can grow.

To ensure that people in towns and rural areas have access to good jobs, the left must develop a place-based industrial strategy that builds on the strengths of local economies. This should have democratic accountability at its heart, with decisions about investment and skills taken by local people. Government investment should focus on 'left behind' areas in order to level the playing field, and the left must put flesh on the bones of the Labour party's plan to establish a network of regional investment banks. The government must also focus on transport connectivity to help bring opportunities to places that have been overlooked.

Fair pay and skills are also central to a good jobs strategy. Alongside measures to strengthen trade unions (discussed below), the left must support sectoral pay bargaining and establish rules that place workers on company boards. A Labour government should also drive up low pay by continuing to raise the rate of the national minimum wage, for younger workers as well as the over-25s, until there is clear evidence that it has reached a level where it risks being a significant drag on employment. Sustained action is also needed to improve skills. For example, the apprenticeship levy could evolve into a wider training levy that funds training opportunities for all employees, and not just apprentices.

Good jobs are only possible if business is able to grow, and if businesses are supported to invest in their workforce. The first step that must be taken in this regard is to support businesses to invest in the technology of the future. While we have a few world-leaders, in every region and every sector, most businesses are not catching up with their most innovative peers (Haldane 2017). For example, just 14% of UK firms are investing in artificial intelligence and the UK is falling behind other countries in research investment (Dellot 2017b). The development of sectoral and local networks of coordination, collaboration and support are essential, something that has been alien to British business culture for too long. The government must also transform investment in digital infrastructure to ensure there is widespread access to technological opportunities and to provide greatly enhanced support for firms entering export markets.

## END EXPLOITATION AT WORK

Precarious, insecure work could increase as the world of work changes, but this is not a technological inevitability. Labour market regulation can shape the future of work without being a bar to innovation. As a start the government should take robust steps to drive out exploitive working practices and ensure that everyone in work has minimum job security. It should prohibit zero-hour contracts, and provide a right for workers to obtain a contract that reflects hours regularly worked.

The left should also consider what it can do to substantially increase the reach and impact of trade unions, which are proven to improve wages and working conditions where they are strong (Freeman and Medoff 1983), but are struggling with a dwindling membership (see Doellgast this volume; BEIS 2017). In Britain trade union density is particularly low in the private sector, and especially in the fastest growing private-sector industries; private-sector membership has fallen from 45% in 1979 to 13% in 2016 (Tait 2017).

To reverse this decline and help workers achieve better terms and conditions of employment, and more productive jobs, a future Labour government should build a new partnership with the trade union movement. Worker voice should be at the heart of all plans to boost productivity and to improve the quality of work, as it is in other jurisdictions, for example in Finland (see Karjalainen this volume). The recent Fabian Society report Future Unions calls for this partnership to include new requirements for employers to halt all union-busting practices and to allow unions into their workplaces, for the creation of sector level forums for employers and unions, and a seat at the table for workers in discussions about the impact of the changing world of work (Tait 2017). These steps could provide the basis for a new deal between unions and a future Labour-led government.

## RENEW THE SOCIAL SECURITY SYSTEM

These labour market policies will not be able to tackle the risk of rising poverty and inequality on their own. The UK also needs to reinvent its welfare state to provide investment and insurance for the rapidly changing labour market. During the years of austerity meted out by the Conservative-led governments, spending on pensions and healthcare was protected, so the balance of expenditure has drifted towards the latter half of life. Meanwhile spending on lifelong learning and working-age social security has plummeted as a share of GDP (HMT 2017, 68). These trends need to be reversed, with new entitlements for skills across adult life and a reinvention of social insurance before pension age. People should be able to obtain economically valuable qualifications at any stage of life – for free when they have not trained to the same level previously, and on a heavily subsidised basis to retrain in a new field at the same level, as in Germany. And meaningful social security supports for training should also exist so that people can take time out of work to reskill.

Social security also needs to provide more for families to ensure that every child lives in a home with the resources they need to develop and thrive. The present government's universal credit system can provide a platform for the reforms that are needed, although the new benefit will need to be a lot more generous than the current design would allow for. If it can be made to work, universal credit should suit the volatility of the modern labour market. Payments are intended to rise and fall automatically each month as people's earnings change or they move in and out of work, so universal credit should be effective at providing a floor if household incomes fall.

The flip-side of this is that universal credit provides only very weak incentives for people to work longer hours or to seek higher pay. Families would have better incentives to increase their earnings if more in-work social security was provided universally rather than being means tested. There is therefore a debate to be had as to how best to strike the balance between a more generous means-tested system and any expansion to the universal child benefit system, perhaps by turning it into a universal basic income for children. But in either case there is a ready source of funding in the tax allowance system, which could be gradually made less generous. Substituting tax-free allowances for children's benefits would divert money from higher earners without dependants to families with children.

Overall the share of national income spent on education and working-age social security should rise, after years of austerity cuts. And since spending on pensions and health is also likely to increase, new sources of revenue will be needed to gradually expand the welfare state as a share of GDP. This will require a fundamental debate on taxation, in the context of the changing economy. First there is a case to be made for the greater use of earmarked taxes and social insurance to legitimise new revenue raising. An expanded role for national insurance and new health taxes are both good options. The UK could even consider ringfenced funds, of the sort common elsewhere in Europe (eg France). Everyone will need to pay a bit more (which will only be acceptable once living standards are rising). But the top third and particularly the top 1% in society should expect the highest tax increases, as currently they pay no more as a share of their income than people with middle incomes.

The balance of tax will also need to be reviewed to ensure that, as the tax share rises, it also raises revenue efficiently and fairly. At present the UK levies relatively heavy taxes on conventional employee labour and business premises. A rebalancing of taxation is needed that might include a shift towards taxing wealth, non-employment income and harmful externalities.

In the long term perhaps the labour share of GDP will decline significantly and a whole new approach to taxation will be needed. But for the foreseeable future the priority of government should be to achieve tax neutrality between similar economic activities that are conducted in different ways. The tax gap between self-employment and employee labour should be greatly reduced and more neutral ways to raise revenue from business are also needed. In particular, technology-heavy businesses that deploy less labour and property need to be appropriately taxed in the places where their sales and profits are generated.

## REFERENCES

BEIS (2017), *Trade Union Membership 2016*, London: Department for Business, Energy & Industrial Strategy.

Bell, T. (2016), 'Prime Minister's Ambition to Help the 2.1 Million "Just Managing" Families Means Tearing Down the "Here and Now" Barriers to Social Mobility', Resolution Foundation, 9 September, http://www.resolutionfoundation.org/media/blog/prime-ministers-ambition-to-help-the-2-1-million-just-managing-families-means-tearing-down-the-here-and-now-barriers-to-social-mobility.

Blundell, R., R. Joyce, A. N. Keiller and J. P. Ziliak (2017), *Income Inequality and the Labour Market in Britain and the US*, Institute for Fiscal Studies Working Paper W17(25), Institute for Fiscal Studies.

Dellot, B. (2017a), '8 Key Takeaways from our New Report on AI, Robotics and Automation', Royal Society for the Encouragement of Arts, Manufactures and Commerce, 20 September, https://www.thersa.org/discover/publications-and-articles/rsa-blogs/2017/09/8-key-takeaways-from-our-new-report-on-ai-robotics-and-automation.

Dellot, B. (2017b), 'Forget Talk of Mass Automation: the UK Needs to Ramp Up Investment in AI or Be Left Behind', Royal Society for the Encouragement of Arts, Manufactures and Commerce (RSA), October, https://www.thersa.org/discover/publications-and-articles/rsa-blogs/2017/10/forget-talk-of-mass-automation.-the-uk-needs-to-ramp-up-investment-in-ai-or-be-left-behind.

DWP (2012), 'Households Below Average Income', Department for Work and Pensions, 14 June, http://webarchive.nationalarchives.gov.uk/20130125093036/http://statistics.dwp.gov.uk/asd/index.php?page=hbai.

DWP (2017), 'Households Below Average Income: an Analysis of the UK Income Distribution: 1994/95–2015/16', Department for Work and Pensions, 16 March, https://www.gov.uk/government/uploads/system/uploads/attachment_data/file/600091/households-below-average-income-1994-1995-2015-2016.pdf.

Evans, G. and J. Tilley (2017), *The New Politics of Class: the Political Exclusion of the British Working Class*, Oxford: Oxford Press University Press.

Freeman, R. B. and J. L. Medoff (1983), 'Trade Unions and Productivity: Some New Evidence on an Old Issue', *Annals of the American Academy of Political and Social Science*, 473: 149–64.

Frey, C. and M. Osborne (2013), *The Future of Employment: How Susceptible Are Jobs To Computerisation?*, Oxford: Oxford Martin School, https://www.oxfordmartin.ox.ac.uk/downloads/academic/The_Future_of_Employment.pdf.

Future Advocacy (2017), *The Impact of AI in UK Constituencies*, London: Future Advocacy, https://static1.squarespace.com/static/5621e990e4b07de840c6ea69/t/59e777fcd7bdce3041b57ac3/1508341775530/FutureAdvocacy-GeographicalAI.pdf.

Gallie, D., A. Felstead, F. Green and H. Inanc (2013), *Fear at Work in Britain: First Findings from the Skills and Employment Survey 2012*, London: Centre for Learning and Life Chances in Knowledge Economies and Societies, Institute of Education.

Haldane, A. (2017), 'Productivity Puzzles', speech, Bank of England, https://www.bankofengland.co.uk/speech/2017/productivity-puzzles.

Harari, D. and M. Ward (2018), *Regional and Country Economic Indicators*, House of Commons Briefing Paper 06924, London: House of Commons.

Harrop, A. and C. Tait (2017), *Universal Basic Income and the Future of Work*, Fabian Society, http://www.fabians.org.uk/universal-basic-income-and-the-future-of-work.

HMT (2017), *Public Expenditure Statistical Analyses 2017*, London: Her Majesty's Treasury, https://www.gov.uk/government/uploads/system/uploads/attachment_data/file/630570/60243_PESA_Accessible.pdf.

Hurst, G. (2017), 'Villages Growing Older as Young Head for the Cities', *The Times*, 22 November, https://www.thetimes.co.uk/article/villages-growing-older-as-young-head-for-the-cities-cvmdl3kk9.

Joyce, R. and L. Sibieta (2013), *Labour's Record on Poverty and Inequality*, London: Institute for Fiscal Studies, https://www.ifs.org.uk/publications/6738.

Low Pay Commission (2016), *National Minimum Wage: Low Pay Commission Report*, London: Low Pay Commission, https://www.gov.uk/government/uploads/system/uploads/attachment_data/file/571631/LPC_spring_report_2016.pdf.

PWC (2017), *UK Economic Outlook*, London: PriceWaterhouseCoopers, https://www.pwc.co.uk/services/economics-policy/insights/uk-economic-outlook.html. , London:, London:

Tait, C. (2016), *A Good Day's Work*, London: Fabian Society, http://www.fabians.org.uk/wp-content/uploads/2016/11/Fabian-Society_A-good-days-work.pdf.

Tait, C. (2017), *Future Unions*, London: Fabian Society, http://www.fabians.org.uk/wp-content/uploads/2017/11/Fabian-Society_Future-Unions-report.pdf.

Taylor, M. (2017), *Good Work: the Taylor Review of Modern Working Practices*, Department for Business, Energy & Industrial Strategy, https://www.gov.uk/government/uploads/system/uploads/attachment_data/file/627671/good-work-taylor-review-modern-working-practices-rg.pdf.

Webb, S. (1918), *The New Constitution of the Labour Party: a Party of Handworkers and Brainworkers: the Labour Programme and Prospects*, London: Labour Party.

# IRELAND

## How to escape the low learning trap in a runaway labour market

## Seán Ó Riain and Amy E. Healy[1]

Ireland is profoundly shaped by the factors that make up the core of contemporary capitalism – including globalisation, financialisation, new technologies and new forms of workplace and labour market flexibilities. Perhaps most fundamentally, Ireland has been moving decisively towards a post-industrial occupational structure, albeit in an uneven manner with rapid digitalisation in technology, market services, and places within the public service that lie alongside other sectors where there has been relatively low adoption of new technologies. The crisis of 2008 hit Ireland particularly hard, with very rapid increases in unemployment combined with government indebtedness. The combination of structural changes and the shock to welfare and public finances since 2008 makes the intersection of work and welfare a vital policy issue, and Ireland an exceptionally apposite case study for examining this interplay.

The Republic of Ireland occupies an interesting place in the world of welfare capitalisms. Economically, it shares significant features with the 'liberal' economies – including relatively low levels of product and labour market regulation, high rates of foreign investment and other capital flows, high levels of market inequality, and volatile business cycles. Nonetheless, we also see significant public efforts to enhance welfare, particularly through benefits and other social transfers. Between these market-centred and welfarist poles is a varied institutional landscape, which has included neo-corporatist social partnership agreements between 1987 and 2009, followed by loose employer–union coordination, alongside a central role for industrial development agencies that are focused on domestic as well as foreign firms (Ó Riain 2014).

How well is Ireland managing to combine the headlong rush into an uncertain future of new technologies, relationships and activities with a social contract, of whatever kind? To examine this we focus on the intersection between the welfare state and the lower-wage end of the labour market, where the challenges are greatest. We first provide an overview of the key features of Ireland's welfare state; we then examine the character of jobs at this lower end of the labour market, and how they are shaped by the use of new technologies; and finally we briefly return to the implications for the welfare system and Irish economic and social development in the future.

## THE IRISH WELFARE SYSTEM

We can think about the Irish welfare system as being simultaneously strong, weak and vulnerable. First, the strength of the Irish welfare system is the transfer system. Figure 26.1 shows the level of inequality within the market, and after taxes and transfers, in a selection of countries, and the percentage reduction in market inequality by those transfers and taxes. Ireland is the only country listed in this table that has both high market inequality and a high proportional reduction in that inequality through the transfer system. That pattern remained fairly consistent throughout the boom of the 2000s, the bust from 2008 until around 2013, and the growth in more recent years. The transfer system faces a major challenge with persistently high levels of market income inequality, but the system also does significant work to reduce that inequality. However, it is telling that market incomes have not become more equal over these years, regardless of the welfare effort being expended to address this inequality.

Ireland's weaknesses are the flip-side of its strengths as it has long been recognised in welfare policy circles that the Irish welfare system is much more effective at redistributing income through benefits and other cash transfers than it is at delivering widely used social services (NESC 2005). In some key areas, particularly childcare, the system is almost entirely private or familial. Training and care supports are crucial in tackling questions of labour market participation and also for reducing market inequality – but after a reasonable performance in the 1990s, Irish efforts in these areas decreased markedly in the 2000s (Ó Riain 2014). These missing services are all the more significant as a 'runaway labour market' increasingly provides medium- to high-skill jobs (OECD 2016) that are out of reach of those at the lower end of the job market. While the overall trend is towards an upgrading of the occupational structure, driven by the growth of professional employment and partly shaped by digital technologies, the distance from those jobs becomes greater,

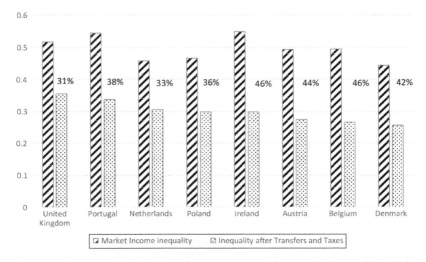

Figure 26.1 Inequality in selected European countries: market inequality (Gini), inequality after taxes and transfers (Gini) and reduction in inequality due to taxes and transfers (%). *Source*: OECD (2014).

especially as education levels rise. Again, the challenge to welfare increases as the labour market changes – but the welfare system relating to services is often found lacking.

Finally, despite the improvement in Ireland's public finances in recent years, the financing of the welfare system remains quite vulnerable. While the transfer system is making a significant financial difference, it depends on a very narrow tax base. This has been built into public policies for at least two decades as the Irish state tries to protect incomes at the lower end by linking tax thresholds to the minimum wage and similar measures. Meanwhile, public policy has created a relatively small tax wedge for employers, particularly in social security contributions such as pay-related social insurance, which are very low compared with other small European countries. Put together, these policies ensure a very small tax effect on costs in labour-intensive, relatively low-productivity firms – but they also weaken the tax base, and do little to encourage firms to enhance learning and upgrade business activities.

Ireland's welfare system is based on using transfers to tackle low incomes in an unequal market. This combines with tax policies designed to support a low-wage labour market, while as services are comparatively poorly resourced (and the enterprise policy historically favoured larger, often foreign, firms over the domestic sector) the gap from the bottom to the top of the labour market remains as difficult to bridge as ever.

## THE IRISH LABOUR MARKET

The welfare system and the labour market appear to combine to continually reproduce a system that generates significant welfare transfer efforts, while also reproducing the conditions that make that effort necessary – even as high-tech sectors have continued to grow steadily and professional employment has consistently expanded. A full understanding of this process requires that we look more closely at the jobs and workplaces that are typical within this segment of the labour market.

These workplaces are shaped by three of the significant trends of the day. First, there is currently major concern regarding the introduction of new technologies, and particularly automation. New technology does not seem to challenge employment levels, which have grown significantly in each of Ireland's post-crisis recoveries – largely following the dynamics outlined in Arnold et al. (this volume). In keeping with their argument, we can see that technology will, at a minimum, significantly restructure work – not just the level of employment, but the kinds of work and how they are carried out. As we will see, this is reflected in the ways that work is organised and how these are changing.

Somewhat separate from this is a second major debate around the nature of employment. Despite the pervasive sense of employment insecurity that many people now feel, many of the statistical indicators do not show a huge increase in the conventional measures of precarious employment. Therefore, we have to dig a little deeper into what precarity means for different workers in different situations.

Finally, the third theme relates to how work itself has been re-organised, not just in the technologies that are used, or the nature of the employment relationship, but in how the work itself is being done, particularly in the emergence and consolidation of systems of work that involve various forms of flexibility.

Table 26.1 and Figures 26.2 and 26.3 summarise some analyses of the European Working Conditions Surveys from 1995 to 2015, which examine each of these issues. We start by examining the typical forms that work organisation takes in Europe today, based on a latent class analysis of these surveys. We can identify three key clusters, defined along two dimensions:

- learning – whether there is an opportunity for learning and whether the job involves complex tasks
- autonomy – how much scope people have at work to make decisions about their own work and how it is done.

Where there is little complexity and little autonomy, we find 'simple' jobs (Holm et al. 2010). Where there is a lot of learning but

Table 26.1    Forms of work organisation and change in the proportion of EU15 workers in each, 1995–2015.

| | | |
|---|---|---|
| Simple (−1.3%) | Lean (+0.8%) | Learn (−3.9%) |
| Simple Pressure (−1.8%) | Lean Pressure (+2.2%) | Learn Pressure (+2.4%) |
| Simple Extreme (+0.4%) | Lean Extreme (+2.2%) | Learn Extreme (−0.3%) |
| Taylor (−0.7%) | | |

*Source*: Author's calculations, based on the European Surveys of Working Conditions (Eurofound 2015).

relatively low autonomy, we find the now classic model of lean production that has been much debated in recent decades, with the influence of Japanese production methods in particular. This involves a lot of pressure being pulled through the system, with many complex tasks but relatively little autonomy. Typically, this is most common in large-scale services and manufacturing. Finally, there is a learning system where workers have a lot of complexity to face, but also a high degree of autonomy.

We can also identify sub-categories. For example, tight control at work creates a pressurised version of the work, and if workers carry out extended (and often unflexible) hours around that pressurised work, this constitutes a more extreme category. Table 26.1 outlines these nine kinds of work (we also include a tenth kind, Taylorism, which is in many respects a mix of simple extreme and lean extreme forms of work organisation). Table 26.1 also shows the change in the proportion of EU15 workers in each of these forms of work from 1995 to 2015.

The Simple and Taylorist regimes in the column on the left are most common in Mediterranean economies. The learning forms of work on the right are strongest in the Nordics and Lean is generally strongest in the UK, Ireland and continental countries such as Germany, France and Austria. Overall, there is a shift towards more pressurised work, but also a growth in the complexity of work. Thus, work is often more interesting, but also more demanding.

How does this relate to new technologies? One well-documented possibility is that when people work with new technologies their

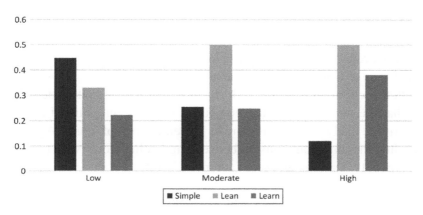

Figure 26.2 The proportion of technology used in each major form of work organisation, Ireland, 2015. *Source*: OECD (2014).

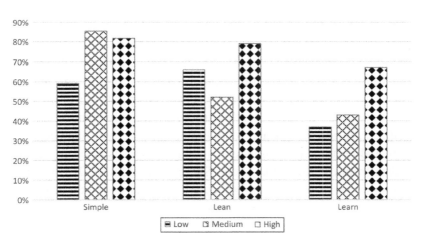

Figure 26.3 The percentage of pressured or extreme forms of work in each workplace type, by level of technology use. *Source*: Eurofound (2015).

work becomes deskilled. However, Figure 26.2 shows that people who do not use a computer very much (or not at all) in their jobs tend to work in 'simple' kinds of job organisation. They do not have access to either technology or learning in the workplace. Higher levels of computer use are associated with more learning at work, and greater technology use is attached to more complex, more interesting work.

However, the picture becomes more complex when we look within the forms of work – Simple, Lean and Learn. Figure 26.3 shows that within each broad form of work organisation, the general tendency is that the more workers use computers the more pressurised they are (more likely to be in Pressure or Extreme forms of work). Again we find this important tension between upgrading work (with more complexity, learning and often autonomy) and at the same time significant control pressures and challenges of flexibility.

The third dimension we outlined is labour market precarity. We draw here on an interesting measure in the European Working Conditions Survey, which includes various kinds of employment contract status. This measure defines workers with a contract of indefinite duration as a permanent contract. There are a series of non-permanent options, including fixed-term temporary contracts, working for an agency, or working without a contract. A fuller discussion would be needed to explain what 'no contract' means in different countries, but Ireland consistently has high levels of people working with no contract – 12.8% in 2015. The only countries with similar levels are the UK and Mediterranean economies like Greece, Spain and Portugal (see Grande this volume). This is also supported by data from the European Social Survey (Eurofound 2015) where the proportion of people stating they are working without a contract is even higher than in the European Working Conditions Survey – and again is significantly higher in Ireland than in most of the rest of Europe.

When we looked more closely at this data we found that a lot of the people in this category in Ireland may think of themselves as permanent workers, but are working without a contract. That is quite different from the nature of precarity in France or Denmark (see Ilsøe this volume, for example). Furthermore, over the last 10 years those workers without a contract are young, work in service or production jobs, in relatively simple forms of work organisation with rare access to learning and little autonomy, with short hours, and likely to be in very small firms with under 10 employees. While some might expect the 'no contract' workers to be freelance portfolio workers, the primary group is in fact workers who we would think of as typically at risk in the labour market.

The interaction of these trends shape the kind of labour market facing people in Ireland coming straight from being welfare recipients. These workers are often in jobs where they are unlikely to use computers, unlikely to be involved in decisionmaking, have little access to learning, and are exposed to different forms of precarious employment. In Ireland today, even as the overall labour market is upgrading in many respects, this part of the labour market is caught in a low learning trap. Many people enter the labour market from education or unemployment with gaps in education, networks, experience and other resources – but the labour market itself is not enabling them to bridge those gaps. Indeed, it is reinforcing them.

## WELFARE'S FUTURE

We conclude by returning briefly to the welfare system and its prospects for meeting the challenges of a world that combines the restructuring of work activities (often increasing worker learning and participation) with new pressures and uncertainties. A policy accommodation around how the labour market and welfare intersect has emerged in Ireland over the last 25–30 years. The Irish polity has implicitly agreed that not much will be done to tackle market inequalities directly, but that support will be provided to make the lower end of the labour market work. This is done partly with transfers, and through the tax system. Governments have pitched the tax thresholds around the minimum wage. Furthermore, policymakers tend to try to avoid imposing too many costs on small employers, especially via a low social security tax wedge and other measures. Those arrangements work – at least in the sense that they achieve the kinds of reductions of inequality we outlined at the beginning, where Ireland carries out a huge amount of work to achieve a medium level of inequality. However, significant challenges remain, which could bring significant financing pressures. 'Work first' policies tend to use the conditions of welfare benefit programmes and entitlements to push people into the labour market, but the Irish labour market does not provide a ladder to learning and sustainable work.

Therefore, it becomes crucial to think about enhancing services – and this should serve to upgrade labour, boost learning, education, care and so on, and also boost employers. Indeed, the Irish state already acts in significant ways to support enterprise – most particularly in high technology sectors. The most well known of these policies are the various tax incentives offered to foreign firms to locate in Ireland, with the low corporate tax rate of 12.5% attracting both major technology firms and political criticism within Europe and the OECD. Even more controversial have been a variety of tax arrangements that enable firms to re-allocate profits, sometimes paying almost no tax in the process – as in the much publicised dispute over the potential payment of a €13bn tax bill by Apple, due in Ireland but enforced by the European Commission. While these extremely low tax arrangements attract some public criticism in Ireland, the low tax regime is firmly instutionalised and supported by almost all political parties. Irish governments have supported international corporate tax coordination in principle, while generally insisting on all changes to take place internationally before any changes are made in Ireland – as is seen for example in the current debates regarding a digital tax. The effect of tax changes on the decisions of the technology giants about where to locate their operations is somewhat unclear; the Irish polity would, in general, prefer not to find out, but would rather delay making any changes for as long as possible.

There are issues of relevance to this debate other than the corporate tax debate, however. Central to these is a persistent dualism within the Irish economy. Historically, the foreign-owned technology sector operated within a broader economy that had a relatively weak uptake of technology – diffusion from the foreign-investment-led enterprise policy into the economy as a whole was very limited. While there have been significant improvements, this pattern still persists. For example, while Ireland has a higher percentage of graduates in science, technology, engineering and maths (STEM) subjects than other EU countries, it lags well behind in overall levels of technological literacy (European Commission 2016). Similarly, while firms' use of social media and related technologies is high, investment in more complex customer and supplier software systems is around the EU27 average (CSO 2017). Nonetheless, questions about the digital economy have moved to centre stage in Ireland's enterprise policy. In the government's encyclopaedic Action Plan for Jobs 2017, five areas are mentioned under the topic 'competitiveness' (DBEI 2017). Workplace innovation, the digital economy and investment in infrastructure are among them – alongside the transition to a low carbon economy, and the ease of doing business. This is a significant change from the Action Plans for Jobs issued by government earlier this decade, where the link between work, technology and enterprise was much less prominent. While the recent action plan includes measures aimed at smaller firms and worker and citizen skills, it remains to be seen how significant the commitment to these initiatives will be in practice – and whether they will suffice to shift Ireland in a serious way to disseminate practices that promote learning in the workplace. There is some promise here, nonetheless, as the public organisational infrastructure exists to begin to develop and extend such an agenda, through local enterprise and employment offices.

Ideally, efforts to upgrade and support development for both firms and workers in the segment of the labour market subject to a 'low learning trap' should also enhance the tax base by giving scope for increased social insurance and a wider income tax base. It is clear that Ireland's combination of a low learning trap in the labour market with a significant welfare effect in transfers and taxes is potentially highly vulnerable, and will remain so as long as welfare and other policies fail to tackle the market inequalities that are at the root of these difficulties. Without policy and political action in this regard, technological change alone will only increase the speed of the runaway labour market without tackling the low learning trap.

## NOTE

1. The research for this chapter was supported by a Consolidator Grant by the European Research Council for the project New Deals in a New Economy, National University of Ireland Maynooth, 2012–2017.

## REFERENCES

CSO (2017) *Information Society – Statistics* Dublin: Central Statistics Office http://cso.ie/en/releasesandpublications/er/iss/informationsociet-ystatistics-enterprises2016/DBEI (2017), *Action Plan for Jobs 2017*, Dublin: Department of Business, Enterprise and Innovation, https://dbei.gov.ie/en/Publications/Action-Plan-for-Jobs-2017.html.

Eurofound (2015), *European Working Conditions Surveys (EWCS)*, Dublin: EurWORK, https://www.eurofound.europa.eu/surveys/european-working-conditions-surveys.

European Commission (2016), *Digital Economy and Society Index 2017 – Ireland*, Brussels: European Commission.

Holm, J., E. Lorenz, B.-Å. Lundvall and A. Valeyre (2010), 'Organizational Learning and Systems of Labor Market Regulation in Europe', *Industrial and Corporate Change*. 19: 1141–73.

NESC (2005), *The Developmental Welfare State*, Dublin: National Economic and Social Council, http://www.nesc.ie/en/publications/publications/nesc-reports/the-developmental-welfare-state/

OECD (2014), *OECD Income Distribution Database (IDD)*, Paris: OECD. Stat, http://www.oecd.org/social/income-distribution-database.htm.

OECD (2016), *Employment Outlook 2016*, Paris: Organisation for Economic Co-operation and Development, http://dx.doi.org/10.1787/empl_outlook-2016-en.

Ó Riain, S. (2014), *The Rise and Fall of Ireland's Celtic Tiger*, Cambridge: Cambridge University Press.

# AUSTRIA

## Challenging the perception of technology as an end in itself

## Jörg Flecker

Austria, a small country at the heart of Europe, has a highly developed welfare state and a long tradition of social partnership. The economy is highly integrated with the German and European production and trade regimes. Since 1990, Austria has also been especially oriented towards central and eastern Europe (CEE). To the Austrian economy manufacturing, financial services and tourism are more important than they are in other EU member states. While the labour market is regulated by law and sectoral level collective agreements, it is also highly flexible and deeply segmented. Thus, the quality of work varies considerably, yet the low-wage sector in Austria has remained relatively smaller than the very large one in Germany. After the period of full employment up to the early 1980s, for many years Austria used to have lower unemployment rates than nearly all other EU member states (Eurostat 2017a). This changed after 2010, when unemployment steadily increased in the aftermath of the financial and economic crisis, which led to the highest number of people out of work since the 1950s (Statistik Austria 2017). The number of people in employment increased at an equal rate, due to a growing population caused partly by immigration.

Trade unions in Austria have been relatively strong by European standards, and have enjoyed comparably high levels of influence on state policy within the country's social partnership arrangements. Yet, the labour movement has been considerably weakened of late by economic structural changes, rising unemployment, reduced membership levels, enforced liberalisation of the labour market, the privatisation of public companies, and intensified economic transnationalisation (Astleithner and Flecker 2017). Inequality has grown substantially, with lower-wage groups facing a loss of real income since the late 1990s and those in higher wage brackets only enjoying moderate gains (Rechnungshof 2016). Simultaneously, the distribution of wealth has become even more unequal, reaching the highest level of inequality within the Eurozone on a par with Germany (Schnetzer and Rehm 2017, 7).

## THE DEBATE IN AUSTRIA

It is against this background that the so-called fourth industrial revolution has triggered debate and now poses challenges to the Austrian social model. Since the term Industry 4.0 was coined in Germany in 2011 (Pfeiffer 2017), labour market actors and research institutions, partly transnational ones, started to promote it in Austria too. The main thrust of their argument was that intensified automation using cyber-physical systems – systems in which physical and software components are deeply intertwined and integrated with the internet – provided the opportunity to further strengthen the economic position of export-oriented companies and to win back manufacturing jobs that had moved abroad (Höhrhan 2016). By way of creating a catchy label to designate diverse and incremental innovations, the 'fourth industrialists' managed to make it a matter of national importance. What is more, some of the most active research institutions, consultancies and companies in Austria called on the whole country to pull together in order not to miss out on these crucial developments. These calls were reminiscent of 'competitive nationalism'

(Butterwegge 1999), which called on the population to pull together no longer for the sake of the nation but for the country as a business location.

While the debate on Industry 4.0 focuses mainly on the important export-oriented manufacturing sector, aspects of digitalisation and of the fourth industrial revolution will also have consequences for a wide range of other sectors, companies and jobs. ICT-based self-service technology and facilities will be further developed in areas such as the banking, retail, travel and public sectors, which will raise concerns about the numbers of people employed in them. However, the new business models based on internet platforms and the gig economy still draw more attention from commentators and policy-makers. These applications of ICT, combined with the new forms of employment, have added fuel to the debate on the future of work, which is often referred to as 'Work 4.0'. Overall, digitalisation has become a topical issue again not only because of its labour-saving potential and the ensuing fears of job loss, but also as a process that is set to disrupt economic structures, labour relations and ways of working. In the remainder of this brief essay I will focus on the particular challenges of employment policy, precariousness and quality of work in Austria.

## EMPLOYMENT

In previous debates on automation and in other countries, one question has been particularly important in the public debate: Will robots take our jobs? There have been strongly divergent assessments of the employment effects both of Industry 4.0 and of the wider processes of digitalisation. While in the beginning horror scenarios heralding massive job loss that were based on studies such as the one by Frey and Osborne (2013) prevailed, more recently researchers have predicted a weaker impact on employment. Nagl, Titelbach and Valkova (2017) argue that 9% of workers in Austria undertake tasks which have a high potential of being substituted by machines. The authors posit that for 80% of all people employed there is a 30–70% risk that their job will be automated. This estimate is lower than the one by Arntz, Gregory and Zierahn (2016), who find that on average 9% of jobs in a selection of Organisation for Economic Co-operation and Development (OECD) countries, and as many as 12% of jobs in Austria, may be automated in future.

It would be mistaken, however, to deduce future employment based primarily on the potential rates of automation associated with Industry 4.0, and how this may play out at workplace level (see Arnold et al. this volume). In the past, assessments of the potential effects on employment of automation have rarely turned out to be accurate. One reason for this has been the emergence of new jobs, business models and whole sectors, which had not been foreseen in the debates, but this should not lead us to give the all-clear prematurely. First, the starting point differs from how things were in the 1980s or the 2000s, when similar discussions regarding the disruptive potential of new technologies on jobs also took place. In Austria, according to the national employment data (Statistik Austria 2017), more than 9% of all workers are currently unemployed or in training courses offered by the public employment service. This high level of unemployment, which is the highest rate since the aftermath of second world war, means that the country desperately needs more jobs and cannot afford to lose more of them – be it 9%, 12% or more.

Second, to compensate for job losses, emerging new products and services and higher growth rates than current levels are required. The record levels of inequality reduce demand and stifle job creation. Today, the richest 1% in Austria own 41% of all assets, while the poorer 50% own only 2.5% of all assets (Ferschli et al. 2017). The distribution of income has also become more unequal. In 2015, men in the lowest quartile earned less than 75% and women some 80% of what these groups had earned in 1998, taking inflation into account (Rechnungshof 2016, 38). Thus, real income has fallen considerably for those who have low wages and a high propensity to consume. As a consequence, people's purchasing power is lower, leading to weaker private demand for new products and services.

Third, the automation of tasks is only one factor that can potentially lead to job losses. In addition, digitisation makes it easier to relocate jobs to lower-cost economies. While Austrian labour costs are lower than those in some EU member states, there is a large wage differential between Austria and neighbouring CEE-countries, and an even wider wage differential between Austria and countries in Asia (see Saxer this volume). We have observed the movement of jobs from Austria to countries with lower-cost bases in the IT sector, in clerical work and in customer service services since the mid-1990s. Restructuring within transnational corporations, business process outsourcing or, more recently, crowdsourcing may have further and considerable effects on Austrian employment.

Fourth, we are witnessing a blurring of the boundaries between paid and unpaid work. Self-service is no longer limited to the retail sector but, given the new opportunities afforded by the internet, has gained currency in sectors as diverse as finance, travel and public administration. What is more, 'prosumption' – where consumers of a good or service also help to produce it – is an important trend that draws consumers or amateurs such as bloggers into value creation in new ways, which thereby reduces the costs of certain jobs in fields such as data entry, design and journalism.

There has been no attempt to reduce weekly working hours in Austria since the 1980s. In view of further potential automation of jobs, the relocation of jobs and the replacement of some paid work by unpaid work, Austrian employment policy needs to better distribute available work among those who want it. One way of doing this is to introduce a 35- or 30-hour working week. While any substantial reduction in working hours would require harmonisation at EU level, possibly through reforming the existing working time directive, Austria may well take a first step as it is among the countries with the longest weekly working hours in the EU (Eurostat 2017b). There is a second opportunity to create jobs in the public sector where employment has been stifled by austerity policies in recent years. Digitisation makes it possible to run public services more efficiently, for example by implementing 'egovernment' applications. At the same time, jobs could be created in areas of the public services where there is a great need for improved provision, such as the health, care and education sectors.

## PRECARITY

From a global perspective, the Austrian labour market is highly regulated. Nevertheless, more and more employment relationships fail to meet social and legal standards deemed to be the norm in the country. Some 8% of workers are now considered to belong to the 'working poor' (Lamei and Heuberger 2017, 5). While forms of employment that deviate from the standard employment relationship are not necessarily precarious, atypical forms of employment still have a greater potential of being precarious – falling short of established standards of job security, minimum income and social security. Digitisation is being used to restructure organisations, for example, as a result of outsourcing work to freelancers that had hitherto been undertaken by employees. Whole business functions including IT and bookkeeping are increasingly being outsourced by service-providing companies.

While these trends have been with us for decades, intensified digitisation increases opportunities for external restructuring, which leads in turn to a fragmentation of employment, where people are increasingly employed under different sorts of contracts and have different employers, although they carry out the same tasks and functions. In some instances, including the aforementioned gig economy, it is increasingly difficult to discern the existence of a traditional employment relationship at all, as workers increasingly find themselves being self-employed when undertaking tasks that were traditionally rendered under a contract of employment, seen most conspicuously in the case of delivery workers with the likes of Deliveroo (Herr 2017).

The quality of employment varies considerably within the service value chains that have emerged (Flecker and Meil 2010). At the bottom end, jobs are often precarious. Call centres that were increasingly outsourced in the 1990s and 2000s are a good example of this (Shire et al. 2009; see also Doellgast this volume). The firms that provide outsourced customer services on behalf of their client companies not only pay lower wages on average, but also tend to use different forms of atypical employment (Flecker 2009). In Austria, the introduction of a 'contract of freelance services' (*Freier Dienstvertrag*) has proven particularly popular, as it has allowed high levels of temporal flexibility at company level while still allowing using external freelancers. Still, when applying this type of contract, companies can circumvent some of the rules, for example those on minimum wages. Stricter enforcement and higher social-security contributions from employers for using *Freie Dienstverträge* have reduced the frequency of such contracts.

In the context of ICT-based restructuring, crowdsourcing (see Berg and De Stefano this volume) involves particularly high levels of 'precarity'. One form of crowdsourcing involves outsourcing tasks over the internet to an undefined group of potential contractors. This type of outsourcing can be facilitated by internet platforms that provide services to both clients and workers. Workers are self-employed but still depend to a large extent on the platform that formally acts only as an intermediary between clients and workers. In practice, however, platform providers bind workers to the platform by setting the rules for their online reputation, by instigating and facilitating competition between 'crowdworkers', and by hindering clients and workers from circumventing the platform. Researching 'crowdworking' in Austria we discovered high levels of precarity in creative industries, in particular among those workers who used the platforms to get access to the relevant markets and to gain an occupational identity. Being formally self-employed, their income is insecure, their working hours are unpredictable and can get out of hand, and they often have to be prepared to undertake unpaid work in order to enhance their online reputation, which they desperately need to procure in order to attract paying clients (Schörpf et al. 2017). The potential for exploitation in these circumstances are clear.

While Austria has a coverage rate of industry-wide collective agreements of nearly 100%, workers can still earn less than the minimum wage if they are self-employed, or indeed have bogus self-employment status – self-employment under conditions for which the law requires an employment contract. It is a major challenge for governments to maintain crucial labour market regulations for workers, in the face of the potentially disruptive impact of digitalisation, which could result in far-reaching restructuring of organisations and jobs. The dynamics of value chains, not only in manufacturing but also relating to digital work, and the proliferation of location-independent jobs considerably widens opportunities for companies and employers regarding organisational choices and forms of employment. To safeguard decent work and to avoid insecure low-wage employment, restructuring processes and new business models need to be evaluated and closely regulated. The chosen forms of employment, the foreseen contributions to social security and so on, need to be inspected before new businesses such as internet platforms for digital work and local personal services such as Uber are authorised. The fact that businesses can now use new forms of flexible employment that can undermine the social rights of workers is not due solely to technological progress, but can also be explained by the turn to neoliberalism, especially since the 1980s.

## QUALITY OF WORK

Societal challenges stemming from digitalisation do not only relate to the number of jobs and the quality of employment, but innovation and restructuring processes may also improve (or degrade) the quality of work. This includes the content of work that is undertaken, the learning opportunities for workers, the stress levels experienced, and the organisation of working hours. It is highly surprising that this issue does not play a more prominent role in the debate in Austria. It was partly used in the promotion of Industry 4.0, where research organisations and companies often sweepingly envisaged a general improvement of working conditions for all as a result, claiming that "people become free for more creative tasks". This argument has been used in all the waves of automation debates since the 1950s, but is no more accurate now than it was before (Flecker 2017).

Digitalisation in general, too, is often assumed to lead to upskilling and higher levels of autonomy at work – as ascribed to the 'knowledge society' in previous decades because work to a large extent consists in producing, distributing and reproducing knowledge. While such a trend can indeed be observed in some areas, increased autonomy may be limited to particular aspects of the labour process, such as temporal or spatial ones, the content of works and the skills associated with it, the dimension of cooperation, and the need for emotional labour (Lohr 2013, 431). And there are persistent tendencies to the contrary, seen for example in the standardisation of work practices. Research on call centres, public administration and shared service centres have provided examples of the standardisation of work in the context of its digitisation (Carter et al. 2011; Howcroft and Richardson 2012; Schönauer 2009).

A further aspect of socio-economic change that is brought about by digitisation is the acceleration of production and communication, which paradoxically does not lead to more free time and leisure for workers, but rather goes hand in hand with an acceleration of the pace of life (Wajcman 2015). While complex societal and cultural developments have contributed to this outcome, it is obvious that people's sense of time has changed in an environment of instant communication. The internet and mobile ICT devices are often seen as contributing to information overload and to increasing levels of stress and burnout. On the other hand, new information and communication technologies are also said to facilitate work–life balance as they make tele-work possible, for example. Although research on the subject is not conclusive, observers tend to agree that the internet and mobile ICT devices can be seen as enabling factors that are contributing to the societal trend of blurred boundaries between work and private life (Jurczyk et al. 2009), which is not only a major challenge for workers and trade unions, but also increasingly shifts the onus of drawing boundaries and limiting work on to the individual.

The debate on digitalisation and Industry 4.0 focuses on technological developments and the consequences these may have on work and employment. It also addresses the skills that are needed and often puts further pressures on workers, for example, those relating to increasing demands from employers for flexibility. Technological determinism assumes a science-driven path of development, and denies the social shaping of technology; this results in technology being designed according to the interests of particular societal groups (Mackenzie and Wajcman 1985). What is more, competitiveness is the main, if not the only, goal of innovation. In fact, economic 'exigencies', as defined by economic elites, were the actual starting point and are what led to the legitimisation of the whole debate around Industry 4.0 (Pfeiffer 2017). The humanisation of work in the context of Industry 4.0 is only being addressed at a rather late stage of the development processes. As digitalisation is currently being used both to enhance work and to degrade it, policies are needed to increase the prevalence of high-quality jobs. At the organisational level, the improvement of the quality of work needs to be a deliberate aim of the development, adoption and application of new technologies, and of the ways that workplaces are organised. Workers and trade unions need to have a greater say in decisionmaking at work, and in the use of technology and work design. Participatory development processes that involve users in the development of technology may also be appropriate to mobilise the knowledge required to create more humane workplaces (see Kenny and Zysman this volume).

There seems to be a double challenge for governments and policymakers. Before it is possible to humanise work through digitalisation, there is a need to perceive technology as socially constructed, and to democratise technology-related decisionmaking. The programme of the new Austrian federal government for the years 2017 to 2022 does not reflect this challenge at all. It sets the goal of turning the country into a trailblazer of digitalisation without stating clearly what should exactly be achieved through digitalisation, apart from 'increased competitiveness' and the vague formula of 'seizing opportunities and avoiding dangers'. It neither specifies directions for the development of technology, nor does it address issues of work and employment. In the past, the far-right Freiheitliche Partei Österreichs (FPÖ), which is now part of the coalition government, presented itself as a 'social homeland party'. However, the new government programme pursues a clearly neoliberal agenda that cannot be expected to contribute to the humanisation of work. On the contrary, the desired deregulation and weakening of labour standards outlined in the programme will likely pave the way for further degradation of work and employment.

## REFERENCES

Arntz, M., T. Gregory and U. Zierahn (2016), *The Risk of Automation for Jobs in OECD Countries: a Comparative Analysis*, Social, Employment and Migration Working Paper 189, Paris: OECD.

Astleithner, F. and J. Flecker (2017), 'From the Golden Age to the Gilden Cage? Austrian Trade Unions, Social Partnership and the Crisis', in S. Lehndorff, H. Dribbusch and T. Schulten (eds), *Rough Waters – European Trade Unions in a Time of Crisis*, 173–96, Brussels: European Trade Union Institute.

Butterwegge, C. (1999), *Wohlfahrtsstaat im Wandel: Probleme und Perspektiven der Sozialpolitik*, Opladen: Leske & Budrich.

Carter, B., A. Danford, D. Howcroft, H. Richardson, A. Smith and P. Taylor (2011), '"All They Lack is a Chain": Lean and the New Performance Management in the British Civil Service', *New Technology, Work and Employment*, 26(2): 83–97.

Eurostat (2017a), 'Unemployment Rate by Age (1983–2016)', http://ec.europa.eu/eurostat/statistics-explained/index.php/File:Unemployment_rate_by_age,_1983-2016_(%25).png.

Eurostat (2017b), 'How Many Hours do Europeans Work per Week?', http://ec.europa.eu/eurostat/web/products-eurostat-news/-/DDN-20180125-1.

Ferschli, B., J. Kapeller, B. Schütz, and R. Wildauer (2017), 'Bestände und Konzentration Privater Vermögen in Österreich', *Materialien zu Wirtschaft und Gesellschaft*, 167, September, Wien: AK Wien.

Flecker, J. (2009) 'Outsourcing, Spatial Relocation and the Fragmentation of Employment', *Competition & Change*, 13(3): 252–68.

Flecker, J. (2017), *Arbeit und Beschäftigung – eine Soziologische Einführung*, Wien: UTB.

Flecker, J. and P. Meil (2010), 'Organisational Restructuring and Emerging Service Value Chains – Implications for Work and Employment', *Work, Employment and Society*, 24(4): 1–19.

Frey, C. and M. Osborne (2013), *The Future of Employment: How Susceptible Are Jobs To Computerisation?*, Oxford: Oxford Martin School, https://www.oxfordmartin.ox.ac.uk/downloads/academic/The_Future_of_Employment.pdf.

Herr, B. (2017), 'Riding in the Gig-Economy: An In-depth Study of a Branch in the App-based On-Demand Food Delivery Industry', AK Working Paper 169, Vienna: AK.

Höhrhan, J. (2016), 'Digitalisierung Braucht Industrialisierung', in J. Fritz and N. Tomaschek (eds), *Gesellschaft im Wandel: Gesellschaftliche, Wirtschaftliche und Ökologische Perspektiven*, Band 5: University, Society, Industry, Münster: Waxmann.

Howcroft, D. and H. Richardson (2012), 'The Back Office Goes Global: Exploring Connections and Contradictions in Shared Service Centers', *Work, Employment & Society*, 26 (February): 111–27.

Jurczyk, K., M. Schier, P. Szymenderski, A. Lange and G. G. Voß (2009), *Entgrenzte Arbeit – entgrenzte Familie: Grenzmanagement im Alltag als neue Herausforderung*, Berlin: edition sigma.

Lamei, N. and R. Heuberger (2017), 'Working Poor: Armutsgefährdet trotz Arbeit?', *Trendreport Arbeit Bildung Soziales*, 1, http://www.forba.at/data/downloads/file/1240-Trendreport_1-2017_Online_FINAL.pdf.

Lohr, K. (2013), 'Subjektivierung von Arbeit', in H. Hirsch-Kreinsen and H. Minssen (eds), *Lexikon der Arbeits- und Industriesoziologie*, 430–37, Berlin: edition sigma.

Mackenzie, D. and J. Wajcman (1985), *The Social Shaping of Technology*, Milton Keynes: Open University Press.

Nagl, W., G. Titelbach, K. Valkova (2017), *Digitalisierung der Arbeit: Substituierbarkeit von Berufen im Zuge der Automatisierung durch Industrie 4.0*, Wien: IHS.

Pfeiffer, S. (2017), 'Industrie 4.0 in the Making – Discourse Patterns and the Rise of Digital Despotism', in K. Briken, S. Chillas, M. Krzywdzinski and A. Marks (eds), *The New Digital Workplace: How New Technologies Revolutionise Work*, 21–41, London: Palgrave Macmillan.

Rechnungshof (2016), *Allgemeiner Einkommensbericht 2016*, Wien.

Schnetzer, M. and M. Rehm (2017), 'Vermögen in Österreich: Erkenntnisse und Herausforderungen', *Trendreport Arbeit Bildung Soziales*, 2017(1): 15–17, http://www.forba.at/data/downloads/file/1240-Trendreport_1-2017_Online_FINAL.pdf.

Schönauer, A. (2009), 'Guten Tag, Hier Spricht Ihr Bürgerservice, Was Kann Ich für Sie Tun?: Restrukturierung im KundInnenservice des öffentlichen Sektors und die Auswirkungen auf die Qualität der Beschäftigung', *Österreichische Zeitschrift für Soziologie*, 34(3): 82–91.

Schörpf, P., J. Flecker, A. Schönauer and H. Eichmann (2017), 'Triangular Love–Hate: Management and Control in Creative Crowdworking', *New Technology, Work and Employment*, 32(1): 43–58.

Shire, K. A., A. Schönauer, M. Valverde and H. Mottweiler (2009), 'Collective Bargaining and Temporary Contracts in Call Centre Employment in Austria, Germany and Spain', *European Journal of Industrial Relations*, 15(4): 437–56.

Statistik Austria (2017), 'Arbeitslose (Nationale Definition)', https://www.statistik.at/web_de/statistiken/menschen_und_gesellschaft/arbeitsmarkt/arbeitslose_arbeitssuchende/arbeitslose_nationale_definition/index.html.

Wajcman, J. (2015), *Pressed for Time: the Acceleration of Life in Digital Capitalism*, Chicago: University of Chicago Press.

# GERMANY

## *Rebalancing the coordinated market economy in times of disruptive technologies*

### Sven Rahner and Michael Schönstein

*The views and opinions expressed in this chapter are those of the authors and do not necessarily reflect the official policy or position of any agency of the German federal government.*

Germany takes a prominent place in the global debate on the future of work. This debate has been triggered by the widely held belief in Anglo-Saxon countries and Germany that digitalisation could lead to a massive loss of jobs (Brynjolfsson and McAfee 2014; Ford 2015). Domestically, the discourse evolved from a technology-focused debate around Industry 4.0 or the fourth industrial revolution to a much wider societal debate on Work 4.0. This was to a significant extent driven by a large public consultation process run by the German Federal Ministry of Labour and Social Affairs (Bundesministerium für Arbeit und Soziales; BMAS) from 2014 to 2016, culminating in a white paper *Work 4.0* (BMAS 2016). A key element of this white paper is the suggestion of a more responsive labour and social policy system that fosters decentralised innovation, based on targeted labour market intelligence and wide stakeholder participation in iterative policymaking processes. Elements of this debate also made their way into international processes, such as the G20 (2017), the ILO Future of Work Initiative (2017) and the revised version of the OECD Jobs Strategy (OECD 2018, forthcoming).

The German debate on the future of work points to a moderate overall impact of the digital transformation on employment in Germany (see Arnold et al. this volume). Nevertheless, many analysts wonder whether the significant structural shift in the German economy and the labour market could potentially erode the foundations of German social policy. Beyond questions about the magnitude of employment effects, evolving employment and labour relations as well as resulting inequalities are front and centre in this debate. The fear of a 'social problem' posed by an army of 'digital day labourers' is connected to the international discourse on the risks of reaching a level of social inequality that it is socially and economically dysfunctional (Atkinson 2015; Fratzscher 2016). Digitalisation could further aggravate the already existing divide within society and accelerate the momentum towards widening inequality. This involves a growing inequality in the distribution of wealth, a widening gap in incomes, a reduction in the number of jobs subject to social security contributions, and more precarious job conditions right up to the emergence of a new lower class at a greater risk of poverty and of certain groups that have inadequate access to social security. At the same time, in a 'society of singularities' a small elite is benefiting from the advantages of digitalisation, such as greater personal freedom in structuring work as well as cultural distinction (Reckwitz 2017).

This chapter summarises the challenges to the German model of differentiated quality production apparent in this debate, and subsequently outlines the three key conflicts that determine the ongoing debate. The final section sets out policy options for the future.


## CHALLENGES TO THE GERMAN MODEL

Germany's coordinated market economy (Hall and Soskice 2001) is characterised by companies focusing on a fixed set of high-quality products, a sufficient number of skilled labourers, a long-term relationship between companies and employees, and a strong relationship to a certain place of production. As Kirchner and Beyer (2016) point out, the very logic of digital platforms is losing these traditionally tight couplings. Germany's diversified quality production (Streeck 1997) and the disruptive, growth-obsessed world of digital platforms are far from a natural fit. Nonetheless, major players of the platform economy try to penetrate the German market and German costumers ask for the convenience they provide. Therefore, the progressing digitalisation of the economy and the world of work are putting the German economic and social model to the test. This has already been affected by an increasing degradation since the early 1990s. Besides the domestic (endogenous) factors, like the consequences of the German reunification and demographic change as well as trends towards knowledge intensive services, international (exogenous) change processes, like deeper European integration and globalisation, have a sustainable impact on successful productivity constellations. Shortages of skilled labour, the decrease in the number of companies and employees covered by collective agreements, and the increase of atypical forms of employment are symptoms of this development. The digital structural change is boosting the problem of the necessary skilled labour supplier and threatens to further erode the social market economy's promise of social balance.

A central structural component of Germany's coordinated market economy is a functionally networked state that operates incrementally and through negotiation (Czada 2000), and employs initiatives to steer the adjustment of the overall political and economic system so as to stay in step with political and social change. Its policy space is restricted by institutional factors, such as the close political coordination between individual states and between states and the federal government, as well as international factors such as European integration and economic globalisation. Schmidt (2006) speaks of "the policy of the middle way", which features an institutional order that tends towards the middle as a characteristic of German domestic government activity and as a reflection of the necessity for the government and the opposition in the Bundestag and the Bundesrat to cooperate on major legislative proposals.

In this context, the question arises in particular to what extent the political forms of cooperation and coordination in the German model can pave the way towards achieving social balance in the process of transformation. A further question is what "institutional complementarities" (Hall and Gingerich 2004) can be identified between the traditional structures of the German model that have grown through time and the new parameters set by the evolution of a digital economy, and if "synergy effects between the different institutions" can be observed (Vitols 2006, 50).

The ongoing digitalisation in the German labour market changes sectors, jobs and tasks. Overall, the German labour market is in good shape. Labour market forecasts look mostly at a period until 2030 and agree that the number of workers is going to remain roughly stable until then, with a slight increase considered likely by some. However, there will be profound structural changes in supply and demand of labour behind this apparent stability.

On the demand side, we see the following:

- Employment will shift across sectors. There will be between 750,000 and 1 million jobs lost in some sectors and a similar number of new jobs created in others. We will see significant employment growth in sectors like business services, health and social care, while the number of jobs will decrease in sectors like public administration, retail or gastronomy. Automation plays a role in this – the OECD forecasts that about 12% of jobs in Germany are likely to be automated over the coming years (Arntz, Gregory and Zierahn 2016; see also Arnold et al. this volume).
- The same OECD study estimates that another 31% of jobs will see significant change because of digitalisation. In addition to employment shifts, job profiles across all sectors and qualification levels are evolving as a result of technological change. This will require skills adaptation across the whole spectrum of qualification

levels and sectors. Whereas technical skills will remain important, increasingly socio-emotional and creative skills will be in demand (Patscha et al. 2017).

Demographic change continues to be a crucial challenge to labour supply:

- A key difference is between rural and urban regions. At an aggregate level, we see that federal states (*Länder*) with more rural areas, like those in the east of Germany, are projected to lose 10–15% of their active population by 2030, while the urban centres will remain stable, and some city states (eg Berlin, Hamburg) will continue to grow.
- In addition, as a result of demographic change, workers are older than in the past, on average, almost everywhere. The average age of the population in Germany today is 43 years, and it will rise to 47 years by 2030 – in large parts of eastern Germany it will be 50 years by then. Crucially, the diversity of workforces will increase not just through the different ethnic backgrounds of workers – in 2016 the number of people with a migration background living in Germany peaked at 18.6 million overall or 22.5% of the population (Statistisches Bundesamt 2017) – but also through having older and younger workers collaborating in teams with the older ones in the majority. The dynamics are also interesting because our younger cohorts tend to enter the labour market at a higher level of formal qualification than earlier ones.

In essence, what we see is an increasingly dynamic labour demand meeting an increasingly diverse and older workforce. Therefore labour market policies need to aim much more at preventing mismatches arising from the disparate development in labour supply and demand than they did in the last decades and be based on a deeper understanding of the underlying mechanisms of work and society in the years to come.

## DICHOTOMIES IN THE GERMAN DEBATE

Against the backdrop of these challenges, three interrelated dichotomies, if not conflicts, characterise the current debate on the future of work and welfare in Germany. They comprise the relation of jobs and incomes, the relationship between humans and machines, and the relationship between work and leisure.

## THE INCREASING DICHOTOMY BETWEEN JOBS AND INCOME

There is an increasing dichotomy of jobs versus income, resulting in technology-driven inequalities. Most analyses of the German labour market find an ongoing polarisation of the labour market (OECD 2017; Spitz-Oehner 2006), though to a slightly smaller extent than that in the US or the UK (Autor, Katz and Kearney 2010; Goos and Manning 2007). Whatever the take on polarisation, all labour market forecasts expect a strong structural shift in employment towards more jobs in services, in particular human services, whose productivity is limited and/or difficult to measure, and a continued but much smaller growth of highly productive jobs in information and communications technologies, professional services and industry. In other words, there will be many jobs, with relatively little income, for example in healthcare, education or social work, and few jobs with relatively high incomes for IT engineers and consultants. Middle-skilled, above-average-income jobs that today are the financial basis of the German corporatist social security system through payroll-based contribution are projected to decrease markedly.

## THE CONFLICT BETWEEN HUMANS AND MACHINES

A second conflict that shapes the German debate is between humans and machines. Though related, the issues arising from this dichotomy are distinct from the often-cited spectre of automation. This conflict plays out, crucially, in dimensions such as skills and health. Machines, such as assistance systems, may augment and complement human skills in many workplaces, ranging from production lines to call centres (Apt et al. 2016). At the same time, they bear risks. First, they may be conducive to de-qualification, as unused skills wither, second, they put pressure on workers to acquire and maintain skills that complement technology, such as communication, creative and social skills (Patscha et al. 2017). But not everyone is apt to do so, which in turn is a key driver behind the polarisation outlined above. A second dimension of the conflict between humans and machines is that machines, in particular robots, may alleviate physical stress and thus support the promotion of physical health (Apt et al. 2016). The automation of routine tasks also implies an increased share of complex non-routine tasks in any given working day, however. This may be stressful for workers, and it leads many workers to perceive an increase in the density of work. This perception goes together with a strong increase in mental-health-related issues. The share of new disability benefits recipients who are unable to work because of mental health problems has increased from 15.4% to 42.9% between 1993 and 2015 (DRV 2016).

## THE CONFLICT BETWEEN WORK AND LEISURE

Related to this (perceived) intensification of work is the conflict between work and leisure. Technology increasingly blurs the temporal and spatial boundaries of work. At the same time, the values that shape workers' attitudes, needs and preferences regarding work and working conditions are increasingly pluralised. Multiple different conceptions of what constitutes a quality job coexist across the population.

A recent study identified seven distinct groups, each with a discrete, distinct system of values about work, ranging from people embracing technology to optimise their productive potential to those who mainly seek a steady income to find meaning in life outside work (BMAS 2016, 32 ff). These two trends, blurring boundaries and pluralisation of value systems, collide, as technological opportunities for some are threats for others. Flexible working times, for example, may bring a gain in autonomy for some, while being a stressor for others (BMAS 2016).

Demographic change and significant urban–rural divides in demand for and availability of infrastructure move this debate to the intersection of work opportunities and care duties. In (growing) German metropolitan areas, and semi-urban areas located close to cities, job opportunities abound, but because of time constraints and the lack of a care infrastructure, care duties are often difficult to handle. For example, there is a significant lack of educators in metropolitan areas (Klemm and Zorn 2017) and an inadequate number of nurses across the whole country (BA 2017). In many rural regions unemployment is higher than in cities, and job opportunities are likely to worsen in the future, especially as digital infrastructure is of a low standard.

## POLICY OPTIONS

To resolve these conflicts within the – challenged – German corporatist system will require policy innovations. Four options are currently discussed by policymakers in Germany (BMAS 2016, 96 ff). They are based on a set of three decisive criteria to shape the fundamental structural change: social partnership, social investment and social innovation:

First, labour market intelligence requires an update. This is not about developing the perfect forecast, nor about workforce planning. Instead, the dynamic of the digital transformation requires continuous monitoring of changes in labour demand and supply. Forecasts are only one part of such a new labour market monitoring – they can take into account demography, skills and regional differences to generate useful insights into emerging mismatches. But, crucially, forecasts will have to be embedded in the German system of social partnership and corporatist labour market policy-making, so insights have to feed into the political debate between government and social partners at the federal level of coordination. It also requires the same approach at the regional level, making regionalised forecasts available to local labour market actors who are crucial in the design and implementation of professional education, such as chambers of commerce and industry and chamber of crafts, as well as labour unions and the regional offices of the Federal Employment Agency.

Second, labour market policy has to be more preventive. To help workers (and not just the unemployed) invest early on and over their whole career in adapting and improving their skills is crucial. This requires counselling, financing and, in the medium term, a legal entitlement to continuous professional development. People need a clear idea of where they stand with their formal and informal competences, and to get orientation about development opportunities to make lifelong learning work for all. This is especially the case for low-skilled workers, workers in small- and medium-sized enterprises (SMEs) and, to some extent, for older workers.

Third, we need new investment in social policies, such as individual activity accounts (see Weber this volume), to complement existing measures and thus accommodate individual needs and wishes. Such accounts would empower individuals to shape employment biographies in a more autonomous manner. It can be used for qualification and further training as well as setting up an enterprise. The individual activity account especially would provide young people with financial scope for personal development, thus opening up new opportunities for them, as it combines individual freedom with social security. It can thus be an instrument to target problems arising from the digital transformation better than a universal basic income could. At the same time, it could take up some of its objectives. This could be a crucial element of a comprehensive transformation strategy for professional and educational transitions throughout the whole career span of workers, and an option to react to the increasingly uneven distribution of wealth and opportunities.

Fourth, we need to enable innovation at the firm level. If we want to shape the future of work we need to involve those who know best: workers and managers on the shop floor. This will require new governance tools. An interesting example are innovation spaces, a project that the German Federal Ministry of Labour and Social Affairs is currently setting up. It aims to implement and experiment with new types of work organisation to respond to the challenges in a new world of work. This comprises a platform for exchange for companies that invest in new learning environment, or new organisational models, for example concerning working time or work place. But it also includes financial support for SMEs to innovate in these areas.

## CONCLUSION

German labour market and social policy is still predominantly targeted at activation. This system is under pressure from endogenous and exogenous factors, leading to significant societal conflicts. The digital and demographic structural change requires a paradigm shift away from the predominant activation-oriented policy system towards an empowering labour and social policy system.

The core task will be providing framework conditions to promote social partnership and social innovation as well as new and additional social investment. Social partnership will require strengthening through legal, non-monetary incentives such as innovation spaces for social-partner-led firm-level reform in areas such as working time and workplace regulation that go above and beyond the current regulatory framework. Social innovation such as socially insuring against the risk of loss of employability rather than (only) insuring the risk of job loss can contribute to an empowering social security system. Following Stiglitz, Sen and Fitoussi (2009), social investment should especially promote the capabilities of people. Given limited resources, there is a delicate balance to find between different infrastructure needs, especially care infrastructure and services in cities versus digital infrastructure and services in the countryside.

## REFERENCES

Apt, W., M. Bovenschulte, E. Hartmann and S. Wischmann (2016), *Digitale Arbeitswelt*, Foresight Study for BMAS (German Ministry of Labour and Social Affairs), Berlin: Institut für Innovation und Technik.

Arntz, M., T. Gregory and U. Zierahn (2016), *The Risk of Automation for Jobs in OECD Countries: a Comparative Analysis*, OECD Social, Employment and Migration Working Paper 189, Paris: OECD Publishing.

Atkinson, A. (2015), *Inequality: What Can Be Done?*, Cambridge, MA: Harvard University Press.

Autor, D., L. Katz and M. Kearney (2006), 'The Polarization of the US Labor Market', *American Economic Review*, 96(2): 189–94.

BA (2017), *Blickpunkt Arbeitsmarkt: Fachkräfteengpassanalyse*, Nürnberg: Bundesagentur für Arbeit.

BMAS (2016), *White Paper Work 4.0*, Berlin: German Federal Ministry of Labour and Social Affairs.

Brynjolfsson, E. and A. McAfee (2014), *The Second Machine Age: Work, Progress, and Prosperity in a Time of Brilliant Technologies*, New York: W. W. Norton.

Czada, R. (2000), Konkordanz, Korporatismus, Politikverflechtung. Dimensionen der Verhandlungsdemokratie', in E. Holtmann and H. Voelzkow (eds), *Zwischen Wettbewerbs- und Verhandlungsdemokratie*, 23–49.

DRV (2016), R*entenversicherung in Zeitreihen 2016*, Berlin: Deutsche Rentenversicherung Bund.

Ford, M. (2015), *Rise of the Robots: Technology and the Threat of a Jobless Future*, New York: Basic Books.

Fratzscher, M. (2016), *Verteilungskampf: Warum Deutschland Immer Ungerechter Wird*, Munich: Carl Hanser.

G20 (2017), *Toward an Inclusive Future: Shaping the World of Work*, Berlin: Federal Ministry of Labour and Social Affairs,

http://www.w20-germany.org/fileadmin/user_upload/documents/
Arbeitsministererkl%C3%A4rung_und_Annex.pdf.

Goos, M. and A. Manning (2007), 'Lousy and Lovely Jobs: The Rising Polarization of Work in Britain', *Review of Economics and Statistics*, 89(1): 118–133.

Hall, P. and D. Gingerich (2004), 'Varieties of Capitalism and Institutional Complementarities in the Macroeconomy: an Empirical Analysis', *British Journal of Political Science*, 39: 449–82.

Hall, P. and D. Soskice (2001), *Varieties of Capitalism: the Institutional Foundations of Comparative Advantage*, Oxford: Oxford University Press.

ILO (2017), 'The Future of Work', International Labour Organization, http://www.ilo.org/global/topics/future-of-work/lang--en/index.htm.

Kirchner, S. and J. Beyer (2016), 'Die Plattformlogik als Digitale Marktordnung: wie die Digitalisierung Kopplungen von Unternehmen Löst und Märkte Transformiert', *Zeitschrift für Soziologie*, 45(5): 324–39.

Klemm, K. and D. Zorn (2017), *Demographische Rendite adé – Aktuelle Bevölkerungsentwicklung und Folgen für die Allgemeinbildenden Schulen*, Gütersloh: Bertelsmann Stiftung.

OECD (2017), *OECD Employment Outlook 2017*, Paris: OECD Publishing. http://dx.doi.org/10.1787/empl_outlook-2017-en.

OECD (2018, forthcoming), *OECD Jobs Strategy*, Paris: OECD Publishing.

Patscha, C., H. Glockner, E. Störmer and T. Klaffke (2017), *Skill and Vocational Development Needs Over the Period until 2030: a Joint Situation Report by the Partnership for Skilled Professionals*, Berlin: BMAS (German Federal Ministry of Labour and Social Affairs).

Reckwitz, A. (2017), *Die Gesellschaft der Singularitäten*, Berlin: Suhrkamp.

Schmidt, M. (2006), 'Die Politik des Mittleren Weges – Die Wirtschafts- und Sozialpolitik der Bundesrepublik im Internationalen Vergleich', in J. Osterhammel, D. Langewiesche and P. Nolte (eds), *Wege der Gesellschaftsgeschichte*, 239–52, Göttingen: Vandenhoeck & Ruprecht.

Spitz-Oener, A. (2006), 'Technical Change, Job Tasks and Rising Educational Demand: Looking Outside the Wage Structure', *Journal of Labor Economics*, 24(2): 235–70.

Statistisches Bundesamt (2017), 'Bevölkerung mit Migrationshintergrund um 8,5 % Gestiegen', Wiesbaden: Pressemitteilung, 1 August, https://www.destatis.de/DE/PresseService/Presse/Pressemitteilungen/2017/08/PD17_261_12511pdf.pdf?__blob=publicationFile.

Stiglitz, J. E., A. Sen and J.-P. Fitoussi (2009), *Report by the Commission on the Measurement of Economic Performance and Social Progress*, French Commission on the Measurement of Economic Performance and Social Progress.

Streeck, W. (1997), 'German Capitalism: Does It Exist? Can It Survive?', in C. Crouch and W. Streeck (eds), *Modern Capitalism or Modern Capitalisms?*, London: Francis Pinter.

Vitols, S. (2006), 'Das "Deutsche Modell' in der Politischen Ökonomie', in V. Berghahn and S. Vitols (eds), *Gibt es einen Deutschen Kapitalismus? Tradition und Globale Perspektiven der Sozialen Marktwirtschaft,* 44–59, Frankfurt am Main: Campus.

# SPAIN

## *After the storm – at the crossroads between employment, job quality and technological changes*

### Rafael Grande

**O**ver the last five decades Spain has undergone an accelerated modernisation process, which has been characterised by major changes in the structure of employment, demographic dynamics and the welfare state. These transformations placed Spain, objectively, in a more prepared position to face the challenges of the so-called fourth industrial revolution than it was to face previous industrial revolutions. However, since the beginning of the 21st century, the development of technological changes and digitalisation in Spain has had to coexist with an economic bubble and employment boom, and a deep economic recession and major employment crisis. In other words, in the midst of the accelerated changes of the fourth industrial revolution, Spain has had to weather quite a storm.

## FROM THE ECONOMIC BOOM TO THE GREAT RECESSION IN SPAIN

From the 1990s onwards, the Spanish labour market began to expand strongly in all sectors, creating approximately 7 million jobs between 1995 and 2007. In this growth, the incorporation of Spanish women into the labour market and the arrival of immigrants stand out. Spain is one of the countries with the largest number of immigrants in Europe. But only a small part of this growth has been due to the emergence of new sectors focused on new technologies and digitisation with highly skilled jobs. To date, economic expansion and employment growth have occurred primarily in labour-intensive and unproductive sectors, especially in the construction and low-skilled services sectors (Bernardi and Garrido 2008).

The economic and financial crisis in 2007 quickly became a profound employment crisis in Spain. Between 2007 and 2013, 16.5% of Spanish jobs were lost, amounting to some 3.5 million jobs. Low-skilled jobs were especially affected. But the crisis did not turn out to be an opportunity for the technology or research sectors because of a lack of public and private investment, and the lack of political initiatives to promote industrial restructuring. Although Spain has begun to experience a slow economic recuperation since 2014, data from The Networked Readiness Index 2016 shows that Spain has regressed in its position with respect to the fourth industrial revolution when compared with neighbouring countries (Baller, Dutta and Lanvin 2016).

On the contrary, during this period there are trends that point towards growth in lower quality employment. First, the economic crisis in Spain has caused a lack of social protection for permanent workers in the primary segment of the labour market as a result of the 2010 and 2012 labour market reforms. And, among the workers of the secondary segment, we observe an increase in job insecurity and growth in temporary employment. An instructive example for this development is the significant rise in the number of 'additional workers' (Humphrey 1940), especially during the first phase of the crisis when adult women entered the labour market intending to balance job losses of male breadwinners and lessening the negative family income effects of the recession. This increase in female employment mainly occurred in the low-skilled position sector, far from the virtuous impacts of technological changes.

Second, a major wage devaluation has led to a loss of purchasing power and to an increase in the levels of the working poor. Relatedly, there has been a decrease in the rate of social security coverage due to the growth in the levels of unemployment (24.5% in 2014, 14% above EU average), which particularly affects less qualified and socioeconomically disadvantaged workers. Together, these factors lead to a significant increase in poverty (29% of the population are at risk of poverty, up from 23% in 2007).

Third, there has been a loss of highly qualified human capital, especially in the areas of health, architecture and engineering, as a result of the migration of young people from Spain to other European countries (Bermudez and Brey 2017; Lafleur and Stanek 2017).

During this storm, the fourth industrial revolution has continued to transform the structure of employment and job quality dynamics. We have to think about what the relationship between innovation and job quality in Spain is. What do we know about the polarisation of the labour market as a result of technological automation? How is the fourth industrial revolution impacting labour policy and the Spanish welfare state model? These are the questions we seek to explore in this short essay.

## THE IMPACT OF COMPUTERISATION: TECHNOLOGICAL CHANGES IN LABOUR DYNAMICS

When Jeremy Rifkin (1995) published his famous work The End of Work, few people in Spain could fully imagine the speed with which the transformation of the economy and labour market through technological changes associated with the fourth industrial revolution would take place. Frey and Osborne (2017) and Bowles (2014) have both estimated that approximately 40–50% of jobs in western society are currently at risk of computerisation. This is because it is not only manual or routine jobs that are being computerised, but also – and increasingly rapidly – non-routine cognitive tasks in the services sector that are at risk. It is timely, therefore, for us to consider the potential positive and negative impacts of the computerisation of jobs on Spanish workers.

First, on the positive side, this digital transformation has led to a significant increase in productivity, partly due to the digitisation and computerisation of many productive processes (see Fernández-Macías this volume). This bodes well for the possibility of sustained economic growth. However, as has already been said, the productive structure and the consequences of the economic and financial crisis have meant that Spain is still far from taking optimum advantage of the virtuous circles of technological change (see Atkinson this volume). For example, in the last decade Spain has not modified its Global Competitiveness Index (4.70), dropping from 29th to 34th place in 2007 to 2017 (Schwab 2017).

Against a pessimistic Luddite vision, many experts are stressing that technological change will not directly destroy jobs but will transform the structure of the labour market by creating new jobs, as happened in previous industrial revolutions. On the one hand, as Arnold et al. (this volume) explain, the potential for automation is arguably much smaller than many estimates suggest. This is because many extant jobs involve tasks that are difficult to automate, and workers often specialise in different non-automatable niches, and in tasks that can be enhanced by the introduction of new technologies, rather than be destroyed by them. On the other hand, the notable thing about these changes is that where there is a greater probability of computerisation in a given sector, there is a greater likelihood of these jobs requiring fewer skills and workers in these sectors, on average, will have lower levels of educational attainment (Frey and Osborne 2017; Levy and Murnane 1992). The implication of this is that low-skilled workers might be reassigned to tasks that require resources of creative and social intelligence that the new generations are more used to. The high levels of educational formation among the young generations of Spaniards (at a level similar to the EU and OECD average, and significantly above the G20 average according to OECD statistics) could place the country in a good position to face this transformation in comparison with previous industrial revolutions.

Finally, among the optimistic aspects of the computerisation of jobs on Spanish workers, there is a positive relationship between innovation and job quality. As in previous industrial revolutions, computerisation and robotisation have enormous potential for improving working conditions, which can translate into greater well-being for workers. In previous work we have analysed the relationship between innovation and job quality. It has been demonstrated that product and process technical innovation has a significant positive effect on the quality of employment (Muñoz-de-Bustillo, Grande and Fernández-Macías 2016, 2017) in European countries as a whole. There is growth in sectors with a higher quality of employment because there is an improvement in the type of tasks to be carried out in the workplace thanks to the introduction of new technologies, and because the increase in productivity can be used – at best – to increase wages or reduce working time.

To deepen the case of Spain, I analyse the relationship between the probability of automation of jobs and the quality of employment. On the one hand, I use the recent work by Frey and Osborne (2017), which seeks to estimate the probability of computerisation for 702 different occupations. Those occupations used as training data are labelled as either 0 (not computerisable) or 1 (maximum risk of being computerisable). On the other hand, with data from the 2015 European Working Condition Survey (EWCS) (Eurofound 2016), I constructed a Job Quality Index (JQI) with five dimensions following the proposal of Muñoz-de-Bustillo et al. (2011).

Figure 29.1 shows the results of this relationship between these two variables for the 39 main occupations in Spain. In general, we observe a negative relationship between quality of employment and computerisation: in Spain the jobs with the greatest risk of disappearing as a result of digitalisation and robotisation are those with the worst job quality. This reinforces the hypothesis that the fourth industrial revolution will progressively imply better job quality by replacing some jobs with others of higher quality.

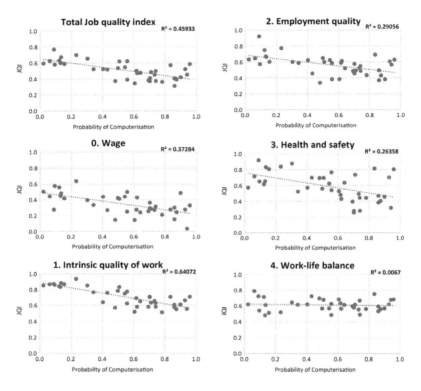

Figure 29.1   Dimensions of the Job Quality Index and probability of computerisation in 39 occupations, Spain, 2015. *Source*: Author's analysis from Frey and
Osborne (2017) and EWCS 2015 microdata.

The data shows that this relationship is different when we disag-
gregate the different dimensions of the JQI. The relationship is negative and intense for wages and, especially, the quality of work. This
is where up to now the digital revolution and robotisation have been
yielding greater job quality. Negative effects are clear, but weaker
between computerisation and employment quality and health and
safety. However, computerisation does not have an effect on work–
life balance. In this respect the improvements depend fundamentally
on labour policies since the employers most associated with the
fourth industrial revolution don't show significant differences in

working conditions related to work–life balance. In the future, as a result of greater levels of productivity, companies and governments may encourage the reduction of working hours at firm level, support men to actively participate in childcare and family life, for example by introducing more generous paternity leave, or take measures to prevent stress caused by greater flexibility, for example by restricting access to emails outside regular working hours.

Second, it is necessary for us to analyse the negative effects of computerisation, when they may interact with the serious effects of the economic crisis in Spain. As discussed above, the fourth industrial revolution has the potential to be a new 'great transformation' and there are social risks for workers associated with these changes (see Palier this volume). Many authors stress that technological change is producing a strong polarisation and segmentation of the labour market in Spain (Anghel, de la Rica and Lacuesta 2014; Sebastián-Lago 2017) and throughout Europe (Fernández-Macías 2012; Goos, Manning and Salomons 2009). The evidence shows that during the last decades the impact of technology is destroying middle-class or middle-skill jobs, a pattern that only increased during the economic crisis. This pattern affects more men than women. At the same time, we see a progressive increase in low-skill jobs in the service sector and a growth in the highest high-skill jobs, with higher remuneration on the occupational scale. These trends will most likely induce a progressive increase in inequality, which is one of the main problems of the Spanish labour market (Arnold et al. this volume). However, as Autor (2015) points out, this polarisation will not continue indefinitely because many middle-skill jobs with relatively good pay do not run the risk of being computerised in the coming decades, but there will be increasing demand for specific vocational skills and professional education, combined with basic technical abilities for the completion of tasks.

Table 29.1 shows the evolution of four categories of employees according to skill levels and occupation type (both white-collar and blue-collar workers) from the current version of the International

**Table 29.1 Evolution of the Job Quality Index and the percentage of workers in four categories of occupations according to skill levels, Spain, 2000–2015.**

| | High-skilled white collar (ISCO codes 1, 2 and 3) | | Low-skilled white collar (ISCO codes 4 and 5) | | High-skilled blue collar (ISCO codes 6 and 7) | | Low-skilled blue collar (ISCO codes 8 and 9) | |
|---|---|---|---|---|---|---|---|---|
| | JQI | workers (%) | JQI | workers (%) | JQI | workers (%) | JQI | workers (%) |
| 2000 | 0.564 | 29.8 | 0.371 | 23.7 | 0.332 | 21.5 | 0.238 | 24.4 |
| 2005 | 0.596 | 30.6 | 0.416 | 23.6 | 0.361 | 20.5 | 0.302 | 24.9 |
| 2010 | 0.656 | 31.8 | 0.441 | 32.1 | 0.425 | 14.7 | 0.338 | 20.9 |
| 2015 | 0.606 | 32.4 | 0.473 | 33.4 | 0.433 | 13.6 | 0.395 | 20.2 |

*Source:* Author's analysis from EWCS microdata and Spanish LFS.

Standard Classification of Occupations (ISCO-88). I analyse the change in the percentage of workers that includes each sector and the evolution of job quality in each category, using the data from the 2015 EWCS and the Spanish Labour Force Survey (LFS). The results show a steady growth of non-manual occupations (white-collar jobs) which are also the categories of jobs with the highest levels of job quality. There has also been a steady decrease of manual-industrial occupations (blue-collar jobs) in relative terms, particularly as a result of the economic crisis and the loss of employment in construction.

This data shows how the Spanish labour market is adapting to a post-industrial society, where the dominant sectors are services in both high- and low-skilled jobs, which have the potential for polarisation. The quality of employment is increases for workers with higher skill sets and non-manual occupations have a better job quality. But job quality has a much higher growth rate from 2000 to 2010 in blue-collar occupations than in white-collar ones. This points to a positive effect of the impact of technological change on non-manual jobs that, in an initial phase, are automating, while also improving the quality of manual jobs.

On the contrary, it is surprising that job quality for high-skilled white-collar workers fell during the period 2010–2015. This helps us to understand the post-crisis effects of labour market and austerity policy and the flexibilisation of the Spanish labour market. These figures and the lower job quality for high-skilled white-collar workers suggest that we cannot expect higher competitiveness and productivity in this segment of the Spanish labour market, which is crucial for a successful transition into a digital economy. Therefore, when we speak of polarisation, as Atkinson (2015) explains, we have to understand that technological change is not exogenous, and its effects depend on the social system and the political economy (see Flecker this volume). Thus, some research has shown that one of the main causes of the deep segmentation of the Spanish labour market is increasing deregulation and the increase of temporary work, which occurred especially during the crisis.

Therefore, finally, among the negative effects of this transformation on Spanish employment, we must consider to what extent these organisational changes, and the development of a new work ethic, are leading to an increase in job insecurity, which (even among high-skill and well-paid jobs) translates into what Sennett (1998) calls the "corrosion of character". On the one hand, in contrast to other types of innovation, organisational innovation and labour flexibility, when applied to different aspects of work, may not be as positive and can lead to a decrease in the wellbeing of individuals. Amid the Spanish economy's incipient recovery, we observe an increase in the rates of temporary work, involuntary part-time work, labour deregulation and outsourcing practices, which is deepening the segmentation of the labour market. This is seen, for example, with 'clickworkers' who are engaged in delivery work with platforms such as Deliveroo, Glovo and foodora. The demand for such work is on the rise because of the growing online trade, which is still based on tasks that are far from being fully automated – transport and delivery services. Workers are engaged as independent contractors or as 'false free-lancers' instead of being considered as salaried workers. Workers endure a reduction in labour rights (see Berg and De Stefano this volume). However, it is clear that digital platforms did not invent precarious work – as Cañigueral (2017) identifies in the Spanish case – and in general a large part of the increase in precarious work is due to the outsourcing of activities that had previously been done in-house.

On the other hand, as has been stated previously, the new models of work organisation have led to increases in productivity, based mainly on a wage adjustment and the demise of the (low productivity) construction sector. Since the late 1980s, in most OECD countries labour share of income has been declining. Among other factors, this trend has led to greater levels of inequality and poverty in increasingly large sections of the population. During the toughest years of the economic crisis in Spain (2008–2013), more than 80% of the fall in Spanish GDP was caused by a decrease of wages.

## POLITICAL DISCUSSION: BEYOND THE WELFARE STATE WEAKNESS

How is the welfare state adapting to this transformation of the labour market? Beyond the weakness of the Spanish welfare state, we start from the idea that, as was the case with previous industrial revolutions, the models of the past will not return because social and labour contexts are completely changed. However, it is necessary to reflect on the future of the welfare state in Spain in light of the impact of the fourth industrial revolution.

First, along with the challenges posed by the fourth industrial revolution, Spain faces a demographic challenge due ageing of the population. By 2066, the population is projected to be around 5.4% smaller than in 2016 (McMurtry 2016). Today, people in Spain are living longer and healthier lives, a fact that Spain should be proud of. However, the demographic situation is being used as an excuse to justify welfare state reforms, and to implement substantial cuts to public expenditure. As Miret-Gamundi and Zueras (2016) affirm, Spain is not facing any lack of workers, but rather a lack of work. There is a lack of capacity in the labour market to employ a large number of workers. In Spain, there has been a significant increase in the number of highly qualified workers in recent decades, which has not been accompanied by equivalent growth in the demand for jobs for highly skilled workers.

Therefore Spain currently faces three important challenges:

- Over-qualification is growing as many workers have higher levels of qualification than are required for the work that they undertake (Ramos 2017).
- Involuntary part-time work and underemployment is increasing. Together with over-qualification, this goes hand in hand with precarious working conditions. As a result there has been a significant drop in the amount of income tax that can be collected, which is depleting the state's ability to cover the cost of paying social benefits.

• Qualified young Spaniards are emigrating, fuelled by the inability
  of young workers to find work in high-skilled, productive sectors.

In short, a change in the orientation of labour policies and public
intervention is needed to better foster the creation of jobs in the
highly productive sectors that are based on information, knowledge
and creativity that high-skilled workers are seeking employment in
(higher rates of employment in the highly productive sectors would
also be a way to solve problems of welfare state resources). Given
the initial difficulty of private investment, it is advisable to promote
medium- and long-term public investment policies that attract the
private sector to the technology and knowledge sectors as a means
of reviving the economy and of creating higher quality jobs.

Although the increase in research and development (R&D) activities should be a priority, from 2009 to 2016 investment in R&D in
Spain declined by 9.1%, representing 1.19% of the GDP in 2016,
compared with 2.03% of the average GDP in the EU. For example,
the renewable energy sector and the number of green jobs were seriously reduced between 2008 and 2015. Despite the low investment
in R&D, proposals such as the plan by the Ministry for the Economy
to develop a strategy on skills for Industry 4.0 are being seen as
positive steps, because they give financial support and technical
training to companies that are seeking to undertake steps towards
the carrying out the necessary digital transformation. Regional policies also have a very important role to play because they provide
much-needed extra resources in this area, although in the medium
term they point to an increase in inequality between Spanish regions.
The best example is the Basque Industry 4.0 strategy of the Basque
country government, which pays special attention to small- and
medium-sized enterprises, worker training and the development of
new technologies.

Second, along with technological changes, there is a growing
tendency on the part of governments and international institutions to
deregulate labour markets and reduce the role of social dialogue by
favouring the individualisation of labour relations. Recent data and

experiences in Spain point to the need to strengthen different social dialogue mechanisms and the means of communication between workers and employers as an effective tool to improve the deterioration of working conditions (Muñoz-de-Bustillo and Pinto 2016).

In order to take advantage of the positive correlation that can exist between technological changes and job quality and social welfare, Spain must counteract the labour policies of recent years that have favoured the reduction of labour rights or the cost of layoffs. For example, the decline in investment in science and R&D has also led to increasing job instability and uncertainty in the careers of many highly skilled and highly productive researchers and workers (see Bell this volume). In the face of this trend, it is necessary to take up a political agenda that prioritises social protection and the adaptation of the welfare state in the context of labour changes that are linked to the fourth industrial revolution. Like other European countries, Spain should start discussing the redistributive model on which a universal basic income or basic income guarantee model is based. These models can encourage redistribution in the face of the growing inequality caused by the increase in part-time and temporary work. If the segmentation of the Spanish labour market continues, other redistributive models should be implemented, for example to implement policies for equality and work–life balance. Proposals such as minimum wage coordination at the EU level (Fernández-Macías and Vacas 2015) may be positive in order for wages to increase, favoured by productivity increases caused by automation and the implementation of new technologies.

Finally, the need to implement new social protection policies makes it necessary for trade unions to adapt. In many cases, trade unions are modelled on outdated Fordist organisations of work, which explains in part low union membership rates among younger workers (see Benhamou in this edition). Updating collective action would make it necessary to strengthen bargaining power and modernise labour relations. It would reveal more rigorously existing precarious conditions in the workplace and emphasise demands to reduce stretched working hours, promote job security, facilitate labour inspections and limit outsourcing of services. What has changed is that union action focuses on specific sectors rather than traditional collective bargaining between employers' organisations and established trade unions, eg the resistance of Coca-Cola workers against a planned factory closure in Madrid and a successful legal battle of Deliveroo drivers over their employment status. In both cases established trade unions were not a precondition for collective action but were empowered by more flexible workers' movements at company level. Whether technology and innovation will leave a positive imprint on job quality in the future economy will largely depend on the degree of impact and success of these new trade union movements.

## REFERENCES

Anghel, B., S. de la Rica and A. Lacuesta (2014), 'The Impact of the Great Recession on employment Polarization in Spain', *Series*, 5(2–3): 143–71.

Atkinson, A. B. (2015), *Inequality: What Can Be Done?*, Cambridge MA: Harvard University Press.

Autor, D. H. (2015), 'Why Are There Still so many Jobs? The History and Future of Workplace Automation', *Journal of Economic Perspectives*, 29(3): 3–30.

Baller, S., S. Dutta and B. Lanvin (ed.) (2016), *The Global Information Technology Report 2016: Innovating in the Digital Economy*, Geneva: World Economic Forum.

Bermudez, A. and E. Brey (2017), 'Is Spain Becoming a Country of Emigration Again? Data Evidence and Public Responses', in J.-M. Lafleur and M. Stanek (eds), *South-North Migration of EU Citizens in Times of Crisis*, 83–98, Springer.

Bernardi, F. and L. Garrido (2008), 'Is There a New Service Proletariat? Post-industrial Employment Growth and Social Inequality in Spain', *European Sociological Review*, 24(3): 299–313.

Bowles, J. (2014), 'The Computerisation of European Jobs', Bruegel, 24 July, http://bruegel.org/2014/07/the-computerisation-of-european-jobs/.

Cañigueral, A. (2017), 'La precariedad laboral no la han inventado las plataformas digitales', *El País*, 6 July, https://retina.elpais.com/retina/2017/07/05/tendencias/1499273411_290872.html.

Eurofound (2016), *Sixth European Working Conditions Survey: 2015*, https://www.eurofound.europa.eu/surveys/european-working-conditions-surveys/sixth-european-working-conditions-survey-2015.

Fernández-Macías, E. (2012), 'Job Polarization in Europe? Changes in the Employment Structure and Job Quality, 1995–2007', *Work and Occupations*, 39(2): 157–82, https://doi.org/10.1177/0730888411427078.

Fernández-Macías, E. and C. Vacas (2015), 'A Coordinated European Union Minimum Wage Policy?', *European Journal of Industrial Relations*, 22(2): 97–113, https://doi.org/10.1177/0959680115610725.

Frey, C. B. and M. Osborne (2017), 'The Future of Employment: How Susceptible are Jobs to Computerisation?', *Technological Forecasting and Social Change*, 114: 254–80, https://doi.org/10.1016/j.techfore.2016.08.019.

Goos, M., A. Manning and A. Salomons (2009), 'Job Polarization in Europe', *American Economic Review*, 99(2): 58–63, https://doi.org/10.1257/aer.99.2.58.

Humphrey, D. D. (1940), 'Alleged "Additional Workers" in the Measurement of Unemployment', *Journal of Political Economy*, 48(3): 412–19.

Lafleur, Jean-M. and M. Stanek (ed.) (2017), *South-North Migration of EU Citizens in Times of Crisis*, Springer.

Levy, F. and R. J. Murnane (1992), 'US Earnings and Earnings Inequality: a Review of Recent Trends and Proposed Explanations', *Journal of Economic Literature*, 30: 1333–81, http://www.jstor.org/stable/2728062.

McMurtry, A. (2016), 'Why Spain's Population is Shrinking by 72 People Every Day', *El País*, 21 December, https://elpais.com/elpais/2016/12/16/inenglish/1481895459_844168.html.

Miret-Gamundi, P. and P. Zueras (2016), 'Breakdown in the Public Pension System: Not in the Name of Demography!', *Perspectives Demogràfiques*, 4: 1–4, http://ced.uab.cat/PD/PerspectivesDemografiques004_ENG.pdf.

Muñoz-de-Bustillo, R. and F. Pinto (2016), *Reducing Precarious Work in Europe through Social Dialogue: the Case of Spain*, University of Salamanca, http://www.research.mbs.ac.uk/ewerc/Portals/0/Documents/Spain-final-report.pdf.

Muñoz de Bustillo, R., E. Fernández-Macías, J. I. Antón and F. Esteve (2011), *Measuring more than money: the Social Economics of Job Quality*, Cheltenham: Edward Elgar.

Muñoz-de-Bustillo, R., R. Grande and E. Fernández-Macías (2016), 'Innovation and Job Quality: an Initial Exploration', QuInnE Working Paper WP5-1-2016, https://www.researchgate.net/publication/317717163_Innovation_and_job_quality_An_initial_exploration.

Muñoz-de-Bustillo, R., R. Grande and E. Fernández-Macías (2017), 'An Approximation of Job Quality and Innovation Using the 3rd European Company Survey', QuInnE Working Paper WP5-3-2017, http://bryder. nu/quinne1/sites/default/files/WP5_3_final.pdf.

Ramos, M. (2017), 'Overqualification and Unemployment in Young People: Pathways to Employment of University Graduates', *Social Observatory of La Caixa*, April, https://observatoriosociallacaixa.org/en/-/sobrecualificacion-y-desempleo-juvenil-dinamicas-de-insercion-laboral-de-los-titulados-universitarios.

Rifkin, J. (1995), *The End of Work: the Decline of the Global Labor Force and the Dawn of the Post-Market Era*, New York: Putnam.

Sennett, R. (1998), *The Corrosion of Character: the Personal Consequences of Work in the New Capitalism*, New York: Norton & Company.

Schwab, Klaus (ed.) (2017), *The Global Competitiveness Report 2017–2018*, Geneva: World Economic Forum.

# PORTUGAL

## *Preparing the next generation*

## Joana A. Vicente[1]

The fourth industrial revolution, characterised by the convergence of digital, physical and biological technologies, will fundamentally alter modern economies on a large scale and at full speed all over the world, and Portugal is no exception.

As a generator of economic value, the revolution has the potential to improve people's quality of life, but while the advantages are clear for those workers who can adapt to the requirements of a new economy and a new labour market, others are in danger of falling behind. Government policy, legislation and economic institutions must not only be adapted to the needs of a faster and more complex economy but must also intervene to lessen the potential negative impacts for the losers of technological development. The relationship between humans and robots must be appropriately weighed and integrated into the professional and personal day-to-day lives of workers and citizens.

Although it has been a major challenge for Portuguese workers and companies – as well as the international companies operating in Portugal – Industry 4.0 has made it possible to achieve advances in multiple areas, such as product quality control, mobility, the use of human capital for functions with higher added value (to the detriment of more routine functions), and new and more active collaborations between technology companies. Gradually, industries are moving away from complete value chains, towards more specialised and focused activities.

## PORTUGAL'S POTENTIAL: 60 POLICY MEASURES

Upgrading business operations is inevitable given that, with the increasing introduction of digitisation and new technologically enhanced production processes, there are fewer and fewer routine jobs.

To counterbalance Portugal's current position vis-à-vis the digital revolution, the Portuguese government announced that it would dedicate €4.5bn (half of this via European funds) of public investment over the next four years to prepare the economy for the fourth industrial revolution. The main aim is to provide technological training to more than 20,000 workers, managers and entrepreneurs, to enable them to face the difficulties created by digitisation, and ultimately to remain in viable employment.

This was announced in January 2017 as the Strategy for Industry 4.0 (BF Consultores 2017), including more than 60 policy measures. Beyond helping workers with the new digitisation processes, their main goal is to bring Portugal to the forefront of this industrial revolution. The policy agenda spans across several different industries, such as trade, tourism, retail, agriculture and the automotive sector. The strategy further envisions the creation of a visa scheme that will enable the recruitment of qualified citizens from abroad, and the provision of incentives for the exhibition of national technology companies at major international trade fairs (eg FABTECH Canada and Mexico, Hannover Messe, IoT Solutions World Congress Barcelona), aiming to share the products and services developed in Portugal in the Industry 4.0 context.

This is the largest single initiative planned by the Portuguese government in its national reform plan, an ambitious set of proposals, which has allowed Mário Caldeira Cabral, the minister for the economy, to state that Portugal is "one of the eight European countries that [has] a strategy for digitisation in industry" (Carvalho 2016). There are 64 companies with a proven background in the application of new technologies involved in this project, alongside various government bodies and trade associations.[2]

Elements of the project are being jointly discussed and implemented by various social actors, including the government and the private sectors, with the aim of tackling different problem areas identified as critical for Portugal:

- human capital qualification: fostering collaboration between universities and the corporate sector (following success cases such as the Science and Technology Park of the University of Porto or Startup Braga with the University of Minho) and developing in-demand qualifications and skills through the education system
- technological cooperation: at the development and implementation level between companies, universities, technology centres, business associations, public bodies and other stakeholders
- start-up modernisation: recognising the important role of start ups in technological innovation, developing measures in line with the national strategy for entrepreneurship (launched in 2016 by the Ministry of Economy, to foster competitiveness and attract domestic and foreign investment).
- financing and investing incentives through public financing policies to develop mechanisms for projects within the scope of Industry 4.0 (such as credit lines to support exports and reinforcement of the technology centres' role); within this, the government's plan includes the allocation of a €7,500 Industry 4.0 voucher to small- and medium-sized companies, which play an important role in Portugal in providing employment and value-added share, helping companies adopt technologies that can absorb disruptive changes in their business models, such as in digital marketing and commerce
- internationalisation: promoting the Portuguese technology industry's positioning in foreign markets and supporting the companies that are in the process of going global

- the need to adopt best practice in standards and regulations, in order to allow the development of technological enablers based on legal guarantees that provide legal and regulatory certainty that increase the supply and adoption of technology.

The final goal is to support high-tech industry and innovation, by trying to bring together the principal actors that play a crucial role in the implementation and development of this revolution: the entities involved in the national reform plan, other policymakers, educators, employers and trade unions. The proposals were sourced from more than 200 entities, and the employers' organisation COTEC Portugal is responsible for overseeing the implementation of the measures.

The fundamental pillars of this strategy are improving training, and strengthening partnerships between large traditional companies, start ups and educational institutions. While this is commendable, a more structured approach would be preferable: examining and measuring the current and forecast human capital shortcomings to address the needs of Industry 4.0, and evaluating what is needed to address these with concrete labour force data to determine the necessary volume and distribution of resources. In this way, shortcomings in important and crucial areas could be avoided, such as tackling the problem of young people who are in not in employment, education or training (NEET), which poses a double threat: as a social problem, and a situation that exacerbates the lack of qualified workers in the country.

## RISKING A LOST GENERATION: YOUTH UNEMPLOYMENT

To counter the potential negative effects that technological change can pose for employees with traditional jobs, the government is focusing on improving training activities for entrepreneurs, managers and other workers, so that all have the necessary technical and managerial skills to prosper in the new working environment. This therefore benefits individuals who already have a job, particularly those who will have to be more closely involved with processes that are likely to be partially or fully automated in future.

However, there are still young people who have difficulties with entering the labour market – 23.9% of the workforce in 2017 (INE 2018) – as they lack skills and training for increasingly digitising economy.

The EU has attempted to counteract high levels of youth unemployment with a number of different measures. For example, the Erasmus+ programme (2014–2020) supports projects designed for youth organisations or groups of young people with a focus on non-formal learning. These include youth exchanges, opportunities for volunteering, training and networking opportunities for youth workers, cooperation for innovation in youth work, and projects to engage young people in a structured dialogue with policymakers. Another example is European Employment Services (EURES), a cooperation network designed to facilitate the free movement of workers within the EU28, and an attempt to compile labour market trends in a way that can be accessed by national labour agencies while serving as a source for individual job vacancy data. Portugal has adopted some measures too: the Active Youth Employment policy, which provides hands-on work-experience opportunities for disadvantaged young people, and the Youth Warranty initiative, a commitment that within four months of leaving the education system or labour market young people will be offered a job, additional education, professional training or internship.

Despite these efforts, youth unemployment is still a serious problem, with severe social and economic consequences for the economy.[3] In 2017, 11.2% of Portuguese young people were NEET, an improvement on 2016 (when 13.2% young people were unemployed, versus the EU28 average of 11.6%) (INE 2018 and Eurostat 2018). These young people are not participating in the fourth industrial revolution, and not receiving the support or gaining the skills needed to face the challenges it presents. As they are not in work, they do not have opportunities to get practical experience. As they

**Table 30.1 Unemployment, youth unemployment and NEET rates in Portugal, EU28 and countries with the euro, 2007 and 2017.**

| Country | Unemployment[1] | | Youth unemployment[2] | | NEET[3] | |
|---|---|---|---|---|---|---|
| | 2007 | 2017* | 2007 | 2017* | 2007 | 2017* |
| Portugal | 8.1% | 8.9% | 16.7% | 23.9% | 11.2% | 11.2% |
| EU28 | 7.1% | 8.6% | 15.5% | 18.7% | 11.0% | 11.6% |
| Euro area | 7.4% | 10.0% | 15.0% | 20.9% | 10.8% | 11.7% |

*Source:* Eurostat (2018).

*Figures are for 2016 for the EU28 and euro area data.

[1]Unemployed persons as a percentage of the labour force. The labour force is the total number of people employed and unemployed. Unemployed persons comprise unemployed persons aged 15 to 74.

[2]Calculated by dividing the number of unemployed persons aged 15 to 24 by the total active population of the same group.

[3]Young people aged 15 to 24 who are not employed (unemployed or inactive) and have not received any education or training in the last four weeks. Data expressed as a percentage of the total population in the same age group and with the same sex.

are no longer in education, they are increasingly at risk of becoming totally disconnected from the labour market.

Youth unemployment in Portugal has fallen as the economy has recovered. It peaked at 38.1% in 2013 and fell to 24% by 2017, though this is still above pre-crisis levels (see Table 30.1). Youth unemployment has also fallen in many other EU countries, though this has been partially driven by increasing numbers of young people being involved in temporary work; unstable and precarious work is becoming increasingly common across the EU.

## LINGERING SKILL MISMATCHES AND PORTUGAL'S POLICY OPTIONS FOR THE DIGITAL AGE

To master the challenges of the fourth industrial revolution, Portugal will have to be able to create high-skill jobs, which is inseparable from the overall challenges that the Portuguese economy faces to ensure durable medium- to long-term growth rates. Current forecasts for the future evolution of potential GDP and productivity growth are not encouraging (in the 0.8–1.2% range in both cases over the next few years, see eg IMF 2017) and structural problems persist (see eg Blanchard and Portugal 201; Gershenson, Jaeger and Lall, 2016).

In these circumstances, youth unemployment – particularly the high rate of NEETs – is a particular challenge. The levels of communication and meaningful cooperation between the Ministry of Labour, Ministry of Education and Ministry of Economy (which is in charge of the Strategy for Industry 4.0) must improve, to achieve the ministries' objectives and to deal more appropriately with the unemployment crises. In addition, despite very significant improvements in educational attainment in Portugal in the past few decades, this has not yet completely fed into the labour market, so Portugal still has one of the lowest proportions of people working (25–64 years) and lowest level of qualifications among the population in the OECD (OECD 2017), with many industrial associations claiming to have difficulty in finding qualified workers (Silva 2017). This lack of qualified workers is increasingly seen as a hindrance to potential growth and new industrial investment, which could result in Portugal being left behind: the lack of supply of qualified workers to meet demand today could lead to a lack of demand for the young, qualified workers of tomorrow.

An adequate bridge must be built to better link education and the modern realities of labour to address this structural gap. Education systems need to provide not only basic skills, but also transferable skills. There should be greater engagement between education and employment, so as to better understand the skills that are currently needed in the market. The fourth industrial revolution is thus an opportunity to address labour market mismatches and imbalances that have existed since before the crisis. There is a need for strategic thinking to improve links between education providers and employers and, at the same time, to make sure that young people are aware of and informed about employability opportunities and requirements.

To better prepare future workers for the fourth industrial revolution, the Portuguese government must help to foster partnerships between educational institutions, enterprises, employers and young people themselves. This government is already attempting to address this with its Strategy for Industry 4.0. Portugal must also focus on young people who are willing to learn new techniques and are more accustomed to new technologies. At 6%, the share of low-skilled NEETs in Portugal is above the OECD average of just over 5% (OECD 2016a). This poses a long-term challenge as this group risks being left behind in the labour market permanently. There is an urgent need to reconnect NEETs with the labour market and to provide them with new career prospects. If Portugal wants to be ahead on this revolution and move forward, it must see this as a long-term investment.

In a broader sense, however, when discussing Industry 4.0 we are talking about transformations that will inevitably occur in the modes of production, which take shape through a deep digitisation across all sectors of the economy, not just automation of industrial processes (Fernández-Macías this volume). This precipitates changes in the work model and, more broadly, the daily lives of workers and citizens. Historically, Portugal has been a laggard in previous industrial revolutions not least as a result of geographical and politico-historical specificities (see eg Costa, Lains and Miranda 2016), which, arguably, might bear resemblance to the technological transformation that is unfolding now.

## PUBLIC DEBATE REGARDING WORK 4.0 IN PORTUGAL

Analysis of the specific effects of this revolution on the Portuguese labour market as has been carried out in other European countries (eg Wolter et al. 2015) is scarce. The Confederation of Portuguese Business expects that "10 to 15 per cent of current jobs in the industrial sector will disappear in the next 10 years, but others [more qualified] will be created" (CIP 2018, 16). In the Portuguese information and communications technology (ICT) sector alone, about 15,000 professionals will be required to fill available vacancies. If potential is met – which requires dealing with the labour market challenges – in the next decade 157,000 jobs will be created in the industrial sector, due to the expansion of the economic activity allowed by the revolution. About 17,500 new jobs will be for specialists in physical sciences, mathematics and engineering. Nowadays, high-tech industries are already considered one of the pillars for Portugal's future growth, alongside the tourism and ICT sectors.

Thus, in Portugal, rather than a widespread increase in unemployment, a change in the type and profile of employment is predicted, with decreasing demand for blue-collar workers and administrative support workers. Demand for mid-level technicians in Portuguese industry will fall, with doctorates and graduates in science, technology, engineering and mathematics becoming increasingly important. However, this trend in demand does not reflect those of labour supply: despite progress Portugal is far behind the leading countries in Europe in its PhD graduation figures, and especially worrisome is the low number of PhD graduates integrating within industry, with only 25% of researchers being employed outside the public sector (OECD 2016b). Industry 4.0 could therefore accentuate the mismatch between demand and supply of workers with appropriate qualifications.

There is still reluctance among some companies to proceed with the necessary investments, although some have already adopted reactive positions and new technologies associated with Industry 4.0 – connectivity, cloud computing and advanced analytics – which allowed Portugal to be ranked 15th out of 29 European economies its digital maturity of domestic companies, according to the Digital Maturity Enterprise Index (Deloitte and Siemens 2015).

The topic has attracted public attention. Meetings and conferences have attempted to gather the multiple social actors and relevant stakeholders in the digitalisation of the economy, particularly government ministries, technology companies, labour and trade unions, and academics. Both socio-economic and labour issues have been addressed, covering subjects such as the modernisation of the economy, competitiveness and productivity within Industry 4.0.

The Tripartite Conference on the Future of Work, organised by the Ministry of Labour, Solidarity and Social Security of Portugal in collaboration with the Lisbon office of the International Labour Organization, was held in Lisbon on 19 October 2016. It involved the prime minister and the employment state secretary from the government side, several academics, representatives of trade unions and the president of the Confederation of Portuguese Business. Focusing particularly on labour market reform challenges, the ministry ultimately recognised the difficulty of giving a homogeneous answer to the challenges of the digitalisation process and a need to adjust the collective contracting to this new reality: "collective contracting will be misfit, namely at the level of the professions committee, which will also imply that we need to look at vocational training and qualifications in a more focused and sharper way" (MTSSS 2017, 62).

There is a consensus among stakeholders to focus on qualifications, since "in the digital era, qualifications are the best weapon against unemployment" (MTSSS 2017, 33). In this respect the future looks more encouraging, as international studies (eg OECD 2015) show that Portugal has improved its qualification levels and quality of education outcome indicators.

Portuguese policymakers agree that the transformation of work is a complex problem, and that a complex policy will be required, even while the exact changes that will take place remain uncertain. Industry leaders and, to a certain extent, labour and trade union representatives are on par with common knowledge on the subject. At the same time, and as in other countries, public opinion is split on potential opportunities and risks of automation, fearing it might result in higher long-term unemployment.

Improving the availability of data and resources devoted to research on this subject is of vital importance to allow for better policy action and for public opinion to be better informed. The success of the transition to Industry 4.0 and Work 4.0 will be determined by the strength of the economy and the balance between the economy, society and citizens in the degree of qualification and skills adjustment. "In order to fully understand the challenge, it is necessary to take a systematic view of the aspirations and needs of different actors for managing behavioural change in organizations and in societies" (COTEC Portugal 2018: 1). Public policies should therefore privilege the training of workers, to allow them to benefit from the advancement of the new technologies, and to meet the growing and often unmet demands of current and potential future companies dealing in high-technology sectors.

Despite robots being the apparent stars of this new technological revolution, as always, the human factor will be decisive not only in reaping its fruits, but in moving it forward. In Portugal, this is particularly clear, given the size of the challenges it faces.

## NOTES

1. IPP and the author would like to thank Luís Teles Morais and Elena Garcia Mañes for the comments and support given to this article.

2. These include among others, the Ministry of Education, Ministry of Economy, Ministry of Science, Technology and Higher Education, Ministry of Labour, Solidarity and Social Security, the Institute of Employment and Professional Training (IEFP), engineering colleges, the Coordinating Council of Polytechnic Institutes, Foreign Services and Borders, COTEC Portugal (Business Association for Innovation) and the Agency for Competitiveness and Innovation (IAPMEI).

3. Here, we adopt the definition of youth unemployment used by Eurostat (2018): "Youth unemployment includes all the youth (people between the ages of 15 and 24, inclusive) who are unemployed". Relatedly, the "Youth unemployment rate is the percentage of the unemployed in the age group 15 to 24 years old compared to the total labour force (both employed and unemployed) in that age group".

## REFERENCES

BF Consultores (2017), 'Indústria 4.0 – Estratégia Nacional para a Digitalização da Economia', Lisbon: Ministério da Economia, http://bfconsultores.pt/2017/03/06/industria-4-0-estrategia-nacional-para-a-digitalizacao-da-economia/.

Blanchard, O. and P. Portugal (2017), 'How to Strengthen the Portuguese recovery', Conference Portugal from Here to Where? Macroeconomics Challenges for the Next Decades, Peterson Institute for International Economics and Bank of Portugal.

Carvalho, M. (2016), 'Portugal Atrasado na Corrida Pela Quarta Revolução Industrial', Público, 23 October, https://www.publico.pt/2016/10/23/economia/noticia/portugal-atrasado-na-corrida-pela-quarta-revolucao-industrial-1748443.

CIP (2018), *O Conceito de Reindustrialização, Indústria 4.0 e a Política Industrial Para o Século XXI – o Caso Português*, Lisbon: Confederação Empresarial de Portugal.

Costa, L. F., P. Lains and S. M. Miranda (2016), *An Economic History of Portugal, 1143–2010*, Oxford: Oxford University Press.

COTEC Portugal (2018), *Work 4.0: Rethinking the Human-Technology Alliance*, Lisbon: COTEC Portugal.

Deloitte and Siemens (2015), *The Digital Enterprise: Europe and Portugal: a Journey to the Future*, Lisbon: Deloitte.

Eurostat (2018), *Unemployment rate from 15-24 years*, http://ec.europa. eu/eurostat/tgm/refreshTableAction.do?tab=table&plugin=1&pcode=te psr_wc170&language=en.

Gershenson, D., A. Jaeger and S. Lall (eds) (2016), *From Crisis to Convergence: Charting a Course for Portugal*, Brussels: International Monetary Fund.

IMF (2017), *2017 Article IV Consultation – Press Release: Staff Report; and Statement by the Executive Director for Portugal*, IMF Country Report 17(278), Lisbon: International Monetary Fund, https://www.imf. org/en/Publications/CR/Issues/2017/09/15/Portugal-2017-Article-IV-Consultation-Press-Release-Staff-Report-and-Statement-by-the-45254.

INE (2018), *Estatísticas do Emprego – 4.º trimestre de 2017*, Destaque – Informação à Comunicação Social, Instituto Nacional de Estatística, 7 February.

MTSSS (2017), *Centenário do Ministério do Trabalho, Solidariedade e Segurança Social: Conferência o Futuro do Trabalho*, Lisbon: Ministry of Labour, Solidarity and Social Security, http://ofuturodotrabalho. mtsss.pt/wp-content/uploads/2017/03/portugues.pdf.

OECD (2015), *OECD Education Policy Outlook 2015, Portugal Country Snapshot*, Paris: OECD Publishing.

OECD (2016a), 'How Does Portugal Compare?', in *OECD Employment Outlook 2016*, Paris: OECD Publishing.

OECD (2016b), *OECD Science, Technology and Innovation Outlook 2016*, Paris: OECD Publishing.

OECD (2017), *OECD Employment Outlook 2017*, Paris: OECD Publishing.

Silva, B. (2017), 'Há Falta de Mão-de-obra Qualificada, do Têxtil às Tecnologias', *Dinheiro Vivo*, 16 July, https://www.dinheirovivo.pt/economia/ha-falta-de-mao-de-obra-qualificada-desde-o-textil-as-tecnologias.

Wolter, M., A. Mönnig, M. Hummel, C. Schneemann, E. Weber, G. Zika, R. Helmrich, T. Maier and C. Neuber-Pohl (2015), *Industry 4.0 and the Consequences for Labour Market and Economy – Scenario Calculations in Line with the BIBB-IAB Qualifications and Occupational Field Projections*, Nuremberg: Institute for Employment Research.

# C

## Low digital density EU countries

# FRANCE

## Moving up the digital ranks?

## Enzo Weber

In recent years, we have witnessed intensive discussion across politics, research, business and wider society surrounding the impact of digitalisation on the working world. The development of digital technology is expected to have a profound effect on the use of human labour, with debates about the new world of employment spanning job sustainability, working conditions, labour market regulation and skills training. This chapter is based on a comprehensive study by the Institute for Employment Research (Institut für Arbeitsmarkt und Berufsforschung; IAB) on digitalisation in Europe (Grass and Weber 2016), which we use to examine the example of France, and the impact of digitalisation on country's economy, as well as the political response to recent change.

## INTEGRATION OF TECHNOLOGY AND ECONOMIC EFFECTS

France was placed 16th on the European commission's 2016 Digital Economy and Society Index (DESI) (European Commission 2016a). The commission classifies France as 'falling behind' because of limited progress in connectivity, development of digital skills and the digitisation of public services. In integrating digital applications in business processes in particular, France takes only 18th place among EU states.

In the Index on the Aptitude Effect of Information and Communication Technologies of 2014, according to Evangelista et al. (2014), France has made progress compared with previous years for example in its rational use of information and communications technology (ICT) in business processes, job placement and education and doubling its index rating among all EU countries between 2004 and 2008.

In 2012 the business processes of French companies made moderate use of mobile applications: in 35% of companies, mobile devices were used to surf the internet, in 40% they were used for email, and in 27% they were used to access cloud applications or exchange servers from outside the companies (Eurostat 2016a). France was not among the leading EU countries in 2014 to integrate multifunctional industrial robots, having 120 industrial robots per 10,000 production employees (International Federation of Robotics 2016).

In 2014, the European commission's Joint Research Centre used data from seven countries – including France – to examine whether there were indications of job losses due to ICT for the period 2007–2010 (Pantea, Biagi and Sabadash 2014). The authors argued that none of the countries examined showed developments in ICT to have a significant impact on employment. Although there were isolated variations, the authors concluded these could not be considered replacement phenomena. Contrary to trends in other countries, the broadband coverage of employees in the French manufacturing sector decreased from 44.7% to 38.8% between 2007 and 2010, while the provision of mobile web-enabled devices increased from 24.3% to 37.3% of employees. The percentage of online sales as a percentage of all sales decreased from 15.4% to 11.5% – another unusual trend compared with the other countries studied. In the service sector the proportion of workers with broadband coverage decreased from 57.3% to 48.1%, but the percentage of employees with a web-enabled mobile device increased to 42.4% from 27.3%. Online sales also decreased, from 7.9% to 6.0% of all sales.

In a 2015 report on the future of employment by 2022, government political consulting agency France Stratégie prepared three different scenarios (Aboubadra, Argouarc'h and Bessière 2015). In the so-called 'target scenario', the authors explicitly include the effects of digitalisation and strong technological progress. Here they expect an increase in productivity of 1% per year and GDP growth of 1.8% per year until 2022. The employment rate would then increase by 0.8% per year, with the unemployment rate dropping from around 10% in 2016 to 7% in 2022.

In 2015, the economic advisory council for the French government outlined potential future changes to the economy due to digitalisation, and made proposals on how to support these through regulation (Colin et al. 2015). With reference to the OECD Digital Economy Outlook 2015, the authors criticised that in France the ICT sector only makes up 4.33% of GDP, compared with an OECD average of 5.5%. In 2014, only 63.6% of companies had a website, while the OECD average was already at 76.2% and France had relatively few ICT specialists among its workforce compared with other countries. According to the advisory council, France suffers a lack of venture capital for business formation; while infrastructure conditions – eg broadband access – are actually good, the regulatory systems of the French economy are by no means ready for a digitalised or even internet economy.

In 2014, the French Ministry of Labour assigned the National Council for Digitalisation with the task of discussing several specific problems related to digitalisation. The council argues that large, medium-sized and small European companies would need to work together closely to achieve successful digital transformation (Conseil National Numérique 2016). Compatible cloud systems, communication and computer programmes for networking various components should therefore take priority and possibly also be subsidised. The council advocates giving systematic support for research networks and their projects in the automobile, healthcare, biotechnology and robotics sectors. At the same time patent law and copyright would need to be adapted so as to regulate the commercial use of open-source and open data options appropriately and compensate contributors.

## EDUCATION AND SKILLS

According to the evaluation of the Digital Economy and Society Index of the EU of the population's basic and advanced computer and internet skills, France performs just above average (European Commission 2016a). More than half (57%) of the population have basic computer and internet skills (compared to an EU average of 55%), but IT specialists only make up 3.5% of the population (compared to an EU average of 3.7%) and, according to the European commission, France has not recently made any considerable progress in this area. However, there is an above average number of STEM graduates among all 20–29 year olds (2.3%, compared with an EU average of 1.8%), but there has been stagnant progress in this area in recent years.

Only around 1.8% of all workers in the manufacturing sector had specific ICT knowledge, with France performing below average in 2012 and showing little improvement since 2008 (Lorenzani and Varga 2014). However, the proportion of the entire employable population in France with general computer skills improved between 2006 and 2014. For example, the percentage of people with moderate to advanced computer skills grew from 57% to 69%. There was more moderate progress among the population in attaining internet skills: the percentage of the employable population with moderate to advanced internet skills grew from 29% to 41% between 2007 and 2013, while the percentage with advanced internet skills was practically stagnant. In 2015, 29% of the employable population had few or no digital skills, while the EU average was just 25% (Eurostat 2016b; 2017).

In addition to its recommendations on the economy, the National Council for Digitalisation provided proposals for education. The committee first recommended conducting a systematic analysis on which skills will be needed in which industries in a digitalised economy. Based on the findings, new forms of training should then be developed to promote improved creativity, abstraction and interpretation skills and focus less on selective knowledge. The report included a call for a right to training and continuing education not directly related to the occupation, and encourages employment agencies to take personal skills as well as aptitudes into account more. Individuals should be given more say in which of the acquired skills they want to emphasise most and which they want to improve in the future. To improve early vocational orientation there should also be more interaction between schools and companies.

In 2015, the French labour ministry asked the personnel manager at Orange, Bruno Mettling, to produce a report on the effects of digitalisation on the working environment. Mettling involved both employer and employee representatives in creating the report, which also addressed topics related to education and skills (Mettling 2015). In order to prevent a painful structural change with major turning points for the population, the report found it would be necessary to incorporate continuing education and special training on the use of digital applications and ICT structurally within the educational system.

The association of trade unions, Force Ouvrière, believes past (continuing) education efforts have been inadequate. In a 2015 position paper Force Ouvrière references a survey that shows 79% of French workers feel the current system does not offer adequate training on the use of new technologies (Force Ouvrière 2015). The aforementioned France Stratégie report on employment in 2022 (Aboubadra, Argouarc'h and Bessière 2015) also demands that in light of the massive decline in employment opportunities to be expected for persons with average qualifications, it would be necessary to improve vocational training provisions in all sectors and further facilitate entry-level career opportunities at a relatively high qualification level.

## DIGITALISATION AND CHANGE IN
## THE WORKING ENVIRONMENT

According to France Stratégie, there has been a casualisation of employment since the 1980s – a trend that has grown since the turn of the millennium due to the increasing use and shortening of limited-term employment. In addition, the percentage of workers with multiple parallel jobs has increased. Since the turn of the millennium, the rate of solo self-employed among the employable population has grown again, after being low for years, and their average income has declined compared with previous years (Jolly and Prouet 2016). Furthermore, pressure on workers has increased because of new organisational structures of labour. Thus, more employees than in the past are stating that automated machine processes are setting the pace for work.

Necessities in the workplace, such as prompt response times to customer enquiries, may in some way also protect many workers against automation. At least this is the belief of France Stratégie experts, who argue it is still quite difficult to have these types of tasks performed by machines (Le Ru 2016). The number of jobs in France with these not easily automated requirements grew by 33% from 1998 to 2013, to 9.1 million total. The economic advisory council for the French government primarily considers labourers, office workers, bank employees and salespeople, as well as less creative elite professions such as certain types of physicians or solicitors threatened by digitalisation and learning algorithms (Colin et al. 2015). However, digitalisation would not simply drive the working population to unemployment but could also free them from routine tasks and have them perform new tasks that require more interaction with people or individual requests and cannot be automated.

Whether digitalisation will result in the net elimination or creation of jobs cannot yet be predicted, according to France Stratégie (cf Jolly and Prouet 2016). In the aforementioned technology-driven 'target scenario', its report on employment in 2022 predicts 212,000 new jobs per year in the medium term, compared with 177,000 in the 'central scenario'. From a purely numerical perspective, in this scenario, newly created jobs, in healthcare and nursing for example, would more than compensate for job losses in administration, for example among clerks. These new jobs may not necessarily be filled with the same people, or those with a similar level of qualification. The authors of the France Stratégie report expect the country's labour market to be less intensely polarised than other countries, such as the US, yet they paint a picture of job profiles drifting apart severely (Kalleberg this volume).

The government's economic advisory council also assumes there will be further polarisation of the labour market. This would primarily leave management or creative jobs for well-trained workers and non-routine jobs for the less qualified. The advisory council refers to a clear U-curve, which already shows the thinning of average qualifications in France between 1990 and 2012. However, in a specific report on polarisation, France Stratégie points out that the thesis on technological progress and digitalisation is not the only explanatory pattern for polarisation. Instead, globalisation (by outsourcing jobs to low-wage countries), fewer channels for social partners to negotiate, deregulation and the transformation of France into a service economy are often listed as the key drivers. France is better equipped, particularly in its social dialogue and regulation, than perhaps the US, and may therefore be able to prevent excessive and uncontrolled polarisation.

The Mettling report assumes that in a few years a high percentage of workers will be working on a mobile basis. Furthermore, digitalisation will result in a massive change towards collaborating and cooperating more, which could lead companies to break with previous rigid and hierarchical forms of control and reporting.

According to the French government's economic advisory council, working modes would change considerably in a digitalised economy. For example, jobs for the low-qualified would rather be offered in the form of freelance work, while digitalisation would facilitate coordination between client and external service providers as solo self-employed. Workers would have the advantage of being able to hold several parallel jobs at once. However, it would be extremely difficult for social security systems or even lending criteria to continue to be completely based on employment, and these systems would need to change. The council specifically calls for taxation systems to improve for the solo self-employed to facilitate transitions between different forms of work, a challenge the National Council for Digitalisation also shares in its aforementioned report. The council generally advocates rediscussing social security and collective representation for the self-employed.

Unions such as Force Ouvrière warn that people could easily be degraded to being servants of technology. The unionists call not to create new forms of contract or employment for the man-machine interaction to prevent degrading people in this system and to maintain securities for workers. Force Ouvrière also stresses that labour in fully automated processes, in some cases merely managing emergencies, is not a trivial matter because of the psychological stress it entails. Force Ouvrière also demands politicians set tight limits for employers over how much they are allowed to monitor employees with the available technologies (Force Ouvrière 2015).

The National Council for Digitalisation also wants to see a focus on the human factor by including criteria such as average employee health in the assessment of the performance of management. Workers should further be granted extended leave or part-time working arrangements in certain situations, for example to undertake research, to participate in continuing education, to attend to social commitments, to form a business, or to allow for professional advancement and adjustment to new challenges. The council further sees the need to adapt employment agencies, which should adjust to companies' changing forms of employment and contract. The council recommends promoting contracts for so-called '*travail en temps partagé*', which have existed in France since 2005, in order to increase flexibilisation within companies. These allow a worker to work simultaneously for several companies or institutions through a contract with a group of employers – and to be paid through the group.

The members of the council also demand adding more data and more reliable information to discussions on alternative forms of social security financing, such as unconditional basic income. A feasibility study should first be conducted on this with a detailed analysis of the economic effects, potential labour displacement and the impact on the supply of labour when introducing a basic income.

The union Confédération française démocratique du travail stresses that technological change could only be used optimally if employees could make a conscious decision on digitalisation and the use of digital applications. There would still need to be the option to also decide against the use of modern technology in some situations. Furthermore, the position of the union is that technology used in the workplace would need to be developed with much greater involvement from the workers, so they will then be able to use this technology to its full potential. Force Ouvrière demands new regulations to limit availability and to set boundaries between work and family time, and stresses that digitalisation should not result in massive crowdsourcing of work with all contractors being responsible for themselves (Degryse 2016). Mettling was not quite as critical on this point, but he also warned: one should contemplate, now, how to incorporate crowdworking and voluntary work in economic and social processes better than in the past without unlegislated areas arising to the detriment of workers or other companies.

Force Ouvrière fears more flexible and decentralised 'normal' employment to hold disadvantages for the working population. Although it recognises the advantages for employees in these forms of work, it also refers to studies that state telecommuters have to manage higher workloads and increasingly to work at night and on weekends. There would need to be safe zones without digital availability; Force Ouvrière touches on the right to digital disconnection.

The Mettling report recommends that working hours and workloads should be modified for digital jobs. With uncharacteristic and increasing contractual relationships and employment or work modes, one can no longer only use fixed working hours in calculations. Instead, the workload also needs to be included. A disconnection 'duty' should be added to the right to disconnection, including workers at all levels learning to use media more deliberately – with companies offering training on this. Telecommuters and mobile workers should be protected against accidents at work. The Mettling report further calls for the planned personal activity account to be used to equip each worker with a certain base of rights, based on their social contributions, which they would then not lose when switching between forms of employment.

## POLITICAL AND PUBLIC-PRIVATE MEASURES

In 2017, the so-called personal activity account (*compte personnel d'activité*; CPA) was launched for every French citizen aged 16 and over. This account is intended to prevent breaches in the rights of the employable, for example when changing from being employed to solo self-employment or other forms of employment. People can collect points in their account, for example through work activity, and government institutions can award points. The points can be used for various purposes, for example to set towards educational activities, financial assistance for business formation, or leave for family obligations or social commitments. The points are not lost if a person's employment status changes.

Even before the CPA, in 2015 the personal education account and the personal account to prevent occupational hazards entered into force, both of which are also specified in the discussion on changes in the digitalised working environment. Employees can use the latter to collect points for exposure to hazards throughout their working life and then use these for specific qualifications for less hazardous positions within the company, shorter working hours or early retirement.

As of 2016, programmes are being implemented in primary and secondary schools – previously, there were only optional courses at the secondary level in specific schools' technical education groups. Upper-level secondary school students can choose a subject called exploring computer sciences and digital work (*enseignement d'exploration d'informatique et de création numérique*). However, according to a European Schoolnet report, teachers are not provided with training to master the skills needed for the new course through the Ministry of Education (Balanskat and Engelhardt 2015).

In 2013 the Ministry of Education, in line with the EU Grand Coalition for Digital Jobs, wanted to create an action plan for how to draw more young people to ICT degree programmes and jobs. That year, there was to be an agreement between companies and the Ministry of Labour on ICT training for the employed or those entering the workforce. Both measures combined were to prepare 3,000 people per year for digital jobs, on top of those already in the B2i training and certification programme for youth and the C2i programme for adults, which both teach digital skills.

The so-called Grand École du Numérique is committed to introducing uneducated and low-qualified people to ICT jobs. This is not a physical educational institution, but rather a construct to support educational institutions and companies in educational projects and initiatives (Grande École du Numérique 2016).

Most recently, a mission statement from President Macron outlined 15 key reforms on digitalisation, including the promotion of investments in start ups, the improvement of internet coverage and the extension of education on digital competencies in schools and professional training (Paquette 2017). Digitising governmental services in general constitutes a strong focus of the Macron administration and is to receive significant funding (Rolland 2017). In addition the Code du Travail (labour legislation), which was reformed in 2017 regarding aspects of collective bargaining in small companies, for example, will be made available online in an understandable and accessible format by 2020 (Absalon 2017; Belouezzane 2017). The system of professional training will be newly regulated along several lines, such as setting up a flexible training contract, a new national standard of minimum remuneration, fiscal support by a single instrument, a strengthened role of industry in the design of vocational education programmes, a business-led certification of apprenticeship, better tailored professional development support to workers, additional finance for the personal training account as well as simplified administration of and access to training. However, the reform proposal has also been criticised for insufficiently addressing digital skills (Sigere 2017).

## REFERENCES

Aboubadra, S., J. Argouarc'h and S. Bessière (2015), *Les métiers en 2022*, Paris: France Stratégie, http://www.strategie.gouv.fr/sites/strategie.gouv.fr/files/atoms/files/fs_rapport_metiers_en_2022_27042015_final.pdf.

Absalon, J. (2017), 'Code du travail numérique: à quoi cela v-a-t'il servir?', Radio Télévision Luxembourg (RTL), 31 August, http://www.rtl.fr/actu/societe-faits-divers/code-du-travail-numerique-a-quoi-cela-va-t-il-servir-7789912733.

Balanskat and Engelhardt (2015), 'Computing our future: Computer programming and coding. Priorities, school curricula and initiatives across Europe', Brussels: European Schoolnet, http://fcl.eun.org/documents/10180/14689/Computing+our+future_final.pdf/746e36b1-e1a6-4bf1-8105-ea27c0d2bbe0.

Belouezzane, S. (2017), 'Réforme du code du travail: ce que contiennent les ordonnances', *Le Monde*, 31 August, http://www.lemonde.fr/politique/article/2017/08/31/reforme-du-code-du-travail-ce-que-contiennent-les-ordonnances_5179082_823448.html.

Colin, N., A. Landier, P. Mohnen and A. Perrot (2015), 'Economie numérique', *Les notes du conseil d'analyse économique*, 26, October.

Conseil National Numérique (2016), 'Travail emploi numerique: les nouvelles trajectores', Paris: Conseil National Numérique.

Degryse, C. (2016) 'Digitalisation of the economy and its impact on labour markets', *ETUI Working Paper* 2016.02, Brussels: ETUI.

European Commission (2016a), 'The Digital Economy and Society Index, Scoreboard France', Brussels: European Commission.

Eurostat (2016a) 'Mobile Connection to Internet', eurostat: Statistics Explained, http://ec.europa.eu/eurostat/statistics-explained/index.php/Mobile_connection_to_internet.

Eurostat (2016b) 'Internet access and use statistics - households and individuals', eurostat: Statistics Explained, http://ec.europa.eu/eurostat/statistics-explained/index.php/Internet_access_and_use_statistics_-_households_and_individuals.

Eurostat (2017) 'Digital economy and digital society statistics at regional level', eurostat: Statistics Explained, http://ec.europa.eu/eurostat/statistics-explained/index.php/Digital_economy_and_digital_society_statistics_at_regional_level.

Evangelista R., Guerrieri P. and Meliciani V. (2014), Taylor and Francis, 'The economic impact of digital technologies in Europe', https://www.tandfonline.com/doi/abs/10.1080/10438599.2014.918438

Force Ouvrière (2015), 'L'impact du numérique sur le travail: ni catastrophisme, ni angelisme, les réflexions de Force Ouvrière s'inscrivent dans le realisme', Réflexions de Force Ouvrière.

Grande École du Numérique (2016), 'Qu´est-ce que la Grande École du Numérique?', press release, https://www.grandeecolenumerique.fr/2016/03/grande-ecole-numerique/.

Grass, K. and E. Weber (2016), *EU 4.0 – the Debate on Digitalisation and the Labour Market in Europe*, IAB Discussion Paper 39.

International Federation of Robotics (2016), *International World Robotics Report 2016*, Frankfurt: International Federation of Robotics, https://ifr.org/ifr-press-releases/news/world-robotics-report-2016.

Jolly, C. and E. Prouet (2016), *L'avenir du travail: quelles redéfinitions de l'emploi, des statuts et des protections?*, Paris: France Stratégie.

Le Ru, N. (2016), 'L'effet de l'automatisation sur l'emploi: ce qu'on sait et ce qu'on ignore', La note d´analyse 49, Paris: France Stratégie.

Lorenzani D. and Varga J. (2014), 'The economic impact of digital structural reforms', Economic Papers 429, European commission http://ec.europa.eu/economy_finance/publications/economic_paper/2014/pdf/ecp529_en.pdf

Mettling, B. (2015), *Transformation numérique et vie au travail*, Paris, http://www.ladocumentationfrancaise.fr/var/storage/rapports-publics/154000646.pdf.

Pantea, S., F. Biagi and A. Sabadash (2014), *Are ICT Displacing Workers? Evidence from Seven European Countries*, JRC Technical Report, https://ec.europa.eu/jrc/sites/jrcsh/files/JRC91122_ICT_displacing_workers.pdf.

Paquette, E. (2017), 'Numérique: les 15 réformes de Macron', *L'Express*, 19 July, https://www.lexpress.fr/actualite/politique/numerique-les-15-reformes-de-macron_1928518.html.

Rolland, S. (2017), 'L'État 100% numérique de Macron coûtera 9,3 milliards d'euros', *La Tribune*, 26 September, https://www.latribune.fr/economie/france/l-etat-100-numerique-de-macron-coutera-9-3-milliards-d-euros-751606.html.

Sigere, S. (2017), 'The Future of Work: a New Deal for Skills in France?', London: Policy Network, 21 November, http://policynetwork.org/opinion/the-future-of-work-a-new-deal-for-skills-in-france/.

# CENTRAL AND EASTERN EUROPE

## *Raising living standards through innovation-driven growth*

## Jan Drahokoupil

The dependent nature of industrialisation and a weak innovation base has made central and eastern Europe vulnerable to economic restructuring related to the introduction of new technologies. An effective innovation policy requires an improvement of the broader institutional environment. A shift to an innovation-driven growth model is needed to sustain a further convergence of living standards between old and new EU member states. This would require a break with the current paradigm, which is based largely on competition based on cost efficiency.

## CENTRAL AND EASTERN EUROPE: A SECOND-RANK EUROPEAN INDUSTRIAL BASE

Framing much of the debate on the impact of the use of digital technologies on manufacturing and its related support services, the concept of Industry 4.0 comes from the discussion in Germany around the future prospects for that country's industrial base. Germany is indeed Europe's manufacturing hub, but there is actually a higher share of industry in terms of value-added and employment in the group of central and eastern European (CEE) countries – including Czechia, Hungary, Poland, Slovakia and Slovenia – than in the supposed European manufacturing power house.[1] The CEE region is thus exposed to possible restructuring that may be induced by the introduction of digital technologies to an even greater extent than is the case in Germany. At the same time, the impact will be different in the CEE countries from elsewhere in Europe, given the region's specific, and somewhat second rank, position in global and regional value chains. Their intermediate-level manufacturing specialisation makes the CEE countries more vulnerable to the restructuring that will be induced by automation and the adoption of digitalisation technologies. At the same time, Industry 4.0 technologies provide an opportunity to upgrade the CEE countries' position and hence to revive the process of catching up with western Europe. However, the CEE bloc needs to address its weak learning and innovation infrastructure to be able to seize the opportunity that the fourth industrial revolution presents.

## DEPENDENCE ON FOREIGN DIRECT INVESTMENT

After much of the industrial base that had been inherited from the Soviet Union collapsed in the early 1990s, the CEE countries were reindustrialised by foreign investors who acquired or inherited firms and, in most cases, through the establishment of greenfield manufacturing sites (Drahokoupil 2008; Myant and Drahokoupil 2010). Taking off in the run up to EU enlargement, the inflows of foreign direct investment (FDI) fuelled rapid growth in the region. Much investment was driven by the exploitation of lower labour costs and the modernisation introduced by FDI failed to develop local innovation systems. Instead, the region relied on the transfer of technology and knowhow through the networks of multinational corporations (Galgóczi, Drahokoupil and Bernaciak 2015). Dependent reindustrialisation thus gave rise to a group of second-rank economies with low research and development (R&D) intensity. In 2015, total R&D spending accounted for 2% of GDP in Czechia, 1.4% in Hungary and for just 1–1.2% in Poland and Slovakia, while it reached 2.9% in Germany.[2]

Dualised economies have emerged, with highly productive, often foreign-controlled firms, paying higher wages, but employing fewer people than domestic firms with less complex products and often in a position of second-tier suppliers to multinationals (Galgóczi, Drahokoupil and Bernaciak 2015). Multinational corporation affiliates also exhibit much higher levels of R&D spending and innovation intensity (Knell 2017). There appears to be little or no growth in domestic R&D activity in most of these countries (although Poland fares better on this indicator). While typically exhibiting superior performance to domestic firms, the local subsidiaries of multinational corporations are themselves in a dependent position in the value chains. These subsidiaries often specialise in activities with low R&D intensity and much of the R&D that does occur is only secondary, such as adapting products for local markets. Subsidiaries have typically been able to upgrade and thus improve employment quality and wages, but upgrading was often not accompanied by an improvement in the value captured by the affiliates (Szalavetz 2015).

Nevertheless, FDI inflows drove a dynamic process of catching up with the EU15 that characterised much of the 2000s (Hunya 2015). The crisis of 2008 was a breaking point. Foreign direct investment inflows stopped and convergence in many CEE countries actually reversed. CEE countries started to grow again in 2013, but the process of convergence has lost its momentum. FDI picked up again, particularly in Czechia and Slovakia, but EU structural fund transfers replaced FDI as the main source of external investment financing for the CEE countries (Hunya, 2017).

## WHY HAS THE FDI-DRIVEN CONVERGENCE DISAPPOINTED?

The FDI-dependent economic model allowed CEE countries to reach output levels that are comparable to that of southern Europe. By 2017, Czechia has reached 84% of EU15 GDP, if differences in price levels are adjusted for purchasing power parity; Slovakia was at 72%, Poland at 66% and Hungary at 64%.[3] The wealthiest of the group thus has well exceeded the level of Portugal (72%) and almost reached the level of Spain (86%). However, capital outflows make actual incomes of these countries somewhat poorer. This is most pronounced in Czechia where the 2016 gross national income was at 78% of EU15, while the Spanish gross national income was almost identical to its GDP (all measured in purchasing power parity).

High profit repatriation, which lowers national incomes, is a dominant characteristic of the FDI-dependent model. In 2016, such capital outflows exceeded 8% of GDP in the Czech Republic in 2016, a value that is high by regional standards. The general difficulty of retaining the value added was expressed also in the low share of wages in national income. Wage convergence thus lagged well behind economic performance. The convergence achievement is, indeed, even less impressive if incomes of workers are compared (see Drahokoupil and Piasna 2017). For instance, in 2017 GDP in the Czech Republic, adjusted for differences in price levels, reached 74% of the German level, but compensation per employee was only about 68% of German levels (adjusted for price differences). The levels in Slovakia, Poland and Hungary were lower, at 64%, 62% and 56% of Germany compensation respectively.[4] There were large wage increases in 2016 and 2017, but these came after a lost decade, and the convergence trend effectively stalled after the crises of 2008.

The wage gap is much wider if measured in nominal terms. In 2017, compensation in Czechia was at 42% of the German level, Slovakia at 40%, Poland at 33%, and Hungary at 31%. While workers face different price levels, particularly for services, a full convergence in price levels would thus also require convergence in real earnings. The price differences for some goods are already low or absent altogether, implying differences in consumption levels that are commensurate with nominal wage differences. Moreover, low prices lead to lower incomes from exported goods and services. In principle, higher prices could harm regional competitiveness, but the evidence suggests that recent wage increases did not affect FDI inflows and export performance in the region (Galgóczi, Drahokoupil and Bernaciak 2015).

Many policymakers thus had second thoughts about the developmental prospects of the FDI-based economic model. In this context, Hungary and Poland have somewhat reconsidered their stance towards FDI, aiming to promote national companies at the expense of foreign investors in the service sectors (Sass 2017). Hungary was most active in this respect, discriminating against foreign investors through sector-specific regulations and taxes that targeted foreign companies that are active in the financial, retail, media and energy markets. However, the approach to investors in export-oriented industrial sectors has not changed in any of the CEE countries. The dependence on multinational corporations thus remains the defining feature of industrial structures in them.

## VULNERABILITIES: WEAK INNOVATION, SKILLS COMPOSITION AND VALUE CHAIN STATUS

The dualised economies with weak innovative performance seem to be a weak basis for reviving a process of convergence that would allow the region to catch up with the west, particularly as far as living standards are concerned. What is more, the second-rank integration in the international value chains makes the region more vulnerable to restructuring through digitalisation and automation.

First, in the last two decades, the countries managed to upgrade the skill composition of jobs through a growth in non-routine cognitive tasks at work, but this was accompanied by an increase in routine cognitive components of jobs, a trend that distinguishes the

CEE region from the advanced economies. Middle-skilled men in the manufacturing sectors and middle-skilled women in the service sectors thus jointly represented 33% of workers in the region in the early 2000s (Keister and Lewandowski 2017). A technology-induced reduction in the demand for routine work would thus affect a large fraction of workers and increase wage inequality in the region. The 2016 OECD assessment of the risk of job loss indeed ranked Czechia and Slovakia as countries most affected by the risk of job losses due to automation, with over 45% of workers in jobs at high and medium risk of automation (Arntz, Gregory and Zierahn 2016; see also Arnold et al. this volume).

Second, automation may represent a threat to the intermediate-level specialisation of the region in the manufacturing activities that provide labour input to international production networks. Industry 4.0 technologies may undermine prior upgrading and innovation achievements as they could become digitalised (eg in production planning, tooling and scheduling) and also undermine future upgrading opportunities in the field of process development (Szalavetz 2017). That would undermine the value capture and retention potential of multinational corporations affiliates in the region. However, the emergence of new manufacturing technologies could even provide incentives for multinational corporations to consolidate manufacturing activities and to reshore the intermediate tasks outside the region.

## DIGITALISATION AS AN OPPORTUNITY

At the same time, digitalisation represents also an opportunity for the region. As demonstrated by Szalavetz (2017) through case studies of multinational corporation manufacturing subsidiaries in Hungary, Industry 4.0 technology adaptation can allow the affiliates to upgrade existing manufacturing facilities, develop 'Industrialisation 4.0'-related competences, and thus benefit from a possible reconfiguration and consolidation of value chains. However, as such upgrading achievements go hand in hand with higher skills requirements, they are necessarily conditional on the availability of skills (Szalavetz, 2017). The case studies indeed showed that securing access to skilled workers was the main challenge and potential constraint in seizing the upgrading opportunities involved in the adoption of digital technologies.

The weaknesses in the skills and innovation systems, and the institutions that underpin them, thus may limit the extent to which these countries can seize the upgrading opportunities offered by Industry 4.0 technologies. There are some promising trends in certain sectors, such as software development, but the overall innovation capacity appears to be relatively weak. Apart from the low levels of R&D (which apply also to business R&D), the region also lags behind in other indicators of innovation capacity, including in the weak links that exist between science and business, the barriers to knowledge diffusion and learning processes that exist, and the insufficient development of digital skills in the workforce (Weresa 2017).

## KEY POLICY CHALLENGES: INNOVATION RATHER THAN CHEAP LABOUR

The key policy challenge for the CEE countries is to create a framework for achieving competitiveness through innovation rather than merely through low labour costs. Given the size of the wage gap, there is scope for wage increases without harming the competitiveness of the countries. Trade unions, particularly in Czechia, have successfully politicised the unsatisfying progress in convergence that has occurred, and have actively campaigned for an 'end to cheap labour' (see Myant and Drahokoupil 2010). Political parties, including the Czech social democrats and the far-right party in Hungary, have taken this up across the spectrum. Employers, as well as the European Commission, have typically responded with the unconvincing argument that any wage increases should not exceed productivity improvements. In any case, in 2016–2017 there were substantial wage increases in many countries, in the context of tight labour markets and the dynamic economic growth that came in that period.

However, economic fundamentals need to change in order for the CEE countries to achieve sustainable convergence in living standards. Addressing the low innovation capacity and skill basis is also key to averting the threats that automation and Industry 4.0 presents for jobs and industrial investment in the region. Improving the learning and innovation infrastructure is also necessary for allowing the companies in the region to take advantage of the opportunities that Industry 4.0 presents.

Governments have discussed tackling digitalisation and supporting a shift to innovation-driven growth across the region. Trade unions had an important role to play putting the challenges of Industry 4.0 on the agenda, particularly in the countries where social dialogue plays an important role (see Jolly this volume). For instance, Czech trade unions have called for a shortening of the working week, and the introduction of a framework for lifelong learning and worker co-determination at company level.

At this point, however, there are scant signs of major changes in the actual policies that are being pursued. The investment support seems to be stuck in the paradigm that encourages new investment through subsidies, with little effective support for the upgrading of existing operations and technological spillovers between foreign and domestic firms (Szent-Iványi 2017). A substantial share of EU cohesion funds was actually earmarked for innovation, but the CEE countries used these funds mainly to investment in hardware and infrastructure rather than enhance their innovation capacity (Ferry 2017).

The conventional advice includes reforming the education and science sectors, increasing the role of development banks, supporting entrepreneurship, and establishing start ups through seed funding and venture capital, boosting business R&D, investing in knowledge diffusion and cluster development, and strengthening local supplier networks around foreign investments (see Kenny and Zysman this volume). However, designing an effective innovation policy is not an easy task as it requires also an improvement of the broader institutional environment. On their own, none of the policies can work as a silver bullet. Building innovation capacity involves a cumulative, path-dependent series of activities and strategies for capacity development and network building. It can only be successful if the paradigm of competing through lower costs is finally left behind.

## NOTES

1. See Eurostat (online data code: nama_10_a10; nama_10_a10_e), available at: http://ec.europa.eu/eurostat/data/database.
2. See Eurostat (online data code: tsdec320), available at: http://ec.europa.eu/eurostat/data/database.
3. Compare macro-economic database AMECO, European Commission (online code: HVGDPR), available at: http://ec.europa.eu/economy_finance/ameco/user/serie/SelectSerie.cfm.
4. Compare macro-economic database AMECO, European Commission (online code: HWCDW), available at: http://ec.europa.eu/economy_finance/ameco/user/serie/SelectSerie.cfm.

## REFERENCES

Arntz, M., T. Gregory and U. Ziehran (2016), *The Risk of Automation for Jobs in OECD Countries: a Comparative Analysis*, Social, Employment and Migration Working Paper 189, Paris: OECD.

Drahokoupil, J. (2008), *Globalization and the State in Central and Eastern Europe: the Politics of Foreign Direct Investment*, London: Routledge.

Drahokoupil, J. and A. Piasna (2017), *What Drives Wage Gaps in Europe?*, ETUI Working Paper 04, Brussels: European Trade Union Institute.

Ferry, M. (2017), 'The Role of EU Funds in Enhancing the Development Potential of CEE Economies', in B. Galgóczi and J. Drahokoupil (eds), *Condemned to be Left Behind? Can Central and Eastern Europe Emerge from its Low-wage Model?*, 153–70, Brussels: European Trade Union Institute.

Galgóczi, B., J. Drahokoupil and M. Bernaciak (eds) (2015), *Foreign Investment in Eastern and Southern Europe after 2008: Still a Lever of Growth?*, Brussels: European Trade Union Institute.

Hunya, G. (2015), 'Mapping Flows and Patterns of Foreign Direct Investment in Central and Eastern Europe, Greece and Portugal During the Crisis', in B. Galgóczi, J. Drahokoupil and M. Bernaciak (eds), *Foreign*

*Investment in Eastern and Southern Europe after 2008: Still a Lever of Growth?*, 37–69, Brussels: European Trade Union Institute.

Hunya, G. (2017), 'Is a Live Dog Better than a Dead Lion? Seeking Alternative Growth Engines in the Visegrad Countries', in B. Galgóczi and J. Drahokoupil (eds), *Condemned to be Left Behind? Can Central and Eastern Europe Emerge from its Low-wage Model?*, 25–46, Brussels: European Trade Union Institute.

Keister, R. and P. Lewandowski (2017), 'A Routine Transition in the Digital Era? The Rise of Routine Work in Central and Eastern Europe', *Transfer: European Review of Labour and Research*, 23(3): 263–79.

Knell, M. (2017), 'R&D Internationalisation and Local Innovation in the Visegrad Group after the FDI peak', in B. Galgóczi and J. Drahokoupil (eds), *Condemned to be Left Behind? Can Central and Eastern Europe Emerge from its Low-wage Model?*, 111–31, Brussels: European Trade Union Institute.

Myant, M. and Jan Drahokoupil (2010), *Transition Economies: Political Economy in Russia, Eastern Europe, and Central Asia*, Hoboken, New Jersey: Wiley-Blackwell.

Sass, M. (2017), 'Is a Live Dog Better than a Dead Lion? Seeking Alternative Growth Engines in the Visegrad Countries', in B. Galgóczi and J. Drahokoupil (eds), *Condemned to be Left Behind? Can Central and Eastern Europe Emerge from its Low-wage Model?*, 47–79, Brussels: European Trade Union Institute.

Szalavetz, A. (2015), 'Upgrading and Value Capture in Global Value Chains – More Complex than What the Smile-curve Suggests', in B. Szent-Iványi (ed.), *FDI to Central and Eastern Europe in the New Millenium*, Vienna: Wiener Verlag für Sozialforschung.

Szalavetz, A. (2017), 'Industry 4.0 in "Factory Economies"', in B. Galgóczi and J. Drahokoupil (eds), *Condemned to be Left Behind? Can Central and Eastern Europe Emerge from its Low-wage Model?*, 133–52, Brussels: European Trade Union Institute.

Szent-Iványi, B. (2017), 'Investment Promotion in the Visegrad Four Countries: Post-FDI Challenges', in B. Galgóczi and J. Drahokoupil (eds), *Condemned to be Left Behind? Can Central and Eastern Europe Emerge from its Low-wage Model?*, 171–87, Brussels: European Trade Union Institute.

Weresa, M. A. (2017), 'Innovation, Human Capital and Competitiveness in Central and Eastern Europe with Regard to the Challenges of a Digital Economy', in B. Galgóczi and J. Drahokoupil (eds), *Condemned to be Left Behind? Can Central and Eastern Europe Emerge from its Low-wage Model?*, 81–109, Brussels: European Trade Union Institute.

# SLOVENIA

## *Grassroots trade unions and the empowerment of the young*

## Aleksandra Kanjuo Mrčela

The fourth industrial revolution is a contested concept that encompasses the advancements in digital technology and the related changes to working and living conditions that have come about since the beginning of the 21st century. Many commentators view new technologies with optimism, and as potentially innovative instruments for positive social change (see Atkinson this volume). Other commentators view new technologies with pessimism, and as a primary cause of social decay. In this essay I will comment on the nature of the contemporary changes to work and to people's lives that has been induced by these changes, and will argue that, contrary to the widely held view of technological change as evolving and influencing society through an inevitable logic of its own, these changes can only be understood as being embedded in the existing social and political context in which they are found.

We will reflect on these changes in an environment that, aside from technological developments, has undergone other substantial change over the last decades. Slovenia is one of the European countries that recently experienced multiple economic and political restructurings, having re-established a capitalist economy, and having introduced multiparty political democracy since gaining political independence in 1991. These changes have placed major demands on Slovenian society, which has had various far-reaching consequences for the different social groups in the country. This has prepared the ground for the specific set of challenges and opportunities that are now faced by Slovenian society regarding the transformation of working and living conditions in the context of the fourth industrial revolution.

## NEW TECHNOLOGIES ARE NOT AUTOMATICALLY BETTER

Contemporary scientific and technological advancements are impressive. Technological innovations are expected to alter radically the performance of education, work, transport and other activities as well as the organisation of health, social security and other systems that are of the utmost important for our lives. Numerous studies now predict that computerisation jeopardises a great deal of existing jobs and that a large proportion of activities currently being performed by workers could already be automatised (see Arnold et al. this volume). Experts in the field expect that artificial intelligence will outperform humans in the next decades, not only in some less demanding tasks (such as driving or performing sales work) but also in writing fiction and non-fiction text, in translation services, and in performing demanding, highly skilled professional work, such as that undertaken by surgeons (Grace et al., 2017; see Petropoulos this volume). Still, as has been the case many times before in history, it is very probable that the predicted changes will be less radical than this, and it remains difficult to foresee all the potential positive and negative consequences that may come to pass for individuals and societies. However, it is almost certain that new technologies will not produce inherently good or bad social results automatically. The impact of new technologies will depend on how they are adopted, which is determined by factors including social norms, expectations and political decisions, as we shall see (see Hofheinz this volume).

In his contribution to the debate around the future of work in the middle of the 20th century, Daniel Bell (1974) argued that services would replace manufacturing in the post-industrial society and that as a consequence, workplaces would be humanised as people would work with people and not just with machines, and that relations between people would be based on bargaining and not conflict. That did not come to pass. Harry Braverman's (1998) estimation that new technologies would not bring any improvement as long as the prevailing production relations remained unchanged. Thus, the notion of work as being primarily profit-oriented proved to be a more accurate prediction. Technological advancements in the past changed living and working conditions only in as much as social relations and norms allowed. To explore this, we can look at the case of the length of paid and unpaid work.

Over recent decades, new technologies have provided us with productivity gains that could have been used to shorten working hours and to improve the working and living standards of workers. Instead, higher rates of productivity emerged alongside higher rates of unemployment, and many of those in employment were required to work even more hours than before. The growing culture of working longer hours seems to be in direct conflict with the potential benefits that are presented by new technologies. Jeremy Rifkin's (1995) analysis points to the fact that the beneficiaries of the productivity gains yielded by technological advancements were shareholders and not workers. Rifkin proposed a new social contract that would affirm the notion of a globalised social economy in which workers would work shorter hours, and where productivity gains provided benefits, not for shareholders, but for society. Historical analysis shows that shorter or longer working hours are not anything to do with technological advancement, but rather are shaped by the strength of organised labour and the bargaining power of workers (or the lack thereof).

The proliferation and widespread use of household appliances in the last century provided for a decreasing burden of unpaid household work, which had primarily fallen on the shoulders of women. However, in spite of this, a combination of rising expectations regarding the nature and standards of household chores (eg regarding cooking and cleaning) and the persistence of the traditional gendered division of labour caused further overburdening of women with domestic responsibilities. It seems that the style of living and the strength of gender equality norms (or the lack thereof) provides for the scope and distribution of unpaid household work, rather than this being anything to do with technological advancement.

## NEW TECHNOLOGIES ARE NOT RESPONSIBLE FOR POOR JOB QUALITY

Technological innovations themselves are socially conditioned and depend primarily on political and social decisions that are made to enable them. For example, we can see today that more and more jobs are mediated by web platforms (see Schor this volume). Workers who perform these jobs enjoy some time and place flexibility, but they also experience many serious problems caused by the insecure nature of their employment, and the lack of labour standards and protectionism, to name a few. The gig economy and crowdsourcing have not flourished because web platforms have enabled them, but because neoliberal discourse has enabled web platforms to function.

Neoliberalism was successful in naturalising the existence of poorer quality jobs. That is why we can observe a paradox: in the time of the glorification of knowledge and the development of advanced digital and technological advancements at work over recent decades, many young, highly educated and digitally competent people all over the world are members of the precariat – the workers who are in the weakest position in the labour markets.

So, instead of expecting too much from digitalisation, we should find the best ways to restore social expectations and the strength of social forces that are the basis for more decent jobs.

## CHANGES IN WORK AND WELFARE IN SLOVENIA IN THE TIME OF DIGITAL REVOLUTION

The latest phase of the digital revolution has been accompanied by other important shifts in Slovenian society. The last 30 years of political and economic turmoil provided Slovenia with valuable experience in managing change. The political and economic reforms that precipitated the establishment of Slovenian state independence were socially and politically demanding. The initial widespread enthusiasm for the new state of affairs in the 1990s was followed by economic and financial crisis, political turmoil, a weakening of previously strong social actors, including trade unions and political parties, and rising dissatisfaction and concerns among the citizenry with the course of change over the last two decades (Stanojević, Mrčela and Breznik, 2016). While strong social dialogue was an important instrument for establishing a consensus that was needed in a time of change, the latest developments reflect a rise of conflictual relations in Slovenia and the country's position in the European and global economy.

At the same time, according to the Digital Economy and Society Index (European Commission 2017), the Republic of Slovenia ranks 17th in the EU and there are ambitious plans on how to improve the country's position in this ranking (MPA 2017). A high degree of digital literacy persists among the population and especially among the youngest Slovenians. According to the EU Kids Online survey, the average index of digital literacy of children aged between 11 and 16 in 25 European countries is 3.1, while Slovenian children are in second place with 4.4 just after children in Finland with 4.6 (RIS 2017).

The younger generations in Slovenia is very well educated and highly digitally literate, which renders them both equipped for, and involved in, digitalisation. However, recent analyses show that young people are especially vulnerable in the labour market, and they are overrepresented in all forms of precarious work (Ignjatović and Mrčela 2016). In 2015, the proportion of young people who were employed for a limited period of time in Slovenia was the highest in

Europe. Younger workers are the cohort that are most at risk of poverty among employed persons in Slovenia. Ultimately, young people now often have limited experience of what had become regarded as the standard forms of employment since the second world war. The uncertainty and exploitation of young people – who often have a lot of knowledge and skills, but cannot obtain what previous generations of workers had regarded as the appropriate remuneration for their work – is particularly characteristic of young 'freelancers' who are forced into risky working arrangements, often supported by new technologies and digital platforms. This generation is experiencing the consequences of ever more individualisation in our societies, flexible employment and competition in the labour market where only the fittest can survive. This is the generation which, if the growth of precariousness does not relent, will in older age be in a significantly worse position than the elderly today.

The precarious position of the younger generation is essentially universal. It remains to be seen how a specific combination of the legacy of the socialist economic system based on the ideology of egalitarianism and solidarity on the one hand, and the only recently embraced neoliberal logic, based on the necessity of privatisation, free markets and competition on the other, will influence the position of young workers in Slovenia. As a reaction to the challenges they face, young people in Slovenia have established a representative association for young workers, which is not a branch of an established professional trade union, but rather exclusively engages and mobilises young people. According to information available to us, this is a unique example in Europe. This organisation is a mixture of a trade union and a social movement and has a very important discursive and symbolic meaning. After decades of distrust and detachment of young people from trade unions, young people are getting organised, and young activists use this form of organisation to partake in collective action (Ignjatović and Mrčela 2016).

Naomi Klein (2017) in her newest analysis of successful strategies for fighting neoliberal politics invests hope in the new social movements that cherish alternative modes of operating based on respect for people, cooperation and the environment. Maybe the ways that young workers in Slovenia are organising and empowering their actions could be seen as an example of this.

## FOURTH REVOLUTION?

Using Wallerstein's understanding of revolutions as involving planet-wide transformations of political common sense, the new movements' activists like Graeber (2013) see this new political common sense as being organised around the expansion of "the zones of freedom, until freedom becomes the ultimate organising principle". If we overcome simplified technological determinism and start to look at technologies as being embedded in social and political structures, we can better understand the potential impact of technological advancements, and also provide informed suggestions on how to shape public policies in order to combine innovation and dynamism with greater social wellbeing. The revolution implies a total transformation of society. If technological and scientific changes that are addressed by the fourth industrial revolution are to realise their revolutionary potential they will have to be accompanied by meaningful social and political transformations that are embedded in a new economic, social and political common sense.

## REFERENCES

Bell, D. (1974), *The Coming of Post-Industrial Society*, New York: Harper Colophon Books.

Braverman, H. (1998), *Labour and Monopoly Capital: the Degradation of Work in the Twentieth Century*, New York: Monthly Review Press.

European Commission (2017), *The Digital Society Index (DESI)*, https://ec.europa.eu/digital-single-market/en/desi.

Grace, K., J. Salvatier, A. Dafoe, B. Zhang and O. Evans (2017), 'When Will AI Exceed Human Performance?', evidence from AI experts, Opensource, 20 November, https://arxiv.org/pdf/1705.08807.pd.

Graeber, D. (2013), *The Democracy Project: a History, a Crisis, a Movement*, London: Penguin Books.

Ignjatović, M. and A. K. Mrčela (2016), *Reducing Precarious Work in Europe Through Social Dialogue: the Case of Slovenia*, Ljubljana: University of Ljubljana, http://www.research.mbs.ac.uk/ewerc/Portals/0/Documents/Slovenia-final-report.pdf.

Klein, N. (2017), *No is not Enough: Defeating the New Shock Politics*, London: Penguin Random House.

MPA (2017), *Digital Transformation of Slovenia*, Ljubljana: Ministry of Public Administration, http://www.mju.gov.si/fileadmin/mju.gov.si/pageuploads/SOJ/2017/digitalna_preobrazba_brosura/Digital_transformation_of_Slovenia.PDF

Rifkin, J. (1995), *The End of Work: the Decline of the Global Labor Force and the Dawn of the Post-Market Era*, New York: Putnam Book.

RIS (2017), 'Use of Internet in Slovenia', Raba interneta v Sloveniji, 20 November, http://www.ris.org/index.php?fl=2&lact=1&bid=11818&parent=27.

Stanojević, M., A. K. Mrčela and M. Breznik (2016), 'Slovenia at the Crossroads: Increasing Dependence on Supranational Institutions and the Weakening of Social Dialogue', *European Journal of Industrial Relations*, 22(3): 281–94.

# LATVIA

## *A case of paradigmatic misalignment*

### Dmitrijs Kravcenko

Current debates around the emergence of the so-called fourth industrial revolution in Europe often consider the interrelations between labour bargaining power and digital infrastructure. Indeed, several chapters in this volume explicitly construct their analysis around these two factors (see Jolly this volume; Zanoni this volume). Latvia is worth paying attention to as an interesting case in this respect. On the one hand, a low degree of unionisation, strong business lobbying powers and an above-average IT infrastructure relative to other EU member states all give Latvia good odds for making decisive progress in digitally revolutionising its economy on a par with larger western liberal capitalist countries. On the other hand, the poor digital literacy of the population and indecisive digitalisation by businesses, compounded by a 'blockbuster' policy for digital innovation, make it seem unlikely that Latvia will be able to undergo a fourth industrial revolution effectively. So where does this leave Latvia? Intent on becoming a regional entrepreneurship hub, Latvia is at risk of becoming a place where government policy and labour legislation begin moving into a digital economy with no one in it.

In this chapter I will first consider how historical emphasis on infrastructure is driving Latvia's strategy of digital development.

I will then offer a way of understanding which type of digital economy is most likely to develop in Latvia and explain the reasoning behind my view. Finally, I will analyse the current state of the digital economy in Latvia and highlight areas requiring more attention as far as the fourth industrial revolution is concerned.

## HOW LATVIA LEARNED THE IMPORTANCE OF INFRASTRUCTURE

While the final shape of the digital economy is still an open question, there are certain emergent characteristics that set this form of market relations apart from its predecessors. Fundamentally, the degree to which any given country will be able to benefit from the fourth industrial revolution will depend on how well the economic actors within that country are able to reconfigure their exchange relations in the digital sphere, and Latvia is no exception. Because a digital economy is in any case an economy, the exchange relations within it will require their own digital marketplaces, complete with an enabling regulatory environment. Bearing all of this in mind, Latvia is an exemplary case of paradigmatic misalignment between government policy, business requirements and technological capability resulting in stagnation.

Located in northern Europe, Latvia is one of the three Baltic states, a member of both the European Union and NATO since 2004, and a historically important transport hub between the west and Russia. Much like its Baltic neighbours, Latvia has been subject to foreign occupation for most of its recorded history. Unlike Lithuania, which has close historical and cultural ties with Poland, both Latvia and Estonia owe their initial statehoods to about 700 years of Germanic rule in one form or another up until 1721, when the regional geopolitical balance shifted in favour of Russia. Known as 'German Baltic provinces' at the time, Latvia and Estonia were considerably more industrialised than Lithuania, which maintained a largely agricultural economy (Norkus 2012). A high degree of urban development and, by the standards of the day, an advanced industrial capacity were made possible in Latvia and Estonia by a developed network of railroads carrying goods and raw materials to and from the ports of Riga and Tallinn.

It is striking just how much historical circumstances with respect to industrial development continue to shape Latvia's foray into the digital economy today. Infrastructure is of supreme importance: in taking advantage of its geographical location and easy access to the Baltic Sea, by the mid-19th century Latvia had propelled itself into the second industrial revolution on the back of ports and railroads. Heavy industry, metallurgy and chemical production made use of a well-educated workforce to achieve world-class standards. At this time, the first universities in the country were built and the foundations of modern Latvian society were laid down. Even throughout the politically and culturally traumatic years of Soviet occupation, Latvia remained one of the most industrialised countries in the region. Despite much of its industrial capacity being obsolete by western standards when Latvia's independence was restored in 1990, the country has since successfully repositioned its economy following the liberal capitalist model, focusing on services and value-added products. Perhaps having learned the lesson in the past of the importance of infrastructure in building up their state and society, Latvians have invested heavily in the new kind of infrastructure – information and communications technology (ICT).

## TELECOMMUNICATIONS: A VEHICLE FOR DIGITALISATION?

Two decades later, Latvia found itself in a remarkable position with respect to ICT development. As recently as 2016, the country's telecommunications infrastructure consistently ranked above the EU average and its speed and coverage was among the best in the world (Belskis 2017). This translated into an affordable, high-speed fibre optic internet connection for most of the population and businesses.

In 2014, the capital city of Latvia, Riga, nominated itself the 'free wifi capital of Europe' on account of its extensive free wifi coverage, which at the time amounted to three access points per square kilometre (LSM 2014). Latvians are well aware of the potentialities that a high-quality internet infrastructure brings to their ability to communicate, access services and even engage in the process of governance. According to the European commission's Digital Economy and Society Index (DESI 2016), Latvia ranks ninth, and above the EU average, for the propensity of individuals to use the internet, with a particular emphasis on access to the news (87% of the population), video calls (55% of the population) and banking (81% of the population). Furthermore, 36% of internet users in Latvia actively participate in egovernment, which can provide all basic services online, is ranked eighth on performance in the EU and shows considerable advances in digitalisation (European Commission, 2017).

Thus, as far as infrastructure goes, Latvia appears to be well positioned for jumpstarting its economy towards digital transition. But what do a digital economy and the associated fourth industrial revolution entail? What do we know about this phenomenon, and how is it possible to distinguish between it and a more traditional web- or network-based service sector, especially given that the revolution towards the digital economy is not yet a foregone conclusion and is still very much in the developing stages? As was pointed out in the introduction to this volume, definitions vary. Schwab (2015) argues for a blurring between the digital and physical spheres of human activity, with an emphasis on the digital sphere gaining prominence relative to the physical sphere, and even becoming more central. On the one hand, this change is thought to be made possible by advances in robotics, nano- and biotechnology, big data and new, more sophisticated algorithms, the sharing economy and the resulting across-the-board automation (Braidotti 2013; Mager 2014; Peters 2017). On the other hand, there are already signs that rapid technological change without an accompanying rise in the skill base of the labour pool, the reconfiguration of the welfare system and a reconsideration of new employment arrangements results in talent shortages, digitalisation-induced unemployment and growing inequality (Schwab and Samans 2016).

Of the various factors driving the digital economy forward, only a selection will be available and, indeed, applicable to countries, such as Latvia, with small research and development industrial bases but strong service sectors amounting to just over 68% of the economically active population in 2016 (CSP 2017). Nanotechnology, biotechnology, big data and advanced robotics are aspects of the fourth industrial revolution that build directly on the extensive industrialisation and market capitalisation experienced during the second industrial revolution, the benefits of which were all but nullified in Latvia during the years of Soviet occupation. Today, the country simply does not have the industrial and financial base needed to make sustained advances in developing these areas. However, with more than one path to digitalisation, Latvia can build on its developed service sector and approach the fourth industrial revolution from the side of automation, algorithms and the sharing economy.

## THE MANY FACES OF THE DIGITAL ECONOMY

Taking a service-centred approach to the digitalisation of its already heavily service-oriented economy is likely to lead Latvia down the path towards what can be broadly described as a sharing and gig economy. These two types of economy are made possible by advances in mobile telecommunications and algorithmic distribution and management of work. In mediating a debate between proponents and opponents of this form of market exchange, Martin (2016) notes the disruptive effect that these two 'entry-level' varieties of the gig economy have on the labour and welfare market. Specifically, the commodification of work that these entail makes for a more flexible but less predictable, and more targeted but less sustainable labour market (De Stefano 2015). The move towards digitalisation of the economy via a sharing economy in Latvia makes sense on at least three levels:

- Latvia has a highly developed telecommunications infrastructure, including mobile speed and coverage (DESI 2016).
- Latvian students still perform above the EU average in science, technology, engineering and mathematics (STEM), although these results have been deteriorating somewhat recently (OECD 2017).
- Most of the Latvian population is concentrated in urban centres, with about half of the total population (and 50% of GDP) found in the capital, Riga.

These three levels translate into a connected, economically dominant workforce that has the skills (or the potential) to engage in algorithm-driven forms of market exchange.

It is important to note that the gig economy and sharing economy as parts of the fourth industrial revolution are two distinct concepts that are often conflated. The term 'sharing economy' refers to an ensemble of marketplaces that, while often digital, need not necessarily be so (Sundararajan 2016). The sharing economy, first and foremost, describes a state of market exchange relations where individuals share personal assets for mutual satisfaction of their needs (see Schor this volume). It is historically a community-based model made scalable by the use of ICT and new forms of algorithmic resource allocation (see Hofheinz this volume). The gig economy, on the other hand, is a new model of organisational design and a configuration of work rather than exchange relations. It is an emergent model of organisational service provision where workers independently carry out disparate, ad hoc 'gigs' for a variety of clients. The gig economy, much like the digital sharing economy, takes advantage of advances in IT, digital technology and various form of algorithmic management in order to allocate, manage and benchmark work. Indeed, the only real point of convergence between the gig economy and the sharing economy is that a number of gig economy platforms do not invest in productive assets but instead rely on freelancers to use their own assets for the completion of 'gigs'.

The reason why this distinction between the sharing and the gig economy is important for understanding Latvia's potential transition into the digital economy has to do with how economic actors within a market think about their work. To reiterate, a sharing economy is a different set of paradigms about exchange relations in a market, whereas a gig economy is a different model of employment relations. The two (or either) are then made digital through yet another ontological level that comes with the fourth industrial revolution – the digitalisation and automation of the economy, actors and markets included.

## A DIGITAL ECONOMY WITH NO ONE IN IT?

Latvia was previously identified as being generally predisposed to digitalisation because of its weak labour unions, advanced IT infrastructure and geographical concentration of economically dominant actors, but it lacks the industrial and scientific base for a more technologically intensive entry into the digital economy. The country therefore seems like a fertile ground from which a comprehensive digital economy based on gigs, with or without the sharing element, should have emerged in recent years. A closer look at employment trends lends further support to this view: the most economically active segment of population is also the one that is more educated and younger, just over two-fifths of the entire workforce are managers and professionals, while one-fifth are skilled workers (CSP 2017). Given that the roots of both the sharing and the gig economy lie with skilled freelancers, work of this type, as well as more egalitarian market exchange relations, should be naturally appealing to most of the Latvian working population. And yet there are no domestic digital markets worth mentioning, the number of people in part-time work is well below the EU average (CSP 2017) and use of Latvia's advanced telecommunications infrastructure is, at best, unrealised (DESI 2016).

While there may be more than a few reasons why the Latvian digital economy is failing to take off despite ostensibly favourable conditions (see Wrobel 2015 for an institutional take on the matter), in this chapter I will argue that the fundamental cause is a paradigmatic mismatch between government policy and development agenda vis-à-vis digitalisation, on the one hand, and some essential socioeconomic behaviours necessary for a working digital economy, on the other. In basic terms, government policy is generally focused on the development of infrastructure and support for high-tech 'blockbuster' enterprises in small numbers, while most of the working population that could provide a critical mass of activity and resources for a digital economy remains uninvolved in digital markets.

Let us first examine the former of these issues – government policy aimed at augmenting infrastructure and fostering the Silicon Valley type of innovative start up. Latvia continues to invest in and develop high-speed internet and to extend its telecommunications infrastructure coverage as before. In 2016, the total value of tangible investment into the sector amounted to €83mn, which is considerable for a country with a population of just under 2 million and a total active workforce of just below 900,000 (Akamai 2017; CSP 2017). Latvia also remained one of the best countries in the EU for its availability of fibre optic networks. In order to capitalise on the developed infrastructure, the Latvian government set out to modernise some of the legislation so as to make the country more innovative and venture-capital friendly. Two particular pieces of legislation are especially relevant in this regard. First, a new law 'on aid to start-up companies', according to which the government will shoulder employers' social contributions on salaries if the business employs highly educated individuals (in order to qualify for full assistance, these individuals must have a PhD) and is engaged in developing and trading innovative products (that would result in a significant improvement on those in current use); second, a bill to regulate ride-sharing services, effectively paving the way for Uber and other such companies to enter the market in Latvia. The two pieces of legislation are brand new, with the law on aid to start-up companies entering into force on 1 January 2017, and the ride-sharing bill on 1 March 2018.

These laws signal a distinctly top-down approach by the Latvian government to the digitalisation of the country's economy. The new law on start-up aid, for example, is explicitly geared at generating 'blockbuster' innovations modelled on Silicon Valley but without the technical and financial capabilities nor the cluster effect. It should be noted that amending the disparity in the ability of Latvian enterprises to raise funds to a degree that could be reasonably expected compared to that of their Californian models is one of the explicit aims of the law (Aseradens 2017). Still, with an explicit aim of helping start only about 20 such enterprises a year it will be difficult to entice existing economic actors to the benefits and opportunities of the digital economy. Nonetheless, this particular way of legislating innovation may succeed in making Riga an attractive destination for regional innovative entrepreneurs (Treija 2018).

The new bill on ride-sharing is likely to be a better introduction to the advantages – and perils – of the nascent digital economy, however (see O'Connor 2016; 2018). Explicitly outlining a regulatory framework for app-based service delivery using electronic payments only, this new bill is Latvia's first pure digital-economy-oriented piece of legislation. It fits well with three of Raisinghani's (2004, 177) 'four pillars of the digital economy', effectively stimulating the development and popularisation of ICT technologies (algorithmic management within the paradigm of the sharing economy under a 'gig' type of organisation) and generating microeconomic change.

Do the two recent pieces of legislation described above constitute a step in the direction of the fourth industrial revolution in Latvia? It is difficult to tell because the preconditions for a digital economy in Latvia differ markedly from those of larger Western countries; however, the overall signs do not paint a promising picture. Socioeconomic trends, as well as policy decisions (the new transport bill notwithstanding) do not point in the direction of a digital economy. As was mentioned at the beginning of this chapter, Latvia is a liberal market economy with weak labour representation, a skilled and educated workforce, a strong service sector, and a world-class telecommunications infrastructure. Furthermore, Latvia has developed effective and comprehensive egovernment and is building up a digitalisation-friendly body of legislation. And yet, economic activity in digital markets is rudimentary and at best peripheral to traditional marketplaces; high-speed internet is used predominantly for recreation, nationwide 'brain drain' is severe, scientific collaboration between the public and private sectors is marginal, and the cornerstone of government policy appears to be built on spawning a 'blockbuster' type of innovation for reasons not wholly pertaining to the goal of stimulating widespread digitalisation of the economy (Akamai 2017; DESI, 2016; Schwab and Samans 2016).

## FINAL THOUGHTS AND AREAS FOR URGENT ATTENTION

To put it simply, most of the economically active population in Latvia is not motivated and has no incentive to engage in digital marketplaces. To complicate matters further, businesses are not digitising despite having the available infrastructure to do so. In fact, Latvia ranks near the bottom of the EU on use of cloud services (Eurostat 2016) and on use of digital technology (DESI 2016). Early signs pointing towards a service-driven digital economy exist, but they do not form any part of the public agenda (Belskis 2017), and those initiatives that are on the public agenda are not even close to being sufficient in propelling Latvia into the fourth industrial revolution.

Far more attention and concentration needs to be focused on the following four areas:

- reversing the decline in STEM graduates, especially in ICT and mathematics
- introducing incentives for the emergence of digital markets (like the new transportation bill stipulating use of digital payments only)

- introducing greater flexibility into employment relations so as to create space for part-time and freelance work
- public procurement of domestic high-tech products and services, as well as mandating the use of collaborative, cloud-based software solutions in relevant industries (eg architecture, construction and design).

Unless the very minimum highlighted by these four points is acted upon, it is quite likely that when some parts of the Latvian economy begin their transition into the digital sphere, there will be no one there to greet them.

## REFERENCES

Akamai (2017), *Akamai State of the Internet Report*, https://www.akamai.com/uk/en/multimedia/documents/state-of-the-internet/q2-2017-state-of-the-internet-security-report.pdf.

Aseradens, A. (2017), *Politikas Veidotājam Jābūt Atvērtam un Elastīgam, Pilnveidojot Jaunuzņēmumu Atbalsta Instrumentus: Likuma Grozījumi Paplašinās Atbalsta Saņēmēju Loku*, Latvian Ministry of Economics, https://www.em.gov.lv/lv/jaunumi/17434-aseradens-politikas-veidota-jam-jabut-atvertam-un-elastigam-pilnveidojot-jaunuznemumu-atbalsta-instrumentus-likuma-grozijumi-paplasinas-atbalsta-sanemeju-loku.

Belskis, E. (2017), *General Overview of [the] Situation in Digital Latvia*, Riga: Ministry of Environmental Protection and Regional Development.

Braidotti, R. (2013), *The Posthuman*, Cambridge: Polity.

CSP (2017), *Darbaspēka Apsekojuma Galvenie Rādītāji 2016*, Gadā, http://www.csb.gov.lv/sites/default/files/nr_17_darbaspeka_apsekojuma_gal-venie_raditaji_2016_gada_17_00_lv_en_0.pdf.

De Stefano, V. (2015), 'The Rise of the Just-in-Time Workforce: On-Demand Work, Crowdwork, and Labor Protection in the Gig-Economy', *Comparative Labor Law & Policy Journal*, 37: 471–505.

DESI (2016), *The Digital Economy and Society Index: Latvia*, https://ec.europa.eu/digital-single-market/en/desi.

European Commission (2017), *14th eGovernment Benchmark Report*, Luxembourg: Office for Official Publications of the European Communities.

Eurostat (2016), *The EU in the World*, Luxembourg: Office for Official Publications of the European Communities.

LSM (2014), 'Riga Names Itself European Capital of WiFi', *Latvijas Sabiedriskais Medijs*, 3 July, https://eng.lsm.lv/article/economy/economy/riga-names-itself-european-capital-of-wifi.a90305/.

Mager, A. (2014), Defining Algorithmic Ideology: Using Ideology Critique to Scrutinize Corporate Search Engines', *TripleC: Communication, Capitalism & Critique, Open Access Journal for a Global Sustainable Information Society*, 12(1): 28–39.

Martin, C. J. (2016), 'The Sharing Economy: a Pathway to Sustainability or a Nightmarish Form of Neoliberal Capitalism?', *Ecological Economics*, 121: 149–59.

Norkus, Z. (2012), *On Baltic Slovenia and Adriatic Lithuania: a Qualitative Comparative Analysis of Patterns in Postcommunist Transformation*, Vilnius: Apostrofa.

O'Connor, S. (2016), 'When Your Boss is an Algorithm', *Financial Times*, 8 September.

O'Connor, S. (2018), 'Algorithms at Work Risk Management by Numbers', *Financial Times*, 6 February.

OECD (2017), *Education Policy Outlook: Latvia*, http://www.oecd.org/education/Education-Policy-Outlook-Country-Profile-Latvia.pdf.

Peters, M. A. (2017), 'Technological Unemployment: Educating for the Fourth Industrial Revolution', *Journal of Self-Governance and Management Economics*, 5(1): 32–41.

Raisinghani, M. S. (2004), *Business Intelligence in the Digital Economy: Opportunities, Limitations, and Risks*, Hershey: Idea Group Publishing.

Schwab, K. (2015), Will the Fourth Industrial Revolution Have a Human Heart?, *World Economic Forum*, 27 October.

Schwab, K., and Samans, R. (2016), *The Future of Jobs: Employment, Skills and Workforce Strategy for the Fourth Industrial Revolution*, Geneva: World Economic Forum.

Sundararajan, A. (2016), *The Sharing Economy: The End of Employment and the Rise of Crowd-Based Capitalism*, Cambridge, MA: MIT Press.

Treija, I. (2018), 'Latvia Launches an Innovative Startup Law and Startup Tax', http://www.eu-startups.com/2016/11/latvia-launches-an-innovative-startup-law-and-startup-tax/.

Wrobel, R. (2015), 'From Independence to the Euro Introduction: Varieties of Capitalism in the Baltic States', *Central and Eastern European Journal of Management and Economics*, 3(1): 9–38.

# POLAND

## *Developing a smart digital agenda*

### Maria Skóra

Every year, one country is spotlighted at the world's biggest trade fair for industrial technology in Hannover. In April 2017, Poland was the chosen partner of this renowned event. With the slogan 'Smart means Poland' the country was presented as moving beyond its standard role of contract manufacturer and transforming into an active player through investments in innovative sectors, such as robotics, industrial IT, digitalisation and automation of industrial processes (Hannover Messe News 2017). Poland has developed tremendously within the last 26 years and has been often portrayed as the frontrunner of social and economic transformation in eastern Europe. Nevertheless, questions emerge: how sustainable will this growth be when confronted by rapid technological change? Which sectors are most vulnerable to the impending risks of the fourth industrial revolution? And what needs to be done to ensure a positive outcome?

In this chapter I set out to outline briefly the status quo in Poland at the doorstep of the fourth industrial revolution and then assess the national public debate on digitalisation and automation. Next, I formulate conclusions with corresponding suggestions for cushioning the effects of the upcoming structural and lifestyle transformation resulting from the likely technological progress.

## ANOTHER REVOLUTION ON THE HORIZON

The effects of ongoing automation and digitalisation are not yet fully known. On the one hand, one study suggests that 47% of all workplaces in the US are at risk of transition or disappearance over the next decade or two (Frey and Osborne 2013). Another study suggests that 30% of the constituent activities of 60% of occupations could be automated with technologies available today (Chui, Manyika and Miremadi 2016). On the other hand, more cautious calculations, like those announced by the Organisation for Economic Co-operation and Development (OECD), find that across 21 OECD countries, on average only 9% of all jobs are automatable – 6% in Korea and as much as 12% in Austria and Germany (Arnold et al. this volume; Arntz, Gregory and Zierahn 2016). While forecasts vary depending on the method applied (occupation vs task-based approach) and the additional factors included in the analysis (eg workplace organisation, investments in technology and education), there is broad expert agreement on which professions are the most susceptible to automation. First, jobs requiring relatively low competences, focused on routine, repetitive activities are at risk. Second, office and administrative work, sales and trade, production and processing will be significantly affected by technological change. Call centre jobs, sales assistance and bookkeeping are also vulnerable to automation (Doellgast this volume). Robots and other machines are also likely to serve as substitutes in the automotive, energy and extractive industries. These potential developments should therefore be of particular relevance for Poland as they account for significant proportions of its labour market.

## A POPULAR DESTINATION FOR OUTSOURCING, TRADITIONAL AND INNOVATIVE SECTORS

After a swift socio-economic transformation on joining the EU in 2004, Poland has become a popular destination for outsourcing and offshoring services. Business services have expanded three times faster than in India (Saxer this volume). Poland was the tenth most popular location in the Quality House Best Outsourcing Destinations 2016 rankings, and the most attractive location in Europe (Quality House 2016). The outsourcing offshoring sector is estimated to have created around 160,000–200,000 jobs in over 900 companies, with business services becoming one of the largest employers in the country (Bogdan et al. 2015). These jobs were mainly concentrated in seven cities and metropolitan areas: Kraków, Warsaw, Wrocław, Katowice, Trójmiasto, Łódź and Poznań (EY Poland 2017).

Industrial manufacturing employs 2.3 million people in total (Włoch 2017). There are currently 180,000 people working in the automotive industry, making it the fourth largest industrial employer in the country. However, there are no domestic car producers, with the industry relying on original equipment manufacturers for Fiat, Opel and Volkswagen. Another important branch of Polish industry is mining, as the country has rich resources of steam coal, coking coal and lignite. More than 80% of the country's electricity comes from coal and lignite. Unlike the ongoing energy transition in many other countries, maintaining the mining industry is considered a strategic pillar of Poland's energy and broader economic security (EY Poland 2017). Whereas the automotive and machine industries are already considerably robotised, coal mining still depends on human labour. While robotisation would improve miners' safety and productivity, it is likely also to result in jobs losses in an already declining industry.

Alongside these traditional sectors, the innovative information technology and computer software sectors in Poland have also grown, and ecommerce is also developing rapidly. However, according to the European Innovation Scoreboard, Poland is less innovative than other European countries. The information and communications technology (ICT) sector generates only 3% of GDP in Poland, one of the lowest percentages of all European countries, even when compared with slightly more advanced Visegrád neighbours (Eurostat Database 2017b). Even though gross domestic expenditure on research and development (R&D) doubled between 2005 and 2015, it continues to lag behind European innovation leaders like Austria, Germany and countries in Scandinavia, as well as south east Asian countries and the US (Eurostat 2017).

The automotive, metalworking, rubber and electronics industries account for 80% of all industrial robots in Poland. The limited use of robots in other branches demonstrates overall low levels of robotisation: in 2015, there were only 19 robots for every 10,000 workers – four times less than the European average (Fandrejewska 2017). If not addressed properly, the consequences of the fourth industrial revolution in Poland could result in profound structural mismatches and perhaps even the implosion of certain industries. Some of the dynamically developing branches of the Polish economy, like the outsourced business-to-business services, accounting, human resources and customer care, are prone to being affected by progressive digitalisation of labour.

## DIGITAL SKILLS

According to opinion polls, the Polish public is aware that digital skills are the key to professional success (Włoch 2017), but these skills are not yet very well developed. Around 80% of all households are equipped with internet access and a computer (Omyła-Rudzka 2017); the online presence of Poles has nearly quadrupled within the last 15 years (Feliksiak 2017). At the same time, only 50% of the population uses the internet at work and the number of digitally qualified individuals is still low (Feliksiak 2017); the share of those with relatively low-level IT skills exceeds the European average (Eurostat Database 2017a). The reasoning behind this is complex. Mass emigration after joining the EU has resulted in a brain drain of young, high-skilled people. The outflow of well-educated workers was partially compensated through economic migration from Ukraine, but there still are generational and competence gaps in the Polish labour market.

## DEBATING THE UPCOMING REVOLUTION

Concerns around the future effects of digitalisation and automation have not been widely discussed in public debates in Poland, and are only beginning to emerge. The liveliest debates are found in the business sector around concerns over digitalisation and robotisation, technological progress, investment opportunities and how 'know-how' transfers can significantly improve competitiveness. Polish entrepreneurs are aware that these processes will soon affect the country. It is crucial for them to catch up with the new reality that technological progress involves investment and postponing immediate profit returns. Nevertheless, the major concern of Polish business is not dealing with the effects of digitalisation but finding sufficient labour. Because of a demographic slowdown there is a visible generation gap in the labour market: 1 in 4 companies have difficulty finding employees with adequate skills, and a third of Polish employers have vacancies due to a lack of appropriate candidates (Fandrejewska 2017). A recent further tightening of the labour market resulted from pension reforms that re-established a lower retirement age for women at 60 and for men at 65; this has reduced the labour supply of older female workers.

While there is some awareness of digitalisation debates in business circles, the topic is barely discussed by trade unions in Poland. Labour unions still largely focus on fundamental problems such as precarious working conditions, low wages and violations of the labour code. This reflects the concerns of Polish employees for whom labour market liberalisation, even more tangible in times of financial crisis, heavily influenced working conditions, terms of employment, and the balance of power. While social dialogue is now being restored, unions' focus is on tangible bread and butter issues.

Trade union density is highest in large-scale industry, which has already undergone significant and successful processes of automation. Tradeable sector and services remain the least unionised sectors of economy. Perhaps this is why concerns about technological progress are not vocally pronounced in public debates. Nevertheless, on the rare occasions they are discussed, the main worries of the Polish trade unions are around the further diversification of work relationships, flexibility and de-standardisation of working conditions, the possible disappearance of some professions, and the substitution of humans by machines in production. To address these challenges, they propose fostering codetermination and union participation in firm decisionmaking processes (OPZZ 2017).

## GOVERNMENT INITIATIVES

The challenges of digitalisation are to some extent being addressed by the socially conservative and mildly Eurosceptic Law and Justice party (Prawo i Sprawiedliwość; PiS), which came to power in October 2015. On a policy level, 're-industrialisation' (a term used by the Polish government for a strategy of reinstating big-scale industrial production in the country) and innovation are top priorities. To meet the challenge of the digital revolution the Ministry of Development launched the Polish Industry Platform Foundation 4.0 (Powstanie Polska Platforma Przemysłu 4.0) within the framework of the government strategy of responsible development (Ministerstwo Rozwoju 2017a). From 2018 onwards, the platform will support the transformation processes of Polish industry to achieve new levels of automation and data exchange in manufacturing technologies. The first so-called Robotisation Act was signed off on 19 July 2017; this amended the tax law allowing entrepreneurs to make a one-off tax depreciation write off when they invested PLN 10,000 (€2,400) or more in new technology for their firm (Ministerstwo Rozwoju 2017b).

While Industry 4.0 is on the agenda, there is no equivalent 'Work 4.0' initiative (Rahner and Schönstein this volume). The issue was recently raised by an employers association, illustrating the high level of awareness in the business sector to future challenges. A recent major conference organised in November 2017 included the Ministry of Education and the Ministry of Family and Labour, and was strongly focused on business solutions, discussing possible changes to the labour code, wages and vocational training. While this demonstrates some concern for the social dimensions of employment, far more attention is being given to the technical aspects of digitalisation than the implications for the regulation of employment.

## CONCLUSIONS

The process of digitalisation and automation in Poland is slow and uneven, so it is likely that the consequences of technological process will be unevenly distributed in particular parts of the economy. The risks are lower in the more traditional mining and agriculture sectors. However, where Poland has successfully attracted foreign investments by offering a highly qualified labour force, a good infrastructure, and an attractive business and financial environment, the risks of the fourth industrial revolution might hit it hard, in particular in the successful business-to-business sector, which is at high risk of digitalisation. Poland could easily be left behind technologically and economically if no measures are taken. If a 'catching up' strategy is implemented too late, this might leave limited capacity for gradual adjustment and the avoidance of structural skills mismatches exacerbated by demographic trends and the brain-drain effects of migration.

In debates in Poland priority has been given to the technical aspects of change, with support for digitalisation, robotisation and innovation largely seen as improving the efficiency and competitiveness of Polish companies. Little attention is paid to how these changes will influence employment opportunities and the labour market. It is to be expected that the changing technological environment will influence not only the nature of work per se, but also employment conditions and lifestyles in general. Fragmentation and digitalisation of working processes will also affect the organisation of work, the division of labour and working times. In times of structural transformation, ensuring social security and labour safety should remain in the spotlight not only for the trade unions, but also when designing governmental strategies.

Meanwhile, in Poland technological modernisation is imagined without sufficient consideration of its social and human aspects. It is evident that there is not much interest in the 'soft' aspects of the technological revolution and they are analysed in isolation from the technological debates. A better understanding of the intersections between technology and society, economic and social policy, and industry and work is much needed. With no bigger vision, without systemic links and a complementary approach in tackling these aspects, the fourth industrial revolution might disrupt the development pattern of Poland.

Therefore, it is necessary to consider now what possible consequences digitalisation and automation might have on the key industry sectors in the country, and long-term strategies should be drafted, to attract investment and launch domestic projects in future-oriented sectors. Although it is difficult to compete with world leaders, increased spending on R&D should be part of this strategy. Technological progress is also likely to affect labour demand, and this requires a proactive, as opposed to reactive, approach in shaping curricula and systemic adjustments in managing educational institutions, anticipating growing industries and demand for skills. Last but not least, a broader public debate on digitalisation and its possible consequences should be initiated in Poland. So far, the mainstream media has not covered the topic in any depth, nor been granted a prominent place in social dialogue. There is a need for a public debate on the possible structural, legal and – most probably – lifestyle changes that will result from digitalisation of labour. Having recently experienced an abrupt socio-economic transformation with the fall of communism, a thorough public debate is necessary not only to prepare industry for the forthcoming changes, but also to secure social peace and cohesion on the way to digital transformation and a smart Poland.

# REFERENCES

Arntz, M., T. Gregory and U. Zierahn (2016), *The Risk of Automation for Jobs in OECD Countries: a Comparative Analysis*, Social, Employment and Migration Working Paper 189, Paris: OECD.

Bogdan, W., D. Boniecki, E. Labaye, T. Marciniak and M. Nowacki (2015), 'Poland 2025: Europe's New Growth Engine', Warsaw: McKinsey & Company, http://mckinsey.pl/wp-content/uploads/2015/10/Poland-2025_full_report.pdf.

Chui, M., J. Manyika and M. Miremadi (2016), 'Where Machines Could Replace Humans—and Where They Can't (Yet)', *McKinsey Quarterly*, 30(2): 1–9.

EY Poland (2017), 'Sectors', in EY Poland, *Doing Business in Poland – edition 2017*, Warsaw: Ernst & Young Poland, 165–78, http://www.ey.com/Publication/vwLUAssets/ey-doing-business-in-poland-sectors/$FILE/ey-dbp-sectors.pdf.

Eurostat (2017), 'R & D expenditure', *Statistics Explained*, February, http://ec.europa.eu/eurostat/statistics-explained/index.php/R_%26_D_expenditure.

Eurostat Database (2017a), 'Digital Economy and Society Statistics: Households and Individuals, Individuals' Level of Digital Skills', 26 April, http://ec.europa.eu/eurostat/data/database.

Eurostat Database (2017b), 'Digital Economy and Society Statistics: Percentage of the ICT Sector in GDP', 14 February, http://ec.europa.eu/eurostat/data/database.

Fandrejewska, A. (2017), 'Dlaczego Martwimy Się Robotyzacją, Skoro to Brak Ludzi do Pracy Staje Się Problemem', *Obserwator Finansowy*, 1 May, https://www.obserwatorfinansowy.pl/tematyka/makroekonomia/dlaczego-martwimy-sie-robotyzacja-skoro-to-brak-ludzi-do-pracy-staje-sie-problemem.

Feliksiak, M. (2017), 'Korzystanie z Internetu', Komunikat z Badań 49, Warsaw: Centrum Badania Opinii Społecznej, http://www.cbos.pl/SPIS-KOM.POL/2017/K_049_17.PDF.

Frey, C. and M. Osborne (2013), *The Future of Employment: How Susceptible Are Jobs To Computerisation?*, Oxford: Oxford Martin School, https://www.oxfordmartin.ox.ac.uk/downloads/academic/The_Future_of_Employment.pdf.

Hannover Messe News (2017), 'Poland at the Hannover Messe 2017 Fair', Hannover Mess, 19 April, http://www.hannovermesse.de/en/register-plan/for-journalists/press-services/press-releases/pressreleases-deutsche-messe/poland-at-the-hannover-messe-2017-fair.xhtml.

Ministerstwo Rozwoju (2017a), 'Powstanie Polska Platforma Przemysłu 4.0', Ministerstwo Rozwoju, 31 May, https://www.mr.gov.pl/strony/ aktualnosci/powstanie-polska-platforma-przemyslu-40.

Ministerstwo Rozwoju (2017b), 'Ustawa o Robotyzacji Podpisana Przez Prezydenta', Ministerstwo Rozwoju, 20 July, https://www.mr.gov.pl/ strony/aktualnosci/ustawa-o-robotyzacji-podpisana-przez-prezydenta.

Omyła-Rudzka, Małgorzata (2017), 'Wyposażenie Gospodarstw Domowych', Komunikat z Badań 125, Warsaw: Centrum Badania Opinii Społecznej, http://www.cbos.pl/SPISKOM.POL/2017/K_125_17.PDF.

OPZZ (2017), 'Digitalizacja rynku pracy', Ogólnopolskie Porozumienie Związków Zawodowych, 19 October, http://www.opzz.org.pl/aktual-nosci/swiat/digitalizacja-rynku-pracy.

Quality House (2016), 'Top Outsourcing Destinations in 2016', Quality House, https://qualityhouse.com/index.php?page=top-outsourcing-des-tinations-in-2016.

Włoch, R. (2017), *Raport Gumtree 2017: Aktywni+ Przyszłość Rynku Pracy*, Warszawa: deLab/Gumtree Polska, http://www.delab.uw.edu.pl/ wp-content/uploads/2017/04/DELabUW_raport_Aktywni.pdf.

# ITALY

## *Prioritising human capital*

## Carlotta de Franceschi[1]

> Replicants are like any other machine. They're either a benefit or
> a hazard. If they're a benefit it's not my problem.
>
> —Bladerunner, 1982

**B**laderunner is set in a 2019 Los Angeles where synthetic humans,
known as replicants, are used in extra-terrestrial colonies as workforce. What looked like fiction in 1982 is, today, not far from reality:
mining and oil companies around the world use autonomous trucks,
drills and trains to boost productivity; people share cars, apartments
and knowledge; books and music are liquid; people manage their
bank accounts, shopping and social life out of a smartphone. More
broadly, automation, robotics, machine learning, ecommerce, the
shared economy and disruptive platforms are changing the way consumers buy, while some industries work at a speed that is hard to for
their employees to cope with.

All around the world these changes are bringing both opportunities and threats and raise fundamental questions about jobs, inequality, welfare and wealth redistribution. In Italy, a country plagued by
the third largest public debt in the world and a deep intergenerational
divide (de Franceschi 2017), policymakers have an even tougher and

urgent mandate. Italy is ranked 25th in Europe on the Commission's measure of digital development (EDPR 2017). The ranking takes into account five factors: connectivity, human capital, use of the internet, digital integration (integration of companies and ecommerce) and digital public services.

## PREVIOUS REFORM EFFORTS

Recent governments have tried to address certain critical issues like broadband connectivity, tried to improve the start-up ecosystem and even launched a dedicated Industry 4.0 package.

Of these measures, the ultra-fast broadband plan has had a particularly positive impact. Launched in 2015 and running until 2022, it is supported by a €4 billion state budget that is attracting private investments, which ensured 72% coverage in 2016 (up from 41% in the previous year).

Measures around improving the start-up ecosystem ('Start-Up Italia' package) have proven less effective. These range from tax reliefs to venture capital, and from lighter bureaucracy to a simplified liquidation process for start ups. On the one hand this package shows both a new and positive attention to the start-up world and a holistic approach to address the issues it faced. On the other hand it seems to lack an understanding of international best practices, market mechanisms and developed innovation ecosystems. First of all, the tax reliefs granted were three times below what is considered the European best practice. Second, in the effort to fill the major venture capital gap with more advanced European economies, the Italian Development Bank seeded a Venture Capital Fund of Funds. This achieved a doubling of available venture capital in the country, but the stock available is still six or seven times less than what is available in Germany or France respectively, as a percentage of GDP (OECD 2016d, 20). The main pitfall of the Venture Capital Fund of Funds (Piol and de Franceschi 2014) promoted by the Italian Development Bank is that it seeded venture capitalists with no prior experience nor international network, both key ingredients in the success and scaling-up of start ups and in the fast development of an already rather underdeveloped local industry.

The Industry 4.0 Plan (September 2016) is a 12-year €18 billion plan consisting of four main areas: tax reliefs for corporate investments and borrowing for investments in hardware and software supporting the Industry 4.0, tax reliefs to train the workforce in the Industry 4.0, dedicated training for students in the Industry 4.0, and competence centres for small- and medium-sized enterprises. The tax reliefs in investments and borrowing were not met with strong demand and were therefore not very effective, while the tax reliefs for personnel training are yet to show meaningful results (Schivardi 2017). On the students' training side, the €220 million dedicated funding for vocational and university training is very positive, although a deeper approach to school, training and university would be advisable. Digital innovation hubs and competence centres are in the process of being activated, yet the European Commission has already warned that their success relies on the effective coordination of government, business associations and the higher education sector (European Commission 2017).

If Italy wants to be a 'winner' rather than a 'loser' in the tsunami brought by the fourth industrial revolution it should first develop a holistic approach to human capital: invest strongly in the school system, review the curricula, prioritise in-school orientation towards both university and the job market, strengthen (particularly vocational) training, upskill the workforce and redesign the university system, with a focus on access, scholarships, interaction with the innovation ecosystem and e-education. Second, Italy should modernise its job market by allowing a convergence of labour and capital favouring tax treatments for long-term equity investment and equity compensation, and provide a welfare safety net for entrepreneurs and non-standard workers. Third, it should focus its industrial policy on attracting the value-added functions of large foreign corporates and promoting the high-tech ecosystem.

## EDUCATION AS THE MAIN CHALLENGE

Education in Italy is a universal and constitutional right. It is an investment to guarantee equal opportunities and social mobility to future generations. However, the execution of this noble intention has been quite poor.

Between 2008 and 2013 public expenditure on education in Italy decreased by 14%, falling to 4% of GDP (versus 5.2% of the OECD average). This decrease reflects a political choice to redirect public expenditure away from education. Second, the percentage of adults who have never used a computer in Italy is almost 1.5 times the OECD average (OECD 2016b). Third, the teacher workforce is the oldest of all OECD countries: in 2014 out of every 10 teachers 6–7 were over 50 (OECD 2016b). Finally, Galletti and Gualdi (2017) observe that according to OECD-PISA Italian students display a significant attainment gap in sciences and maths (Italy ranks 26 out of 28 EU countries considered in the OECD).

Italy has one of the worst social mobility scores in Europe (Darvas and Wollfs 2016) and the highest number of young people not in education, employment or training. Public expenditure in education is significantly lower than the OECD average, penetration of tertiary education is weak, and subject choice is poorly matched to the job market demands of today, let alone those of the future (OECD 2016a, 2016b). When assessing the human capital of the country's digital evolution the European Commission observes that Italy has 26% fewer science, technology, engineering, and mathematics (STEM) graduates, 29% fewer ICT specialists as a percentage of the working population and 21% fewer adults with basic digital skills than the European average (European Commission 2017).

In a fast-paced world, where careers might be increasingly shorter as machines quickly make up the skill gap with humans, education and training are key to giving people the valuable skills that will allow them to enter or stay in the job market. Countries that invest in education and training are more likely to prevail in the future global economy than others.

What should Italy do then to best prepare its youth for the employment of the future? How can it provide continuous on-the-job training and retrain people who are out of work or in industries that have been disrupted?

## MAKE INVESTING IN SCHOOLING A PRIORITY

If Italy wants to be prepared for the fourth industrial revolution the school system should be redesigned for a new concept of literacy and required learning. In particular, the generational renewal of the teaching workforce should provide an opportunity to review curricula by refocusing and improving the quality of STEM subjects, critical reasoning and logic, and skills such as network collaboration, creativity and critical judgement. Mandatory curricula should also include entrepreneurship, coding (Galletti and Gualdi 2017) and finance.

## FIX THE WAY STUDENTS ARE ORIENTED TOWARDS UNIVERSITY AND JOBS

According to Galletti and Gualdi (2017) Italy is the worst country in Europe for 'skill activation' (the ability of students to transition to the job market) because of the low employment of recent graduates and high university and training dropout rates. They also point out that when choosing a training track (university vs vocational programme) Italian students are more influenced by their school than students from other European countries. Furthermore, lacking solid career advice from counsellors, many students seek help from their families who can offer biased, often uninformed, advice that contributes to inequality and lack of social mobility (Forti 2017). On this point Ferrari and Carlana (2016) highlight that education choices in Italy are strongly influenced by the socio-economic conditions of the families and the education level of the parents. As a result, education is not a tool of social mobility. Instead, children's levels of education tend to remain anchored to those of their parents.

Highlighting the findings of a research project,[2] Zucchini, Lecce and Caputo (2016) recommend that high school students should be given two sets of options for their compulsory work-based training scheme ('alternanza scuola-lavoro' – introduced by the Buona Scuola reform). One set would allow students to attend university classes, receive credits, complete their university programme and enter the job market earlier. The other set would be for students who have not yet decided their track and would include classes focused on university and job orientation, and involve the participation of corporations and external parties. Students would be allowed to choose between regular internships, university credits and the orientation track according to objective criteria that assess their predisposition towards the chosen area of study or job.

## IT'S NOT JUST ABOUT EDUCATION, BUT ALSO ABOUT TRAINING . . . AND RETRAINING

Italy must first make sure that even workers without a college degree can participate in the economy of the future by strengthening the vocational training system.[3] Galletti and Gualdi (2017) recommend improving attractiveness and understanding of vocational training in Italy. They point out how this type of training in Italy is delegated to the regions, with big differences not just in the number of absorbed funds but also in effectiveness. The percentage of young people employed among those who followed a vocational training versus a technical or professional high school track is 62% versus 50% in the north east, 55% versus 39% in the north west, 30% versus 39% in the centre, and identical (28%) in the south. In the northern regions we do not only observe higher employment from the vocational training but also lower average costs to run the programmes and higher participation. Based on these findings Galletti and Gualdi (2017) identify two policy priorities: the harmonisation of the systems among regions and a strict evaluation of the various funded projects.

Second, Italy must make sure that people who lose their job are properly retrained and upskilled. Galletti and Gualdi (2017) recommend binding workers who lose their job, and who are also eligible for a monthly voucher to be spent on training, to join the relocation programmes in the first few months of unemployment. At the moment they can join at any time during the 24 months that unemployment insurance covers them, and evidence from other countries shows that these programmes are more effective when people enrol in them during the first period of unemployment.

## UNIVERSITIES MUST EMBRACE URBANISATION AND TECHNOLOGY . . . OR DIE

The first university in the world was founded in 1088 in Bologna, Italy. Almost a thousand years later, in 2016, the Italian tertiary education attainment is among the lowest ranked in the OECD, with only 18% of the Italian population having a university degree compared with an OECD average of 36% (OECD 2016b). In addition, more than 30% of the Italian workforce with tertiary education studied art and humanities, compared with an OECD average of 19% (OECD 2016b). In 2015, 39% of students graduated in arts, humanities, journalism and information versus 23% of the OECD average, leading to a serious mismatch in the country's job market, with the business association Unioncamere commenting that it was "impossible to find" STEM graduates (Zucchini, Lecce and Caputo 2015).

Three policy proposals could help increase the number of STEM graduates. First, after assessing policy recommendations by successful Italian entrepreneurs and venture capitalists in the global digital sector we call for the number of scholarships for students and PhDs in engineering and computer sciences (Piol and de Franceschi 2014) to be increased. Second, despite the serious skills mismatch, in Italy access to engineering schools is capped, but not access to humanities schools. To balance this, last year the dean of Milan University tried to cap access to degrees in literature, history, philosophy and geography. The students' union successfully objected, appealing to the administrative court and winning. We propose that policymakers should be held accountable and restrict the offer of degrees in humanities and journalism and lift the cap on engineering schools.

Third, Italy has to rethink the way it organises and provides higher education. In the past 20 years there has been a proliferation of peripheral universities across the country whose quality and cost are often questionable. Today the best and most innovative universities are located in large metropolitan areas (Anvur 2016). Furthermore, universities located in urban areas also engage in more corporate partnerships and produce more start ups; their research feeds into local innovation ecosystems and strengthens them (Andes 2017). Universities located within innovation districts generate more economic value as they are part of a bigger network, leading to strategic interplay between firms, entrepreneurs and research labs.

For these reasons Italy should strengthen universities in large metropolitan areas and rationalise the peripheral ones by asking bigger universities to provide online versions of their curricula. Italy should also foster competition between foreign and Italian universities on online curricula by assigning a voucher to the top university students who want to access e-education, which can be spent on either credited Italian or foreign courses. Finally it should shut down peripheral universities that do not excel. In this way Italy will be able to leverage technology to provide better education to students who cannot afford to relocate or have to work while studying in a cost-effective way.

## IT'S NOT ONLY ABOUT EDUCATION AND TRAINING, IT'S ALSO ABOUT WORK AND CAPITAL . . . AND THE APPROACH CAN NO LONGER BE IDEOLOGICAL

Two characters are deeply rooted in the Italian imagination: Don Camillo (a democratic Christian priest) and Peppone (a communist mayor). Both are deeply committed to their beliefs and antagonise each other openly in a small village right after the second world war. Their stories appeal to all generations for their ideological positions that make them extremely relevant even in today's Italy.

The strong political dichotomy between capital and labour in Italy is not simply out of fashion, but is becoming very detrimental to the development of society and its ability to cope with globalisation and technological progress.

Policymakers should prioritise creating quality jobs and reducing wealth inequality. Nowadays, this is only possible when workers can participate in the company's success through equity compensation, at all levels. They should also empower and support entrepreneurship, as the process of innovation will blur the lines between entrepreneurs, innovators and employees. Long-term capital gains of start-up owners and employees, stock options and equity compensation in general should have a more favourable tax treatment than they have now. Policymakers should also create a welfare package for – and extend unemployment protection to – entrepreneurs, nonstandard workers, contractors and freelancers.

## ITALY NEEDS MORE HIGH VALUE-ADDED JOBS TO FIGHT INEQUALITY

High value-added jobs are the least threatened by automation. In general, hi-tech sectors create three times more jobs in their ecosystem than manufacturing ones (Piol and de Franceschi 2014). Italy should work towards attracting successful international corporations and promoting employment and entrepreneurship in high-tech industries.

From 2014 to 2016 Italy made a promising start by supporting companies that hired PhDs or STEM graduates in research functions by making 35% of their costs tax deductible (for up to €200,000 per company and for a maximum of 10 hires per company). In France innovative start ups were supported between 2004 and 2016 by fully exempting them from social contributions for researchers and research and development (R&D) managers. Italy should borrow the same measure, extending it to all companies and include ICT specialists as well as graduates and PhDs in STEM. It should also seek to apply a hyper-amortisation for small- and medium-sized enterprises onto R&D expenditures and make tax deductible the acquisition cost of start ups and other companies (Piol and de Franceschi 2014). This way it would promote a virtuous cycle of investments, innovation and growth.

As Italy is gearing up for the elections, the different parties are appealing to the public in the effort to convince the electorate on crucial issues. At the heart of the debate are immigration, taxes and pensions. Education, training, innovation, research and industrial policy have slipped off the discussion. Media and influencers barely talk about the risks and opportunities of the fourth industrial revolution and most of the public probably ignores the problem.

Klaus Schwab, founder and executive chairman of the World Economic Forum, said,

> We must develop a comprehensive and globally shared view of how technology is affecting our lives and reshaping our economic, social, cultural, and human environments. There has never been a time of greater promise, or greater peril.

If Italy wants to be prepared, it should embrace a revolutionary and very long-term vision, at least as revolutionary and as long term as the challenges that it is actually facing.


## NOTES

1. I am grateful to Gabriele Diana, associate at Action Institute, for the great work and support on this chapter. I would also like to convey my thanks to Chiara Bellucci, associate at Action Institute, who supported me on collecting data for the first draft.

2. The project was conducted for Action Institute to assess and improve recent school reforms within the broader context of EuFactor, a joint

campaign of the European Commission and the European Parliament to influence 16–19 year olds to take STEM careers.

3. In 2017 the OECD estimated that 53% of the population in Italy is expected to graduate from a vocational programme in their lifetime (OECD 2016c).

## REFERENCES

Acemoglu, D. and D. Autor (2011), 'Skills, Tasks and Technologies: Implications for Employment and Earnings', in O. Ashenfelter and D. Card (eds), *Handbook of Labor Economics*, vol. 4, Amsterdam: Elsevier.

Andes, S. (2017), *Hidden in Plain Sight: the Oversized Impact of Downtown Universities*, Washington: Brookings, https://www.brookings.edu/research/hidden-in-plain-sight-the-oversized-impact-of-downtown-universities.

Anvur (2016), 'Rapporto sullo stato del sistema universitario e della ricerca 2016', Roma: Agenzia Nazionale di Valutazione del sistema Universitario e della Ricerca.

Darvas, Z.and G. B. Wolf (2016), *An Anatomy of Inclusive Growth in Europe*, Brussels: Bruegel, http://bruegel.org/2016/10/an-anatomy-of-inclusive-growth-in-europe/.

De Franceschi, C. (2017), *Un passato che grava sul futuro*, Milan: Action Institute.

European Commission (2017), *Europe's Digital Progress Report (EDPR) for Italy 2017*, Brussels: European Commission.

Ferrari, A. and M. Carlana (2016), *BuonaScuola: autonomia, merito e valutazioni*, Milan: Action Institute.

Forti, A. (2017), *Italy, No Country for Young People?*, Organisation for Economic Co-operation and Development, 4 December, https://oecd-skillsandwork.wordpress.com/2017/12/04/italy-no-country-for-young-people/

Frey, C. and M. Osborne (2013), *The Future of Employment: How Susceptible Are Jobs To Computerisation?*, Oxford: Oxford Martin School, https://www.oxfordmartin.ox.ac.uk/downloads/academic/The_Future_of_Employment.pdf.

Galletti, F. and F. Gualdi (2017), *Skills Mismatch in Italia: analisi e scelte di policy in uno scenario in rapida evoluzione*, Milan: Action Institute.

OECD (2016a), *Big Data: Bringing Competition Policy to the Digital Era*, Paris: OECD Publishing.

OECD (2016b), *Education at a Glance 2016: OECD Indicators*, Paris: OECD Publishing.

OECD (2016c), *Skills Matter: Further Results from the Survey of Adult Skills*, Paris: OECD Publishing.

OECD (2016d), *Entrepreneurship at a Glance 2016*, Paris: OECD Publishing.

Piol, A. and C. de Franceschi (2014), 'Finanziare l'Innovazione – Costituzione di un Fondo di Fondi di Venture Capital', follow up note, Rome: Action Institute.

Schivardi, F. (2017), 'Industria 4.0: Incentivi sì, ma Solo all'Innovazione', *LaVoce*, 11 November.

Zucchini, G., G. Lecce and A. Caputo (2016), *Alternanza Scuola–Lavoro: Come Garantire un Arricchimento del Capitale Umano?*, Milan: Action Institute.

# GREECE

## *In search of growth, work and welfare after the crisis*

## Sotiria Theodoropoulou

The fourth industrial revolution is driven by the fusion of techno-logical developments such as the increases in processing capacity and the shrinking size of computers, the lower cost of data storage, the expanded access to affordable internet facilities, artificial intel-ligence and robotics (Schwab 2016). This fusion produces a cumu-lative transformative impact on economies, which goes far beyond the technology-related economic sectors, and affects even industries such as retailing, transport and construction (Mulas 2016).

Following the widespread diffusion of technology, entrepre-neurship and innovation, both cornerstones of sustained economic growth, have become more affordable and delocalised. Innovation increasingly becomes 'open'; it is being co-created by large firms, entrepreneurs and other actors, and comes from start ups located in more and less advanced economies, which creates new growth opportunities, especially for the latter (Mulas 2016).

The potential consequences posed by the fourth industrial revolu-tion have already sparked a significant debate on employment and work around the world. The two most hotly debated factors are the prospect of automation and robots displacing humans from jobs, and the rise in employment in the so-called 'gig' or 'platform economy'. The jobs most at risk of being automated are routine ones, whether cognitive or manual. This is likely to exacerbate the polarisation in the labour market, with jobs being created largely at the highly paid and lower paid ends of the spectrum (see Arnold et al. this volume). It is also likely to increase the pace of change in the skills that increase the employability of humans, which are likely to develop in directions that are difficult to predict (see Atkinson this volume). In view of these developments, softer skills such as creativity, communication, critical thinking and the ability to work collaboratively become ever more important for employability in the future (see Benhamou this volume).

On the other hand, while the spreading of platform or gig employment can improve the matching of labour demand with labour supply (see Aubrey this volume), it also arguably shifts risks from employers and clients to workers. This shift can undermine the relevance of the standard employment relationship for the provision of workers' protection, and may have a negative impact on work and employment conditions (Drahokoupil and Piasna 2017; Doellgast this volume).

This contribution will look into the potential policy priorities that may be used to harness the opportunities, and may minimise the threats for work and welfare posed by the fourth industrial revolution for Greece, which is a particularly interesting case in this respect. Traditionally, a country with weak industry, and with an economy oriented towards low and low-to-medium levels of technological penetration in manufacturing and services, and a 'digital laggard', Greece has been the EU member most badly affected by the recent Eurozone crisis, as has been well documented. Attempts to find a more sustainable growth model and to undertake reforms to the organisation of work and welfare are thus a pressing concern for Greek policymakers. While the fourth industrial revolution could present growth opportunities for Greece, unless key policy initiatives are taken it could also exacerbate the existing problems of precarity and inequality in the labour market, and may pose challenges to the financing and strengthening of the Greek social safety net.

The chapter is structured as follows: the next section provides a broad-brush picture of the effects of the recent crisis in Greece. The following section discusses the strengths and weakness of Greece vis-à-vis the requirements for taking advantage of the fourth industrial revolution and the opportunities and threats that the fourth industrial revolution presents for Greece. Using this analysis, the final section proposes a range of policy priorities for Greek policymakers.

## GREECE: A TRAUMATISED ECONOMY AND SOCIETY EMERGING FROM THE CRISIS

Greece has been experiencing a deep economic, social and political crisis since 2009. Between 2008 and 2013, real GDP per head in Greece fell by 26% and the average annual real GDP per head growth rate has been 0.5% ever since. Real gross investment declined at an average annual rate of 11% since 2008, compared with an average annual rate of decline of 0.8% in the euro area and of 0.5% in the EU28 (own calculations based on data from AMECO, the annual macro-economic database of the European Commission's Directorate General for Economic and Financial Affairs). Between 2010, when the first economic adjustment programme was put in place, and 2015 labour productivity per hour worked in the total economy declined at an annual average of 1% (own calculations using EU KLEMS data)

By 2016, Greece had eliminated its government budget deficit, which stood at 15.1% of GDP in 2009. To that end, real public spending (excluding interest payments) in Greece had fallen to 81% in 2016 from what it had been in 2010 while the country's gross public debt had reached 181% of its GDP. By 2016, the country's current account balance, at 15.8% of GDP in 2008, was also virtually eliminated, with reduced imports (and therefore consumption) accounting much more for this adjustment than increased exports. Up until the crisis, Greece's growth model relied on domestic demand. The Greek tradables sector has been rather anaemic and has specialised in low- to low-to-medium technology goods and services.

The economic crisis painted above was matched by a social meltdown. Starting at 7.8% of the labour force in 2008, and 21% for young people (18–24 year olds), the average Greek unemployment rate peaked at 28.7% in 2013, falling to 23.6% in 2016, 78% of which represented the long-term unemployed who had been without work for over a year. Youth unemployment peaked at 60% in early 2013 before declining to 43.7% in the second quarter of 2017. Almost a million jobs (net) were lost between 2008 and 2016. Despite the developments in youth unemployment capturing the news headlines, two-thirds of these job losses concerned people of prime working age (25–49 year olds), mostly men. This was a grave development for a labour market and welfare state model that has been geared towards the protection of the male breadwinner. By 2016, only about half (52%) of Greek residents aged 15–64 were employed, the lowest rate in the EU28. Meanwhile, the involuntary part-timers as a share of total part-timers had increased from 44% in 2008 to 72% in 2016, which suggests that there has been a large increase in underemployment. The crisis has also stripped Greece of a large part of its workforce; Greek workers either became long-term unemployed or left the country in search of (better) job opportunities elsewhere.

The risk-of-poverty rate (anchored to 2008 incomes) rose from 20% to 48% between 2008 and 2016. Moreover, during the crisis, unemployment and the risk of poverty became much more tightly linked than before, which aggravated the risks of social exclusion for the jobless. In-work poverty stood at 19% in 2016.

The concurrent internal (labour cost) devaluation and fiscal adjustment policies which Greece had to pursue in exchange for receiving financial support resulted in fundamental changes in labour relations, and in the social security, pensions and healthcare systems.

Total social protection spending as a share of GDP contracted from 27.4% of GDP in 2012 to 26.1% of GDP in 2015 (the year for which the latest provisional data are available from Eurostat). Social protection functions such as unemployment and healthcare were not spared from cuts. By 2015, 11% of Greeks stated that they had unmet healthcare needs because they could not afford healthcare. Spending on unemployment benefits declined from 1.7% of GDP in 2011 to 1.1% of GDP by 2015 while spending on healthcare benefits declined from 6.8% of GDP in 2010 to 5.1% of GDP in 2015. The Greek labour market, which was already highly segmented before the crisis, underwent changes that increased employers' flexibility, while also reducing workers' security, as employment protection legislation was eased for both regular and fixed-term contracts (Matsaganis 2018, forthcoming).

Last but not least, the crisis has led to major changes at the political and electoral levels. The electoral power of the two parties that alternated in government during the 1974–2009 period more than halved from a joint share of 77% of votes in October 2009 to 32% in January 2015. Most starkly, support for the Socialists (the Panhellenic Socialist Alliance; PASOK) dropped from 44% to 4.7% of the vote during this period. There have been four general elections in Greece, and five different governments since 2009, the last four of them being, unusually for Greece's most recent history, coalition governments with weak or fragile parliamentary majorities. The number of parties represented at the parliament has risen from four to five to eight, with at least two of them being classified as 'anti-systemic' parties, which has led to a fragmented and polarised multiparty system. At the same time, abstention from the general elections has increased from 29% in 2009 to 44% in 2015, which reflects – among other things – a disillusionment of voters with politics following the economic collapse and the harsh economic adjustment programmes that were imposed in exchange for financial support from the country's international creditors.

Despite the large number of reforms that have taken place in Greece since 2010, there has yet to emerge a concrete and realistic national vision that is widely shared across parties of what economic, but also work and welfare model, the country should be steered towards – let alone a strategy for realising any such goal. The economic adjustment measures requested by the Troika of the EU, European Central Bank and International Monetary Fund (or Quadriga from 2015, following the inclusion of the newly created European Stability Mechanism) in exchange for financial support have for the most part prioritised an accounting approach aimed at meeting fiscal targets. There has been less concern about the effects of measures on the emergence of a sustainable growth model, and concerns about their social impact have only been reported since 2015. The failure of the Greek parties – alternating in government from the 1970s until as late as 2015 – to reach even a minimal consensus on how the high costs of economic adjustment should have been strategically distributed, the continued divisive rhetoric in the public policy debate, and the chronically deficient engagement of Greek policymakers with expert knowledge and subsequent continuous failures in policy learning (Monastiriotis and Antoniades 2009) do not inspire optimism for the future, in this respect at least.

For example, a strategy for developing the digital economy is a precondition for taking advantage of the fourth industrial revolution. In November 2016, the current government published its national digital strategy for the period 2016–2021 and established a ministry of digital policy, telecommunications and information, with a specific secretariat for digital policy. The strategy document contained several priorities, including one on integrating important Greek sectors into the fourth industrial revolution. This strategy has not been the first of its kind. In fact, every government since the 1990s had published a similar document of its own. As Katsikas and Gritzalis (2017) argue, the problem with these strategies is that their time horizon always exceeds the term of each government and the next government taking office always disregards the strategy of their predecessors, which results in no strategy ever being fully implemented.

## THE FOURTH INDUSTRIAL REVOLUTION AND GREECE: STRENGTHS, WEAKNESSES, OPPORTUNITIES AND THREATS

According to the European Commission's European digital progress report on Greece for 2017 (European Commission 2017), Greece is classified as a 'digital laggard' in Europe. While it scores fairly low in all of the dimensions (such as connectivity, human capital, use of the internet, integration of digital technology and digital public services) of the Digital Economy and Society's Index (DESI), it also presents some strengths in certain areas, such as the fixed broadband coverage of households, the number of science, technology, engineering and maths (STEM) graduates, the proportion of people engaging in online activities, the proportion of firms using social media and electronically sharing information, the share of internet users that engage with egovernment services, and the provision of open data. On the other hand, Greece has the lowest share of information and communications technology (ICT) specialists in total employed persons in the EU, a rather low share of the population with at least basic digital skills, very low take-up rates of mobile broadband and subscriptions to fast broadband, and very low online provision of public services.

In principle, the fourth industrial revolution presents growth opportunities for Greece. First, the changing open, affordable and delocalised nature of innovation in the context of fourth industrial revolution opens up opportunities for the creation of firms that provide high-tech innovative services and products that help the economy to move away from its specialisation in low- and low-to-medium technologies. Such innovative services and products could be provided from Greece to anywhere in Europe or the world. These firms could start small (for example, with start ups) and, if successful, grow to attract foreign direct investment, a flow that the Greek economy will have to rely on to start growing again, given the constraints on public spending as part of the country's bailout arrangements, which are likely to last for decades, and given the high rate of non-performing loans that Greek banks have been saddled with.

Second, following investment, new technologies that are emblematic of the fourth industrial revolution could be introduced in more traditional sectors to lower the costs of production while improving productivity and the quality of products or services, which could ultimately improve competitiveness in the economy. Third, automation and digitalisation could allow the provision of public services at a lower cost, thus helping to relieve some of the pressures on the Greek government budget, which are expected to remain for decades until the public debt to GDP ratio recedes to levels that pose fewer risks to the economy. The development of egovernment is also paramount for promoting digitalisation in an economy.

While such developments would generate income, they are unlikely to generate large numbers of jobs (again, with many potential new jobs coming in the form of relatively small start ups) and they are also likely to lead to job losses or to a shift of jobs towards less dynamic services sectors that depend more on domestic demand. Moreover, whether any productivity gains from innovation and new technologies will result in productivity growth at the aggregate level will depend on whether demand for the products and services of these sectors will increase commensurably. In turn this will depend on whether there is sufficient income across the economy to support demand for the products of these sectors and, insofar as these new products are digital, whether digital skills and fast internet access are widespread enough to support demand.

Digital platforms can provide a valuable tool for remaining employed in a labour market where jobs under more classic employment relationships are scarce, while also providing a source of income for Greek households, which on average lost a quarter of their income since the onset of the crisis. However, platform employment can involve pitfalls, as it is often precarious, insecure, undeclared and subject to sub-standard working conditions (for example as regards health and safety). Undeclared work can in turn result in a lack of social security coverage for workers and to lower contributions to the system overall (Drahokoupil and Piasna 2017). These risks are particularly important in Greece, which has been traditionally characterised by a large informal sector where employment regulations are systematically violated, while the financing of the social security system has also suffered from the high unemployment and job loss rate, especially among men.

## POLICY PRIORITIES FOR HARNESSING THE POTENTIAL BENEFITS OF THE FOURTH INDUSTRIAL REVOLUTION IN GREECE

Given the above mentioned strengths and weaknesses of Greece and the opportunities and threats that the fourth industrial revolution can present for the country, what should be the policy priorities for the Greek governments in order to enable the country to make the most of the fourth industrial revolution?

First, and in order to move up from the 'digital laggards' group in Europe, policymakers need to understand the importance of adopting a consistent digital strategy that will last beyond changes of political parties in office. The likelihood that the current national strategy might have a different fate appears slim. The aforementioned de-alignment of voters from the two parties that alternated in government between 1974 and 2009, the change in the Greek electoral law towards a system that is closer to simple representation, and the maintenance of divisive rhetoric in national politics, at least from the part of the current government parties, taken together do not bode well for any elevation of the question of the digital strategy to a national priority. That does not give much hope for the creation of a strategy that can survive the term of any government, while the 'reform technology' of the country is also weak (Monastiriotis and Antoniades 2009).

A second priority should be to maximise as far as possible the capacity of as many citizens and firms as possible to use and participate in the digital society. For this, the education system needs to integrate the acquisition of digital skills from an earlier stage, and affordable training opportunities should be available for older people. The education system should also equip students with the 'softer' skills that will shield them from being replaced by robots in the future. Digitalising public administration would also be an indispensable step in that direction, thus providing incentives for citizens to acquire and use these skills, while also contributing to improved transparency and efficiency in public administration.

A third priority would be to establish a business environment that is friendly for innovative start ups. Elements of such an environment would be a more efficient judicial system, and a more predictable and transparent taxation system, coupled with the provision of high-quality public and social services, especially if taxes are high. Stronger links between start ups and university research, in which Greece is actually highly competitive, would also help.

A fourth priority should be the rethinking of employment and social protection (see Palier this volume). Employment in the platform economy should be brought under the regulation that governs more traditional forms of employment, in order to secure the participation of platform workers as contributors to, and ultimately as beneficiaries of, the social protection system, and to create the basis for better working conditions, provided that the enforcement of regulation will also improve (see Berg and De Stefano this volume). Recent reforms in the unemployment insurance system have been a step in the right direction for extending coverage to self-employed people. However, they have also been subject to biting budget constraints, whereas the eligibility rules failed to adjust to the realities on the ground and resulted in only a limited extension of the coverage (Matsaganis 2018, forthcoming).

More generally, the inevitable disruptions in the way that work and welfare are organised as a result of the necessary adoption of a new growth model for Greece, and given the advent of the fourth industrial revolution, suggest that social protection should become less tightly linked to the employment relationship, and more closely associated with fiscal residence. The recent deployment of a (means-tested) guaranteed minimum income is a first step in the right direction.

## REFERENCES

Drahokoupil, J. and A. Piasna (2017), 'Work in the Platform Economy: Beyond Lower Transaction Costs', *Intereconomics: Review of European Economic Policy*, 52(6): 335–40.

European Commission (2017), *Europe's Digital Progress Report (EDPR) 2017 Country Profile: Greece*, https://ec.europa.eu/digital-single-market/en/news/europes-digital-progress-report-2017.

Katsikas, S. K. and S. Gritazlis (2017), 'Digitalization in Greece: State of Play, Barriers, Challenges, Solutions', in A. A. Paulin, L. G. Anthopoulos and C. G. Reddick (eds), *Beyond Bureaucracy*, 355–75, Cham: Springer.

Matsaganis, M. (2018, forthcoming), 'Austerity and the Welfare State in Greece: the Case of Labour Market Policies', in S. Theodoropoulou (ed.), *Welfare States and EU Austerity: the Case of Labour Market Policies*, Brussels: European Trade Union Institute.

Monastiriotis, V. and A. Antoniades (2009), *Reform That! Greece's Failing Reform Technology: Beyond 'Vested Interests' and 'Political Exchange*, London: The Hellenic Observatory, London School of Economics and Political Science.

Mulas, V. (2016), 'How Can Countries Take Advantage of the Fourth Industrial Revolution?', World Bank blog: Private Sector Development, 13 October, http://blogs.worldbank.org/psd/how-can-countries-take-advantage-fourth-industrial-revolution.

Schwab, K. (2016), 'The Fourth Industrial Revolution: What it Means, How to Respond', The World Economic Forum Agenda, 14 January, https://www.weforum.org/agenda/2016/01/the-fourth-industrial-revolution-what-it-means-and-how-to-respond.

# D

# Global perspectives

# CANADA

## Opportunities for the many?

## Juan Gomez and Rafael Gomez

Speculation on how technology can transform work and society, in either positive or negative ways, is hardly novel. It goes as far back as Aristotle's Politics, where he describes an "(inanimate) instrument" that "could do its own work, at the word of command or by intelligent anticipation" (Carol 2010), removing among other things the need for subordinates and giving deep thinkers more time to brood over life's bigger meaning.

In the modern era, conventional wisdom is that innovation forms part of a continuous process of creative destruction, with some jobs eliminated, but over time many more added. From this perspective, the correct societal response is to embrace technological change while managing its downsides, whether it is the loss of employment, growing skill mismatches or rising inequality.

Yet, more than 2,000 years after Aristotle, the comforting premise of more gain than pain from technological change is being questioned. The feeling that 'this time is different', with employment creation being overwhelmed by its destruction, has grown. Advancements in such areas as artificial intelligence (AI) are purportedly happening so quickly and of such a monumental scale that even high-skilled workers (eg doctors and lawyers) are under threat

(Suskind and Suskind 2016). Sensationalised reports of killer robots supplanting humans and triggering civilisational collapse are finding a ready audience in today's world of 'trending' and 'clickbait' media. Everyone from Stephen Hawking to Vladimir Putin to Yanis Varoufakis are weighing in with apocalyptic warnings of what the fourth industrial revolution and its technologies could augur for the world (Embury-Dennis 2017; Hearn 2016; Karpukhin 2017).

## UTOPIA, DYSTOPIA OR THE SAME OLD SCENE?

For some, of course, the fourth industrial revolution is not all doom and gloom. 'Techno-optimists' like MIT's Erik Brynjolfsson and Andrew McAfee see us "living in a time of astonishing progress with digital technologies" that will create vastly more wealth and – provided these benefits are broadly shared throughout society – greater opportunity as well (Brynjolfsson and McAfee 2014). Likewise, World Economic Forum (WEF) founder Klaus Schwab in his book The Fourth Industrial Revolution sees technologies like AI, robotics, 3D printing and biotech as having the potential of lifting "humanity into a new collective and moral consciousness based on a shared sense of destiny" (Poole 2017, citing Schwab).

Meanwhile, somewhere between pessimists and optimists lie economists like Robert J. Gordon, who argues that from a productivity and innovation standpoint we have been going downhill since the 1970s. Gordon (2016) sees a future of stasis or 'secular stagnation' as it is technically known, highlighting the Depression-era fears of economists such as John Maynard Keynes and Alvin H. Hansen, who saw a tendency for productivity and growth in mature economies to slow down (Gomez and Lamb 2013). In this middle-range scenario, the most important contributions of the digital revolution have already occurred. Sure, innovations will continue, but they will be evolutionary and not revolutionary according to Gordon (2016).

Irrespective of where one stands, there's no denying that technology in today's disembodied and intangible economy is qualitatively different from the goods-producing economies of yesteryear (Wolf 2017). This point is illustrated by Jonathan Haskel and Stian Westlake (2017) who note that the tangible assets of Apple, the world's largest company by market capitalisation, account for a meagre 4% of its $880bn market value. Likewise, Google, Alphabet and Microsoft have relatively little in the way of fixed assets (Mak 2017). What makes these firms highly valued are elements not considered in traditional cost accounting, particularly brand-equity, data management and supply-chain expertise.

However, the emergence of these tech giants takes us back to the days of America's gilded age when industrial giants like Standard Oil and Carnegie Steel dominated the economic landscape. And as in the gilded age, tech is creating its Rockefellers and JP Morgans in the form of Jeff Bezos and Mark Zuckerberg. Eight of the world's most highly valued companies are now technology businesses.[1] The total market capitalisation of these companies is $4.7tn, a startling 30% of the combined market capitalisation of the other 92 companies that make up the world's 100 richest firms (Wolf 2017). People are beginning to notice, which is perhaps why the Financial Times recently declared that only monopolies could deliver such super-normal profits and valuations (Wolf 2017).

Like in the gilded age, the monopolistic and cartel-like position of these tech titans is contributing to an enormous concentration of wealth and power with highly worrying implications for workers, communities, small enterprises and our democratic institutions. The fall of labour's share of GDP in the US and many other countries and commensurate rise in inequality since the 1980s is well documented (Piketty 2013) and has now been linked to the rise of these 'superstar firms' (Frick 2017).

While some of this concentration is undoubtedly due to higher productivity and innovative capacity, we should not discount the agency costs that this kind of corporate power creates. The top five US tech firms (Google, Facebook, Apple, Amazon and Microsoft) now outspend Wall Street 2:1 on lobbying to fight 'unfavourable' regulation (Solon and Siddiqui 2017). Moreover, the rent-seeking activities of these firms, which include complex tax avoidance schemes, starve governments of revenues they need to maintain vital public infrastructure. As Haskel and Westlake point out, this does "no good for the economy . . . but instead (is) about slicing the existing economic pie to the exclusive benefit of the intangible investor" (cited in Mak 2017).

## CANADA'S QUANTUM LEAP?

For mid- to small-sized countries like Canada, a very real challenge is how to play in a technology game fraught with so many risks. Certainly, there's no shortage of opinions on the subject. In Canada people in a myriad of thinktanks, consultancies and government agencies talk of job losses, economic inequality and societal dislocation (Lamb and Lo 2017), as new technologies replace workers and perhaps even make government obsolete (Johal 2017). One of the country's longest running public affairs TV programmes, The Agenda, recently devoted a full hour in primetime to debate whether the rise of robots and AI means the end of work (Paikin 2017).

Not to be outdone, Canada's prime minister, Justin Trudeau, garnered international headlines at a public event hosted by a Canadian physics research institute. In response to a reporter's slightly sarcastic suggestion that he explain quantum computing, according to news accounts Trudeau surprised reporters by explaining the basics of this technology and stunned physicists in attendance with his understanding of their field (Wells 2017).

Trudeau's bona fides as something of a techno visionary were cemented by his 2016 speech at the WEF. Notably, Trudeau argued that the fourth industrial revolution would not be successful unless it created real opportunity for the many, not just the elite attending the conference in Davos; something he felt Canada 'gets' (Trudeau 2016). It was also a speech in which the prime minister sought to erase the reputation that Canada was simply a purveyor of natural resources. Instead the new Canada, in Trudeau's words, was all about "resourcefulness", using our brains more than our brawn, as it were. These and other interventions prompted founder and executive chairman of the WEF, Klaus Schwab, to state that he "couldn't imagine anybody who . . . represent[s] more the world which will come out of this [fourth industrial revolution] than Trudeau" (Wells 2017).

The big question, now almost two years on from the Davos speech, is to what extent does Canada 'get' it or, more precisely, how well is it prepared for the challenges of creating shared prosperity in a time of rapid technological change? In attempting to respond to this question, it is useful to take a step back in time for both inspiration and insight into how Canada will perhaps navigate the fourth industrial revolution.

## EXPO 67: CONSOLIDATING THE THIRD AND VISUALISING THE FOURTH INDUSTRIAL REVOLUTION

In 2017 Canada marked two important and related milestones: the 150th anniversary of its founding in 1867 as a confederation of former British colonies and the 50th anniversary of Expo 67, the world's fair hosted by the city of Montreal. For Canadians with memories of Expo 67, in particular baby-boomers, a recent flurry of documentaries, articles and exhibitions were an opportunity to revel in some unabashed nostalgia. Often described as the best world's fair ever,[2] Expo 67 was more significantly a giant incubator for innovations in new media, architecture, design and laying the foundations for the growth and vibrancy of Canada's creative industries. Famed Canadian communications theorist Marshall McLuhan saw it as a mosaic "of culture and media, a global rendezvous unlike any before. What is happening today around the world" McLuhan proclaimed "is what is happening at Expo" (Fargo 2017).

From its conception to its implementation, Expo 67 was also emblematic of an increasingly 'entrepreneurial' Canadian state. It embodied a notion, which economist Mariana Mazzucato (2015) today calls on governments to embrace, to create markets and not just fix them. State-owned enterprises like Hydro Quebec, TV Ontario and the Canada Development Corporation – often referred to as 'crown corporations' – shaped industries and created important national markets in energy, aerospace, culture or transportation to name just a few. Such policies reflected a pragmatic economic nationalism, which though not eschewing foreign trade and investment reflected what historian Kenneth McNaught (1969) noted was a consensus among Canadians on the need to maintain control of the country's key economic sectors.

Certainly, the success of this approach was borne out by results. By the 1970s Canada had become one of the world's most prosperous economies. And, remarkably, in little over a decade (from 1965 to 1977), the country became a modern welfare state. Under the leadership of prime ministers Lester B. Pearson and, later, Pierre Elliot Trudeau (father of our current PM) Canada there were major enhancements to post-secondary education, physical infrastructure, pensions, unemployment insurance, income support and public housing, and the rollout of universal healthcare. The scale of this transformation was evident in Canada's largest province, Ontario, where the government built and opened nine public universities in just under 10 years. Moreover, as Canadian economist Pierre Fortin observed in his obituary of the prime minister, the 'Just Society', as it was defined by Trudeau, would contain the core of an effective human capital strategy: "a full-employment policy, a good income security policy (with few adverse work incentives), a redistributive income tax policy, a major effort in education, a fair minimum wage, and freedom to unionise" (Fortin 2000). A strategy that would produce significantly less poverty and inequality than its southern neighbour.

To be sure, Canada would not entirely free itself of the ills afflicting industrialised nations during the 'stagflation' period of the 1970s, whether it was inflationary pressures, labour conflict or terrorism and separatism in Quebec. Nonetheless, Canada demonstrated itself much more resilient than many of its counterparts in dealing with these socio-economic challenges. Canada's positive response to the oil shock of the early 1970s, in particular, proved that the best shock absorber is a sound combination of proactive and adaptive public policies and a diverse economic base. This is a lesson today's policymakers should keep in mind.

## IN 2017, WITH ECHOES OF 1967, THE PENDULUM SWINGS PROGRESSIVE ONCE AGAIN

Like much of the industrialised west, from the 1980s to the early 2000s, Canada followed the standard playbook of neoliberal and third-way orthodoxy, and suffered as a result with its unemployment rate rising above and GDP per-capita falling below the US for the first time in the postwar period. Fortunately, this tendency to embrace neoliberal nostrums did not extend to deregulation of the financial sector, sparing Canada the worst effects of the Great Recession (eg, no Canadian bank required a bailout following the financial crash of 2008).

Since 2009, Canadian governments have embraced approaches with echoes of the entrepreneurial and welfare state of the 1960s and 1970s. This is evident in the realm of fiscal and macro-economic policy where the federal government is making some not insignificant investments in physical and social infrastructure and forecasting modest deficits over the next several years. While not proportionately as large as those of the 'Just Society', these public investments and the rhetoric surrounding them marks a sea change.

In the context of the fourth industrial revolution, a major emphasis is being placed on innovation, skills development and modernising labour legislation. Though not quite a full-blown industrial strategy, the federal government launched its Innovation Superclusters Initiative, which will invest substantial sums in areas, such as machine learning and AI. Interestingly, the fund also seeks to invest in projects that cross-pollinate high tech in more traditional sectors like agriculture, retail and energy. And while the development of AI is most often associated with Silicon Valley, Canada has 'the' leading researcher in the field, Professor Geoff Hinton, who as a recent New York Times article noted, is "helping underpin a wave of new developments in the field" (Tam 2017).

In skills development, federal and provincial governments are meeting the growing demands of the knowledge economy by blending investments in apprenticeship, work-based learning and improved labour market information. This is buttressed by what is already a world-class primary, secondary and post-secondary educational system (Conference Board of Canada 2014; Coughain 2017).

Perhaps most promising are changes to labour and income support policies, which are responding to the increasingly low-wage and precarious nature of employment in the so-called gig and platform economies. In the country's provinces, which have jurisdiction over most workplaces, policies like increased minimum wages, support for collective representation, giving workers a greater say in scheduling, equal pay for contract and casual employees, and stronger enforcement of labour legislation (eg hiring more inspectors) are becoming the norm.[3]

Ontario (Canada's most populous province), like Finland, is also piloting a basic income programme, a concept that is not without its detractors on the left and right, but which has thus far attracted mainstream support (Segal 2016). It must be stressed, however, that a basic income is based on a not unreasonable demand from capital, particularly tech, for a *quid pro quo* of sorts. In exchange for allowing flexibility in employment relationships (and as some critics charge, allowing tech companies to get rich by mining our personal data and exacerbate income polarisation) support for basic income protection that provides a floor against employment loss is offered. In more than just a rhetorical sense, many tech captains of the industry support the basic income, though for some this is still a public relations exercise by which Silicon Valley can play 'good cop' to Wall Street's 'bad cop', and there is concern that the existing welfare state will be replaced with a threadbare basic income.

## SO, DOES CANADA GET IT?

So, returning to the question we posed earlier, does Canada, as the prime minister suggests, 'get it' when it comes to creating shared prosperity in a time of the fourth industrial revolution? The answer, it would seem, is a very qualified yes.

In general, Canada's focus on innovation, skills and modernising labour standards moves the country in the right direction. Canada, as noted, has the potential for a first mover advantage in fourth industrial revolution areas like machine learning and AI, with the city of Toronto already being recognised as an international hub for these activities. For decades, University of Toronto Professor Geoffrey Hinton worked on what was thought to be an arcane area of mathematics known as 'neural nets' but now, along with a group of Canadian-trained students, his work is part of the team developing cutting-edge AI technology (Gray 2017). And the world's biggest tech companies are throwing millions of dollars into Canada's neural net research programme, hiring many of Hinton's students, who now run or conduct AI research at Apple, Twitter, Google and Facebook (Gray 2017).

This emphasis on neural nets and machine learning also helps to rebalance the economy from an overreliance on natural resources. Neural nets, developed by Canadian talent, are already powering most of the voice recognition software in mobile phones. They recognise faces in pictures and can distinguish different diseases on radiological scans, in some cases more accurately than humans can. This new fourth industrial revolution focus makes us more 'resourceful' and crucially builds in resilience and diversity, something that is needed given the inevitable ups and downs of the economic cycle and the very real potential for future 'black swan' events in capital markets. Likewise, the focus on fundamentals like education and economic supports for displaced workers will help reduce inequality and mitigate what could be difficult transitions for some industries in the fourth industrial revolution.

## FINAL THOUGHTS

Unfortunately, there are some dark clouds that overshadow the rosy picture. Notwithstanding the well-documented need for AI specialists, code writers and so on, there is perhaps too much of a tech-centred focus on the labour market side, which ignores opportunities for meaningful employment in other sectors. It is no secret that in Canada, as in other advanced economies, aging demographics are driving massive growth and demand for personal services and care-based work (Osterman 2017). Currently, these jobs are low paid and do not require a high degree of skill or qualifications to practice. But this does not have to be the case. Why not work to transform these jobs into more skilled occupations? Indeed, just a moderate amount of additional education and technology could improve job quality for workers and outcomes for care recipients. The objective should be to advance innovation and productivity improvements across all sectors and occupations, not only tech.

The lengths many Canadian politicians and regional economic development specialists are willing to go – often involving large tax breaks and subsidies – to attract the 'big' established tech firms are also worrying. They do this in the hope that they can transform a region's economic fortunes with more jobs and growth. This was certainly evident during Amazon's recently announced public tender process for the location of its second North American headquarters, during which Toronto and several other Canadian regions clamoured to make their community Amazon's new home.

This approach produces splashy headlines and ribbon cutting ceremonies for politicians, but empirically we know that growth is more reliably correlated with the number of small independent firms based in a region or city (Glaeser, Kerr and Kerr 2015; Gomez, Isakov and Semansky 2015). Local tech investors know this all too well, which is why they are pleading with politicians to focus their efforts on supporting smaller, successful Canadian start ups (eg Shopify and Thalmic Labs) instead of rolling out the red carpet for Amazon (Lacavera 2017), which has no shortage of money but a less than stellar record in the treatment of its global workforce (Head 2014).

Likewise, it was disappointing that Waterfront Toronto, a world-renowned state-owned entity responsible for managing North America's largest urban regeneration project, effectively handed over to Alphabet (Google's parent company) the redevelopment of a Toronto waterfront district called Quayside. Google envisions Quayside as a tech-rich and data-informed neighbourhood, using AI to create a safe, sustainable and affordable place to live. But as some open data advocates have observed, it may be less an urban planning initiative and more about a private actor insinuating itself into a city's urban infrastructure and harvesting data for virtually no cost (Wylie 2017). Also concerning is "how this model may further erode the technological capacity of the state; and what that does to our ability as a nation to operate independently of technology vendors" (Wylie 2017).

Although there is value in partnering with firms such as Google to improve the urban environment, it is perplexing that the city did not consider local tech players in addition to international expertise. This is an approach the agency has already successfully executed on redevelopment projects such as Corktown Common (Waterfront Toronto 2017).

Overlooked as well is the issue of how much control citizens (in their roles as workers and more broadly as voting citizens) should have over the deployment of fourth industrial revolution technologies at work and across society (see Crouch this volume). This points to the need for a reinvigorated democracy extending from the shop floor to the floor of parliament, so as to ensure multiple voices, not just well-paid lobbyists, shape our economic future (Gomez and Gomez 2016).

Given the global reach and increasingly monopolistic position of today's tech giants, Canada also needs to think about how it can work with two of its biggest trading partners, the EU and US, to ensure that fair and open market access extends to smaller, nationally based tech players.

In a domestic context, it is also critical that Canada give serious consideration to a call from open data advocates for a national discussion about our information, related public infrastructure, and the degree to which we want private actors based in Silicon Valley influencing our governance and public services (Wylie 2017).

To conclude, the fourth industrial revolution once again calls for a pragmatic nationalism that keeps Canada open to the world while at the same time seeking to preserve what is good and unique about the country.

## NOTES

1. Five companies (Apple, Alphabet and Google, Microsoft, Amazon and Facebook) are American, two are Chinese (Alibaba and Tencent) and one (Samsung) is South Korean.

2. The New York Times at the time praised its "sophisticated standard of excellence (that) almost defies description" (Wall 2017).

3. Finally, also notable from an income support standpoint is the federal government's announcement of a new housing benefit for lower income Canadians. Again, this is a very real and practical response to the emerging prosperity and employment gap resulting from the new economy and the fourth industrial revolution. For more information on the housing benefit, see Canada's National Housing Strategy (Government of Canada 2017).

## REFERENCES

Aristotle (350 BCE), *Politics*, translated by Benjamin Jowett, Boston: MIT Classics.

Brynjolfsson, E. and A. McAfee (2014), *The Second Machine Age: Work, Progress, and Prosperity in a Time of Brilliant Technologies*, New York: W.W. Norton.

Caroll, S. (2010), 'Aristotle on Household Robots', *Discover*, 28 September, http://blogs.discovermagazine.com/cosmicvariance/2010/09/28/aristotle-on-household-robots/#.Wjp99jRG272.

Conference Board of Canada (2014), *Provincial and Territorial Ranking: Education and Skills.* Rankings. Ottawa: The Conference Board of Canada.

Coughlan, S. (2017), 'How Canada Became an Education Superpower', BBC News, 2 August, http://www.bbc.com/news/business-40708421.

Embury-Dennis, T. (2017), 'Capitalism is Ending Because it has made itself Obsolete, Former Greek Finance Minister Yannis Varoufakis Says', *The Independent*, 18 October, http://www.independent.co.uk/news/world/europe/yannis-varoufakis-capitalism-ending-obsolete-former-greek-finance-minister-artificial-intelligence-a8006826.html.

Fargo, J. (2017), 'Expo 2017: Utopia, Rebooted', *The New York Times*, 22 June, https://www.nytimes.com/2017/06/22/arts/design/expo-2017-utopia-rebooted.html.

Fortin, P. (2000), 'Pierre Elliott Trudeau: 1919–2000', *Globe and Mail*, 9 October, http://v1.theglobeandmail.com/series/trudeau/grosuc_oct9.html.

Frick, W. (2017), 'The Real Reason Superstar Firms are Pulling Ahead', *Harvard Business Review*, 5 October, https://hbr.org/2017/10/the-real-reason-superstar-firms-are-pulling-ahead.

Glaeser, E. L., S. P. Kerr and W. R. Kerr (2015), 'Entrepreneurship and Urban Growth: an Empirical Assessment with Historical Mines', *The Review of Economics and Statistics*, 97(2): 498–520.

Gomez, R. and J. Gomez (2016), *Workplace Democracy for the 21st Century: Towards a New Agenda for Employee Voice and Representation*, Broadbent Institute Discussion Paper.

Gomez, R. and D. Lamb (2013), 'Demographic Origins of the Great Recession: Implications for China', *China & World Economy*, 21(2): 97–118.

Gomez, R., A. Isakov and M. Semansky (2015), *Small Business and the City: the Transformative Potential of Small-Scale Entrepreneurship*. Toronto: University of Toronto Press.

Gordon, R. J. (2016), *The Rise and fall of American Growth: the US Standard of Living since the Civil War*. Princeton, N.J.: Princeton University Press.

Government of Canada (2017), *Canada's National Housing Strategy*, Ottawa: Government of Canada.

Gray, J. (2017), 'U of T professor Geoffrey Hinton Hailed as Guru of New Computing Era', *Globe and Mail*, 7 April, https://www.theglobeandmail.com/news/toronto/u-of-t-professor-geoffrey-hinton-hailed-as-guru-of-new-era-of-computing/article34639148/.

Haskel, J. and S. Westlake. *Capitalism Without Capital: the Rise of the Intangible Economy*. Princeton: Princeton University Press.

Head, S. (2014), 'Worse than Wal-Mart: Amazon's Sick Brutality and Secret History of Ruthlessly Intimidating Workers', *Salon*, 23 February, https://www.salon.com/2014/02/23/worse_than_wal_mart_amazons_sick_brutality_and_secret_history_of_ruthlessly_intimidating_workers/.

Hearn, A. (2016), 'Stephen Hawking: AI will be 'Either Best or Worst Thing' for Humanity', *The Guardian*, 19 October, https://www.theguardian.com/science/2016/oct/19/stephen-hawking-ai-best-or-worst-thing-for-humanity-cambridge.

Johal, S. (2017), 'Technology Will Make Government as we Know it Obsolete – and That's a Good Thing', *Mowat Centre*, 29 November, https://mowatcentre.ca/technology-will-make-government-as-we-know-it-obsolete-and-thats-a-good-thing/.

Karpukhin, S. (2017), 'Putin: Leader in Artificial Intelligence Will Rule World', *CNBC*, 4 September, https://www.cnbc.com/2017/09/04/putin-leader-in-artificial-intelligence-will-rule-world.html.

Lacavera, A. (2017), 'Amazon Bid the Wrong Move for Toronto, Tech Investor Says', Interview by Matt Galloway. *Metro Morning*, CBC, 3 October, http://www.cbc.ca/news/canada/toronto/programs/metromorning/don-t-roll-out-red-carpet-for-amazon-tech-investor-says-1.4318398.

Lamb, C. and M. Lo (2017), *Automation Across the Nation: Understanding the potential impacts of technological trends across Canada*. Toronto: Brookfield Institute.

Mak, R. (2017), 'Invisible Forces: Review of Capitalism without Capital by Jonathan Haskel and Stian Westlake', *Reuters*, 1 December, https://www.breakingviews.com/features/review-firm-ideas-for-a-world-of-soft-assets/.

Mazzucato, M. (2015), *The Entrepreneurial State: Debunking Public vs Private Sector Myths*, London: Anthem Press.

McNaught, K. (1969), *The Pelican History of Canada*. Baltimore: Penguin Books.

Osterman, P. (2017), *Who Will Care for Us: Long-term Care and the Long-Term Workforce*, New York: Russell Sage Foundation.

Paikin, S. (2017), 'The Agenda with Steve Paikin: Rise of Robots, End of Work?', TVO, 6 December, https://tvo.org/video/programs/the-agenda-with-steve-paikin/rise-of-robots-end-of-work.

Piketty, T. (2013), *Capital in the Twenty-First Century*, Cambridge, MA: Harvard University Press.

Poole, S. (2017), 'The Fourth Industrial Revolution Review – Adapt to New Technology or Perish: Review of The Fourth Industrial Revolution by Klaus Schwab', *The Guardian*, 6 January, https://www.theguardian.com/books/2017/jan/06/the-fourth-industrial-revolution-by-klaus-schwab-review.

Segal, H. D. (2016), *Finding a Better Way: A Basic Income Pilot Project for Ontario*, Government of Ontario Discussion Paper, https://www.ontario.ca/page/finding-better-way-basic-income-pilot-project-ontario.

Solon, O. and S. Siddiqui (2017), 'Forget Wall Street – Silicon Valley is the New Political Power in Washington', *The Observer*, 7 September, https://www.theguardian.com/technology/2017/sep/03/silicon-valley-politics-lobbying-washington.

Suskind, R. and D. Suskind (2016), *The Future of the Professions: How Technology Will Transform the Work of Human Experts*, Oxford: Oxford University Press.

Tam, P.-W. (2017), 'Tech Roundup: Canada Spends to Keep AI Experts Home', *New York Times*, 10 April, https://www.nytimes.com/2017/04/10/technology/tech-roundup-canada-spends-to-keep-ai-experts-home.html.

Trudeau, J. (2016), 'The Canadian Opportunity', address at the 2016 World Economic Forum in Davos, 20 January, https://pm.gc.ca/eng/news/2016/01/20/canadian-opportunity-address-right-honourable-justin-trudeau-prime-minister-canada.

Wall, D. (2017), 'Expo 67: Canada Stars on the World Stage', *Journal of Commerce*, 3 July.

Waterfront Toronto (2017), *Corktown Common*. Toronto: Waterfront Toronto, http://www.waterfrontoronto.ca/nbe/portal/waterfront/Home/waterfronthome/projects/corktown+common.

Wells, J. (2017), 'Innovation Key to Fixing Trudeau's 'Resourcefulness' Problem', *The Toronto Star*, 14 January, https://www.thestar.com/business/2017/01/14/innovation-key-to-fixing-trudeaus-resourcefulness-problem-jennifer-wells.html.

Wolf, M. (2017), 'The Challenges of a Disembodied Economy', *Financial Times*, 28 November, https://www.ft.com/content/a01e7262-d35a-11e7-a303-9060cb1e5f44.

Wylie, B. (2017), 'Think Hard Before Handing Tech Firms The Rights To Our Cities' Data', *Huffington Post*, 8 November, http://www.huffingtonpost.ca/bianca-wylie/think-hard-before-handing-tech-firms-the-rights-to-our-cities-data_a_23270793/.

# US

## *Balancing risks and improving job quality in a changing economy*

## Arne L. Kalleberg

The confluence of technological changes linked to the so-called fourth industrial revolution will have a profound bearing on a wide range of issues, providing opportunities and creating threats for workers and employers and reconfiguring the organisation of work and welfare in all countries. I focus here on two major impacts of the fourth industrial revolution on the future of work in the US: its effect on the quantity of jobs as reflected in employment and unemployment related to automation, and the quality of the jobs in the earnings that will be available to workers. This dynamic world of work will require workers to change jobs more often, and to learn new skills and adapt to new situations. These changes in the organisation of work will also require a new social contract among workers, the government and business.

### THE FOURTH INDUSTRIAL REVOLUTION

The term fourth industrial revolution refers to recent and fundamental changes in the organisation of work and labour market behaviours that is being driven by digitisation and IT: the availability of big data, industrial robotics, the internet of things (see Fernández-Macías this volume), artificial intelligence (AI; see Petropoulos this volume), and the continued growth of precarious and polarised employment relations in the US. Descriptions of the fourth industrial revolution emphasise the profound impacts generated by the combination of digitisation and IT that are fusing physical technologies (eg 3D printing, self-driving cars), digital technologies (eg online platforms such as Uber and distributed computer systems such as blockchains) and biological technologies (eg genetic editing and engineering) in innovative ways. The convergence of these three technologies is the central feature of the fourth industrial revolution (Schwab 2016).

The spread of information and communications technology has had, and will continue to have, deep effects on productivity (see Soete this volume), the wage distribution (see Doellgast this volume) and long-term economic growth. Automation will require new skills and eliminate others (see Aubrey this volume). Income inequality is likely to grow and become increasingly linked to differences in skills and educational credentials. Wealth inequality is also likely to continue to grow given the enactment of tax policies favouring the rich under the current administration.

There is disagreement over the consequences of the fourth industrial revolution for the quantity and quality of jobs. It is generally assumed that automation will have important effects on the number and nature of jobs, though there is less agreement on the number of jobs that are likely to be eliminated or be created and their characteristics.

## AUTOMATION AND EMPLOYMENT AND UNEMPLOYMENT

Concern over machines wiping out jobs has had a long history, famously represented by the early example of the destruction of machines by Luddite movements among English textile artisans of the early 19th century. In 1964, President Lyndon B. Johnson created a commission to assess the likelihood that productivity growth would exceed the demand for labour. The commission concluded that while technology eliminated some jobs, it would not eradicate the need for work as new jobs would be created; hence, machine substitution of labour does not replace human labour but rather displaces workers from one part of the economy to another (Autor 2015). At the same time, the commission recognised the reality of technological disruption and recommended policies to cope with its consequences: a guaranteed income, job creation by the government, and free education at community or vocational colleges, among others.

Similar concerns have re-emerged with the advent of the fourth industrial revolution. Again there are worries that we are headed into a 'jobless future' in which technological changes will reduce the demand for human labour. As in the past, these anxieties are likely overblown, as the destruction of some jobs will be accompanied by the creation of others.

The numbers and types of jobs that will be eliminated and created are less clear, however. Frey and Osborne (2017) examine occupations that could be automated and conclude that current technological changes will make it possible to replace about half of the jobs in the US with machines in the next 10 to 20 years. They found that jobs at the greatest risk of being automated were occupations involving transportation, logistics, office and administrative support, and production. The jobs in these industries are routine in nature and typically involve rules-based logic that computers are particularly good at replicating (Levy and Murnane 2013).

By contrast, Arntz, Gregory and Zierahn (2016) focused on the automation of the task content of jobs within occupations and concluded that Frey and Osborne's occupation-based approach overstates technological possibilities (see Arnold et al. this volume). They suggest instead that on average across 21 OECD countries only 9% of jobs are potentially automatable since workers in automatable occupations often perform non-routine interactive tasks, which are less amenable to automation. They also emphasise heterogeneities among countries in the share of automatable jobs, depending on factors such as investments in automation technologies and differences in education. Moreover, Arnold et al. argue that the labour-creating effects of technological change are likely to exceed its labour-eliminating effects, at least in Europe.

Any job whose tasks and overall functions can be digitised is likely to be automated. Those at the highest risk of losing their jobs to automation are low-skilled employees in industries such as manufacturing or customer service, since their tasks involve recognisable patterns that are more easily programmable and replaced by computers. Ford (2015, xiv) takes a fairly extreme position by arguing that no job is safe from the rise of robots:

> while lower-skill occupations will no doubt continue to be affected, a great many college-educated, white collar workers are going to discover that their jobs, too, are squarely in the sights as software and automation and predictive algorithms advance rapidly in capability.

But not all jobs are liable to be automated. Recent technological advancements such as the development of autonomous cars and the possibilities of 3D printing have provided insight into the skills needed for new jobs created by these advancements that only humans can perform (Ford 2015). The human mind has strengths that allow it to perform certain tasks that computers cannot:

> The human mind's strength is flexibility – the ability to process and integrate many kinds of information to perform a complex task. The computer's strengths are speed and accuracy, not flexibility, and computers are best at performing tasks for which logical rules or a statistical model lay out a path to a solution (Levy and Murnane 2013, 9).

Requirements for jobs that are less likely to be automated include extensive education and experience, critical-thinking and problem-solving ability, and adaptability and creativity; these are all skills which humans, and not computers, possess. Brynjolfsson and Mitchell (2017) agree that there are a number of tasks that machine learning is unlikely to be able to do, such as those that require unstructured tasks and complex reasoning, or planning that depends on common sense and experience.

Moreover, as automation and smart technology become more prevalent, new jobs will be created alongside those created by AI. Human workers will be required to "complement the tasks performed by cognitive technology, ensuring that the work of machines is both effective and responsible – that it is fair, transparent, and auditable" (Wilson, Daugherty and Morini-Bianzino 2017). Because humans possess skills and strengths that computers do not, there is likely always to be a place for humans to complement and augment the tasks done by machines.

Other technological changes will redefine some jobs rather than eliminate them. AI and other technological innovations will change the way in which the expertise of a wide range of professions is made available to society (Susskind and Susskind 2015). Lawyers, for example, will likely face changes in their occupation to keep up with technology, possibly creating systems that offer legal advice rather than offering legal advice themselves (Mahdawi 2017).

## IMPACTS ON THE QUALITY OF WORK

The transformation of employment relations in the US that began in the 1970s led to a growth of high-skilled, well-paid jobs as well as low-skilled, low-wage and short-term jobs. This labour market polarisation has enhanced economic inequality, as well as job and economic insecurity, in the US (Kalleberg 2011).

The gig economy – generally characterised by short-term engagements among employers, workers and customers – illustrates the polarisation of opportunities spawned by the fourth industrial revolution. In this sense, the gig economy is not new. Instead, it represents a digital version of the offline atypical, casual, freelance or contingent work arrangements characteristic of much of the economy before the middle of the 20th century and that have reappeared in the past 30 years (Kalleberg and Dunn 2016).

Although jobs in the gig economy (see De Stefano and Berg this volume; Schor this volume) differ from our traditional definitions of good jobs (stable jobs providing health and retirement benefits), the reality of the gig economy is more nuanced than many of the most critical portrayals: it produces both good and bad jobs (Kalleberg and Dunn 2016). Platforms such as Upwork, for example, provide relatively high wages and enable workers to have high control over their work, while Uber offers somewhat high wages at the expense of worker control. The rapid expansion of the gig economy has attracted the attention of the media, social scientists and the public at large. While it is still a relatively small slice of the American economy (Katz and Krueger 2016), it is growing rapidly and is liable to become increasingly prominent in the future.

Looking ahead, education and skills are likely to be the source of the main divisions in the labour market. Workers with creative, social and other in-demand skills will have greater market power and thus be better able to adapt to the increasingly dynamic technological environment. Consequently, they should be able to take advantage of the greater opportunities for mobility among employers. On the other hand, those without such market power are most vulnerable in the changing labour market. These are the low-skilled, less-educated workers who do not have the resources to develop necessary skills or find new jobs when their old ones are automated (Sorgner 2017). In addition, demographic differences defined by gender, age, race, ethnicity and immigration status are associated with factors that affect the ability of members of these groups to obtain well-rewarded jobs. The challenge here is to provide all people with access to the opportunities for skill acquisition so as to be competitive in the labour markets shaped by the fourth industrial revolution.

## NEW RISKS, NEW SOCIAL CONTRACT

"The challenge we face is to come up with new forms of social and employment contracts that suit the changing workforce and the evolving nature of work" (Schwab 2016, 49). Automation and AI will eliminate some jobs, redefine others and create new ones. While the relative size of these categories is somewhat unclear, what is certain is the need to provide people with the skills and social protections to cope with these changes. In order to tackle these issues, policies should maintain flexibility for employers yet still provide individuals with ways to mitigate the negative consequences produced by such flexibility. In every case, we need to consider individual and group diversity in access to education and skills and in employees' ability to use them in the labour market.

Examining the experiences of other rich democracies that face challenges similar to those of the US provides insights about strategies to help individuals cope with the uncertainty and insecurity associated with the upheavals produced by automation and technological change. The idea of flexicurity – prominently illustrated by Denmark and the Netherlands (see Keune and Dekker this volume; Ilsøe this volume) – offers a general way of conceptualising the needed risk structures by involving both employers and workers in a cooperative effort (European Commission 2007). Flexicurity is an appealing concept in that it offers a narrative about how employers and labour markets can have greater flexibility and workers can still be protected from the insecurity created by employers' search for such flexibility.

It is essential to have more robust social and economic protections to collectivise the risks associated with technological change. This includes basic forms of social insurance such as health insurance and health and pension benefits that are provided to all workers, regardless of their employment status. Particular attention must be paid to needs related to aging, the care of children and the elderly, and work–family balance. The provision of such a safety net should be the highest priority for economic and social welfare in the US in order to alleviate the threats of new technology and to harness its potential.

These social protection policies need to be complemented by a second set of essential strategies: providing greater access for all to early childhood and formal education as well as lifelong education and retraining in order to prepare people for the inevitable changes that will occur in jobs. The evidence shows that early childhood education is vital for providing the foundational skills and abilities that are crucial for the acquisition of additional skills later in life. For example, a recent study by Garcia et al. (2016) that followed children from birth until age 35 found that high-quality care during the earliest years enabled both mothers and children born into disadvantage to be more engaged in the work force, have higher skills, and be more active participants in society. Moreover, active labour market policies and private and public partnerships (such as those between community colleges and businesses) are needed to enhance lifelong education and retraining so as to prepare people for the inevitable changes in jobs that I have discussed above.

Third, revisions to social labour regulations and laws are needed to protect those in both regular and non-regular employment. Many of our current labour regulations and laws were formulated on the assumption of a standard employment relation (see Berg and De Stefano this volume). Current debates over whether Uber drivers are employees or independent contractors, for example, illustrate the ambiguity that currently exists about the new forms of employment relations that have been created by the fourth industrial revolution. A prominent policy suggestion here is to establish a third category between independent contractor and employee, such as 'dependent contractor'. While such a third classification would acknowledge the complexity of modern work arrangements, it is likely that this would encourage employers to classify more employees this way in order to forego their obligations to provide benefits and to deprive employees of social and statutory protections.

## POSSIBLE FUTURES

The rapidity of changes in technology and the organisation of work in the US should make us cautious about making predictions about the future. Nevertheless, recognising how and why these changes have occurred is essential to identifying the opportunities and coping with the challenges associated with technological innovations. We can imagine negative as well as positive scenarios.

It is relatively easy to envision a variety of dystopian futures, as we can only extrapolate from current trends. The confluence of forces related to globalisation, technological change, the financialisation of firms' organisation of work (see Kenney and Zysman this volume) and weak worker power (see Jolly this volume) may well continue and extend key social and economic trends. These include the expansion of low-wage jobs, outsourcing and subcontracting of the production of goods and services to lower-wage firms, growing polarisation between good and bad jobs and increasing economic inequality, expansion of digital platforms creating short-term and poorly protected jobs (the 'Uberisation' of the economy), and so on. Moreover, many of the implications of the automation of jobs are still unclear, fuelling fears that it will reduce drastically the need for workers.

It is more difficult to imagine utopian possibilities, given the priorities of current political and economic debates in the US. Creating the necessary conditions for any optimism requires strengthening and expanding social welfare protections and providing active labour market policies to facilitate job mobility. These are basic for giving people the skills and education to thrive in the new employment relationships between employers and workers.

But more comprehensive and long-term solutions will require more basic changes. One optimistic scenario is Beck's (2000) notion of an emerging 'post-full-employment society' or 'multi-activity work society', which defines work as something beyond market work, wherein people are able to shift their actions over the course of their lives across formal employment (albeit perhaps working fewer hours), parental labour and civil labour (labour in the arts, culture and politics, which helps the general welfare). The latter activity could be rewarded with 'civic money' that is not a handout from the state or community but a return for engaging in these activities. Each person would control her own time-capital that she can allocate to different activities over time. Beck advocates that paid work and civil labour should complement each other and calls for greater equality of housework and outside care work with artistic, cultural and political civic labour in the voluntary sector, which he believes will help create a gender-neutral division of labour. The idea of work as going beyond paid labour is a notion also espoused by Supiot (2001), Vosko (2010) and Standing (2011), among others.

If we are to define work formally as something beyond paid market work, it is essential to decouple economic security and social protection from market work and labour force status. One increasingly popular option, which was also raised as a policy recommendation in the early 1960s in response to the threats posed by automation, is that of a universal basic income that would provide a foundation of economic security. This idea is still very controversial for economic, political and cultural reasons, though we need to know more about how such unconditional grants affect labour market behaviours before evaluating its potential. Alternatively, the US might adopt social welfare protection systems that are relatively generous, inclusive and universalistic, where welfare benefits were provided to all citizens. The Affordable Care Act 2010 was a step in this direction, though it has yet to be fully implemented.

We may also need to reconceptualise our understanding of what constitutes value in a society. The commonly used economic indicator of value, the GDP, is increasingly unable to capture developments such as widening inequality and the rise of precarious work. Alternative, 'beyond GDP' indicators of wellbeing could shift the emphasis from measuring economic production to assessing the multiple dimensions of peoples' wellbeing.[1] This idea, unfortunately, has not gained much traction in the US and has lost momentum in Europe in the past few years. To some extent this reflects both the difficulties in measuring indicators of wellbeing other than GDP as well as the economic pressures on governments in the wake of the economic crisis of the late 2000s. Nevertheless, the profound changes to the economy that will accompany the technological changes discussed above are likely to make economic value as measured by the GDP increasingly problematic.

The likelihood that one or another of these dystopian and utopian scenarios will happen depends on whether we are able to implement the kind of social contract I have described above. This, in turn, rests primarily on the ability of workers to summon sufficient power resources to counteract the power of business and corporations and to exert significant influence on government policies.

## NOTE

1. The Report by the Commission on the Measurement of Economic Performance and Social Progress (Stiglitz, Sen and Fitoussi 2009) explores problems with the GDP indicator and alternative indicators to measure wellbeing.

## REFERENCES

Arntz, M., T. Gregory and U. Ziehran (2016), *The Risk of Automation for Jobs in OECD Countries: a Comparative Analysis*, Social, Employment and Migration Working Paper 189, Paris: Organisation for Economic Co-operation and Development.

Autor, D. (2015), 'Why Are There Still So Many Jobs? The History and Future of Workplace Automation', *Journal of Economic Perspectives*, 29(3): 3–30.

Beck, U. (2000), *The Brave New World of Work*, translated by Patrick Camiller, Cambridge: Polity Press.

Brynjolfsson, E. and T. Mitchell (2017), 'What Can Machine Learning Do? Workforce Implications', *Science*, 358: 1530–34.

European Commission (2007), *Towards Common Principles of Flexicurity: More and Better Jobs through Flexibility and Security*, Brussels:

Directorate-General for Employment, Social Affairs and Equal Opportunities.

Ford, M. (2015), *Rise of the Robots: Technology and the Threat of a Jobless Future*, New York: Basic Books.

Frey, C. B. and M. A. Osborne (2017), 'The Future of Employment: How Susceptible are Jobs to Computerisation?', *Technological Forecasting and Social Change*, 114: 254–280.

Garcia, J. L., J. J. Heckman, D. E. Leaf and M. J. Prados (2016), *The Lifecycle Benefits of an Influential Early Childhood Program*, University of Chicago, Human Capital and Economic Opportunity Global Working Group Paper, 2016-35.

Kalleberg, A. (2011), *Good Jobs, Bad Jobs: the Rise of Precarious and Polarized Employment Systems in the United States, 1970s-2000s*, New York: Russell Sage Foundation.

Kalleberg, A. and M. Dunn (2016), 'Good Jobs, Bad Jobs in the Gig Economy', *Perspectives on Work*: 10–13, 74.

Katz, L. F. and A. B. Krueger (2016), *The Rise and Nature of Alternative Work Arrangements in the United States, 1995–2015*, Cambridge, MA: National Bureau of Economic Research, http://www.nber.org/papers/w22667.

Levy, F. and R. J. Murnane (2013), *Dancing with Robots: Human Skills for Computerized Work*, Washington, DC: ThirdWay, http://content.thirdway.org/publications/714/Dancing-With-Robots.pdf.

Mahdawi, A. (2017), 'What Jobs Will Still Be around in 20 Years? Read This to Prepare Your Future', *The Guardian*, 26 June, http://www.theguardian.com/us-news/2017/jun/26/jobs-future-automation-robots-skills-creative-health.

Schwab, K. (2016), *The Fourth Industrial Revolution*, New York: Crown Business.

Sorgner, A. (2017), 'The Automation of Jobs: a Threat for Employment or a Source of New Entrepreneurial Opportunities?' *Foresight and STI Governance*, 11(3): 37–48.

Standing, G. (2011), *The Precariat: the New Dangerous Class*, New York: Bloomsbury.

Stiglitz, J. E., A. Sen and J.-P. Fitoussi (2009), *Report by the Commission on the Measurement of Economic Performance and Social Progress*, Commission on the Measurement of Economic performance and Social Progress, http://ec.europa.eu/eurostat/documents/118025/118123/Fitoussi+Commission+report.

Supiot, A. (2001), *Beyond Employment: Changes in Work and the Future of Labour Law in Europe*, Oxford: Oxford University Press.

Susskind, R. and D. Susskind (2015), *The Future of the Professions: How Technology Will Transform the Work of Human Experts*, Oxford: Oxford University Press.

Vosko, L. F. (2010), *Managing the Margins: Gender, Citizenship, and the International Regulation of Precarious Employment*, Oxford: Oxford University Press.

Wilson, J., P. R. Daugherty and N. Morini-Bianzino (2017), 'The Jobs That Artificial Intelligence Will Create', *MIT Sloan Management Review*, 23 March, http://sloanreview.mit.edu/article/will-ai-create-as-many-jobs-as-it-eliminates/.

# INDIA

## *Livelihoods in a digital age of manufacturing*

### Marc Saxer

Every month, more than 1 million jobseekers enter India's labour market, but although it is an investors' darling, India's employment generation track record has been disappointing. Despite great efforts, Delhi seems unable to repeat the east Asian economic miracle. Many of India's challenges are home made. Simultaneously the global window for export- and manufacturing-led development is closing. What does digital automation mean for the emerging economies in Asia? And how can India, under these circumstances, create livelihoods for its billion people?

## THE DIGITAL REVOLUTION ACCELERATES THE RACE FOR DEVELOPMENT

In a number of Asian countries, most notably China, wages are rising (Johnson 2017). This is particularly significant in those countries which have already passed the Lewis turning point – the point at which the supply of surplus labour from rural areas for employment in cities is exhausted – and the reserve army of cheap labour in the agricultural sector has dried up, as well as in aging societies where the total labour pool is shrinking (Das and N'Diaye 2013). While labour costs are rising in many emerging economies, digital automation increases productivity in the old industrial countries. Total costs of manufactured goods in some emerging economies are approaching those of the US (New York Times 2015; Sirkin, Zinser and Rose 2014). All things considered, manufacturing in the US is only 5% more expensive than in China (Dumaine 2015). The combination of higher energy efficiency and the tumbling labour costs makes manufacturing in the old industrialised countries competitive again. The shrinking differential between labour costs in developed and emerging economies erodes the incentives for offshoring, which has been one of the major drivers of globalisation over the last decades.

The deglobalisation trend is accelerated by the need to react more quickly and flexibly to the demands of consumers. In the clothing and garment industries, shelf lives are getting increasingly shorter. Hence, long shipping times are the Achilles heel of fast-moving consumer markets, so the time it takes to ship from factory to shelf will increasingly rival labour costs as the main motivator in inventors' calculations. Consequently, multinational companies like Walmart, Ford and Boeing, as well as small- and medium-size companies, have increasingly started to reshore production facilities back to their parent countries – they have started to reintroduce manufacturing after having previously undertaken production overseas. The Reshoring Initiative (2017), a non-profit organisation, estimates that 260,000 jobs have been created in the US as a result of this trend.

Whether this trend will be accelerated by populist promises to 'bring jobs back home', or if it will be only robots who return to the old shores, remains to be seen. The US has already withdrawn from the Trans-Pacific Partnership. Given the dark political clouds on the horizon it can no longer be taken for granted that western markets will stay open for Asian exports. While digital automation is accelerating, globalisation seems to be going into reverse. In 2016, global trade has been growing slower than global GDP, for the first time since 2001 and for only the second time since 1982 (WTO 2016).

The global capital flow collapsed as a share of global GDP in the wake of the global financial crisis since 2008, and it is not yet recovering (Donovan 2016). Some have even argued that global supply chains are beginning to disintegrate (Economist 2017). These deglobalisation tendencies are particularly worrying for Asia, the primary benefactor of open world markets. Asia's emerging economies would therefore be wise to rethink their orientation towards exports.

These trends may spell the end of the export- and manufacturing-led developing model which worked so well for many east Asian countries. The fourth industrial revolution will affect economies at the top, middle and bottom of the global value chains in different ways, and it makes a difference if population sizes are stable or continue to grow, and how big domestic markets are. All of these cases deserve an analysis on their own. This chapter will focus solely on the impact of digital automation on the Indian labour market.

## THE IMPACT OF DIGITAL AUTOMATION ON THE INDIAN LABOUR MARKET

Actually India seems to be under a lucky star. A benign global environment of low oil prices is leaving room for public spending on infrastructure and encouraging consumption. The giant consumer market attracts a plethora of multinational companies. Japan, partly out of geopolitical rivalry with China, invests heavily in India. Given its massive surplus of cheap labour, India should be in a good position to compete for the labour-intensive industries currently leaving China (Government of India 2017).

However, even under these benign circumstances, India is unable to create jobs. The shiny new factories on its coasts are almost entirely empty of people. Whereas 20 years ago millions of rural workers could make a living in the growing number of factories in China, today robots have taken over in India. In fact, while continuing to attract international investment from often foreign-owned firms, India loses 550 jobs per day (Mehta and Kulkarni 2016).

So, while today no new jobs are created despite high growth rates, what will happen in a future when algorithms and robots start to replace human labour (Hindustan Times 2016a)? The World Bank gloomily predicts that a whopping 69% of jobs in India could potentially be automated (Kim 2016). Outside the highly competitive export sectors, however, it remains unlikely that cheap labour would be automated, at least in the medium term. For an economy that is notorious for its poor track record in job creation, the combination of high population growth and accelerating automation gives cause for concern (Palanivel. 2016). According to some estimates, by 2050 there will be 280 million more people in the job market in India than there are now (Mishra 2016). What will happen if the aspirations of these internal migrants remain unmet and if frustrations and tensions rise (Kumar 2017)? Addressing these worries, Indian president Pranab Mukherjee attributed this slow employment generation to the rapid tendency for machines to replace humans, and has called for a paradigm shift (Hindstan Times 2016b). Today, the debate over jobless growth has moved to the top of the political agenda.

Nonetheless, the Indian government is hoping that a surging manufacturing sector could absorb millions of jobseekers. The ambitious programme Make in India aims to increase the GDP share of manufacturing from 12% today to 25% by 2022, hoping to provide employment for 100 million people (IBEF nd). The government's chief economic adviser, Arvind Subramanian, has pointed out that in order to achieve this, India would have to reverse the country's longstanding trend of premature deindustrialisation (Subramanian 2014).

Dani Rodrik observed that in a globalised market manufacturing moves on as soon as wages start to rise, which leads to premature deindustrialisation in newly industrialising economies (Rodrik 2015). By the time manufacturing in South Korea accounted for its highest proportion of jobs, incomes were around $12,700 annually. In India, factory employment started to decline as a share of employment when income was around $3,300 annually (Zhong 2015). Meanwhile, breakneck international competition will increase the pressure to automate. India's shiny automobile or smartphone factories are already populated in large part by robots. Now, other domestic industries are starting to automate (Bhattacharya, Bruce and Agrawa 2015). Hence, even if the manufacturing share of GDP increases, it is unclear if this would create many more jobs.

Certainly, new employment will be generated in the manufacturing sector, and old jobs will survive thanks to their competitive cost. Still, it seems safe to assume that in future manufacturing will not play the central role in employment generation in India as it did in Europe and East Asia in the past. If the historical window for export- and manufacturing-led development is closing, India has to find an alternative path (Economist 2015).

## HOW CAN INDIA CREATE LIVELIHOODS IN THE DIGITAL AGE?

With the traditional route to development closed, the search for alternative development models is in full swing. Former central banker Raghuram Rajan warned against an export- and manufacturing-led model, and advocated an approach that focuses on the domestic market instead as an answer to the expected slowdown in global trade (Rajan 2014). Indeed, with a population of 1.25 billion, and a rapidly growing middle class, India has one of the biggest domestic markets in the world. Even if labour costs start to rise, multinational companies will keep their foot in these 'future markets'. However increased consumption demand depends on rising wages, and in a jobless growth scenario such wage increases seem unlikely. Besides, India has had to learn the painful lesson of how too much focus on the domestic market can undermine incentives for technological innovation.

Some contributors have pointed out that the bulk of Indian workers are still in the agricultural sector. However, the need to increase productivity in the agricultural sector would only accelerate the freeing-up of surplus labour, and will increase the migration pressure on the urban centres, many of which are already bursting at the seams. On the other hand, the emergence of ethics and health conscious young, urban, middle-class consumers offers opportunities for organic farming, local products and even urban farming. Producing high-quality agricultural products for this niche market can be a source of decent jobs for agricultural workers.

Green growth offers new opportunities for development. The International Renewable Energy Agency estimates that renewable energy employed 8.1 million people around the world in 2015 (IRENA 2016). In India, reaching the government's goal of producing 100 GW of solar energy through photovoltaic sources by 2022 could generate a further 1.1 million jobs in construction, project commissioning and design, business development, and operations and maintenance (Mukul 2016). With its domestic focus, the construction industry seems to be better shielded against international competition than other sectors. There is also enormous potential to create clean employment in jobs that might be created by initiatives designed to achieve energy efficiency.

With the manufacturing sector in decline, and given the notorious labour surplus in the Indian agricultural sector, all hopes lie in the service sector being the next job-creating machine. This is where the digital revolution can create new opportunities. With its millions of highly educated workers, India is in a good position to compete in the globalising service markets. The National Association of Software and Services Companies suggest that India aims to capture 20% of market share in the 'internet of things' sector, which may be worth as much as $300bn (Mehta 2016). India aspires to build a $35bn cyber-security product and services industry by 2025, and to generate a skilled workforce of 1 million workers in the security sector (Mehta 2016). Multinational corporations have long started to outsource parts of their back offices (Benner 2014; Leimeister and Zogaj 2013). India, in particular, has attracted many of these services from telephone hotlines to IT emergency assistance services, to accounting to coding. Compared with western workers, who are increasingly being deprived of social security, decent wages and workplace codetermination, the gig economy may still offer a way for Indian workers to get ahead. Accordingly, domestic worker app companies that bring together households with domestic workers are expanding at a rate of 20–60% each month. However, while digital crowdsourcing platforms allow employers to choose from offers originating in labour markets that have vastly different wage levels, this extreme competition between the global labour reserve armies drives a race to the bottom in labour standards, where only the lowest wages tend to prevail. This competition will increase even more as digital automation accelerates. Whether the global division of labour in the services sector will keeps its promise of job creation remains to be seen.

What does the future hold for workers of work in India? The educated, entrepreneurial and flexible Indians seem poised for success in the digital economy. India's cosmopolitan middle classes are therefore likely to continue to grow. However, what will happen to the billion plus Indians who do not have such a background? East Asia's success formula, built around export- and manufacturing-led growth, offers little hope. It is hard to understate the social and political backlash to be expected if the aspirations of millions of workers are frustrated. It seems that India's fate will be decided by the speed with which the country manages to shift to a new development model. Whether any of the currently debated models can work is an open question. In the global race for development, India is at risk of running out of time. Encouragingly, its thinkers and decision-makers seem to have recognised the challenge. Now it is up to all of us to support them in finding the first development model for the digital age.

## REFERENCES

Benner, C. (2014), Crowd Work – Zurück in die Zukunft – Perspektiven digitaler Arbeit, Frankfurt am Main: Bund Verlag.

Bhattacharya, A., A. Bruce and S. Agrawa (2015), Future of Indian Manufacturing: Bridging the Gap, New Delhi, Mumbai, Chennai: The Boston Consulting Group.

Das, M. and P. M. N'Diaye (2013), *Chronicle of a Decline Foretold: Has China Reached the Lewis Turning Point?*, IMF Working Paper 12/26.

Donovan, P. (2016), *Global Economic Perspectives: the Continued Collapse of Globalisation*, UBS Global Research.

Dumaine, B. (2015), 'US Manufacturing Costs Are Almost as Low as China's, and that's a Very Big Deal', *Fortune*, 26 June, http://fortune.com/2015/06/26/fracking-manufacturing-costs/.

Economist (2015), 'The Future of Factory Asia', *The Economist*, 12 March, http://www.economist.com/news/briefing/21646180-rising-chinese-wages-will-only-strengthen-asias-hold-manufacturing-tightening-grip.

Economist (2017), 'In Retreat: the Multinational Company is in Trouble', *The Economist*, 28 January, http://www.economist.com/news/leaders/21715660-global-firms-are-surprisingly-vulnerable-attack-multinational-company-trouble.

Government of India (2017), *Economic Survey 2016–2017*, New Delhi: Oxford University Press.

Hindustan Times (2016a), 'Job Growth in 8 Sectors at 7-year Low: Govt Data', *Hindustan Times*, 16 April, http://www.hindustantimes.com/india/job-growth-in-8-sectors-at-7-year-low-govt-data/story-UkWVLA-9jQyZJZuNCWXI3BO.html.

Hindustan Times (2016b), '1.35 Lakh Jobs Created in India in 2015, Lowest in Seven Years: President', *Hindustan Times*, 16 November, http://www.hindustantimes.com/india-news/1-35-lakh-jobs-created-in-india-in-2015-lowest-in-seven-years-prez/story-G2v47WgMDkjvtEYb-CyHtXK.html.

India Brand Equity Foundation. 'Role of Manufacturing in Employment Generation in India', New Delhi: India Brand Equity Foundation, https://www.ibef.org/download/Role-of-Manufacturing-in-Employment-Generation-in-India.pdf.

International Renewable Energy Agency (IRENA) (2016), *Renewable Energy Employs 8.1 Million People Worldwide, Says New IRENA Report*, Abu Dhabi: IRENA, http://www.irena.org/newsroom/press-releases/2016/May/Renewable-Energy-Employs-81-Million-People-Worldwide-Says-New-IRENA-Report.

Johnson, S. (2017), 'Chinese Wages Now Higher than in Brazil, Argentina and Mexico', *Financial Times*, 26 February, https://www.ft.com/content/f4a260e6-f75a-11e6-bd4e-68d53499ed71.

Kim, J. Y. (2016), 'The World Bank Group's Mission: To End Extreme Poverty', speech, 3 October, Washington, DC: World Bank.

Kumar, R. (2017), 'Jobs Are Crying Need of the Hour', *Mail Today*, 1 March, http://epaper.mailtoday.in/1121300/mt/Mail-Today-Issue-March-1,-2017#page/10/2.

Leimeister, J. M. and S. Zogaj (2013), *Neue Arbeitsorganisation durch Crowd-Sourcing: eine Literaturstudie*, Arbeitspapier der Hans-Böckler-Stiftung, Reihe Arbeit und Soziales 287.

Mehta, P. (2016), 'Sustaining Transition to a Digital Economy', Mint, 28 December, http://www.livemint.com/Opinion/VLD7KCJi2xCbLN0d-hY3bxK/Sustaining-transition-to-a-digital-economy.html.

Mehta, P. and A. Kulkarni (2016), 'It Is Time to Address India's Abysmal Job Creation Record', *The Wire*, 25 November, http://thewire.in/82017/india-abysmal-job-creation-record/.

Mishra, A. R. (2016), 'India to See Severe Shortage of Jobs in the Next 35 Years', Live Mint, 28 April, http://www.livemint.com/Politics/Tpql-r4H1ILsusuBRJlizHI/India-to-see-severe-shortage-of-jobs-in-the-next-35-years.html.

Mukul, J. (2016), 'India Global 5th in Green Energy Jobs, China on Top', *Business Standard*, 26 May, http://www.business-standard.com/article/economy-policy/india-global-5th-in-green-energy-jobs-china-on-top-116052600701_1.html.

New York Times (2015), 'The Rising Cost of Manufacturing', *The New York Times*, 2 August, https://www.nytimes.com/interactive/2015/07/31/business/international/rising-cost-of-manufacturing.html?_r=0.

Palanivel, T., T. Mirza, B. N. Tiwari, S. Standley and A. Nigam (2016), *Asia-Pacific Human Development Report: Shaping the Future: How Changing Demographics can Power Human Development*, New York: United Nations Development Programme, http://www.asia-pacific.undp.org/content/dam/rbap/docs/RHDR2016/RHDR2016-full-report-final-version1.pdf.

Rajan, R. (2014), 'Make in India, Largely for India', the Bharat Ram Memorial Lecture, New Delhi: Reserve Bank of India, https://www.rbi.org.in/scripts/BS_SpeechesView.aspx?Id=930.

Reshoring Initiative (2017), 'Reshoring Initiative Goals and Accomplishments', Reshoring Initiative, http://www.reshorenow.org/blog/reshoring-initiative-goals-and-accomplishments/.

Rodrik, D. (2015), *Premature Deindustrialization*, NBER Working Paper 20935, http://www.nber.org/papers/w20935.

Sirkin, H., M. Zinser and J. R. Rose (2014), *The Shifting Economics of Global Manufacturing: How Cost Competitiveness Is Changing Worldwide*, Chicago: BCG Perspectives.

Subramanian, A. (2014), 'Reversing Premature De-industrialisation in India', *Ideas for India*, 26 May, http://www.ideasforindia.in/article.aspx?article_id=293.

WTO (2016), 'Trade Statistics and Outlook', press release 779, Geneva: World Trade Organization.

Zhong, R. (2015), 'For Poor Countries, Well-worn Path to Development Turn Rocky', *Wall Street Journal*, 24 November.

# CONCLUSION

## *Political realities and a reform agenda for the digital age*

# Max Neufeind, Florian Ranft and Jacqueline O'Reilly

For progressive politics, the task remains of how to develop a public policy agenda that addresses the challenges of this new wave of 'destructive creation'. This task comes at a time of exceptional volatility in European and North American politics, significant shifts in geopolitical power from west to east, and a profoundly changing global economic order where new forms of capitalism, with greater levels of state intervention, are emerging in countries such as China, Russia and India. These transformative shifts were accelerated by the global financial crisis of 2007/08, whose unanticipated magnitude led to a great recession, the worst global economic decline since the 1930s (IMF 2009).

The consequences of the great recession for the people of Europe have been painful and long lasting. They have increased the economic divide between southern and northern Europe and impoverished many in Eastern Europe. With increasing rates of economic divergence, social exclusion and poverty in countries that were hit the most by the crisis, levels of trust in political institutions have also deteriorated among EU citizens (Muro and Vidal 2014; see Theodoropoulou this volume). As a consequence of these major economic and social forces, the European political landscape has profoundly changed with voters questioning traditional allegiances and party affiliations (Dassonneville and Hooghe 2017; Hernández and Kriesi 2015). These developments have polarised and fragmented party systems across Europe and have led to the rise of a new generation of challenger parties on the left and right (Hobolt and Tilley 2016). It has also undermined the power of traditional centre-right and centre-left parties who are being electorally squeezed, and find it increasingly difficult to build coalitions.

This shake up of the centre ground has meant that governing coalitions commonly include more than two parties (Belgium, the Netherlands and Norway), rightwing populist parties (Austria, Finland, Norway and Poland), or are formed as minority governments (Denmark, Ireland, Portugal, Spain and the UK). Progressives are often relegated to nothing more than spectators. In some countries, the electoral success of rightwing populist parties has made it difficult to form any stable government at all, as was seen in the 2018 elections in the Czech Republic and Italy. Only in very few cases have progressives broken the mould, notably in France and Portugal, where they remain electorally potent.

Adding to this post-crisis socio-economic and political era of uncertainty are new technologies and the debate on the robotisation of work that have left many people disorientated about their personal future and prosperity. There is not only increasing uncertainty about what the future of work will look like (Benhamou this volume) and whether there will be enough jobs to go round (Arnold et al. this volume), but also how new forms of employment will be regulated (Berg and De Stefano this volume) and what the consequences of change will be for the environment, racial discrimination and inequality (Schor this volume). Although there is an intellectual debate unfolding, to which this volume seeks to contribute, in modern economies traditional political concepts, solutions and narratives are no longer resonating with large parts of the electorate.

In this phase of 'diffuse nervousness' (Braun 2018) people feel that politics needs a fresh start and must offer, among other essentials: affordable housing, modern infrastructure, world class education, social and health care, a secure workplace and a sustainable economy that creates jobs, growth and higher wages. Yet, the solutions on offer from traditional parties do not seem to be convincing. Arguably, this explains the rise in support for populists who have successfully exploited this vacuum with anti-establishment strategies, claiming that traditional parties are unable to respond to these challenges by highlighting the dangers of migration and open borders (Goodwin 2011).

There is a risk that the effects of digitalisation may exacerbate the next populist backlash, which could be directed at machines and their owners. This makes it more relevant for progressives to offer a convincing narrative that addresses the concerns of voters and at the same time recognises the vast economic opportunities for business, industry and the public sector that this revolution presents. There is time for policymakers to respond to the challenges outlined in this volume. But it is imperative for them to be better prepared and develop a deeper understanding of the changes that lie ahead. This requires the identification of new concepts of work and the role of business and the state in the promotion and provision of modern social welfare and social dialogue systems (see Jolly this volume; Palier this volume). These new concepts need to explain how a friendly environment for growth, innovation and job creation, with high-quality training and education and fair taxation of firms and corporations, can be developed. Such an approach also needs to include a more rigorous consideration of the social and political – not only industrial – consequences of an economy where value is increasingly created from intangible assets, including data, data-sharing, branding and marketing (Hofheinz this volume).

Soete argues in this volume that the third industrial revolution was dominated by a sense of technological determinism and international competitiveness during the 1980s. Despite the belief in developing a malleable European model of the information society, the speed of change made it feel impossible to govern; liberalisation and deregulation became the default options. This created the feeling that there was no capacity for policy action to address the threats of job loss and low productivity. This sense of incapacity cannot be repeated with the advent of the fourth industrial revolution.

In this book the scene-setting theoretical chapters and case studies offer insights into the current state of the debates about the future of work in Europe, what the challenges and solutions are, and who the main actors are that may promote and precipitate change. We can identify a number of responses where new coalitions of actors emerge to develop existing concepts of work and labour relations and to address some of the negative consequences of digitalisation at work (Flecker this volume; Kanjuo Mrčela this volume).

The chapters often highlight the social and political response to the main challenges of the fourth industrial revolution, which have more on offer for policymakers and politicians than just liberalisation and deregulation. The contributions also offer brief yet comprehensive analyses from experts, and perspectives from different countries, which catalyse the debates at regional, national and supra-national level. The book makes it clear that countries are moving at different speeds. Our comparison of the different levels of digital density, even within the EU, illustrates the variety of challenges different social and political actors face. Such a comparative perspective has until now been surprisingly lacking in the vast volumes of research on the fourth industrial revolution.

As people feel increasingly insecure about what the future of work will mean for them, there is a need for democratic discourse and control relating to socio-technical changes caused by digital advancements. While conservatives and right-wing populists offer easy solutions to complex scenarios, either by protecting vested interests or deregulating industries, the centre left must claim leadership by providing individuals with strong safety nets and empowering tools in a new work environment, and by advancing a narrative of an open and updated society.

This book illustrates that we are at a key political juncture where these issues need a more informed public policy-based discussion about the direction of change, a debate that has not yet received the attention it deserves. Otherwise we risk sleep walking into a potentially turbulent political environment where the disruptions created by technological change are blamed on other social groups and minorities. There is a chance for progressives, but they have to discuss it more rigorously and must project themselves more resolutely into the future.

So what should a progressive agenda on work in the digital age encompass? We believe the following constitute the crucial building blocks for progressive policymakers:

- Don't fall for the dominant discourse. Developing and using the right maps is essential and helps to see beyond the disruption talk.
- Get serious about high-quality initial education and training. That's more than teaching kids how to code.
- Build institutions that guarantee secure transitions and foster employability. Focus on enabling good transitions for everyone.
- Translate employment standards and social protection into the digital age. Recognise technology as an enabling force.
- Update tax and transfer policies to tackle income and wealth inequality. Aim to distribute ownership more widely.
- Re-invent the state as the lead investor. Go for mission-oriented innovation.
- Mind the regional gap. Make regional development great again.
- Broaden your view. Envision a good working society that includes all forms of work, paid and unpaid.

## FRAMING: FROM HYPE TO DISCOURSE AND SCENARIOS

A progressive agenda on work in the digital age must be based on a critical analysis of the current discourse around digitalisation. We must talk about factors including interests, power and control. The idea that technology itself will deliver fast and clear-cut solutions to social problems ('technological solutionism') is misguided and dangerous. So is the notion that technological innovations render only one distinct model of work in the future possible ('technological determinism') (Benhamou this volume). In fact, we have to talk about the different possible futures of work – with some that will possibly be more desirable than others.

To have any effect, a progressive agenda must be more than merely a list of measures that are needed for societies to adapt to the coming change. Any progressive agenda must present policies that explicitly seek to shape the future of work. Progressives recognise that a world of work where technology autonomously shapes all aspects of human action is a myth; in fact the opposite is true. Since human decisions shape how technology is implemented, the question is: Who makes those decisions and what consequences do they have? How do we develop a discourse about the types of technologies being developed in the workplace and wider social life, and the purposes they serve for different social groups? Only then can we begin to define the conditions, and the rules and norms through which the digital revolution can improve the living standards of all members of our societies, rather than just those of a privileged few. Critically, technology is not only about jobs becoming automated. Technology will also define the kinds of new jobs that we will end up with in the future, and how jobs that we currently have may change (Bernhardt 2017). The language surrounding the fourth industrial revolution, including terms like 'Industry 4.0', is embedded in certain discourses and pursued by actors with their own interests; we must not neglect the political dimension of this revolution (Pfeiffer 2017).

Progressives must be sure to make use of the right 'maps', as O'Reilly (2017) puts it, to make sense of the digital transformation. Downplaying technological disruptions does not help, nor does being blinded by the relentless disruption talk – 'automation angst' (see Arnold et al. this volume). New technologies might pose new challenges for policymakers, but the basic questions remain the same. How can policymakers equip citizens with the skills that will be needed to thrive in the future? How can governments guarantee decent work and social protection for all? How can productivity gains be shared fairly? Engaging with key stakeholders through social partnership arrangements remains vital for governments and policymakers to establish better ways of promoting equity and prosperity. Addressing the challenges of the fourth industrial revolution effectively will require institutions to be transformed, as many contributions to this volume have argued. Progressives should call for meaningful reform, which is something different from a 'disruption' of the status quo. The future of work remains unknown and somewhat unpredictable, but that should not leave us feeling paralysed.

There are key policy challenges that progressives must address now, regardless of how future scenarios will materialise. Focusing on the implications of change at the individual level draws attention to policies that affect successful transitions throughout the life course: transitions from school to work, and between jobs and different forms of employment and working time arrangements.

## INITIAL EDUCATION AND TRAINING: EQUIPPING EVERYONE WITH THE RIGHT SKILLS

Digitalisation will lead to major changes in the demands for skills. However, it is unclear to both businesses and policymakers precisely what skills will be needed (Aubrey this volume).

Much of the debate on the digital transformation of the labour market has been in relation to skills-biased technological change (where high skills yield a wage premium that rises over time), routine-biased technological change (demand for routine skills decreasing over time) and capital-biased technological change (productivity-enhancing technological advances reducing labour's share of aggregate output) (Berger and Frey 2016). While the latter two are important, the race between developments in technology and investment in skills is pivotal for labour market outcomes (Martin 2018). One answer to the challenges posed by skills-biased technological change lies in making education and training more widely available to all citizens over their life course, regardless of income or age.

The importance of education in science, technology, engineering and mathematics (STEM) has become central to discussions about the future of work in the digital age, but focussing on STEM alone will not suffice (see de Franceschi this volume). Teaching young people how to code is useful, but does not solve the problem. Autor (2015) expects the future workforce of advanced economies to feature a significant proportion of 'T-shaped' skill profiles that combine specific vocational skills with transversal foundational middle skills including literacy, numeracy, adaptability, capacity for problem solving and common sense. With nurses, teachers, construction supervisors, tradespeople or physical therapists we find such profiles that bring together technical skills with interpersonal interaction, flexibility and adaptability to offer services that are uniquely human (Autor 2013).

It is crucial to understand that the increasing use of digital technologies at work is raising the demand for skills along four lines (OECD 2016a). Generic ICT skills involve being able to use technologies in daily work; specific ICT skills include programming, developing and managing; complementary ICT skills allow processing complex information, communicating with co-workers and clients, and solving problems. However, all three require sound levels of general cognitive skills as a prerequisite. While enhancing the provision of new digital skills we also need to recognise that the general cognitive skills level of a substantial proportion of the workforce in advanced economies is already today below or at the level of computer capabilities (Elliott 2017; OECD 2016c). Proficiency in problem solving in technology-rich environments is relatively low for the majority of adults in advanced economies (OECD 2016b). Thus, legitimate demands for substantial investments in digital skills have to be complemented by investments in non-digital skills. The challenge is that the need for investment in non-digital skills might even surpass that which will be required for developing digital skills (Elliott 2017).

So how can the skills challenge be tackled? There is general agreement on the importance of early childhood education (Kalleberg this volume; MGI 2017) and high-quality future-oriented primary and secondary education, which includes generic, specific and complementary ICT skills and a change to how core subjects are taught, with increased emphasis being placed on conceptual understanding and problem-solving (Levy and Murnane 2013). Where generic ICT skills are insufficiently developed on a broader scale (see in this volume Drahokoupil for central and eastern Europe and de Franceschi for Italy), updating syllabuses and curricula in primary and secondary schools must be a priority to prevent a 'lost generation' of young people with low competences in the key information-processing skills that are in increasingly high demand in the labour market (Martin 2018). Policymakers should look to Sweden, which has been successful in integrating ICT skills in its curricula (OECD 2016d).

The idea of complementary ICT skills has to be taken seriously in tertiary education. 'Hard' technical knowledge and skills alone will not be enough (Kremer and Went this volume). Workers in an Industry 4.0 manufacturing scenario will need higher levels of 'soft' skills, such as the capacity for trans-disciplinary collaboration, an understanding of how the material and the abstract level of production processes are linked, or the ability to act confidently in conditions of uncertainty (Pfeiffer 2015). Italy's plan Industria 4.0, for example, dedicates €220 million to vocational and university training that is focused specifically on the fourth industrial revolution (de Franceschi this volume).

The emphasis on STEM fields has to be expanded to an emphasis on STEAM, that is, the interaction of STEM subjects with arts and humanities (Land 2013). For example, the French National Council for Digitalisation recommends the promotion of creativity, abstraction and interpretation skills while focusing less on static knowledge (Weber this volume).

In addition, it seems crucial not only to focus on university-based tertiary education, but to update vocational training and to foster its attractiveness. Routine-biased technological change has the potential to produce a polarised labour market with the middle being hollowed out. High-quality vocational training with a significant component of work-based learning is one key measure that may prevent this from happening. The stigmatisation of non-university tertiary education as a second choice option to university education remains a problem in some countries. Where vocational training is more widespread, occupational profiles must be modernised and training methods opened up. This does not mean that occupational profiles become imposed by bureaucratic decree but rather that government provides the right framework for social partners to become actors in this process. Trade unions and employers associations possess deep knowledge of industries and service sectors, which can help gather data on skills demands and identify key challenges in adapting to the fourth industrial revolution. Pfeiffer (2015) emphasises that vocational schools must be modernised, and that teaching staff must be offered continuing education and training opportunities, particularly with regard to new learning methods and accruing digital skills.

Finally, we need better intelligence-based careers advice for school leavers about future skill demands. Too often there is insufficient information for school leavers to understand whether demand is increasing or decreasing for certain occupations, leading to uninformed career decisions (see in this volume de Franceschi for Italy and Aubrey for the UK). Counselling will not be based on perfect forecasts, which we do not have, but should rather focus on robust individual strategies to promote the development of relevant and adaptable skill sets.

## SECURE TRANSITIONS AND EMPLOYABILITY: AN ACTIVE WORKING LIFE FOR ALL

While getting initial education and training right is necessary, it is not sufficient for tackling the challenges of the fourth industrial revolution for two reasons:

- Skills demand will change, so frontloading skills is of limited effectiveness.
- Most of the workforce in 2030 is already in employment today, therefore more attention needs to be focused on maintaining and improving their employability.

As Arnold et al. (this volume) emphasise, the main challenge for labour and social policy in the digital age is not the elimination of human labour by technology. The risk of jobs being eliminated through automation tends to be overestimated in the public discourse as the task composition of jobs, the macroeconomics of technology diffusion, and hurdles to digitalisation are not fully taken into account. While the net employment effects of new digital technologies could be small, this does not preclude massive structural changes. The demand for human labour is likely to increase in sectors such as IT and education, but there could be a substantial reduction in the number of jobs in manufacturing industries, where the use of machines and technical equipment is widespread (Arnold et al. this volume).

Structural change also unfolds within occupations. When machines take over tasks that are comparatively easy to programme and automate, human labour is mainly needed for less routine and skill-intensive tasks that involve creativity and social interactions. Thus, occupations change markedly with regard to task composition and skill requirements (Arnold et al. this volume).

If the challenge is about a future with different jobs, not one with no jobs, the main problem is one of matching. In a worst-case scenario, advanced economies will see high levels of technological unemployment and high levels of skilled labour shortages at the same time. Therefore, ensuring employability over a person's life becomes the primary objective for policymakers. To prevent large-scale structural skill mismatches between workers and jobs, opportunities for upskilling and reskilling as well as for developing transferrable skills must be expanded (see Karjalainen this volume).

Addressing the challenges outlined above begins with acknowledging that the digital transformation will lead to a more 'fluid' world of work. Rates of job turnover are likely to increase within companies as well as between sectors and occupations. The task content of jobs will change faster. The answer to this 'fluidity' is to provide for secure transitions for those who have to change jobs, and employability for those whose jobs change.

Let us begin with transitions. Since protecting companies from technology-based disruptions does not seem to be economically or socially desirable (Atkinson this volume; Kalleberg this volume), workers have to be provided with secure transitions between different jobs and occupations. Job security measures must be translated into a comprehensive set of policies that ensure that workers who lose their jobs are taken care of and given access to training and new skills that will allow them to return to the labour market.

The term 'flexicurity' has been used to describe reforms in this direction that have been implemented in recent years most notably in the Nordic countries, and most prominently illustrated in Denmark and the Netherlands (see Ilsøe this volume; Keune and Dekker this volume). While the term is often misused as a catch-all phrase, progressives should focus on its essence as an explicit alternative to the mantra of liberalisation and deregulation. Obviously, flexicurity is not a simple one-size-fits-all tool. It depends heavily on institutions, for example, the tax-based social security and training systems in Denmark, and a culture of consensus between the social partners. Tripartite agreements between business, unions and the government are at the heart of the Danish flexicurity model along with extensive active labour market policies. The implementation of this model presents significant challenges in countries lacking these features.

A progressive version of flexicurity should not be about promoting any kind of mobility but rather about 'good transitions' (Ranft and Thillaye 2015; Schmid 2003), which allow people to end up in desirable positions and to have a meaningful career. The overall goal is not the creation of a flexible labour market per se, but rather to enable more people moving into higher quality jobs or to maintain a continuity of employment (O'Reilly, Cebrián and Lallement 2000). To achieve this, flexicurity measures must be embedded in a broader paradigm of prevention. Most importantly, such a paradigm would comprise improved access to life-long learning. In most advanced economies life-long learning is an empty phrase. Adult participation in education and training activities varies vastly across the countries covered in this volume, from high rates in the Netherlands, the Nordic countries and Canada to low participation rates in southern Europe, Slovakia, Poland and France (Martin 2018).

In most countries examined in this volume, institutions that mitigate the effects of structural change for individuals are reactive. For example, access to unemployment insurance and corresponding reskilling measures are often only granted once redundancy has taken place. Söderqvist and Arnold et al. (this volume) emphasise that reforms will need to push existing institutions to introduce proactive measures that are focused on the individual, particularly those groups whose skill levels would otherwise fall further and further behind the rising skills requirements. This would also need a change in culture and narratives, with upskilling and reskilling becoming an integral part of a successful working life (Hofheinz this volume; Keune and Dekker this volume).

Such a prevention paradigm must consist of two building blocks: financing and allowing people to make informed choices. Upgrading skills and taking time off to do so needs to be financially viable for people. Those with the greatest need for upgrading their skills – particularly those in non-standard employment, workers in small- and medium-enterprises, or the non-employed – often do not have access to necessary financial resources to invest in their skills. Here, governments can play an important role, for example by creating individual activity accounts. France recently introduced a measure to spread access to education over the lifetime with the '*compte personnel d'activité*' (Weber this volume). The account runs throughout the working life and is not attached to an employment contract. Whether the current model will allow for substantial investments in upskilling or reskilling remains to be seen. Germany is discussing the implementation of more generously funded 'individual activity accounts' (Rahner and Schönstein this volume). Up to €20,000 per individual could be used for qualification and further training as well as for starting a business. The individual activity account would particularly provide younger people with financial scope for personal development.

If the financial barrier is overcome, institutions must support individuals to make sound investments in their human capital. To accomplish this, an encompassing and sound careers advice infrastructure is needed. The German government is discussing the proposed introduction of a legal entitlement to careers and continuous education advice based on labour market forecasting (Rahner and Schönstein this volume). In Finland, trade unions play a key role in career counselling (Karjalainen this volume). No matter who provides it, counselling has to be located at the regional and local levels, as Aubrey (this volume) points out. To help individuals track their human capital investments and to help future generations make more informed choices lifetime digital individual learning records, as suggested in the Taylor report (Taylor 2017), seem promising. For a comprehensive approach to skills advice and development, policymakers should look to Singapore and its Skills Future initiative (Ng 2017).

Measures of primary prevention (preventing displacement by automation) have to be complemented by measures of secondary prevention (reducing the risk of longer-term unemployment). Sweden, for example, has been very successful with the model of job security councils helping redundant workers to retrain and find new employment (Söderqvist this volume; OECD 2015). These councils began as private unemployment offices that were owned by employers' associations and trade unions with a focus on white-collar professionals, but now they cover most of the Swedish workforce. Transposing this model to other countries would depend on fostering social partnership, which is seen as an essential precondition. Another option to be considered is using publicly funded employment, something Germany is currently experimenting with (Bauer, Fertig and Fuchs 2016), for secondary prevention.

Finally, understanding the role of policies at the workplace level is crucial when it comes to fostering employability over the life course. Workplaces have to become 'learnplaces'. Workplace-based measures of reskilling and upskilling have to be available for all workers, not only for those in standard forms of employment (Keune and Dekker this volume; Doellgast this volume). However, Crouch argues that 'non-employees' working on digital platforms are less likely to be seen as an asset to be invested in. Meanwhile, systems design at the workplace level is equally important. To enhance human capabilities and skills development, technology must be designed with human factors in mind (Taylor 2017). In addition, progressive policymakers must seek to link the issues of employability and working time. Technology has the potential to allow for more individual working-time arrangements to fit in with different stages of the life course. Life phase oriented working time arrangements improve workers' health, wellbeing and motivation and are therefore a crucial factor for fostering employability (Chung, Kerkhofs and Ester 2007). While there are clearly very differentiated patterns of the take up of these flexible working time arrangements by gender, age and ethnicity (O'Reilly and Fagan 1998), facilitating an active working life for all will be a major challenge in the digital age, especially as new employment platforms emerge.

## EMPLOYMENT RELATIONS AND SOCIAL PROTECTION: SAFEGUARDING STANDARDS

Digital platforms that mediate work, such as Upwork or Amazon's Mechanical Turk, and platforms that provide services, such as Uber or Airbnb, transform the nature of work. Platforms may improve labour market efficiency and increase opportunities for flexible employment. Yet, depending on the national regulatory frame-work, they potentially erode the standardised relationship between employers and employees that is needed to finance and deliver social protection and benefits in most advanced economies (Berg and De Stefano this volume; Huws et al. this volume; Schor this volume).

So far, the amount of gainful employment that is delivered through digital platforms is the subject of considerable controversy. Some experts doubt that digital platforms will lead to more than a marginal rise in self-employment (Atkinson this volume), while others argue that that the phenomena are already more widespread than official statistics now reveal (Hill 2015a). Nonetheless, by their very architecture, including the inherent network effects, digital platforms have the potential for a vast diffusion and for the creation of an internet-based 'distributed workforce' in which it is increasingly difficult to enforce national labour laws. Furthermore, digital platforms might catalyse some of the ongoing trends towards a destandardisation of employment relationships (Schor this volume; Weil 2014). Unregulated, the proliferation of platform business models could lead to a two-tier workforce and society (Benhamou this volume; Tyson 2015). On the one hand, there could be an upper tier populated by fully employed highly skilled workers with state- or employer-provided benefits (Howcroft and Rubery this volume), alongside highly skilled self-employed individuals who finance their own benefits. On the other hand, there could be a lower tier populated by contingent middle- and low-skill workers, with low pay and little social security (Berg and De Stefano this volume). However, it is important to note that the disruptive potential of digital platforms also applies to highly skilled knowledge workers (Boes et al. 2017; Crouch this volume).

At the moment, the main challenge that digital platforms pose to policymakers might be the inherent ontological ambiguity over what a firm is, who an employee is according to labour law, and what constitutes an employment relationship (Kalleberg this volume; Keune and Dekker this volume). Social policy and labour law require clear answers to these questions, particularly when benefits are financed through employer and employees contributions, and when representation and social protection depend on an employee status.

Broadly there are four options, which are discussed in more detail here:

- the adaption and enforcement of existing statuses to move (some) platform workers towards an employee status
- the creation of a new, hybrid status halfway between employees and independent workers
- the expansion of some rights and benefits currently reserved for employees towards independent workers
- the creation of one single worker status for all.

First, many commentators and analysts describe a widespread misclassification of dependent platform workers as independent contractors. To contain this trend a modern and enforceable definition of dependent and independent employment and of the relationship between platform workers and their employers would be needed. Prassl (2015) calls for the promulgation of guidelines that provide clear definitions of self-employment relating to tax, insurance contributions and social protection entitlement, where the onus of proof rests with the employer rather than the worker. The issue of classification is currently being debated in several countries, for example, France, Germany and the Netherlands. There are a number of major legal cases in the UK and the European Court of Justice (Berg and De Stefano this volume) as well as some legislative reforms in Italy and Spain (Jolly this volume). Based on an updated definition of the status of a 'worker', and what this means, platforms could be required to provide regular benefits and protections for workers who are essentially full-timers – those who work over a certain number of hours a week (see Schor this volume). However, this could lead platforms employers to make sure workers never reach this threshold.

Second, there is an international debate on the establishment of a new, hybrid category of employment halfway between independent contractors and employees. In the US and the UK the introduction of a 'dependent contractor' status is being discussed, and Spain and Italy have already introduced new definitions in labour law reforms

(Jolly this volume). Proponents argue that such measures acknowledge the complexity of modern working arrangements and could extend 'employee-like' statuses so those with this status receive adequate and high-quality social protection. The recently introduced Belgian federal law on the platform economy (Zanoni this volume) actually creates a third employment status in addition to employees and the self-employed: individuals who offer services on platforms occasionally have to register as self-employed but pay a reduced tax rate, which is levied from the platform employer. However, progressives should be aware of the risk of introducing such a third category as employers might seek to classify more employees in this way to avoid providing social contributions, benefits and entitlement to statutory protections (Kalleberg this volume).

Third, some of the rights associated with standard employment could be extended to the self-employed, for example representation on works councils, through collective organisation and in collective bargaining (Berg and De Stefano this volume; Keune and Bekker this volume). The new categories of emerging self-employed workers associated with digital work platforms are not easily subsumed into the established institutional framework of labour relations (Jolly this volume). But platform workers have shown their willingness to organise. Granting platform workers the right to collective bargaining would require solutions to issues of competition law that can arise, as the recent case of Uber in Seattle shows (Miller 2017). Where platforms largely accept their responsibility as employer, as is the case in Sweden, unions and platforms should come together to integrate collective agreements with the platform firms' software and make them mutually compatible, as Söderqvist (this volume) argues. Organising dispersed platform workers is a major challenge for unions, although there have been some significant examples of new unions emerging for example in relation to Deliveroo riders and Uber drivers in the UK (Berg and De Stefano this volume). Mainstream unions are also developing new organisational strategies to target these groups of workers (Vandaele 2018). Progressive policymakers need to think about how to make organising easier for platform workers.

The need to expand rights also applies to basic social protection. Schor (this volume) argues that platform workers lack basic welfare provision, and platforms work best when workers participate freely and without compulsion. This requires access to social measures to reduce workers' dependency. Therefore, the self-employed should be included in basic social protections, particularly pension and disability insurance systems, and (maybe) unemployment benefits. For example, Germany aims to include the self-employed in the statutory pension insurance system (Rahner and Schönstein this volume).

The French National Council for Digitalisation advocates a revision of the social security and collective representation status of the self-employed (Weber this volume). Obviously, the crucial question will be who pays for welfare provision. Keune and Bekker (this volume) argue that the respective costs could be carried either by the companies through social contributions, as with regular employees or, alternatively, all fiscal incentives and tax allowances for the self-employed could be used for social security coverage instead. To allow for the former, the non-trivial issue of portability has to be solved. Some ideas on how to address this issue are emerging. Hill (2015b), for example, proposes an individual security account to be established for each worker. Any business that hires that worker would pay the employer's share of social security costs on a pro-rata basis into this account, based on the number of hours that a worker works for any given business. Recently, US Senator Mark Warner introduced the Portable Benefits for Independent Workers Pilot Program Act, which would establish a pilot programme for innovations (Portable Benefits Bill 2017).

Besides social benefits, ensuring minimum wage and, possibly, minimum hours has become a key issue. Here, technology can play a crucial role (Berg and de Stefano this volume). The online freelance marketplace Upwork, for example, offers its corporate clients the option of paying by the hour, as it can monitor the workers by recording their keyboard strokes and mouse clicks and by taking random screenshots of a worker's activity. Including a minimum wage into the algorithmic back-end of platforms such as Uber would be a technological triviality. Keune and Bekker propose introducing regulations that would guarantee a minimum number of hours of work to be paid that take into account the average number of hours worked over a reference period. This is already the case for zero-hour contract workers in the Netherlands.

And finally, a fourth option would be to create one single worker status for all (France Stratégie 2016) whereby everyone regardless of their employment situation has the same rights to access training and social benefits. The principle would be to go beyond the distinction between wage earners and self-employment, creating a universal status for all, defining a right of professional activity encompassing existing statutes. It is argued that a single worker status category would make it easier for people to switch more easily from one job to another and give everyone equal access to training and social protection (France Stratégie 2016, 7). For instance, this would require the creation of a unified pension scheme or personal activity account that would cover everyone, across all sectors regardless of employment status. This concept of a single and common protection of all would lead to profound transformations of the architecture and financing of the welfare state, including simplifying its active and passive labour market policies. However, this option has rarely been discussed outside France and the UK (see Future of Work Commission 2017) and it remains to be seen whether it can resonate in other European countries.

What an updated welfare system that mitigates the risks for digital platform workers will look like is affected by institutional path dependencies of the specific welfare state regimes (Palier this volume): a Bismarckian solution will differ from a Nordic or liberal one. Still, progressive policymakers should not expect digital platforms to disappear but take the need for reform upfront.

Education, employability and social protection of individuals in the future world of work are essential to a progressive agenda. In addition, broader challenges related to tax policy and capital ownership as well as the provision of infrastructure and stimulus for innovation need to be addressed at the governmental level.

## TAX AND TRANSFER POLICIES: ADDRESSING INCOME AND WEALTH INEQUALITY

Recent technological change is producing vast profits and rents for some 'superstar firms' (Autor et al. 2017) and winner-take-all incomes for some individuals working for the most successful firms (Atkinson this volume; Appelbaum, 2017; Haskel and Westlake 2017). Guellec and Paunov (2017) illustrate how rents from digital innovation typically go to shareholders, investors, top executives and key employees of such 'superstar firms', while the wage pressure on average workers only increases.

To the extent that the ongoing digital transformation contributes to these trends, three questions have to be addressed:

- Is the tax burden on (dependent) employment adequate?
- Are gains in productivity distributed fairly?
- Is the level and concentration of private ownership of the means of production appropriate?

The business and technology community frequently refers to earned income tax credits (EITCs) to address income polarisation and the decrease in workers' share of national income. EITCs raise income and work incentives by subsidising incomes. Brynjolfsson and McAfee (2014) suggest an expansion of EITCs to ensure that the benefits of innovation are more equitably shared. Without doubt, EITCs have proven effective in the US and the UK (Hofheinz this volume). However, it is difficult to raise significantly the after-tax incomes of workers in low-productivity low-skill industries for the simple reason that wages cannot exceed the output of the worker (Atkinson this volume). EITCs will not suffice, and a broader rebalancing of taxation is required.

It can be argued that as machines become better at substituting human labour, taxing workers' incomes has increasingly negative effects on employment. Arnold et al. (this volume) raise the question of whether lower tax rates for capital income than for wage income create disincentives to using human labour as an input factor. An adjustment of the relative tax burdens, they argue, could lead to more positive employment effects in the context of the digital transformation. Bailey and Harrop (this volume) call for rebalancing taxation, including a shift towards taxing wealth, non-employment income and negative externalities such as greenhouse gas emissions. One might also think of the global, coordinated wealth tax as prescribed by Piketty (2014). However, the technical obstacles to taxing wealth, related to issues of global assessment and enforcement, are severe and require further consideration. Therefore, progressive policymakers should focus on updating national regulations on inheritance tax, top marginal income tax rates and capital gains tax.

With regard to the (re)distribution of productivity gains, leaders in politics, business and civil society frequently promote the idea of a 'robot tax', where a tax is levied on the use of robots, for example. Bill Gates (cited in Delaney 2017) famously argued that a robot tax could finance jobs in the care, health or education sectors. EU lawmakers considered a proposal to tax robot owners to pay for the retraining of workers who lose their jobs, but ultimately rejected it. Proponents of a robot tax face the question how to avoid discouraging innovation. Atkinson (this volume) describes proposals that call for the taxation and regulation of robots as "progress-killing ideas". This does not necessarily apply to big platform companies that profit from network effects (Soete this volume) and accumulate vast profits. Thus, the European Commission's recent proposal to tax large digital companies' revenues at a common rate based on where their users are located, rather than where they are headquartered, seems sensible (Guarascio 2018).

Considering the difficulties that are related to taxing wealth, it makes sense to think about distributing the means to generate wealth instead. Kremer and Went (this volume) and Freeman (2015) argue that by pluralising the ownership of the means of production, for example robots, productivity gains can be shared without disincentivising innovation.

Three options to pluralise ownership are discussed here: social wealth funds, non-classical business forms, for example platform cooperatives, and tackling the ownership of data.

First, several commentators and analysts argue for the introduction of some form of social wealth fund through which to distribute the returns from technological progress more widely and to boost consumption demand (Kremer and Went this volume; Lansley 2016). The proposals differ with regard to who pays into the fund and what the fund should be used for. While Fratzscher (2018) suggests an inheritance-tax-based sovereign investment fund to invest in future-oriented industries, Varoufakis (2017) suggests establishing a fund-based returns system on all capital that is used to pay for a universal basic dividend to all citizens. Setting up social wealth funds would be an effective and practical way for progressive policymakers seriously to address the concentration of wealth in the hands of the few in the digital age.

In many debates, distributing the returns from technological progress is linked to a universal basic income, which has both supporters and detractors, from economists to CEOs, entrepreneurs and activists. For progressives, however, a universal basic income is not the answer to the labour and social policy challenges posed by the fourth industrial revolution, for technical (OECD 2017) and political reasons (Hassel 2017). More sophisticated commentators allude to Ulrich Beck's (2000) "multi-activity society", where civic labour is supported by a state-funded social wage, or to Frithjof Bergmann's concept of "new work" (van Gelder 1994), to name only two. All of these models have their flaws. But they also pose relevant questions and can provide us with inspiration to understand how we conceptualise work and address issues around income and ownership that are so central.

Second, in many countries there is a rich tradition of non-classical business forms, from worker cooperatives to mutual benefit societies or social enterprises (Borzaga, Salvatori and Bodini 2017). Examples like Mondragon, the Basque corporation and federation of worker cooperatives, demonstrate that these non-classical businesses can flourish in the 21st century economy. Scholz and Schneider (2017) and others argue that particularly cooperatives should be rediscovered since they have a huge potential for rendering the rising platform economy more equitable (see Schor this volume; Berg and de Stefano this volume). Digital cooperatives are digital platforms that are collectively owned and democratically governed by workers (and sometime by users as well) to guarantee pay, representation and security. They particularly flourish in the ride-hailing business in the US (for example Juno) but can also be found in the care or cleaning sectors (for example 'Up and Go'). Digital co-operatives show that the efficiency gains of digital platforms (which should be welcomed in low productivity sectors, see O'Reilly 2017) can go hand in hand with decent work. It is crucial for progressive policymakers to understand that digital platforms are based on technological building blocks that can be combined in very different ways, leading to very different business models and societal outcomes. Progressives should be at the forefront of such innovative regulatory frameworks as well as taxation and funding mechanisms that encourage digital platform models to promote decent work and benefit society at large. For some sectors even state-owned digital platforms could be an option, as Howcroft and Rubery (this volume) allude to.

Third, spreading ownership within our societies could also lead to the ownership of data being regulated, based on the argument that this data 'belongs' to citizens and is increasingly becoming a crucial factor of production (Fratzscher 2018). Obviously, issues of collective ownership or taxing multinational corporations may not be workable within national borders and may require a coordinated effort in the context of the EU or the World Trade Organization, as Keune and Dekker (this volume) explain.

In sum, digitalisation of work raises a number of significant challenges for developing new tax and transfer policies to address the emerging and widening disparities in income and wealth. A further dimension of the way inequalities are presenting themselves relates to issues of investing in infrastructure, innovation and supporting regional development.

## INFRASTRUCTURE AND INNOVATION: INVESTING IN THE FUTURE

The digital era creates demands for new investments in public goods and infrastructure. These include physical infrastructure related to housing, renewable energy, care for the young and the aging, as well as digital infrastructure with open source software, public data and digital courseware, to boost inclusive growth. Just as the industrial economy needed roads, sewers and public libraries to prosper, new kinds of digital public goods are needed, not only to drive innovation and employment but also to rejuvenate the democratic project so the benefits are more widely distributed.

To deliver inclusive growth in the digital age we need innovation policies that are different from traditional industrial policies that supported targeted industries. Historically, government, in the form of the 'entrepreneurial state', has funded risky and most pioneering research activities (Mazzucato 2013). In many cases these have contributed to significant technological advances creating and shaping markets, and increasing growth and prosperity; the internet itself would not exist without massive public investments in basic and applied research. In recent years, despite the advent of many innovative technologies these have not had the equivalent effect on productivity growth (Gordon 2016). To improve living standards this 'productivity paradox' must be addressed (Atkinson this volume; Soete this volume). Government will be central in the third wave of digitalisation (Case 2017), which is expected to have major productivity effects on health, education, transport, energy and food. For progressives, the role of government should be one of a lead investor and smart regulator. Innovation cannot be left to the private sector alone. It will depend on flourishing cross-sectoral innovation networks, where the state as catalyst is "sparking the initial reaction" (Mazzucato 2013). Since growth has not only a rate, but also a direction, innovation policy must be mission-oriented (Mazzucato and Caetano 2015): the state must set the direction of travel, based on public and political debates specifying society's 'grand missions', while at the same time enabling bottom-up experimentation and learning, and developing new and fragile innovations.

## TAKING A REGIONAL PERSPECTIVE

In many advanced economies, GDP per capita in the richest and poorest regions has been diverging over the past two decades (Chazan 2018). 'Good workers' and 'good firms' are increasingly colocated in large cities (Dauth, Findeisen and Suedkum 2016). Many of those citizens who will be most severely hit by digital transformation and globalisation are spatially concentrated and relatively immobile (Suedekum 2017). In addition, the social prestige associated with urban life has increased (Florida 2002). Many policies proposed above – for example on education and training or secure job-to-job transitions – can only become effective if they account for dramatic regional differences. Understanding regional differences with regard to the effects of the digital transformation and the capacities to deal with them must be a defining characteristic of a progressive agenda on work in the digital age. 'Solving' intensifying regional economic disparities by increasing spatial labour mobility, as it can be observed in the US, does not seem to be viable – nor politically desirable. Notably, Gidron and Hall (2017) show how regional decline and a loss in subjective social status increase support for the populist right. Therefore, progressives must revitalise regional development, to demonstrate that the digital transformation is about not only urban co-working spaces and start-up incubators, but also better working and living conditions for all. In particular, regional ecosystems centred on innovation and digital technologies must be better understood, promoted and nourished.

In the digital age, the regional and global levels are closely intertwined. Regional ecosystems are connected to and embedded in international ecosystems, and global value chains can become global value networks (Srai and Christodoulou 2014). It is crucial for policymakers to understand where countries, regions and companies are positioned in these global ecosystems and value networks. Progressive policymakers should take an active role in nurturing high value activities involving emerging technologies that seeks to secure decent work for their citizens.

## CONCLUSION: UPDATE, RECHARGE AND RELOAD THE CONCEPT OF WORK IN SOCIETY

As evidenced by the rich and diverse range of contributions to this volume there is no lack of ideas about how to address the challenges of the fourth industrial revolution across a number of dimensions. By drawing on a wealth of cross-national evidence we are able to spotlight areas of effective policymaking, and draw attention to factors that have contributed to this. A progressive agenda needs to equip everyone with the right skills, ensure stable employment transitions across the life course, safeguard social standards and create innovative transfer policies that can both stimulate innovation and capture the rewards in a more inclusive way.

We call on progressive policymakers to broaden their view and to envision a good working society in the digital age, which includes and values all forms of human work: paid and unpaid, in industry and in services, dependent and self-employed. Progressives should take a more comprehensive perspective and engage in a debate on the working society that includes work in a broader sense (Kalleberg this volume). A large proportion of work is undertaken not in formal gainful employment but in family labour (caring for children or parents) or voluntary civil labour (in the arts, culture and politics sectors), which all contribute to the general welfare. Without this kind of work our societies could not function. As Howcroft and Rubery (this volume) argue, we need to recognise and value this unpaid, caring and voluntary work more adequately.

Work in the digital era requires us to update, recharge and reload our concept of a good society.


## REFERENCES

Appelbaum, E. (2017), 'What's Behind the Increase in Inequality?', Washington DC: Center for Economic and Policy Research, http://cepr.net/images/stories/reports/whats-behind-the-increase-in-inequality-2017-09.pdf.

Autor, D. H. (2013), *The 'Task Approach' to Labor Markets: an Overview*, Discussion Paper 7178, Bonn: Institute for the Study of Labor.

Autor, D. H. (2015), 'Why Are There Still So Many Jobs? The History and Future of Workplace Automation', *Journal of Economic Perspectives*, 29(3): 3–30.

Autor, D., D. Dorn, L. F. Katz, C. Patterson and J. Van Reenen (2017), *The Fall of the Labor Share and the Rise of Superstar Firms*, NBER Working Paper 23396, http://www.nber.org/papers/w23396.

Bauer, F., M. Fertig and P. Fuchs (2016), *Modellprojekte öffentlich geförderte Beschäftigung in NRW: Teilnehmerauswahl und professionelle Begleitung machen den Unterschied*, IAB-Kurzbericht, 10/2016, Nürnberg: Institut für Arbeitsmarkt- und Berufsforschung.

Beck, U. (2000), *Brave New World of Work*, Cambridge: Polity Press.

Berger, T. and C. Frey (2016), 'Structural Transformation in the OECD: Digitalisation, Deindustrialisation and the Future of Work', *OECD Social, Employment and Migration Working Papers*, No. 193, OECD Publishing, Paris. http://dx.doi.org/10.1787/5jlr068802f7-en.

Bernhardt, A. (2017), 'Beyond Basic Income: Claiming Our Right to Govern Technology', *Medium*, 11 May, https://medium.com/@a.d.bernhardt/can-we-imagine-governing-technology-eb4b58092b81.

Boes, A., T. Kampf, B. Langes and T. Luhr (2017), 'The Disruptive Power of Digital Transformation: New Forms of Industrializing Knowledge Work', in K. Briken, S. Chillas, M. Krzywdzinski, and A. Marks (eds), *The New Digital Workplace: How Technologies Revolutionise Work*, 153–76, Basingstoke: Palgrave Macmillan.

Borzaga, C., G. Salvatori and R. Bodini (2017), *Social and Solidarity Economy and the Future of Work*, Geneva: International Labour

Organization, http://www.ilo.org/wcmsp5/groups/public/---ed_emp/---emp_ent/---coop/documents/publication/wcms_573160.pdf.

Braun, S. (2018), 'Deutschland Steht Unter Erheblicher Spannung', interview with Naika Foroutan, *Die Süddeutsche Zeitung*, 24 January, http://www.sueddeutsche.de/politik/integration-deutschland-steht-unter-erheblicher-spannung-1.3837398.

Briken, K., S. Chillas, M. Krzywdzinski and A. Marks (eds.) (2017), *The New Digital Workplace: How New Technologies Revolutionise Work*, Basingstoke: Palgrave Macmillan.

Brynjolfsson, E. and A. McAfee (2014), *The Second Machine Age: Work, Progress, and Prosperity in a Time of Brilliant Technologies*, New York: W. W. Norton & Company.

Case, S. (2017), *The Third Wave: an Entrepreneur's Vision of the Future*, London: Simon & Schuster.

Chazan, G. (2018), 'Germany's Economic Engine Fails to Power Struggling Rural Regions', *Financial Times*, 27 February, https://www.ft.com/content/c6edf308-1875-11e8-9376-4a6390addb44.

Chung, H., M. Kerkhofs and P. Ester (2007), *Working Time Flexibility in European Companies: Establishment Survey on Working Time 2004–2005*, Dublin: European Foundation for the Improvement of Living and Working Conditions.

Dassonneville, R. and M. Hooghe (2017), 'Economic Indicators and Electoral Volatility: Economic Effects on Electoral Volatility in Western Europe, 1950–2013', *Comparative European Politics*, 15(6): 919–43.

Dauth, W., S. Findeisen and J. Suedekum (2016), *Spatial Wage Disparities – Workers, Firms, and Assortative Matching*, http://www.ieb.ub.edu/files/PapersWSUE2016/WSUE2016_Suedekum.pdf.

Delaney, K. J. (2017), 'The Robot that Takes Your Job Should Pay Taxes, says Bill Gates', *Quartz*, 17 February, https://qz.com/911968/bill-gates-the-robot-that-takes-your-job-should-pay-taxes/.

Elliott, S. W. (2017), *Computers and the Future of Skill Demand*, Paris: OECD Publishing.

Florida, R. (2002), *The Rise of the Creative Class: and How It's Transforming Work, Leisure, Community, and Everyday Life*, New York: Basic Books.

France Strategie (2016), 'Nouvelles formesdu travail et de la protectiondes actifs', Paris: France Stratégie. https://francestrategie1727.fr/wp-content/uploads/2016/03/17-27-nouvelles-formes-du-travail-et-de-la-protection-des-actifs.pdf.

Fratzscher, M. (2018), 'Warum zahlt uns Google nicht eine Nutzungsge-bühr?', *Die Zeit*, 23 February, http://www.zeit.de/wirtschaft/2018-02/digitalisierung-vermoegen-staatsfonds-soziale-teilhabe-ungleichheit.

Freeman, R. B. (2015), *Who Owns the Robots Rules the World*, Bonn: IZA World of Labor, https://wol.iza.org/uploads/articles/5/pdfs/who-owns-the-robots-rules-the-world.pdf?v=1.

Future of Work Commission (2017), Report of the Future of Work Commisison, London. https://d3n8a8pro7vhmx.cloudfront.net/campaigncountdown/pages/1052/attachments/original/1512946196/Future_of_Work_Commission_Report__December_2017.pdf?1512946196.

Gidron, N. and P. A. Hall (2017), 'The Politics of Social Status: Economic and Cultural Roots of the Populist Right', *British Journal of Sociology*, 68(SI): 57–84.

Goodwin, M. (2011), *Right Response: Understanding and Countering Populist Extremism in Europe*, London: Royal Institute of International Affairs.

Gordon, R. J. (2016), *The Rise and Fall of American Growth: the US Standard of Living since the Civil War*, Princeton: Princeton University Press.

Guarascio, F. (2018), 'EU Plans New Tax for Tech Giants up to 5 percent of Gross Revenues', Reuters, 26 February, https://www.reuters.com/article/us-eu-tax-digital/eu-plans-new-tax-for-tech-giants-up-to-5-percent-of-gross-revenues-idUSKCN1GA25R.

Guellec, D. and C. Paunov (2017), *Digital Innovation and the Distribution of Income*, NBER Working Paper 23987, http://www.nber.org/papers/w23987.

Haskel, J. and S. Westlake (2017), *Capitalism Without Capital: the Rise of the Intangible Economy*, Princeton: Princeton University Press.

Hassel, A. (2017), 'Unconditional Basic Income is a Dead End', Social Europe, 1 March, https://www.socialeurope.eu/unconditional-basic-income-is-a-dead-end

Hernández, E. and H. Kriesi (2015), 'The Electoral Consequences of the Financial and Economic Crisis in Europe', *European Journal of Political Research*, 55(2): 203–24.

Hill, S. (2015a), 'How Big is the Gig (Economy)?', *Medium*, 9 September, https://wtfeconomy.com/how-big-is-the-gig-economy-e674c7986a28.

Hill, S. (2015b), *New Economy, New Social Contract: a Plan for a Safety Net in a Multiemployer World*, Washington, DC: New America, https://static.newamerica.org/attachments/4395-new-economy-new-social-contract/New%20Economy,%20Social%20Contract_UpdatedFinal.34c973248e6946d0af17116fbd6bb79e.pdf.

Hobolt, S. B. and J. Tilley (2016), 'Fleeing the Centre: the Rise of Challenger Parties in the Aftermath of the Euro Crisis', *West European Politics*, 39(5): 971–91.

IMF (2009), 'World Economic Outlook, April 2009: Crisis and Recovery', *World Economic Outlook*, Washington: International Monetary Fund.

Land, M. H. (2013), 'Full Steam Ahead: the Benefits of Integrating the Arts Into STEM', *Procedia Computer Science*, 20: 547–52.

Lansley, S. (2016), *A Sharing Economy: How Social Wealth Funds can Reduce Inequality and Help Balance the Books*, Bristol: Policy Press Shorts.

Levy, F. and R. J. Murnane (2013), *Dancing with Robots: Human Skills for Computerized Work*, Washington DC: Third Way, https://dusp.mit.edu/uis/publication/dancing-robots-human-skills-computerized-work.

Martin, J. P (2018), *Skills for the 21st Century: Findings and Policy Lessons from the OECD Survey of Adult Skills*, IZA Policy Paper 138, Bonn: IZA – Institute of Labor Economics.

Mazzucato, M. (2013), *The Entrepreneurial State: Debunking Public vs. Private Sector Myths*, London: Anthem Press.

Mazzucato, M. and P. C. Caetano (eds.) (2015), *Mission-orientated Finance for Innovation: New Ideas for Investment-led Growth*, London: Policy Network.

MGI (2017), *Jobs Lost, Jobs Gained: Workforce Transitions in a Time Automation*, McKinsey Global Institute, https://www.mckinsey.com/mgi/overview/2017-in-review/automation-and-the-future-of-work/jobs-lost-jobs-gained-workforce-transitions-in-a-time-of-automation.

Miller, C. (2017), 'FTC and Uber Align to Stop New Seattle Law for Ride-Hail Drivers', *The Recorder*, 7 November.

Muro, D. and G. Vidal (2014), 'Mind the Gaps: the Political Consequences of the Great Recession in Europe', blog, LSE Euro Crisis in the Press, London School of Economics, http://blogs.lse.ac.uk/eurocrisispress/2014/06/10/mind-the-gaps-the-political-consequences-of-the-great-recession-in-europe/.

Ng, P. T. (2017). 'The Future of Lifelong Learning in Singapore', in H. J. Malone, S. Rincón-Gallardo and K. Kew (eds), *Future Directions of Educational Change: Social Justice, Professional Capital, and Systems Change*, 205–222, New York: Routledge.

O'Reilly, J., I. Cebrián and M. Lallement (eds.) (2000), *Working Time Changes: Social Integration Through Transitional Labour Markets*, Cheltenham: Edward Elgar.

O'Reilly, J. and C. Fagan (eds) (1998), *Part-time Prospects: International comparisons of part-time work in Europe, North America and the Pacific Rim*, London and New York: Routledge.

O'Reilly, T. (2017), *WTF?: What's the Future and Why It's Up to Us*, London: Random House Business.

OECD (2015), 'Back to Work: Sweden Improving the Re-employment Prospects of Displaced Workers', Paris: OECD Publishing.

OECD (2016a), *Skills for a Digital World: 2016 Ministerial Meeting on the Digital Economy*, OECD Digital Economy Paper 250, Paris: OECD Publishing.

OECD (2016b), *Skills for a Digital World: Policy Brief on the Future of Work*, Paris: OECD Publishing.

OECD (2016c), *Skills Matter: Further Results from the Survey of Adult Skills*, OECD Skills Studies, Paris: OECD Publishing.

OECD (2016d), *Skills for a Digital World: Working Party on Measurement and Analysis of the Digital Economy*, Paris: OECD Publishing.

OECD (2017), *Basic Income as a Policy Option: Can It Add Up?*, policy brief on the future of work, Paris: OECD Publishing.

Pfeiffer, S. (2015), *Effects of Industry 4.0 on Vocational Education and Training*, *MANU:SCRIPTS*, Vienna: Austrian Academy of Sciences.

Pfeiffer, S. (2017), 'Industrie 4.0 in the Making – Discourse Patterns and the Rise of Digital Despotism', in K. Briken, S. Chillas, M. Krzywdzinski and A. Marks (eds), *The New Digital Workplac: How Technologies Revolutionise Work*, 21–41, Basingstoke: Palgrave Macmillan.

Piketty, T. (2014), *Capital in the Twenty-First Century*, Cambridge: Harvard University Press.

Portable Benefits Bill 2017 (2017), US Senate, 115th Congress, 1st session, https://www.scribd.com/document/349414506/Portable-Benefits-Bill-05-25-2017.

Prassl, J. (2015), *The Concept of the Employer*, Oxford: Oxford University Press.

Ranft, F. and R. Thillaye (2015), 'Rapidly Changing Labour Markets: Is EU Flexicurity Still the Answer?', in C. Reuter, R. Bazillier, G. Cozzi, A. Crespy, F. De Ville and A. Wigger, and on behalf of SOLIDAR: M. Claassens, B. Saenen and E.-M. Schneider (eds), *Progressive Structural Reforms Proposals for European Reforms to Reduce Inequalities and Promote Jobs, Growth and Social Investment*, 193–208, Warszawa: Oficyna Wydawnicza ASPRA-JR.

Schmid, G. (2003), 'Activating Labour Market Policy: "Flexicurity" Through Transitional Labour Markets', in J.-P. Touffut (ed.), *Institutions, Innovation and Growth*, 68–96, Edward Elgar.

Scholz, T. and N. Schneider (eds) (2017), *Ours to Hack and to Own: the Rise of Platform Cooperativism, a New Vision for the Future of Work and a Fairer Internet*, New York: OR Books.

Srai, J. S. and Christodoulou, P. (2014), *Capturing Value from Global Networks: Strategic Approaches to Configuring International Production, Supply and Service Operations*, Cambridge: University of Cambridge Institute for Manufacturing.

Suedekum, J. (2017), 'Besser als das Arbeitslosengeld', *Frankfurter Allgemeine Zeitung*, 23 September, http://www.faz.net/aktuell/wirtschaft/arm-und-reich/wie-kann-der-staat-wettbewerbsverlierern-helfen-15210042.html.

Taylor, M. (2017), *Good Work: the Taylor Review of Modern Working Practices*, London: Department for Business, Energy & Industrial Strategy.

Tyson, L. D'A. (2015), *How Can We Protect Workers in the Gig Economy?*, World Economic Forum, https://www.weforum.org/agenda/2015/11/how-can-we-protect-workers-in-the-gig-economy/.

Vandaele, K. (2018), 'How Can Trade Unions in Europe Connect with Young Workers?', in J. O'Reilly, J. Leschke, R. Ortlieb, M. Seeleib-Kaiser and P. Villa (eds), *Youth Labor in Transition*, New York: Oxford University Press.

Varoufakis, Y. (2017), 'A Tax on Robots', Project Syndicate, 27 February, https://www.project-syndicate.org/commentary/bill-gates-tax-on-robots-by-yanis-varoufakis-2017-02?barrier=accessreg.

Van Gelder, S. (1994), 'New Work, New Culture: an Interview with Frithjof Bergmann', *Context*, 37, https://www.context.org/iclib/ic37/bergmann/.

Weil, D. (2014), *The Fissured Workplace*, Cambridge, MA: Harvard University Press.

# ABOUT THE AUTHORS

**Daniel Arnold** is a researcher at the research department Labour Markets, Human Resources and Social Policy at ZEW, Germany. His research focuses on the impact of working conditions on the wellbeing of workers.

**Melanie Arntz** is assistant professor at the University of Heidelberg, and currently serves as acting head of the research department Labour Markets, Human Resources and Social Policy at the Mannheim Centre for European Economic Research (Zentrum für Europäische Wirtschaftsforschung; ZEW), Germany. She is a member of the German Economic Association's panel on regional theory and politics and is co-editor of the Journal for Labour Market Research. Her work focuses on individual and collective reactions to changing labour market conditions, including the digitalisation of work and the internationalisation of production processes.

**Robert D. Atkinson** is the founder and president of the Information Technology and Innovation Foundation. An internationally recognised scholar, he is shaping the debate on a host of critical issues at the intersection of technological innovation and public policy. His work on technology and innovation-related topics ranging from tax policy, advanced manufacturing and productivity to global competitiveness has been widely published. Having served under the Clinton, Bush and Obama administrations, he is a valued adviser to policymakers around the world.

**Thomas Aubrey** is a senior adviser at Policy Network and director of the Centre for Progressive Capitalism. Thomas is chief executive officer and founder of Credit Capital Advisory and publishes on credit risk management and macro strategy, particularly on the impact of credit on the wider economy and its implications for asset allocation and business cycle measurement. Previously, he ran several analytics and research businesses and spent a number of years as an international management consultant in Europe, North America and Asia, and was responsible for turning around failing companies.

**Olivia Bailey** is the deputy general secretary of the Fabian Society, UK, and previously worked there as research director. In the 2017 general election, she was the Labour party candidate in the constituency of Reading West. Before she joined the Fabian Society, she worked as political adviser to a member of Labour's shadow cabinet, specialising on Labour's policy development and political reform. Before this Olivia worked as a political analyst for the BBC, as the chair of Labour Students and as an elected officer at the National Union of Students. Currently, she is also chair of the Labour Women's Network.

**Kate Bell** is head of the Economic and Social Affairs Department at the Trade Union Congress (TUC), and leads the TUC's work in many key areas of economic and social policy. Before joining the TUC, Kate worked as head of policy and public affairs for a local authority. Before this she served as work and pensions adviser to Ed Miliband during his period as leader of the Labour party. Kate also worked for the charities Child Poverty Action Group and Gingerbread.

**Salima Benhamou** is an economist at the Paris School of Economics and is professor of international macroeconomics at the Paris-Dauphine University, France. She also works at the office of the French commissioner general for strategy (France Stratégie). Her areas of expertise include human resource practices, organisational and technological innovation, responsible business practices and well-being at the workplace. Previously, Salima has worked at the Centre for Economic Performance at the London School of Economics.

**Janine Berg** is a senior economist at the International Labour Organization, based at the Conditions of Work and Equality Department. She specialises in the economic effects of labour laws and has authored several books and numerous articles on employment and labour market institutions. Since joining the International Labour Office (ILO), Janine has provided technical assistance to ILO constituents on policies for generating jobs and for improving working conditions. She was awarded a doctor of philosophy (PhD) from the New School for Social Research in New York, US.

**Colin Crouch** is a professor emeritus of the University of Warwick, UK, and is an external scientific member of the Max Planck Institute for the Study of Societies at Cologne, Germany. His most recent books include Post-Democracy (2004), The Strange Non-death of Neoliberalism (2011), Making Capitalism Fit for Society (2013), Governing Social Risks in Post-Crisis Europe (2015), The Knowledge Corrupters: Hidden Consequences of the Financial Takeover of Public Life (2015), Society and Social Change in 21st Century Europe (2016) and Can Neoliberalism Be Saved from Itself? (2017).

**Carlotta De Franceschi** co-founded Action Institute in 2012 and has served as its president ever since. She was senior economic adviser on banking and finance to the Italian prime minister from 2014 to 2015 and head of banking solutions and public finance for Italy. Before this she worked for Credit Suisse, Morgan Stanley and Goldman Sachs. She is a member of the Bretton Woods Committee and a former Aspen junior fellow. Ms De Franceschi graduated in Business Administration from Bocconi University, Italy, and holds a master's in business administration (MBA) from Harvard Business School.

**Valerio De Stefano** is a research professor of labour law at KU Leuven University, Belgium. Previously, he has worked at the ILO in Geneva, Switzerland, where he carried out research in non-standard employment, work in the 'platform' (gig) economy, labour dispute resolutions and human rights in global supply chains. While obtaining his doctoral degree from Bocconi University, Italy, he was a part-time associate at the Employment, Pensions and Benefits Department at Freshfields Bruckhaus Deringer limited liability partnership (LLP) in Milan, Italy, where he worked as a postdoctoral fellow with visits to Clare Hall College at the University of Cambridge and University College London, UK.

**Fabian Dekkker** is a policy researcher at Regioplan Policy Research, focusing on flexible employment, new technology, labour mobility and youth unemployment. Prior to this he worked in the Netherlands as a social researcher at the Verwey-Jonker Institute, the Netherlands Scientific Council for Government Policy and Erasmus University, and as a lecturer at Utrecht University. He obtained his master's degree and PhD in Sociology from Erasmus University, Rotterdam.

**Virginia Doellgast** is associate professor of comparative employment relations at Cornell University's School of Industrial and Labor Relations. Her research focuses on the impact of collective bargaining and labour market institutions on inequality, job quality, and worker voice. Some of Virginia's past projects include comparative studies of organisational and work restructuring in the European and US telecommunications and call centre industries. She is the author of Disintegrating Democracy at Work: Labor Unions and the Future of Good Jobs in the Service Economy (2012) and the co-editor of Reconstructing Solidarity: Labour Unions, Precarious Work, and the Politics of Institutional Change in Europe (2018).

**Jan Drahokoupil** is a senior researcher on multinational corporations at the European Trade Union Institute (ETUI), Brussels, where he coordinates research on digitalisation and the future of work. His broader expertise lies in political economy and development issues, particularly in the context of eastern European countries. He obtained his PhD in 2007 from the Central European University, Hungary. He has published widely on transition economies, including the political economies of Russia, Eastern Europe and Central Asia.

**Enrique Fernández-Macías** is a research manager in the employment unit at Eurofound, Dublin. He has a PhD in economic sociology from the University of Salamanca, Spain, where he worked as a lecturer and a researcher before joining Eurofound. His main research interests are in the areas of job quality, occupational change and inequality. In his current role he is responsible for the European Jobs Monitor, among other projects. He is also the coordinator of Eurofound's research activity on the implications of the digital age for work and employment.

**Jörg Flecker** is a professor at the University of Vienna, and head of the Department of Sociology. His work includes the international comparison of changes to employment systems, research on transnational value chains as well as dynamic networking of organisations, and the quality of work. Previously, he worked as scientific director at the Forschungs- und Beratungsstelle Arbeitswelt (FORBA), an independent research institute in Vienna specialising in social science research into work and employment.

**Juan Gomez** is director of research and policy and senior partner at Think Tank Toronto. He is a public policy specialist and served most recently as vice president for policy and government relations at the Toronto Region Board of Trade, and previously as head of economic strategy for the region of Greater Manchester in the UK. Juan has senior-level government experience with ministries and agencies within the Government of Ontario, Canada, such as the Ontario Realty Corporation, the Ministry of Training Colleges and Universities, Ombudsman Ontario and the Ministry of Municipal Affairs and Housing. One of his most recent works, co-authored with Rafael Gomez, Workplace Democracy for the 21st Century, was published by the Broadbent Institute in 2016.

**Rafael Gomez** has a bachelor of arts (BA) and master's in economics (MSc) degrees, and a PhD in industrial relations. Since receiving his PhD he has taught and has undertaken research at various international institutions such as the London School of Economics, the Central Bank of Spain and Glendon College, York University, UK. Since 2009 he has been professor of employment relations at the University of Toronto and is currently the director of the Centre for Industrial Relations and Human Resources. He is the author of several books and over 70 articles and chapters in edited volumes.

**Rafael Grande** is a researcher and senior lecturer in the Department of State Law and Sociology at the University of Málaga, Spain. A member of Networks and Social Structures (University of Málaga) and Labor Market, Migrations, and Health (UIC-Castilla y León, Spain) research groups, Rafael's research focuses on stratification in the labour market, demography and international migration. He obtained his master's and PhD in Latin American economics studies from the University of Salamanca, Spain. He is also an editor of the journal Encrucijadas Revista Crítica de Ciencias Sociales.

**Terry Gregory** has been a member of the research department Labour Markets, Human Resources and Social Policy at ZEW, Germany, since 2009. As a senior researcher in the field of changing labour markets, Terry conducts research into empirical labour economics and regional economics. His special interest lies in the labour market consequences of digitisation and automation, labour market inequalities and the impact of minimum wages. Terry Gregory studied economics at the University of Bonn, Germany, and at the Charles University in Prague, Czech Republic, and received his doctoral degree from the University of Regensburg, Germany.

**Andrew Harrop** is the general Secretary of the Fabian Society, UK. He has led the society's research on economic and social policy as well as on the future of the Labour party. He was previously director of policy and public affairs for Age UK and a vice president of the Foundation for European Progressive Studies. He has been a Labour party activist since he was 18 and was a parliamentary candidate in the 2005 general election.

**Amy E. Healy** is a comparative, quantitative sociologist and is currently the Postdoctoral Research Fellow for the European Social Survey, Ireland at Mary Immaculate College, University of Limerick. While she has published across a range of topics and disciplines, her primary research interests are in sociology, specifically related to: work, consumption, stratification and religion.

**Paul Hofheinz** is president and co-founder of the Lisbon Council, a Brussels-based independent, non-partisan thinktank and policy network. An experienced journalist and editor, Paul Hofheinz frequently appears on Bloomberg, CNBC and the BBC as a commentator on economic reform and European politics. Before he launched the Lisbon Council, Paul worked as a writer and editor at The Wall Street Journal, covering such diverse topics as financial-market regulation, European integration, emerging markets and Russian politics. He also served two years as managing editor of Central European Economic Review.

**Kaire Holts** is working towards a PhD, and is a research fellow at the University of Hertfordshire, UK, within the Creative Economy Research Centre. Before joining the research team at the University of Hertfordshire, Kaire worked for the ILO and the UN Institute for Training and Research in Geneva, Switzerland.

**Debra Howcroft** is professor of technology and organisation in the People, Management and Organisation Division of Alliance Manchester Business School, UK. She is co-editor-in-chief of the journal New Technology, Work and Employment, and has served on the editorial boards of Information Systems Journal, Information Technology and People, Journal of Information Technology, Journal of Strategic Information Systems and the Qualitative Review of Accounting and Management.

**Ursula Huws** is professor of labour and globalisation at the University of Hertfordshire Business School, UK, where she is currently directing the Dynamics of Virtual Work project at the European Cooperation in Science and Technology and carrying out other research on creative labour. Ursula is the editor of the international interdisciplinary journal Work Organisation Labour and Globalisation. She has a background in developing and managing large international research projects in Europe, the Americas, Asia and Australia.

**Anna Ilsøe** is associate professor at the Employment Relations Research Centre (Forskningscenter for Arbejdsmarkeds- og Organisationsstudier; FAOS) at the Sociology Department of the University of Copenhagen, Denmark. She is president of the Danish Sociological Association and a member of the editorial board of the Nordic Journal of Working Life Studies. Her primary fields of research include company-level bargaining, digital labour markets, working hours, labour market segmentation and the private sector.

**Cécile Jolly** works at France Stratégie, specialising in new occupational structures and the future of work. She is also the director of activities at the thinktank Association travail emploi Europe société (ASTREES). Cécile has an MBA from ESSEC (École supérieure des sciences économiques et commerciales) Business School, Paris, and a master's degree in the politics of the Arab world from Institut d'études politiques de Paris (Sciences Po). Cécile previously worked for the French Ministry of Defence, the Commissariat général du Plan and its institutional successor, the Centre d'analyse stratégique.

**Arne L. Kalleberg** is a Kenan distinguished professor of sociology at the University of North Carolina at Chapel Hill. US. He is also an adjunct professor in the Kenan-Flagler Business School, the Department of Public Policy, and at the Curriculum in Global Studies. Arne has served as the secretary of the American Sociological Association and as its president. He is currently the editor of Social Forces, an International Journal of Social Research.

**Jenni Karjalainen** is a former special adviser to the Finnish minister of labour, and currently works as a senior policy adviser at the Finnish Union of Professional Engineers. Before this she worked for Miltton and the Finnish Ministry of Employment and the Economy.

**Martin Kenney** is a professor in community and regional development at the University of California, Davis, US, is a senior project director at the Berkeley Roundtable on the International Economy in the US, and a senior fellow at the Research Institute for the Finnish Economy, Finland. His research focuses on the dynamics of entrepreneurial high-technology regions, university-industry technology transfer, the development of the venture capital industry, and the impacts of new technologies on industrial structures and labour relations. He is an editor at the world's premier innovation research journal, Research Policy. He has given over 250 lectures at universities, government agencies and corporations in Europe, Asia and North and South America.

**Maarten Keune** is a professor at the University of Amsterdam where he holds the chair in social security and labour relations and the directorship of the Amsterdam Institute for Advanced Labour

Studies. Previously, he held various positions at the ILO in Geneva, and at the ETUI in Brussels. He has published widely on industrial relations, the labour market and welfare state developments, and European integration.

**Dmitrijs Kravcenko** is assistant professor of organisational behaviour at the University of Sussex. His research interests centre on questions of collective memory, knowledge integration, management theory and the role of technology in shaping the future of work. He completed his ESRC-funded doctoral studies at the University of Warwick Business School, IKON Research Unit. Dmitrijs is founder and host of the Talking About Organizations Podcast, innovator in mobile and distance learning for higher education, and pioneer in academic audiobook publishing.

**Monique Kremer** is professor of active citizenship at the Faculty of Social and Behavioural Sciences at the University of Amsterdam's, the Netherlands. Her research focuses on citizens in the welfare state, and explores questions such as: how do changing citizens and changing welfare states interact? Who is or is not considered a citizen? How can we describe citizens as 'involved'? Kremer's research is mainly comparative in the European context and qualitative in nature. She has served as a senior academic staff member of the Dutch government's independent thinktank the Scientific Council for Government Policy since 2004. In 2007, she received the award Best Young Sociologist from the European Sociological Association.

**Aleksandra Kanjuo Mrčela** has been president of the Slovenian Sociological Association since 2017. Aleksandra is professor of economic sociology and the sociology of work at the Faculty of Social Sciences, University of Ljubljana, Slovenia, where she is also a researcher at the Organisations and Human Resources Research Centre at the Faculty of Social Sciences. Aleksandra's teaching, research and consultancy activities are in the fields of industrial relations, gender and economy, ownership and changes post-privatisation in Slovene companies.

**Max Neufeind** is a researcher and policy advisor on the future of work with a focus on emerging technologies and innovative work practices. He is a lecturer at the Hertie School of Governance and a policy fellow at the Berlin-based thinktank Das Progressive Zentrum. Recently, he was a John F. Kennedy memorial policy fellow at the Centre for European Studies at Harvard University, US. Max holds a PhD from ETH Zurich and master's degrees from the London School of Economics and Mannheim University. His views and opinions expressed in this book do not necessarily reflect the official policy or position of any agency of the German federal government.

**Seán Ó Riain** is Professor of Sociology at the National University of Ireland Maynooth. His current research is on the comparative sociology of European workplaces, the political economy of Ireland and Denmark, and change in state and governance institutions, with a focus on new deals in the new economy. The research in this paper was funded by a European Research Council Consolidator Grant, New Deals in the New Economy.

**Jacqueline O'Reilly** is Professor of Comparative Human Resource Management at the University of Sussex Business School. She was coordinator of a EU funded large-scale research project STYLE: Strategic Transitions for Youth Labour in Europe (www.style-research.eu) (2014-17) and is the UK lead on the EU funded project NEGOTIATE, examining how young people deal with early career insecurity (www.negotiate-research.eu) (2015-18). Her research focuses on fairness at work, international comparisons of gender and labour market transitions across the life cycle and on labour market policy evaluation.

**Bruno Palier** is director of research at the Centre d'études européennes at the National Centre for Scientific Research (Centre national de la recherche scientifique; CNRS) at Sciences Po, France, and is honorary professor in welfare state research at the University of Southern Denmark, where he undertakes research into welfare reforms in Europe. Previously, he was the scientific coordinator of a European network of excellence Reconciling Work and Welfare in Europe (RECWOWE) and is currently a member of the board of the European Social Policy Association Network (ESPANET), a member of Research Committee 19 of the International Sociological Association, and a member of the steering committee of the European Politics and Society section of the American Political Sciences Association.

**Georgios Petropoulos** is a resident research fellow at Bruegel in Brussels. He is a Greek citizen and his research focuses on industrial organisation, competition policy and the digital economy. Georgios has extensive research experience from holding visiting positions at the European Central Bank in Frankfurt, Banque de France in Paris and the research department of Hewlett-Packard in Palo Alto, US. Georgios has been a speaker at many international academic conferences and workshops, and has some economic consulting experience from spending a summer at Compass Lexecon in Madrid, Spain. He is the founder and first editor-in-chief of the student magazine TSEconomist and co-founder of the TSEconomist student association.

**Sven Rahner** is a policy advisor and lecturer at the Hertie School of Governance in Berlin, Germany. His research focuses on the future of work and welfare in the digital age. He previously worked as a policy advisor in the committee on labour and social affairs at the German Bundestag. He holds a master's in political science from the University of Heidelberg and a PhD in economics and social science from the University of Kassel, both in Germany. Sven is the author of Architekten der Arbeit (Architects of Work), a collection of interviews on the future of work with leading political thinkers.

**Florian Ranft** is head of policy and international at Policy Network, senior research analyst at the Centre for Progressive Policy and policy fellow at Das Progressive Zentrum. He holds a diploma in politics from the University of Potsdam, and a PhD in politics from the University of Greifswald, both in Germany. Florian has lectured and undertaken research in international politics at a number of top-tier universities, research institutes and international organisations in Europe, America and Africa.

**Jill Rubery** joined the University of Manchester Institute of Science and Technology in 1989, having previously worked at the Department of Applied Economics at Cambridge University, where she had been a fellow of New Hall and Director of Studies in Economics. From 1991 to 1996 and again from 1998 to 2007 she acted as coordinator of the European Commission's group of experts on gender and employment. In 2006 Jill was elected a fellow of the British Academy and an emeritus fellow of New Hall, University of Cambridge.

**Marc Saxer** is head of department for the Asia and Pacific office and the coordinator of the Asia-Europe Economy of Tomorrow project at the Friedrich-Bert-Stiftung, Berlin, Germany. His work focuses on the processes of transformation and democratisation. Previously, Marc headed the Friedrich-Ebert-Stiftung (FES) Thailand and India offices and coordinated the global working lines on security, energy and climate policy. He holds a master's of law from Hamburg University and a master's in political science from the Free University of Berlin, both in Germany.

**Michael Schönstein** is a senior policy adviser and lecturer at the Hertie School of Governance in Berlin, Germany. He specialises in trends that drive skills demand, in the labour supply and more broadly on the future of work. Previously, Michael worked as an economist at the OECD in Paris. Before that he was a policy adviser and consultant in various federal ministries in Germany. Michael holds degrees in economics, international relations, and public policy.

**Juliet Schor** is professor of sociology at Boston College, US. She studies trends in working time, consumerism, the relationship between work and family, environmental sustainability, women's issues and alternative, sustainable economies and societies. A graduate of Wesleyan University, Schor received her PhD in economics at the University of Massachusetts, both US. Before joining Boston College, she taught at Harvard University for 17 years in the Department of Economics; she served on the Committee on Degrees in Women's Studies. Schor is a co-founder of the South End Press, the Center for Popular Economics and the Center for a New American Dream. She is also the vice chair of the board of the Better Future Project.

**Maria Skóra** is senior project manager at Das Progressive Zentrum, Berlin. She formerly worked for the Humboldt-Viadrina Governance Platform in Berlin and advised the All-Poland Alliance of Trade Unions in Warsaw. Maria led the research group Social and Fiscal Policy of the project A Future Agenda for Eastern and Central Europe, which was jointly organised by Das Progressive Zentrum and FES in 2013–2015.

**Fredrik Söderqvist** is an economist at the Swedish private-sector white-collar trade union Unionen, the largest trade union in Sweden, and a PhD student at the Blekinge Institute of Technology in Sweden. Frederik's research focuses on structural change, labour market regulations and institutions. He is a former expert to the Swedish government's Digitalisation Commission.

**Luc Soete** is a professorial fellow at Maastricht University in the Netherlands, where he was rector magnificus until September 2016. Previously, Luc was director of the research and training institute at the UN University – Maastricht Economic and Social Research Institute on Innovation and Technology (UNU-MERIT) in Maastricht, and professor of international economic relations and director-dean of the Maastricht Graduate School of Governance at Maastricht University. Luc is a member of the Advisory Council for Science, Technology and Innovation (De Adviesraad voor Wetenschap, Technologie en Innovatie; AWT) and the Royal Dutch Academy of Arts and Science (Koninklijke Nederlandse Akademie van Wetenschappen; KNAW). Luc's research is strongly embedded in innovation studies, and focuses on the nature, origin and determinants of innovation.

**Neil Spencer** is a reader in applied statistics at the University of Hertfordshire, UK, and the director of its Statistical Services and Consultancy Unit. Neil is a fellow of the Royal Statistical Society and a chartered statistician. He has been undertaking contract research and consultancy work in statistics alongside more traditional research for over 20 years.

**Susanne Steffes** is an assistant professor at the University of Cologne, Germany, and a senior researcher at the research department Labour Markets, Human Resources and Social Policy at ZEW. Her research focuses on the effects of human resource management on job quality and in particular on the impact of human resource management on employee retention, the optimal design and the effects of flexible work, and the effects of personnel development and equality of opportunities on individual careers.

**Dag Sverre Syrdal** is a statistical consulting associate and doctoral candidate at the University of Hertfordshire, UK. Dag's research focuses on human-machine interaction, interaction prototyping for novel technologies and research methodologies.

**Sotiria Theodoropoulou** joined the ETUI as a senior researcher in 2010. Her research interests include macroeconomic policies and economic governance in the EU, with a focus on the effects of crisis responses and fiscal austerity on macroeconomic and labour market performance and on labour market and social policies. Before joining ETUI Sotiria worked as economic policy analyst at the European Policy Centre in Brussels, as a researcher for the programme Knowledge Economy of the Work Foundation in London, and as an associate fellow for the European programme of Chatham House. Sotiria spent several years teaching economics and public policy at the

University of Athens in Greece, and at the London School of Economics, King's College London and Birkbeck College in London.

**Joana Vicente** is a research fellow at the Institute of Public Policy in Lisbon. She graduated with a BA in economics at the Lisbon School of Economics & Management (Instituto Superior de Economia e Gestão; ISEG) (2012) and holds a master's in economics and public policy (2015) from the same institution, with a minor in finance and public administration. Joana's master's thesis focused on corporate governance in state-owned enterprises in Portugal, with a case study of the public transport company Carris. Joana has previously worked as a tax consultant at Deloitte in the Transfer Pricing Department.

**Enzo Weber** is head of the research department Forecasts and Macroeconomic Analyses at the Institute for Employment Research of the German Federal Employment Agency, Nuremberg, Germany. He researches on labour markets, macroeconomics, forecasting, financial markets as well as econometrics. In labour studies his works cover macroeconomic labour market development, labour demand and supply, unemployment, labour market reforms, labour market dynamics, demographics and pensions, as well as technological change and digitalisation. Previously, Enzo held a postdoctoral position at the University of Mannheim and was junior professor of economics at the University of Regensburg, both in Germany. He has a degree in economics and a PhD from the Free University, Berlin, Germany.

**Robert Went** works as an economist at the Dutch Scientific Council for Government Policy (Wetenschappelijke Raad voor het Regeringsbeleid; WRR). He focuses on the future of work. He has studied general economics and obtained his doctorate with a thesis on globalisation. He has previously worked as project manager at the Netherlands Court of Audit (Algemene Rekenkamer). At the WRR he participated in the innovation renewed project, directed the Development Cooperation Project Group and participated in the project group responsible for the publication How Unequal is the Netherlands?

**Patrizia Zanoni** is a professor at the Faculty of Business Economics at Hasselt University, Belgium, and a professor in organisation studies at the Utrecht University School of Governance, in the Netherlands. Patrizia's research focuses on the role of social identities, including gender, ethnicity, disability and age, in struggles over symbolic and economic power within and across organisations. Patrizia regularly acts as a scientific adviser in policy committees and projects whose aim is to foster equality in companies, public administration bodies, interest organisations, schools and universities.

**Ulrich Zierahn** is a senior researcher at the research department Labour Markets, Human Resources and Social Policy at ZEW, Germany. His research currently focuses on the consequences of technological change, international trade and offshoring for the dynamics of individual labour market careers, and the economic performance of regional labour markets.

**John Zysman** is a professor of political science at the UC Berkeley, US, and co-founder and co-director of the Berkeley Roundtable on the International Economy. He has written extensively on European and Japanese policy and corporate strategy. John's research interests include comparative politics, western European politics and political economy. His publications include Manufacturing Matters: The Myth of the Post-Industrial Economy (Basic Books, 1987) and Governments, Markets, and Growth: Finance and the Politics of Industrial Change (Cornell University Press, 1983). John's work has made him a frequent guest speaker, and a key adviser to governments and corporations in Europe, Asia and the US on how to deal with globalisation and how to enhance competitiveness.

Lightning Source UK Ltd.
Milton Keynes UK
UKHW02f2356250518
323231UK00006B/86/P